P9-DFF-187

THE ABINGDON
PREACHING
ANNUAL
2001

THE ABINGDON PREACHING ANNUAL 2001

EDITED BY

Charles Bugg

ABINGDON PRESS
Nashville

THE ABINGDON PREACHING ANNUAL 2001

Copyright © 2000 by Abingdon Press

All rights reserved.
No part of this work may be reproduced or transmitted in any form or by any means, electronic or mechanical, including photocopying and recording, or by any information storage or retrieval system, except as may be expressly permitted by the 1976 Copyright Act or in writing from the publisher. Requests for permission should be addressed to Abingdon Press, P.O. Box 801, 201 Eighth Avenue South, Nashville, TN 37202-0801.

This book is printed on recycled, acid-free, elemental-chlorine–free paper.

ISBN 0-687-08197-1
ISSN 1075-2250

Scripture quotations, unless otherwise indicated, are from the *New Revised Standard Version of the Bible,* copyrighted 1989 Division of Christian Education of the National Council of the Churches of Christ in the United States of America. Used by permission. All rights reserved.

Scripture quotations noted RSV are from the *Revised Standard Version of the Bible,* copyright © 1946, 1952, 1971 by the Division of Christian Education of the National Council of the Churches of Christ in the USA. Used by permission. All rights reserved.

Scripture quotations noted NIV are taken from the HOLY BIBLE: NEW INTERNATIONAL VERSION®. Copyright © 1973, 1978, 1984 by International Bible Society. Used by permission of Zondervan Publishing House. All rights reserved.

Scripture quotations noted NEB are from *The New English Bible.* © The Delegates of the Oxford University Press and The Syndics of the Cambridge University Press 1961, 1970. Reprinted by permission.

Scripture quotations noted NKJV are taken from the New King James Version. Copyright © 1982 by Thomas Nelson, Inc. Used by permission. All rights reserved.

Scripture quotations noted KJV are from the King James or Authorized Version of the Bible.

Scripture quotations noted Message are from *THE MESSAGE.* Copyright © Eugene H. Peterson, 1993, 1994, 1995. Used by permission of NavPress Publishing Group.

Scripture quotations noted JBP are from The New Testament in Modern English, by J. B. Phillips. Copyright © 1972 by J. B. Phillips.

Invocations and benedictions are from *Invocations and Benedictions for the Revised Common Lectionary,* compiled and edited by John M. Descher. Copyright © 1998 by Abingdon Press. Reprinted by permission.

00 01 02 03 04 05 06 07 08 09—10 9 8 7 6 5 4 3 2 1

MANUFACTURED IN THE UNITED STATES OF AMERICA

CONTENTS

❦

CONTENTS

CONTENTS

CONTENTS

AUGUST

SEPTEMBER

CONTENTS

OCTOBER

NOVEMBER

CONTENTS

THE ABINGDON
PREACHING
ANNUAL
2001

INTRODUCTION

How do you teach preaching? It's a good question! The person who asked the question was dressed in overalls bearing the name of a moving company. He was helping me pack my books as I prepared to leave the parish to return to the seminary to teach preaching.

Our conversation reflected people from two different worlds. He did his job well, but let's say he didn't reflect a lot of "spiritual sensitivity." Church was not high on his list of priorities. He had no idea what a seminary was. The preaching he had listened to was likely loud and long. Given his comments, the preaching models he had heard had probably never read a preaching text-book, and were suspicious of any type of education that would "ruin" heartfelt preaching. So the man in the overalls asked, "How do you teach preaching?"

I'm not sure of all that I said. I told him a few things I empha-sized in class. Then I talked about trying to help people discover and develop the gifts that God had given them. Like some ser-mons we preach, my answer was more than he needed. If the man in the overalls ever thinks about it anymore, he probably still wonders, "How do you teach somebody to preach?"

I wonder that myself sometimes. In fact, I often wonder how any of us has the courage or the gall, or whatever it takes to pre-sume to tell people about God. The apostle Paul talked about God's putting divine treasure into earthen vessels. That giant of our century, Gardner Taylor, called the very act of preaching a "presumptuous" business. And yet, some of us continue to try to preach and even to teach others how better to communicate the divine treasure in our earthen vessels.

Why? I'm going to venture a response. We are *called* to preach. Either that or we, of all people, are most presumptuous. Called to preach? It's a response, not "the answer." We can argue about the call. At times, we may feel this call more keenly. However, there are other times when we prepare or preach sermons when we feel alone—as if God has exited the stage. Yet, what keeps us at it, if not the call? Most of us who began our preaching ministry thinking we were really good at it have had our grandiosity stripped by the relentless rhythm of preparing sermons, or by the folks who heard us and who were never different for the experience. That's humbling—to preach and to realize on any given Sunday, most people vote, "no decision."

But we preach because somewhere in the depths of who we are, we feel compelled to give shape to the vision of the Holy One and to give voice to the needs of our congregants. This book is designed to help all of us to fulfill our calling. The sermon briefs and helps are not intended to substitute for our work with the biblical text. Hopefully, the words which are written will spur us to ponder more deeply both the biblical words and the lives of our listeners.

I want to express my gratitude to Abingdon Press for asking me to help with this and next year's *Annual*. I also want to thank all who have offered their insights and inspirations as they have composed the words that comprise this book. Finally, I want to salute all who preach. We get discouraged. We wonder if anyone is listening. Sometimes we are tempted to become the insurance agents our mothers told us we should be. However, we are called to preach. I salute you.

Charles Bugg

SERMONS FOR
SPECIAL
DAYS

TASTING COMMUNION

❦

GALATIANS 3:23-29

It's been ten years, but it could have happened yesterday.

Our daughter, Sarah, was two years old. She and I had just done the grocery shopping and were sitting on a bench in front of the grocery store waiting for my wife, who was to pick us up after running some errands.

We were sharing the bench with another person, a man who, from all appearances, was going through hard times. His clothes were worn and dirty, his face was unshaven, and he was eating what must have been his breakfast—maybe his lunch and dinner, too—a can of Vienna sausages.

As we waited for Elizabeth, Sarah did the usual two-year-old thing—hopped and jumped and twisted on the bench between this man and me, looking up and down and all around, humming and clucking and so on. Before I knew what had happened, she had shuffled over to the other end of the bench, reached into the can of Vienna sausages that this stranger was holding, and pulled one out for herself, as though this were some church picnic.

I didn't know what to say or do. I heard all the stock parental messages making their claim inside my head: "Don't take things from strangers," "You have to ask for things nicely," "You don't know where that's been," and the rest. I heard them all loud and clear, well rehearsed from childhood on, but this time none of them made it to speech. I suppose I was so taken by Sarah's innocent gesture that I couldn't bring myself to chide her.

Children, of course, have a hard time seeing the walls the rest of us see. Walls of propriety. Walls of etiquette. Walls of hygiene. Walls of class, education, color. Walls of fear. Walls of prejudice. Children don't generally see those walls or know those separating rules the rest of us have studied so well.

Apparently, neither does God. "In Christ Jesus you are all children of God through faith," Paul writes to the Galatians. "There is no longer Jew or Greek, there is no longer slave or free, there is no longer male and female; for all of you are one in Christ Jesus."

We could spend weeks talking about how fundamentally important each of the distinctions Paul names would have been in his day: Jew and Gentile; slave and free; male and female. Books have been written about how carefully and forcefully separations between these groups were maintained. Yet with a few strokes of a quill pen, Paul announces their eradication.

Imagine Montagues and Capulets—together. Irish Protestant and Irish Catholic—together. Israeli Jews and Palestinian Arabs—together. An investment banker and a day laborer trading stories on the city bus. Liberal and conserative Christians with an open Bible between them, listening to each other. A brother and sister who haven't spoken since the estate was settled; a former husband and wife; parents and their estranged daughter. Imagine two people who share a bed and the toothpaste, but little besides that in the haste and hurry of their days. Imagine them together, in Christ.

This table is built on words such as those from Galatians. And so to eat from this table is to lay down whatever claim we have to isolation from anyone else, whether it's our spouse or our supervisor. It is to let go of any position of superiority or inferiority, moral or otherwise, in order to free our hands for sharing the loaf and the cup. We are all guests together here, with the same host, invited to hop and jump and twist on the same bench, and even eat out of the same can.

Today especially, World Communion Day, we are reminded that it's a small can we're invited to eat out of. The world is, in the words of a friend, a "small marble." The Lord's table is the world's table, which means it will seat as many as come—people from north and south, theologically and ideologically and geographically, and from east and west, economically and racially and culturally. All will be seated at this one table, seated close enough to rub elbows when we reach for another sausage. Close enough for the children among us and those with the gift of childsight to see what God must see: family.

"All of you are one in Christ Jesus," writes Paul, "And if you belong to Christ, then you are [together] Abraham's offspring, heirs according to the promise." Hear that? This isn't just a philosophy of "go along to get along"; goodwill for the sake of appearances; get through this religious thing arm in arm and then we can go our separate ways again. We are *family*—grafted together in a blood kinship, you and I—through Christ. You and I, and every other strange or despised, labeled or dismissed, feared or put down person and group under the sun. Stuck with each other. Like it or not. Family.

We may protest that the biblical idea of covenantal family applies more narrowly than is suggested in this passage; but we have only to pull out those books I mentioned earlier, the ones that talk about how dramatically Paul's blurring the lines between Jew/Gentile, male/female, slave/free defied both culture and conviction. God is done, Paul seems to be saying, with name-calling. Except for one name, held in reserve, to be used universally among God's people: children.

There is a beautiful scene from the movie, *Places in the Heart,* that years later I still carry with me. Set in Waxahatchie, Texas in 1935, in the heart of the Depression, the movie tells the story of the town sheriff, accidentally killed by a young man who is drunk and wielding a gun. The sheriff's widow and children struggle to make ends meet without him, facing all kinds of adversity and forging all kinds of unanticipated friendships in the process.

The very last scene of the movie is set in the local church on a Sunday morning. The pastor is reading from 1 Corinthians 13:1: "If I speak in the tongues of mortals and of angels, but do have not love, I am a noisy gong or a clanging cymbal." Then communion is shared. As the elements are passed from person to person, one says to the next, "The peace of God." The camera follows the plate of bread as it moves down one particular aisle. There's the widow, Mrs. Spaulding, taking the bread; she then hands the plate to the person next to her—it's her husband, the sheriff, alive again! Right away we know we are in some other world, the next world. "The peace of God," she says to him. And he takes the plate from her, and a piece of bread.

Then the sheriff hands the plate to the person next to him—it's the young man who accidentally killed him, who was himself put to death for the careless deed. "The peace of God," the sheriff says. Others from the long and dramatic story are there, too:

there's the drifter and the blind man, both of whom were courageous in helping the Spaulding family through their crisis; there's
the merciless banker; the couple whose marriage is nearly split
apart by unfaithfulness—they are there, too, holding hands as
they pass the plate to one other. Everyone is there, at this table
we call communion, the table built upon these Galatian words—
no more Jew and Greek, inside and outside, us and them.

The walls we put up God doesn't seem to recognize. Children
don't either. As we grow out of the innocence of childhood, we learn
rules of separation between things, classes, categories, kinds, colors,
and cultures. But maybe as we continue to grow, by the grace of
God, we grow to appreciate the irrelevance of those rules, and the
deeper reality of family ties that bind even the most remote, most
alienated, most despised individuals or groups in Christ.

When you come to the table today, who needs to have your
offer of reconciliation extended? Who needs to hear you say to
them, "The peace of God"? When you come to this table, who
remains outside *your* table of acceptance? They're probably
there for good reason: "They would never eat at my table, and I
would never eat at theirs." And yet, the disturbing—and delightful—word of Scripture is that such estrangement grows tiresome
over time and finally has no place in the family of God's children.
God has greater things in mind for us, together.

It's been ten years since that strange incident outside the grocery store, but it could have happened yesterday. In fact, it could
happen today.

Sarah toddled back across the bench with her Vienna sausage,
pulled fresh from the can of the stranger who was now a little less
of one. He had raised his eyebrows and shown a toothless grin; I
think he was warmed, flattered maybe, by this little go-between
and her freewheeling antics. By now she had nibbled a bite off
the end of her little sausage, and now wanted to share the rest
with me. "Here, Daddy."

What would *you* say? I heard the voices: "You don't know
where that's been." "We don't take things from strangers." I
heard the voices, and then took her little wrist, guided the
sausage to my mouth, and took a bite. I was surprised at how it
tasted. It tasted like—communion. (Paul L. Escamilla)

PRODIGALS ON THE ROAD

LUKE 15:11-32

Three men, family to one another, yet relating so differently in the circumstances they encounter. Most Christians know this famous parable of Jesus, a lesson to remind us that God loves us unconditionally and that we are always welcome into God's household, no matter how far away we have wandered or how long we've been gone. The elder son's story also reminds us that even those of us who remain close to God's house have a special place in God's heart as a special child and member of God's family. And I believe that the father's story has much to teach as well, not just about who God is and how much we are loved, but also about who God calls us to be as a Christian family and how we are to treat one another in this family whether the fellow family member has stuck by our side and pleased us at every step of the journey or wandered far and wide for years forgetting we were even here.

The story of the Prodigal Son is surely the story of all of us here, for have we not all been either a prodigal or an obedient child or a loving parent waiting patiently and hopefully for a loved one to return to the fold. And so this morning, I invite you to enter into the worlds of each of these three people. In today's world, family means many things to many people, and if Jesus were telling the parable to us, the characters could just as easily be three very good friends, three members of a Bible study, or even three sisters. But this morning, I'll portray the characters as a family, a family of women, a mother and her two daughters-struggling with the different roads they have chosen.

The Mother Speaks

I love my family, but even so, the house seems kind of empty these days. I wait and wait for my daughter to return. If I knew how to track her down and drag her back, I probably would. Yet,

I know that would only push her away further. I've learned a lot about being a parent and a friend since she left. She'll probably never know how very much she's taught me about waiting patiently, forgiving freely, loving unconditionally.

> I'll be waiting, I may be young or old and gray counting the days
> But I'll be waiting, and when I fin'lly see you come, I'll run when I see you, I'll meet you.[1]

The Younger Daughter Speaks

I've been gone for a long time. By now, everyone back home has probably forgotten all about me. It seemed like such a good idea at first, striking out on my own, seeing the world, tasting the fruit of life on the wild side, figuring out who I was without worrying about what Mom or Dad or any of the neighbors thought. But somewhere along the line, I began to realize that being in the family wasn't all that bad. I think I even knew more about who I was when I was with them. Anyway, it doesn't matter now. The best I could hope for would be a place in the servant quarters. Maybe it's time to go back, tell Mom I know that I messed up. I sure don't deserve to live in the house with my sister whose been right there all that time, but maybe I can work with the other servants. They certainly live better than I'm living right now. And I know my mom, she'd never turn anyone away who needed a place to live and a job to earn a living. Her heart is so big, her love so stubborn, her hope so persistent. I could learn a lot from being back in her house.

> It's your stubborn love that never lets go of me; I don't understand how you can stay;
> Perfect love embracing the worst in me, how I long for your stubborn love.[2]

Maybe it's time to go home.

The Elder Daughter Speaks

I've always lived here, always known I was loved, since the day my mom first held me in her arms for all the family to see, and she beamed her proudest smile at his first born daughter. It's a safe place, warm and comfortable, loving and kind. Mom has pushed me along when I've needed to grow and learn new things, helped me along when I've messed things up. Even now that I'm an adult, I still keep making mistakes, but I learn from them and find new ways to grow. I don't think I could do that if I were out on my own—like my little sister. I wouldn't know who I was or how to survive if it weren't for the warm love I feel right here in this very house. Now that my sister is back, it's been hard to know how to react. I mean, Mom had seemed so sad for so long, and it's good to see her happy again. I just start to wonder if she beamed more proudly when my sister was born. Maybe she won't want to keep teaching me about the household and how to run the family. What if she doesn't know how to love both of us at the same time? Oh no, here comes Mother now, all smiles. And my sister trailing behind. I wonder if they'll understand what I'm going through.

> I have found a place where I can hide, it's safe inside your arms of love
> Like a child who's held throughout a storm, you keep me warm in your arms of love.[3]

The Prodigals Meet: The Younger Daughter Speaks

Hello, sister. I'm sorry to have been away so long. I don't expect you to greet me with a big hug or anything, but I did want to let you know how much I've learned from you. Yes, I see how you've grown and changed. You've managed to find yourself without ever leaving this place. I want that for my life. I want to know the peace and contentment you have.

Maybe if I stick around long enough, I'll understand a little more about this family and Mom's love than I did when I left. Maybe you and Mom can both help me.

> In the place I found where I can hide, It's safe inside your arms of love
> Like a child who's held throughout a storm, you keep me warm in your arms of love.

May we know the patience of waiting upon the Lord.
May we know the love that is waiting for us.
May we share that love with those whom we meet
and those who are far away from us.
May we go forth in God's arms of love. (Mary Scifres)

1. (From "The Prodigal" ["I'll Be Waiting"], by Amy Grant, Gary Chapman, and Robbie Buchanan. Copyright © 1985 Bug and Bear Music, Nanacub Music, Riverstone Music Inc., Bug and Bear Music Exclusive by LCS Music Group Inc. In Amy Grant's *My Songs* [Nashville:Word Music].

2. "Stubborn Love," by Amy Grant, Gary Chapman, Sloan Towner, Brown Bannister, and Michael W. Smith. Copyright © 1982 Meadowgreen Music Co. and Handrail Music, Meadowgreen Music Co. Administerd by Tree Publishing Co. In Michael W. Smith's *The Songs* [Nashville: Word Music].

3. "Arms of Love," by Gary Chapman, Michael W. Smith, and Amy Grant. Copyright © 1982 Bug and Bear Music of Meadowgreen Music Co., Bug and Bear Music Exclusive by LCS Music Group Inc. In Amy Grant's *My Songs* [Nashville: Word Music].

REFLECTIONS

Introduction to the Monthly Meditations

I think it's safe to assume that nobody buys this book because of the monthly devotionals. You purchase a volume like this to stock your pantry with ingredients that may help you feed your people for a year—that's why you want the sermons and sermon briefs. You buy it also to shop for language that may help your people express their worship of God—that's why you want the calls to worship, the prayers, the benedictions. Any thought of this book as a source for feeding yourself or enriching your own worship of God may come in, at best, a distant third. That's all right. Other sources abound, classical and contemporary, to assist you in your own soul feeding and worship.

But there's wisdom, I think, in the publisher's decision to weave into this book twelve meditations for your personal use. As you busily scan all these worship resources and sermon resources for meeting the needs of others, the meditations show up once a month to raise their hands and remind you: You've got your own needs too. The cook had better eat. Who can feed others without having been fed? Who can lead in public prayer who has not entered the sanctuary of his or her own silence to listen and to pray?

These meditations were very deliberately prepared as nourishment for the minister's personal table, and especially for those who preach and lead worship. Though we are no different from anyone else, the nature of our work presents us with unique seductions, dangers, and needs. Just as many people in a given part of the country will flock to the same vacation spot, most ministers, sooner or later, will show up in the same desert.

My current vocation is with seminarians, preparing them especially for their work as preachers and leaders of worship. Before this, for seventeen years, I was a pastor. Inevitably, I have tried in these reflections to offer the kind of nourishment that I've hungered for in my own experience as a pastor and preacher. In preparing these twelve little meals, I've stirred in some concerns, questions, realities, needs, hopes, and encouragements that keep showing up on my own plate.

I have chosen to base these reflections on biblical texts, believing that the same Scriptures we preach to the community also want a private word with us. Specifically, I have chosen in most of these reflections to sit beside various persons in the biblical story who, in different ways, may offer clues and helps to our situation. So you won't be sitting down alone to these meals. You'll be joined at the table by Jesus and the disciples, Mary of Bethany, Mary Magdalene, Simon Peter, Ezekiel, Paul, Naomi and Ruth, Moses, a psalmist, the second Isaiah, and Zechariah the priest. Good company, all.

In previous editions in this series the devotionals have included prayers for you to pray. I chose a different path. My intention was to offer words that would open you to your own reflections and prayers. So it's my hope that you'll follow the time-honored parental table advice: Don't gulp your food, chew it well, take your time, don't run off from the table, be still and let it digest. And don't forget to say your prayers. (Paul D. Duke)

REFLECTIONS

❦

JANUARY

Reflection Verse: "Come away to a deserted place all by your-
selves and rest a while" (Mark 6:31).

Jesus in the Gospels has a way of disappearing. After his baptism he disappears forty days into the desert. After a long day's
work in Capernaum, he disappears before dawn to a solitary
place. After feeding the multitudes he disappears onto a mountain. And on his last night, though he knows they will find him,
he disappears into that lonely garden.

It's probably not enough to say that Jesus loved lonely places.
More likely, he needed them. Who could give what he gave and
not be bone-weary? Who could see what he saw and not need to
lift his eyes to the stars, or hear what he heard from the people
and not need to salve his ears with silence? He knew a psalm that
said, "O that I had wings like a dove! I would fly away and be at
rest." He lived in the rhythm of engagement and retreat.

Once he told his disciples to take a retreat, but it was only after
he'd made ministers out of them. He had sent them out preaching and healing with nothing but the clothes on their backs, the
sticks in their hands, and a partner at their sides—nothing but
themselves, for the Power would have to flow *through* them.
After that experience came his new invitation: Peter, get your golf
clubs. James, bring your fly rod. John, bring a book. All of you
sprout wings of a dove with me and disappear. Now you know
what you need. You've emptied your cup, so carry it into the
waterfall of retreat. "Come away and be at rest."

If you're a minister, you don't need me to tell you what makes
you so hungry for personal renewal; but let me name some of
what we're up against anyway. In the first place, we are reposi-
tories of other people's pain. We become receptacles of grief,
loneliness, rage. We hear terrible secrets. People who come to us

may leave with a lighter step, shoulders a little more lifted. They have been unburdened. What they don't know is that it got on us. Sorrows and sins do not vanish away; someone bears them away. We claim this of Christ, and a priest is a sacramental embodiment of that bearing. It has to be born away from us too.

But there's more. Burning in our bones there are—or at least used to be— beautiful dreams for a more faithful church and for a better world. But we've got the best seats in the house for the disappointment of dreams: so much narrowness and greed and death. Jesus called the Twelve to retreat just after the news that Herod had murdered John the Baptist. So we must step back, having buried too many friends and too many dreams.

This doesn't even count our disillusionment with ourselves. How we have never managed to live up to our own preaching. How fraudulent we can feel. And how often we have exhausted ourselves giving out more than is in us to give, breaking off pieces of ourselves and handing them out to everyone like the Eucharist!

Christ calls us to come often to the other side of the table, to be nourished, restored, and cured of our messianic seriousness. Even the Messiah did the dance of engagement and retreat, engagement and retreat. Is this too what he means when he says, "Follow me"?

It means saying our prayers—our own unprofessional, secret, stammering prayers. It means listening to the silence. It means getting good rest and good play, letting ourselves be loved, letting someone else be priest to us.

When I was a pastor I made annual retreats to a Benedictine monastery and seminary. Usually I worshiped with the monks and seminarians, but on one visit I chose to remain in complete solitude. A strange thing happened on my last morning. I was minding my own business, writing a letter down by the lake, when a pickup truck pulled up behind my private bench. A student jumped out of the truck, mumbling, "Gotta find an altar!" I said, "*What?*" He said, "We're having mass out here by the lake." He set up some benches to make an altar right in front of me. He told me his name; I said I was Paul. He asked what I did. I said I was a pastor. He said, "Well, Father Paul, join us for mass. You can help lead if you like." I said I wasn't a Catholic, but he was off in a rush and never heard me.

Knowing it was against house rules for me to partake of the Eucharist, I decided to move into the woods to finish my letter. But when the group arrived for mass, my new friend spotted me through the trees. "Hey Father Paul, come join us!" Again I protested, but he was already introducing me to his friends as Father Paul. I gave up, gratefully, and joined them. I never had a sweeter communion. A young priest in sport shirt and sunglasses led us. The New Testament lesson nearly knocked me down: the story of Ananias coming to a blind Paul and calling him, "Brother." And when we passed the peace at the end, one after another they came and said, "Peace of Christ, Father Paul."

Sometimes Christ must call to ministers on a note of laughter. Maybe your own name belongs in one of the following blanks, on the voice of a playful, insistent Christ: Father _____, Mother _____, come round to the other side of the table, you hungry, fortunate guest. Soon enough you'll be host again. It happened with the Twelve. In no time thousands of people showed up and there was a picnic of loaves and fishes to be organized, just as you will soon be feeding your own little multitude again. But remember that, for us, feeding always follows being fed. The steps to the dance of ministry go forward and back, out and in. Listen carefully and notice: it's the rhythm of your living heart. (Paul D. Duke)

JANUARY 7, 2001

❧

Baptism of the Lord

Worship Theme: We rejoice that in our baptism we are called to follow Jesus, revealed by God as the Anointed One who brings healing to the nations.

Readings: Isaiah 43:1-7; Acts 8:14-17; Luke 3:15-17, 21-22

Call to Worship (Psalm 29)

Leader: The voice of the LORD is over the waters;
the God of glory thunders,
the LORD, over mighty waters.

People: **The voice of the LORD is powerful;
the voice of the LORD is full of majesty.**

Leader: The LORD sits enthroned over the flood;
the LORD sits enthroned as king forever.

People: **May the LORD give strength to his people!
May the LORD bless his people with peace!**

Pastoral Prayer:

God of all glory, you have called us by our name and led us through perilous waters: Lead us now by your Holy Spirit to show your love to those we meet at work, at school, at home, and in places of recreation. Let your presence be known through us to the sick and sorrowing, to the hungry and those in prison, to the victims of violence and disaster. Surround all families with your love and encourage them with your Spirit that, like your Son, our children may grow in wisdom and in years and in favor with you and all humankind. Give us grace to know the names of children in need, to accept with your Son our ministry to love the world. Strengthen us in the promises made at our baptism, for we remember with joy and grateful praise your gift of new life through Jesus Christ, your beloved Son. Amen. (Blair G. Meeks)

SERMON BRIEFS

A TIME TO SPEAK PLAINLY

ISAIAH 43:1-7

"I have called you by name, you are mine." Strong words.
"I will be with you." "I am with you." Powerful words.
"I am the LORD your God, the Holy One of Israel." The words of God. "I love you."

A time comes in every meaningful relationship to speak plainly. Whether that relationship is romantic or a parent-child bond or a close friendship, the time comes. A word must be spoken to define the relationship. This word is powerful. It carries feelings, intentions, and promises. Ambiguity may precipitate this word. A couple asks, "Where is this relationship going?" Or the word may come at a milestone. The child leaves home, and the parent must express everything in a parent's heart in a few words. Sooner or later, the time comes.

I. A Time for the Nation

This time came for Israel during exile in Babylon. The armies of Babylon had invaded Judah, destroyed Jerusalem and the temple, and carried most of the people into exile. Life in Babylon posed a dangerous threat to the people of God. Their God seemed less powerful than the gods of Babylon, who, after all, had been victorious. They also found plenty of prosperity to go around in Babylon. Why not embrace Babylonian ways and cash in?

God's people had suffered. Now they were tempted. The time had come for God to speak plainly. So the prophet speaks a word

33

of healing and hope. The God of Jacob had formed this people, and the same God would re-form them. The people wonder if God has abandoned them; and God says, "You are precious in my sight, and honored, and I love you." As they worry about their future, they hear, "Do not fear, for I am with you."

II. A Time for the Nations

God speaks these words again at the baptism of Jesus. The prophet of the exile had seen Israel as the chosen servant of God and a light to the nations. Jesus took this role upon himself, standing for Israel and calling the nations to the one true God. As the prophet had known, God's love is for all people; each one created by God, each one called by name.

III. A Time for You

God speaks these same words to you. The time comes when you must hear them. A relationship exists between you and your creator, even if you are not aware of it or intentional about it. This relationship has a history: God created you. Jesus died for you. And now God claims you with a word of love: "You are precious in my sight, . . . and I love you."

Once you hear this word, you respond. It is inevitable that you answer. What you answer depends on you. God's word is decisive. You cannot change who God is or who you are. But you can choose whether or not to reciprocate God's love. You can be called by God's name or not. You can trust God to lead you back from exile, or you can try to cash in by pretending to be someone you are not. I believe our choices have integrity, that how we answer matters. God does not seem to coerce followers. Instead God woos us with a word softly spoken and a promise. I hope that you can appreciate that word the way the exiles did. The discerning among them saw it as life. It gave them hope and purpose. It meant everything. At just the right moment, God said just the right thing. Like someone deeply in love, they could not say no. I wish for you the same. (David Mauldin)

"A LIFE-TRANSFORMING MISSION"

ACTS 8:14-17

Many have referred to this text as an "episcopal" visit made by Peter and John. The two apostles were sent to Samaria to confirm and complete the successful missionary work performed there by Philip, the evangelist. Not to be confused with Philip the apostle, Philip the evangelist was originally one of the seven men appointed by the apostles to take care of tables, while the apostles devoted themselves to prayer and teaching the word (Acts 6:1-6). However, with Saul persecuting the church (Acts 8:1-3), these seven men and others were scattered from Jerusalem to places in the Diaspora. Many of them, including Philip, began preaching the word and proclaiming Jesus as the Messiah to those who would hear. Through Philip's powerful proclamations, many people believed in Jesus Christ, were baptized, and healed of their infirmities. One of those who came to believe was Simon the magician, who used to trick people into thinking that he was the power of God with his magic.

But no longer was the power of God mistaken after Peter and John prayed and then laid hands upon these newly converted Samaritans. Upon receiving the Holy Spirit, it was quite evident that what had been confirmed and completed was a life-transforming mission, leaving the lives of these Samaritans and all involved never the same again.

For what is discovered from the life-transforming mission of Acts 8:14-17 is a threefold tale of joy. First of all, there is confirmation and affirmation through Philip's work and Peter and John's mission that God's word will be received by those who previously have no familiarity with it. All we must do is share it. While Jesus passed through Samaria and had several encounters there (Luke 17:11-17; John 4:1-31), the proclamation of the gospel and the spread of Christianity had not reached the Samaritans until Philip's arrival. Yet through Philip's proclamation, it was received readily and with great joy (Acts 8:8). We can be encouraged as we travel domestically and internationally that as we preach the word, strangers shall receive the word. Jesus said, "You will be my witnesses in Jerusalem, in all Judea and Samaria,

35

and to the ends of the earth" (Acts 1:8). "And I, if I be lifted up from the earth, will draw all men unto me" (John 12:32 KJV).

Second, we find that God's word can and will break down deep-seated divisions among our races and nationalities. Philip, a Jew, normally would not have had any dealings with Samaritans, nor Samaritans with Jews. And, under normal circumstances, Peter and John, who were Jews themselves, would not have ventured to Samaria either. Generational disagreements over which group represented the true children of Abraham, and the location of the actual temple of worship were but a few of the issues keeping these parties separated. But the revelation of 8:14 and Philip's experiences in the previous verses of chapter 8 demonstrate that not only was the Holy Spirit liberating and healing people from their infirmities, the Holy Spirit was destroying strongholds that for generations kept people apart. In our racially charged and often segregated world, we need to know that the Holy Spirit we claim to possess and proclaim has the power to unite divided people.

Third, this life-transforming mission of Acts 8:14-17 encourages us as present day apostles to act with authority. While many can, have, and will debate over when and how the Holy Spirit is conveyed upon those converting to the faith, the fact remains that Peter and John acted with authority to initiate the presence of the Holy Spirit coming into the lives of the Samaritans. We, too, today, must take authority. For there are many Christians in our midst who have received the word, been baptized, but are still awaiting the life-transforming power of God's Holy Spirit. As leaders of the faith, through prayer and other spiritual disciplines, we must be intentional in inviting the Holy Spirit to come into the lives of those we encounter.

As God's messengers, we will be sent on many a journey to bless and uplift the people of God. May our visits, like Peter and John's, be life-transforming as well. (Joseph Daniels)

WHAT'S ON YOUR BANNER?

LUKE 3:15-17, 21-22

John the Baptist was not the sort of person you'd want as head of your church's evangelism committee. From everything we read about him in the Gospels, he didn't call on newcomers to the neighborhood. On the contrary, if you wanted to talk to him, it had to be on his turf. Nor would you want him on the finance committee. Anyone who feels free to yell at pillars of the church and say, "You brood of vipers! Who warned you to flee from the wrath to come?" is not likely to increase per-member giving.

In fact, you wouldn't even want to invite John the Baptist home for Sunday dinner after the worship service. He was the first-century equivalent of a street person, wearing odd, smelly clothes and contributing a handful of dead bugs to the hors d'oeuvres tray.

It is not surprising, then, that we hear a hundred sermons about Mary and Martha for every *one* about John the Baptist. It may sound preposterous, therefore, when I suggest the reading from the Gospel presents John as a *model* for you and me as individuals. He demonstrates how to prepare for God's coming, receive the Lord, and proclaim the truth about Christ to others.

I. John the Baptist Desired Christ Above All Else

The depiction of John in Luke 3 shows John as someone whose earnestness and devotion threaten the complacent, vague religiosity to which we are often accustomed. As a member of a priestly family, John could have enjoyed a measure of security and status within the religious community. No human forced him into an ascetic life in the Judean wilderness, to preach repentance or announce the coming of the Messiah. John's words in verses 16 and 17 are an expression of longing: longing for God's Promised One. Having "prepared the way" and baptized multitudes in preparation for the Kingdom, John received Jesus as the fulfillment of prophecy. John desired, and announced, and received the Lamb of God—and was blessed in seeing Jesus face-to-face, as Savior and Friend. John the Baptist is an example for us, calling us to make our first order of business seeking with all our might to know, to understand, to encounter Jesus Christ.

II. John the Baptist Sets the Standard
for Christian Witness

John's words in Luke 3 may strike us as tactless and unpolished, but he was also transparent and forthright in summoning all to behold the Lord's Anointed. It is appropriate that his story is retold during Epiphany, a season commemorating the "showing forth" of Christ to the world. If John the Baptist were in our congregations today he'd be after us to announce the Messiah to everyone, in the plainest language, without discrimination or judgment. He'd announce it to those who are seeking and those who would think he had lost his mind; to people who already know Jesus Christ and to others who have never been inside a church.

I know a congregation that was celebrating its one hundredth anniversary. At one time there were over 2,000 members; now the church seldom has more than 40 on a Sunday. So I was surprised when they scraped together money for a huge banner announcing the centennial, to hang outside facing a busy street. The slogan was even more surprising: "Celebrating 100 years of community service." Community service? Was that what they'd been about for the last century? Did community service sustain their forebears and send out missionaries? Was it the foundation of their faith and ground of their hope? John the Baptist's banner announced, "Here is the Lamb of God who takes away the sin of the world!" (John 1:29). What is written on your banner, on mine, on our church's? God grant us the courage of John the Baptist to seek the Messiah with all our strength, to receive him with all our heart, and to bear witness to all the world that here is the Son of God. (Carol M. Norén)

JANUARY 14, 2001

❦

Second Sunday After the Epiphany

Worship Theme: As Jesus revealed the overflowing generosity of God's abundant gifts, let us joyfully accept the gifts of the Spirit to use in service to God.

Readings: Isaiah 62:1-5, 1 Corinthians 12:1-11, John 2:1-11

Call to Worship (Psalm 36:5-10):

> *Leader:* Your steadfast love, O LORD extends to the heavens, your faithfulness to the clouds.

> *People:* **Your righteousness is like the mighty mountains,**
> **your judgments are like the great deep;**
> **you save humans and animals alike, O LORD.**

> *Leader:* How precious is your steadfast love, O God!
> All people may take refuge in the shadow of your wings.

> *People:* **They feast on the abundance of your house,**
> **and you give them drink from the river of your delights.**

> *Leader:* For with you is the fountain of life;
> in your light we see light.

> *People:* **O continue your steadfast love to those who know you,**
> **and your salvation to the upright of heart!**

Pastoral Prayer:
Gracious God, giver of abundant gifts, your Son was first

revealed through an act of astonishing extravagance at the wedding feast of his friends. Teach us to accept with grateful hearts the outpouring of your generous Spirit and to live, guided by that same Spirit, for the common good. Grant that we may know the strength of our gifts and perceive the needs of those around us as we strive to bring to others your light and comfort. Be with us as we engage in counseling, teaching, healing, interpretation, discernment, and service, according to the abilities given us, for we know that we are called by you and that you give us a new name to announce your delight in our readiness to be your people. Give the sick and those in distress a place of refuge beneath the shadow of your wings, in the name of Jesus Christ our Lord. Amen. (Blair G. Meeks)

SERMON BRIEFS

A VISION OF THE PUT-UPS

ISAIAH 62:1-5

God will not be silent until Zion (Jerusalem) has been rebuilt. Her salvation will be as visible as a burning torch from a distance in the darkness. Nations will know that Jerusalem has been vindicated. The restorative glory of God will be seen through the *old but new* city.

Jerusalem will be called by a new name. Some scholars believe this new name is found in verse four where it's stated that Jerusalem will be called "My Delight Is in Her." In addition, after the reconstruction has been completed the surrounding land will be designated as "Married." Others believe that the name is not revealed. Regardless of scholarly argumentation, it's obvious that the new name represents a change in status and condition.

This Scripture has implications far beyond its historical context. For example, at present, there is talk of spending billions of dollars to reconstruct the Balkans, Yugoslavia, Macedonia, and other countries of the area. One wonders if they will be given a new name. An even more poignant question has to do with why reconstruction is even necessary. Why can't people live together peacefully? Why is war necessary? Isn't there a better way? If we weren't bent toward destruction, couldn't our energies and funds that are used to reconstruct war zones, be channeled into other works of mercy in the world? Nevertheless, it seems that humankind has this innate desire to tear down so that it can build up. Perhaps we should be bold enough to call it by its right name, *sin*.

This entire concept was made simple for me as I began to reflect theologically about a visit to my son's school. My wife and I attended a parent-teacher conference regarding our first experience with a year-round school. The most profound thing I heard was not about the new schedule which includes half of the summer, but when the teacher told us that her classroom specializes in *put ups*. "In other words, we will not tolerate *put downs* in this class." I came away thinking that this is a constructive approach, the loving touch, the way of God. Now, everytime I drive by the school or deliver my son to class, I'll think of it by a new name, "The School Of The Put Ups."

What if every church was intentional about taking the new name of *Put Ups* and living out the vision of what the name implies. Unfortunately, the church is often a place very much like the rest of the world. Put downs are the order of the day. If we could only hear the prophecy of Isaiah with open ears, perhaps we would begin to specialize in building up instead of tearing down. (Jim Clardy)

GIFTS OF THE SPIRIT

1 CORINTHIANS 12:1-11

It's important not to be "uninformed" (v. 1) about something as central to the faith as spiritual gifts, especially for a people coming from paganism, in which they had a whole different orientation. Those new Corinthian Christians need to make a quantum leap from dumb, silent idols to a God who actually speaks and enables people to speak the truth as well. What comes out of their mouth will determine the source. The Spirit of God *affirms* Christ's lordship and anyone *denying* it would not be speaking by the Spirit.

41

The basic concept of the Spirit's *flow* is profoundly important information for them to assimilate, Paul says. They must make a dramatic shift from a stone-solid idol—dead and silent—to an ethereal, fluid Spirit—living and really communicating! In fact, this Spirit is the communicator for God, as the body's blood system is the "communicator" for the heart, keeping the whole person enriched with every "vitamin and mineral" and even the vital "oxygen" it needs to be alive. The Spirit is the *life-blood* of the Church, and when Christians share its gifts, we become the vessels through which this life-blood passes.

I just returned from a denominational, statewide meeting of pastors and lay delegates. We began the meetings with our mission statement, which was happily accepted, except for one amendment. Between the affirmation of commitment and the envisioned goals, one pastor suggested we add the phrase: "by the power of the Holy Spirit," which we all realized, of course, was absolutely necessary.

I. Same Source

"One God, one Spirit" was a new concept for many then and if we're honest, it may be for many of us too. We too can think of ourselves as unconnected and as even in competition. We might read between the lines here and understand that Paul has heard of some people flaunting their gifts, especially the gift of speaking in tongues. Paul could be both angry and fearful about this perversion of priorities. But instead of scolding them, he speaks as if responding to a question, in a positive "vein," to *help them learn* about spiritual gifts, lest they be ignorant.

First, because these gifts all come from the same Spirit, no one can take credit for them personally, *and* their differences would be minor compared with their unity in the source.

II. All for One and One for All

Second, the gifts are all "for the common good," (v. 7) or they are not spiritual gifts (v. 3). If the talent does not nurture the life-blood supply of the community of faith, then it's not from the Spirit, no matter how impressive or adroit the exercise of it.

As Paul lists the gifts, we do well to inventory our community stock of them too. In our church, how is the availability and flow of wisdom, knowledge, faith, healing, miracles, prophecy, discernment, tongues, and interpretation of tongues? Paul lists tongues last, and surrounds it by the gifts of discernment and interpretation, giving the clear message that the tongues are of no use at all without those other gifts that must accompany them if they are to have any meaning for the church. Interdependence in this complex capillary system is the other equalizer.

For the true free and clear flow of these gifts through the "system" in the church, they must be celebrated as "gifts" from the Spirit, to be used for the good of the whole system. Those setting themselves above the others, with their physically blatant show of speaking in tongues, for instance, must note that this gift is last on the list. It's not the most important by any means, and it's useless without several other companion gifts to assist them. Even who gets which gift(s) is totally activated by the Spirit (v. 11), so no one need be tempted to give anyone but God all of the glory for those gifts.

But perhaps the most important (often missed) thing to be *informed* about here is that every single one *is* given some gift of the Spirit (v. 7). At the same meeting I mentioned earlier, the lay leader asked all of the ministers to stand. It was, you know by now, a trick question. *Everyone* should have been standing because all clergy and laity alike are called to *exercise* the spiritual "muscle" they have in the spiritual gifts every single one has received! (Kathleen Peterson)

A SAVIOR IN A COMMON PLACE

JOHN 2:1-11

The context of this story is that of a celebration of a first-century wedding. Jesus is present, not teaching or doing miracles (at first) but just attending as a guest, enjoying the festivities. It is sometimes difficult to imagine Jesus sitting back and relaxing, enjoying a good joke, being normal. Yet, this passage makes clear that Jesus was present as a guest. In the midst of normalcy, the miraculous can happen. It happens in this story and perhaps that concept is what we should glean for our own lives from these verses.

I. A Problem That Calls for Less Than a Savior (vv. 1-3)

Midway through the festivities of the wedding reception, the wine runs out. Jesus' mother approaches him for assistance with the problem. The bridal family was responsible for catering the entire affair, which could last for days, so this was no minor societal infraction. In reality, however, this problem could be solved with a little human ingenuity. It certainly was not a matter that called for the intervention of the Creator of the cosmos and Savior of humanity.

By Mary's request for Jesus to perform a rather menial task, she does not seem to recognize who Jesus is in the grand scale of things. She does not seem to identify her son as the Messiah. Jesus notes that his time for being "unveiled" as the Messiah was not at hand. However, he does move immediately to assist in this minor human dilemma.

Are we shocked that Jesus is willing to assist in such a trivial matter? Perhaps in our lives we look only for the "God-sized" problems for which we request divine assistance. Notwithstanding her failure to grasp his true identity, Mary requests help for a "human-sized" problem. Jesus' willingness to help seems to indicate that he will meet us at our point of need, even if it is a need that does not require a Savior to assist us.

II. Common Vessels for Miraculous Activity (vv. 5-8)

Mary recognizes the authority of Jesus and directs the servants to follow whatever he instructs them to do. This is certainly good advice. If Jesus is willing to become involved in our crisis (regardless of its magnitude) obedience to his directives are important. He will make a way even if he seems to be utilizing unconventional means to accomplish his purpose for our good. That seems to be God's "mode of operation" when assisting us. God uses ravens to feed prophets, widows to provide during famine, a few loaves and a couple of fish to feed five thousand, and twelve disciples to turn the world upside down.

Jesus directs the servants to six stone water jars that were used for ceremonial washing. Although used for ceremonial purposes, the stone jars were quite common in the first century. How many hours did the guests and servants walk past the water jars and not even give them a second thought? Even after the crisis of a lack of wine, the jars hardly commanded anyone's attention. Jesus points out the common vessels to the servants because he chose to use them for his service.

We may well miss the opportunity to participate in the work of Christ because we fail to appreciate the important use of common vessels. If we are always looking toward the big moments, we may miss him in the mundane hour. If we always look toward the supernatural vessels for his activity, we may well miss being part of the miracle. The fact is God uses common vessels for demonstrating God's power.

III. The Lord over Physics (vv. 9-11)

As the servants follow the instructions of Jesus, a miracle of physics takes place. One substance (water) is transformed into another (wine). So authentic is this transformation that the master of the banquet commended the bridegroom for bringing out the best wine at the end of the celebration. Not only is this a supernatural activity, but it is one that is done with a touch of class (the best wine).

In our crises, we are bound by circumstances. The laws of physics apply. For every action (physical, emotional, relational, financial, or spiritual), there is an opposite and equal reaction. We cannot escape our dilemma; it is a trap of finite humanity. However, it is important that we understand that God is not limited nor bound by these "laws" of physics, God is the Lord over the laws of physics. The laws conform to God's nature. Indeed, God can move mountains, calm seas, heal leprosy, raise the dead, and forgive sin. If God can remove the sting of death for us, surely God is not limited to assist in lesser crises. Our dilemma may not call for a Savior, but that is exactly who is on the side of the believer. (Joseph Byrd)

JANUARY 21, 2001

❦

Third Sunday After the Epiphany

Worship Theme: God's word fills us with joy and calls us to join the ministry of Jesus in bringing good news to the poor, justice to the oppressed, and healing to the sick.

Readings: Nehemiah 8:1-3, 5-6, 8-10; 1 Corinthians 12:12-31*a*; Luke 4:14-21

Call to Worship (Psalm 19:1-2, 7-10, 14):

Leader: The heavens are telling the glory of God;
              and the firmament proclaims his handiwork.

People: **Day to day pours forth speech,**
              and night to night declares knowledge.

Leader: The law of the LORD is perfect, reviving the soul;
              the decrees of the LORD are sure,
              making wise the simple;
              the precepts of the LORD are right,
              rejoicing the heart.

People: **The commandment of the LORD is clear,**
              enlightening the eyes;
              the fear of the LORD is pure,
              enduring forever;
              the ordinances of the LORD true
              and righteous altogether.

Leader: More to be desired are they than gold,
              even much fine gold;
              sweeter also than honey,
              and drippings of the honeycomb.

People: **Let the words of my mouth and the
meditation of my heart
be acceptable to you,
O LORD, my rock and my redeemer.**

Pastoral Prayer:

God of all peoples, you have called us to be the Body of Christ: Lead us away from dissension and guide us by your Spirit to care for one another, knowing that if one member suffers, we all suffer. Open our hearts to the urgency of Jesus' words that this very day we may join him in proclaiming good news to the poor and bereft, recovery of sight and insight to those who stumble, release to those held captive by political or spiritual tyrannies, and an end to all that oppresses your children. Refresh us with your teachings; let us rejoice in hearing your word again as if it were new to us, for your voice is sweet and precious to our ears, and you are our strength. Defend us from all that separates us so that we may be one as you are one with Christ and the Holy Spirit. In Christ's name we pray. Amen. (Blair G. Meeks)

SERMON BRIEFS

LATE SUMMER READING

NEHEMIAH 8:1-3, 5-6, 8-10

Okay, I confess. I suffer from what antiquarian book expert Nicholas Basbanes calls the "gentle madness." It's in the genes. Some of my earliest memories of vacations have something to do with books. Summer reading lists for the subsequent fall term at school is one such memory. Each student had three books that were required reading, and each of us was strongly urged to pick three optional books to read and report on the first day of class. But my fondest memories are of going to secondhand bookshops with my father. To this day, I can spend hours browsing, unaware of the passage of time and current events. My wife, a lover of books herself, even has trouble getting me out from among the overstacked shelves of books in secondhand and antiquarian shops when we're on vacation.

It must have been a high-charged emotional time when Ezra

the scribe brought forth the scrolls containing the Law of Moses, set them on a makeshift pulpit, and began reading from them. The people were granted entrance into the strange, new world of the Bible: the history of their deliverance; their arrival in the promised land in which prosperity flowed like milk and honey; and above all, the story of the God who chose and loved these people above all others, even when they were at their stubborn and stiff-necked worst. Having recently come out of deportation and exile, hearing their story would have been incredibly moving.

Books are such wonderful things. Venerating them somehow comes naturally. One feels the slight swell of pride when a priest holds up the Bible in a service of worship and kisses it before gingerly laying it down upon the lectern. Some even bend over the page opened to the day's reading and kiss the page in homage to the Word of God. There is something at once uplifting and moving, as if the horizontal and vertical aspects of life come together at the intersection of all that is holy. It happens in synagogues, too. Whenever the Torah scrolls are removed from their special place and carried out into the congregants, they kiss or touch the scrolls as they pass through their midst.

I miss seeing such veneration. When Ezra, who was both scribe *and* priest—a true literate religious functionary—opened the scroll, the people stood up. Such veneration is a lost rite in our churches. In this day of easy sophistication, fast food (which isn't as fast as it used to be), instant communication and gratification, and constant global change, such homage to a centuries-old text is meaningless at best, perhaps even pointless. The people who received the Law of Moses and its interpretation were overcome with tears of great joy. Perhaps it takes a cataclysmic event to bring such heartfelt sentiment to bear when we hear the Word of God read in our midst. A holocaust or a war, perhaps?

When my wife and I toured the beaches of Normandy, France, last year, we made a brief stop at Amaranches, where the floating harbor was constructed to throw off the Axis powers as D-Day loomed near. There were a couple of World War II veterans in our group, one of whom had landed in Normandy. To see his face, the occasional tear creeping down his cheek, hat in hand as he read the plaques and paid homage to the markers and respect at the gravesites, was very moving. After that trip, rest assured that he went home with great rejoicing because he understood what he had seen and heard at Omaha Beach. (Eric Killinger)

PUTTING IT ALL TOGETHER

1 CORINTHIANS 12:12-31*a*

The connectedness through their shared "life-blood" infusion by the Spirit that Paul just described (vv. 1-11), is now complemented by his inspired image of each Christian as part of one common physical body. Just as they are all mystically "one body *in* Christ" (Romans 12:5, emphasis added), so they are also one, as "the body *of* Christ" (1 Cointhians 12:27, emphasis added). In his careful description of how the human body functions as an integral unit, with many different parts, each having its own special function (every one important and necessary for optimal life), Paul draws an indisputably accurate picture of how our bodies work. (1 Corinthians 12:14-26).

Then, just like the prophet Nathan's surprise: "You are the man!" (after supposedly talking to King David about something else), Paul throws out his clincher: *"Now **you** are the body!"* (1 Corinthians 12:27*a*, emphasis added). This classic prophetic "gotcha" sequence sends us back into the preceding description to examine again how it applies with the new understanding of what it really was all about.

I. Equal and Not Separate

It's a picture that gets bigger and bigger as we look at it. Again it is the Spirit (1 Corinthians 12:13) that unites us with everyone who is baptized into Christ's body. Our imagination cannot even conceive how huge an organism the many members of this body have created.

We hardly even know the immediate local extent of it in our midst. That reminds me of a couple, Sally and Joe, who decided to sit up front in the sanctuary one Sunday because their little daughter was going to be in the Christmas pageant, and they wanted to be sure they could see her. Before that, like everyone else, they'd always sat in their usual pew.

The woman they sat next to greeted them with a hearty smile and said she was so happy to welcome them. "Where are you two from?" She asked. A bit embarrassed and confused, Sally answered, "The back."

Studies have shown that small churches often unconsciously *resist* growing beyond the size where everyone can know everyone else because it is a hard comfort zone to move out of.

Paul is more concerned with honor and respect for each part of the church's body, than total familiarity with it. There is an undercurrent here of competition for prominence and the highest honors among members. If the human body were to function in that way, Paul points out, that would be ridiculous and disastrous. All the parts are clearly interdependent. None of them can function except as they are connected to the whole, and the smallest and "less respectable" (1 Corinthians 12:23) parts are absolutely necessary and "clothed" with greater respect because they need it more. It should be just the same in the body of Christ, which consists of all the members of the church, who must take care similarly of everyone. We are linked as closely to each other as the parts of our own body in Paul's analogy, and each one is just as important to the whole. So it follows that pain and honor felt in any "member" will be felt throughout. This stretches our imagination again, but in our hearts we know it's true.

II. Specialization

Obviously everyone can't fulfill the same function in the physical or the church body. Many different roles are needed. In the list we see so many opportunities for ministry that seem to have fallen into oblivion in our assembled bodies. Instead of: "Are *all* apostles?" we might ask: Are *any* apostles? (1 Corinthians 12:29, emphasis added). Can we consider the criterion from Acts 1:21 to be a present possibility? If not, since these seem to imply a specific, now-past, period in Jesus' life, how about the rest of the list?

Instead of: Are *all* prophets, miracle workers, healers, speakers of tongues or interpreters of tongues? we might ask if we have *any* of these. Thank God for teachers still being around, eh. What about all those other gifts of the Spirit?

We do well to cherish unity and respect in the body of Christ, and to honor our differences as they make us able to do and be more. But if most of the gifts Paul lists are largely missing for us, we might better look at that too. We read this so familiar passage so often, so well and still manage to hardly notice that most of the gifts mentioned seem to be missing today. Could that be worth pondering?

Taking up your cross does not mean martyring yourself for someone else, to whom you then shift the responsibility of being the part of the body that you alone, personally and uniquely, are called to be. That would be too easy and too worldly. It also puts an impossible burden on the recipients of your martyrdom because it robs them of their own unique role and they can't live out yours. There is a cowardice that calls itself humility and obedience in service to what turns out to be the world and not God. "But strive for the greater gifts" (1 Corinthians 12:31). The world hungrily awaits the success of *that* striving. (Kathleen Peterson)

FIRST THINGS

LUKE 4:14-21

This first month of the year is a time when people think about their hopes and aspirations for the future. We promise ourselves we'll lose weight, or learn a new skill, or work on a relationship or do something else—if not for the first time, making it a priority in the months to come. Beginnings, or firsts, function as milestones; benchmarks against which we measure our progress. When we mark the "first" of anything, or make a fresh beginning, we do it with the implicit understanding that it's important. That's true in our lives, and it is true in today's reading from the Gospel. The fourth chapter of Luke is about "first things."

You'll notice that today's reading is from the fourth chapter, and not the first. In earlier chapters, Luke tells us about the birth of Jesus, his presentation to Simeon and Anna, and that episode in the temple when Jesus was twelve. But the event depicted in this morning's lesson is offered as the *first words* spoken in Jesus' public ministry. It's no accident, this arrangement of material. Luke quotes Jesus as saying, "The Spirit of the Lord is upon me, because he has anointed me to bring good news to the poor. He has sent me to proclaim release to the captives and recovery of sight to the blind, to let the oppressed go free, to proclaim the year of the Lord's favor." That's how Jesus introduces himself in the Gospel of Luke. That's what Luke thinks is of first importance.

It is certain that Luke didn't believe "The Spirit of the Lord is upon me" were *literally* Jesus' first words in ministry. Luke acknowledges that Jesus had been teaching in other synagogues and working wonders elsewhere in Galilee before he came to his hometown. But Luke places the event in the synagogue at Nazareth in first position, in the important slot. He's signaling to readers that the most significant thing they can know from the very start is that Jesus is the Christ. He is the fulfillment of all the messianic prophecy in the Old Testament. The Greek term "Christ" and the Hebrew word "Messiah" mean the same thing: *God's anointed*. The Gospel writer is staking a claim about Jesus here. He's not putting words in our Redeemer's mouth, to make it a better story. But he's arranged the material so that right from the start there is the assertion that whatever other stories you may have heard about Jesus, whatever other religious ideas you have, Jesus is the one you've been waiting for. He's the answer to human longing. God Almighty sent his Son to fulfill a unique, never to be repeated role in the universe.

Luke reports that "the eyes of all in the synagogue were fixed on him." The people in that congregation had gathered on the Sabbath all their lives. For generations they'd sung their hymns and said their prayers and heard their leaders speak about One who was to come: a Savior and deliverer. They'd memorized the scriptures about the coming Messiah. They waited and watched, hoping the Anointed One would come in their lifetime. Is it any wonder, then, that when they heard Jesus speak, people were amazed? Jesus' first recorded words of ministry announce that their time of waiting is over.

As we think about that synagogue service in Jesus' hometown, what he said and what the people's reaction was, we are moved to consider some fundamental questions about ourselves and our faith. Is the first thing Jesus says about himself the first thing we say *about* him? Is "Jesus Christ is Lord" the primary message we communicate about ourselves, as individuals or as a church? Luke announces the Messiah before he relates anything else the Savior said or did. I wonder if the same can be said for us. Do the programs of your church, the order of service, the investment of time and energy and the way visitors are treated all proclaim that Jesus Christ is Lord of all and *first* of all in our lives?

This chapter in Luke also raises the question of how we respond to Jesus Christ in our midst. Without jumping the gun on next Sunday's Gospel reading, we can see there were at least two reactions on the part of his contemporaries. In the synagogue, Jesus' words were met with astonishment and surprise. This came from the people who had been waiting for the Messiah, who were familiar with the scriptures concerning him, who had known Jesus as a boy. And the other response, which came from people both inside and outside the community of faith, was praise and glory to God; spreading the news about him through all the surrounding country; bringing others to meet the Savior. And the wonderful thing about Jesus in the Gospels is that when he comes, it's always to a level playing field. No one has an inside track or can bank on pedigree or years of service.

So it is with us at the start of a new year. Whatever our history is, whether we're outsiders, newcomers to the faith, or pillars of the church, Jesus has the same promises for us all: good news; release; recovery of sight; liberty; the year of the Lord's favor. The Christ who could give even a thief on a cross a fresh beginning comes to us with the offer of new life. How shall we respond in this season of Epiphany, a word that means "to show forth"? Will we hear him? Receive him? Glorify God and show others where he may be found? Let us pledge to make him first in all we are and all we do: Jesus the Messiah; our Alpha and Omega; the beginning and the end. (Carol M. Norén)

JANUARY 28, 2001

❧

Fourth Sunday After the Epiphany

Worship Theme: God calls us, young and old, women and men, to be witnesses; and we will know God's presence, as Jesus did, even when we are rejected for speaking God's word.

Readings: Jeremiah 1:4-10; 1 Corinthians 13:1-13; Luke 4:21-30

Call to Worship (Psalm 71:1-6):

> *Leader:* In you, O LORD, I take refuge;
> let me never be put to shame.

> *People:* **In your righteousness deliver me and rescue me;**
> **incline your ear to me and save me.**

> *Leader:* Be to me a rock of refuge,
> a strong fortress, to save me,
> for you are my rock and my fortress.

> *People:* **Rescue me, O my God, from the hand of the wicked,**
> **from the grasp of the unjust and cruel.**

> *Leader:* For you, O LORD, are my hope,
> my trust, O LORD, from my youth.

> *People:* **Upon you I have leaned from my birth;**
> **it was you who took me from my mother's**
> **womb. My praise is continually of you.**

Pastoral Prayer:
God of the prophets, you know us and consecrate us before we are born: Be with our young people that they may speak your jus-

54

tice at an early age. Give them hope that they may expect to serve you their whole lives long; give them faith that they may grow in understanding and see you face-to-face; give them love that they may find the courage to embrace those whom others have forgotten. O God, all of us tremble at the awesome prospect of being called as your messengers "to pluck up and to pull down," "to build and to plant"; we know that even your Son was reviled for his words of truth. Be our rock in a weary land; teach us the ways of kindness and patience; prepare us to endure for the sake of your gospel and to rejoice in your steadfast promises. We praise you for the gift of Jesus Christ our Savior. Amen. (Blair G. Meeks)

SERMON BRIEFS

GOD'S INVITATION

JEREMIAH 1:4-10

Despite scholarly speculation as to how old Jeremiah was when the word of the Lord came to him, there is no way to know exactly. Even though Jeremiah's protestations to God included the plea, "I am only a boy," the Hebrew word rendered as "boy" in the NRSV can mean anything from "child" to "youth" to "apprentice." It is not likely that Jeremiah's chief concern, years later as he dictated this opening passage to Baruch, was to make sure his readers could calculate his date of birth. His point was to reveal how intimidated he was by his own sense of inadequacy and his awareness of the gloriously awesome burden of receiving and having to deliver the very Word of God.

Like other prophets—Moses stuttering before the burning bush (Exodus 3:1–4:16), Gideon negotiating for signs on the threshing floor (Judges 6:1-27), Ezekiel eating a scroll from his trembling hand (Ezekiel 2:1–3:3), and Amos, minding his own sheep (Amos 7:14-15)—Jeremiah was as unsure of his own potential as a prophet as he was struck by the urgency and scope of what Yahweh expected him to do. Yet apparently, God had set him apart, with a particular time and place and mission in mind, before he was even born. Moreover, God had already anticipated his every excuse—poor communication skills, no work experience—even one Jeremiah tried to hide: weak knees. "No problem," God says. "I'll be with you every step of the way. I'll put my own word in your mouth to say. I'll even stand beside you if I have to." All in all, a pretty sweet deal.

In truth, though, we are glad it was Jeremiah and not us. We wouldn't wish Jeremiah's life on our worst enemy, not to mention ourselves. Jeremiah lived in excruciating anguish over having to deliver a pronouncement of judgment, having to witness the unfolding destruction of his people and Jerusalem, and having to suffer the consequences of being a thorn in the side of priests, prophets, and people alike, all who refused to listen. We prefer that Jeremiah's call not be a model for us. We would prefer to read the first chapter of Jeremiah as a benign reminder that God does not discriminate by age or experience.

A common pattern in the biblical narrative when God calls is for the one called to either drop the phone or hand the receiver to another. Consequently, many of us presume from this pattern when the divine call comes today, it comes only to those whose peculiarly spiritual dispositions, capacities and experiences have left them especially susceptible to being called in the first place. In other words, God does not "call" just anyone. Whew!

What Jeremiah describes in verses 4-10, however, is how God called "just anyone." What Jeremiah confirms is that God sought him out in the womb, long before any peculiarly spiritual dispositions or capacities had formed, long before he had studied any Scripture or attended any worship or bowed his head for any prayer, and marked him as a prophet.

The claim of this opening chapter of Jeremiah is not simply that God knows us even before we know ourselves. The amazing claim of these few verses is that, in knowing and consecrating us fully at our creation, God can invite us at any time, to receive and to be the bearers of God's particular Word to a particular people for a particular purpose. God's claim on us includes the right to call us in spite of inadequacy, inexperience, and wobbly knees. While the specifics may vary—and at times not be very specific— the potential purpose and risk of bearing a prophetic message is the same for us as it was for Jeremiah. For Jeremiah, the Word

God gave him carried the power to "to pluck up—and to plant."
For us God's Word continues to hold the frightening potential to
tear down and to build up. And in our day there continues to be a
need for both actions—among the nations as well as in the
church. Thankfully, Jeremiah continues to remind us that such a
Word does not require a specially equipped bullhorn to be heard.

Just a birth certificate. (Mark Price)

THE ESSENTIAL INGREDIENT

1 CORINTHIANS 13:1-13

In the passages that proceed our scripture for today, Paul has
been using figurative language to talk to the Corinthians about all
their bickering. He uses the various parts of the *physical* body to
show them how ridiculous it is for members of the same "body"
of believers or *church* to argue among themselves about who is
greater because they are *all* necessary for the whole "body" to be
complete.

From there he goes on to his famous hymn of love, introducing
it by saying: "But strive for the greater gifts. And I will show you
a still more excellent way" (1 Corinthians 12:31).

The greatest epiphany, of course, in this *season* of epiphanies,
is to see *love* and to see *how to* love. And this often involves seeing things *differently* from how we have seen them in the past.

I heard a story that illustrates how this kind of *shift* in the way
we look at things can make the *apparently impossible*, possible.
It's about a man who loved his money very much. In fact, he was
such a miser that in his will he stipulated that he wanted all his
money to be buried with him. He was going to take it with him
after all. At his funeral there were three friends: a priest, a doctor, and a lawyer. After the funeral, the priest said: "Well, I have a
confession to make. I'm a bit ashamed, but when no one was
looking, I took a little of the money out of one of the envelopes in
the coffin. It was so sad to see it just buried and after all it's for a
good cause."

The doctor then said, "Yes, I took some too. And I'm ashamed,
but I just couldn't let it all go into the ground. So I slipped a little

more than you, actually," he said to the priest. "I took one whole envelope."

"I'm ashamed of both of you," the lawyer said. "Stealing from a dead man! I took all the rest of his money, all the other envelopes. But I didn't steal it. *I* put in a *check* for the full amount." Totally legal, and profoundly in touch with the truth of this situation. The *check* was just as good to the dead man as the cash would have been. It just took a *new* way of thinking about it to release the gifts.

And finding your way through to how to make *love* viable in a situation where it *seemed* impossible, *that* epiphany is like this story in another way too because it can make you very rich—in *spiritual* resources—the most important kind. The lawyer thought about the situation in a different way and got all the rest of the money. When you find the different way of looking at the situation that has stopped you from loving before, then the way is opened to releasing a flood of resources to enable love to use that *same* key to open other impasses. So our range and repertoire of love grows.

The Ultimate Priority

In I Corinthians 13 Paul gives us a "lucky list" of thirteen ingredients in love, which is not a sentimental feeling for him, but a series of clearly defined spiritual disciplines. You know the list and a sermon could be preached on each of these aspects of love.

But the central point here is that in all this talk about gifts and graces, none of them are worth a fig leaf without love. In other words, you can say and do everything *magna cum laude* and still get it all wrong. Love is the leaven in the loaf, the oil in the lamp, and the life-breath in the body of believers.

It's interesting too that love is mainly proactive in Paul's list. Only five of its aspects are defined by what it does *not* do. We cannot be faithful in the fullness of love's expression by what we don't do. Although it is always a good day when we can win the battle without ever having to draw our sword and that is love's way.

Love also has longevity on its side. All those other gifts get finished finally. We grow out of all the things of this world, as a child matures into adulthood. We will be similarly transformed to clarity of vision and fullness of understanding beyond our comprehension now. Paul's vision is of a completeness that totally transcends all worldly things. This puts the competition about gifts and honors on a clearly ephemeral sandy shore, *this side* of "Jordan."

So what's left? Seek to live in love, use your unique spiritual gifts for the common good, and trust God.

We have a lovely family in our church with two daughters named Faith and Grace. The grandfather tells the parents: "You have Faith and Grace, but no Hope!" He's kidding, of course. But he would never, even joking, have said: "No *Love.*" We don't joke about that because it is the ingredient above all others that makes or breaks the stew of life. (Kathleen Peterson)

NO RESERVATIONS ACCEPTED

LUKE 4:21-30

Some sermons just don't get the response you want. Some preachers don't preach the message you want to hear. And some reporters don't seem to give enough details for it all to make sense. That appears to be the case in this morning's reading from the Gospel. Jesus had returned to his hometown of Nazareth. It was after his baptism in the Jordan, and the voice from heaven saying, "this is my beloved Son"; and after his temptation in the wilderness. His ministry to people in Galilee had attracted public attention. He cast out demons. His fame spread throughout the region.

But playing before the home crowd can be a difficult and painful experience, as any professional sports team can tell you. You're not only expected to live up to the advance publicity; this audience makes demands on you as none other does. These people feel as though they own you, as though they're entitled to a share in your triumphs and accomplishments. That is the way the people of Nazareth apparently reacted to Jesus. The leaders of the synagogue invited Jesus to be their guest teacher, let him

choose his own text, and ran some publicity in the *Nazareth
Daily News*. The longtime members reminded each other that
this was Joseph's oldest boy. Some may have bragged that they'd
lived just down the street from his family. They listened to him
read from Isaiah and waited for their favorite son to do them
proud.

Jesus knew what was going on. He understood better than the
people in the pews did what they wanted him to say and do. In
Luke's Gospel, the synagogue at Nazareth is more than a local
congregation; it symbolizes the dreams and hopes of all Israel at
the time. And in the few sentences recorded here Jesus disappointed them, rejected their claim, and announced God's
promises through him were for someone else.

They hoped for a messiah to fulfill their expectation of God's
promise to the Jews—but Jesus spent time with outcasts. They
wanted Jesus to perform better wonders than he'd done in
Capernaum—but Jesus said, "a prophet is without honor in his
own country," and he performed no miracles in Nazareth. They
wanted to hear of God's special care for Israel—but Jesus
reminded them, through reciting their own history, that God was
not obligated to render special services to any of them.

The misguided souls at Nazareth synagogue thought they were
somehow entitled to reserved places in the kingdom of God;
Jesus showed them no reservations were accepted. Places of
honor at the messianic banquet would not be granted because of
one's place of birth or ancestry, one's prestige or pocketbook, but
only by God's gracious initiative, as God willed. Frustrated and
denied at every turn, it's no wonder the people of the synagogue
turned on Jesus. The Son of the Most High could not be owned
by a special interest group.

This is a revolutionary text, if we take it seriously. The grace of
God, made known in the promises Jesus fulfilled, has nothing to
do with human ideas of deserving and entitlement. If we believe
this, it can turn our lives and our church and our world upside
down. What good news for most of us, caught up in the futility of
trying to stake a claim on God's love. What a relief to stop trying
to force the Holy Spirit's hand by how many hours we spend at
the church, the number of committees we serve on, the size of
our pledge. We'd be free from the tyranny of competing with

others to be the most deserving of power from on High. How differently we would see ourselves if we repented of the sin of presuming we are not as needy as the widow of Zarephath, as helpless as Namaan the leper. Gratitude and wonder and a holy joy would be ours as we realized redemption is our unmerited gift in Jesus Christ.

Imagine what could happen in the church if we received God's word to us in this text. We'd be delivered from the temptation to regard budgets and building programs as barometers of divine favor, and instead praise God for these signs of his beneficence even to the likes of us. We could abandon the pious disguises used to justify our vanities and self-interests. Thanking God that Scripture has been fulfilled in our hearing, every aspect of our worship and mission would proclaim the year of the Lord's favor to those folks over in Capernaum, outside the household of faith: the homeless, the imprisoned, and other present-day lepers.

And imagine how different the world will be when people no longer try to claim the Son of God as their private property. What blessed peace will come when nations no longer act as though their faith entitles them to this piece of land or that border; a divine right protected with the blood of their children. When all followers of Jesus heed the warning in today's Gospel, they will cease to regard one village or nation or race as more chosen and deserving than another. What relief for the world's poor, its captives, its blind and oppressed—all precious in our Lord's sight— when the power to consume most of the world's goods is not taken as a sign of God's favor.

The faithful of Nazareth insisted that the wonder-worker of Galilee belonged to them and that they deserved more than others. But Jesus makes clear there are no reservations accepted at God's banqueting table. The invitation is issued by grace where the Spirit wills, and those who insist on their rights will find the promise is given to others. Like the Nazarenes, we are not entitled to divine power. Jesus the Messiah does not belong to us—but by the mercy of God only, we may belong to him. (Carol M. Norén)

REFLECTIONS

❦

FEBRUARY

Reflection Verses: "He called the twelve and began to send them out two by two, and gave them authority over the unclean spirits" (Mark 6:7). "After this the Lord appointed seventy others and sent them on ahead of him in pairs . . ." (Luke 10:1).

If Jesus sent his disciples two by two into their ministries, what makes any of us think we can go it alone? Ministry is no solo affair. This calling is weighty enough, it always takes at least two to carry it.

Why *did* he send them in pairs? Because each one was dumb enough to get lost by himself or herself and likely to need bailing out by a buddy? Because when the strangest things started happening, each disciple would ask, "Did that really *happen*?" and needed someone to reply, "It really did"? Because the law says it takes two to constitute a witness in Israel?

He must have had his reasons, but we're in no position to read his mind. What we can do is reflect on our own reasons for needing partnerships in this vocation. By "partnership" I don't mean a formally appointed copastor or colleague, though one of these could do the trick. What I mean is a bonafide brother or sister. I mean a friend of the heart, the kind who walks beside us in all weathers, shoulders grief and joy with us, and gives us a piece of his or her mind when we need it. It could be anyone. It could be more than one—an assortment of sisters, a bevy of brothers.

Taking a cue from the text, one purpose of such companionship is to keep us uncluttered. Jesus makes a point of sending the Twelve empty-handed into their work, strips them of all equipment but sticks in their hands and a partner at each of their sides. They have no resource kits, no *Preaching Annual* (!), no external validation, security, or crutch—nothing to "use" or hide behind.

All they get to take is *who they are and what is within them to give*. Scary! And having sent us on this journey of a self-without-props, Christ requires a brother or sister at our side. It suggests that real and uncovered selfhood, indispensable to ministry, may elude us without fellow travelers to help us get to it and stay with it.

More than thirty years ago, Carlyle Marney wrote vividly, to say the least, of this necessity: "To be of a proper new breed, somewhere, sometime, somehow, someone must rub my nose in the offal of my real motives that moved me to seek a ministry of high-calling. Without this confrontation of self-soul I am never housebroken and continue to soil the temple. . . . I cannot face these primal powers of Original Sin alone. It takes a . . . brother [or sister], or some other beloved, to midwife me on this labor. It's a journey to depth—never possible alone . . . to fish that old cistern out and properly label its old skeletons and carcasses of primal powers. . . . And one can drown down there, in the waters of his new-birth, unless he begins early to see also an Original Salvation, namely even there I had been loved" (*The Coming Faith*, [Nashville: Abingdon Press, 1970], pp. 142-43).

So our need for a friend of the heart is a need for someone to help us go down to a deeper honesty, a more authentic selfhood. The old word for our calling—"Parson"—meant simply, "person." It was understood that a minister's chief function was to be a true human being among the people, a real presence, a revelatory self. Jesus pointed to the necessity for this when he directed his disciples to go empty-handed. He pointed the path to it not only by giving them each his authority but also by giving them each a partner. No one gets down to solid selfhood alone.

Not to mention that it's just a whole lot more fun to have a friend in it with you—a Laurel to your Hardy, a Thelma to your Louise, a Silas to your Paul. Can you imagine either Paul or Silas sitting all *alone* in that Philippian jail in the midnight hour and managing to sing up an earthquake? Outrageous joy rises in the back-and-forth of joined voices, contagious courage, shared fire. The surest cure for our timidity and faithless despair is a sister or brother who knows better of us, who needs better from us, and can pitch in to help us both lift up our hearts.

Have you heard the reason that mountain climbers tie themselves to each other? They say it's to keep the sane ones from going home! How good to be tied to people who are the right kind of crazy.

Yes, there's a necessary solitude too. You apparently know this, for here you are all alone with this book in your hand. To be a "Parson" is to embrace the loneliness of selfhood too. There is private work to do, interior struggles to face, no substitute for silence, and we must say our own prayers. Even so, if you listen very carefully inside your own silence, what you may often hear is a prompting toward another: To whom do I need to confess what I have just realized about myself? Or who can help me bear this grief? Who can help me sort out this confusion? With whom can I share this thrilling new vision? Or who needs me to be such a friend of the heart for them?

If you have a good friend, maybe today would be a very good day to say your most hearty thanks—to God and to them. If you have found yourself lately too much alone, today might be a good day, without excuses, to ask why. Is it possible that today would be a very good day to pick up the phone and make a call? (Paul D. Duke)

FEBRUARY 4, 2001

❦

Fifth Sunday After the Epiphany

Worship Theme: The voice of Jesus tells us not to fear for he is with us; then Jesus calls us to gather others into the embrace of God's love.

Readings: Isaiah 6:1-8 (9-13); 1 Corinthians 15:1-11; Luke 5:1-11

Call to Worship (Psalm 138:1-6, 8):

> *Leader:* I give you thanks, O LORD, with my whole heart;
> before the gods I sing your praise;
>
> *People:* **I bow down toward your holy temple**
> **and give thanks to your name**
> **for your steadfast love and your faithful-**
> **ness. . . .**
>
> *Leader:* On the day I called, you answered me,
> you increased my strength of soul.
>
> *People:* **All the kings of the earth shall praise you,**
> **O LORD,**
> **for they have heard the words of your**
> **mouth.**
> **They shall sing of the ways of the LORD,**
> **for great is the glory of the LORD.**
>
> *Leader:* For though the LORD, is high, he regards the lowly,
> but the haughty he perceives from far away.
>
> *People:* **Your steadfast love, O LORD, endures**
> **forever.**
> **Do not forsake the work of your hands.**

Pastoral Prayer:

Holy God, the whole earth is full of your glory, and yet we are afraid. You know our fear; you know our failings; and you promise to blot out our sins and remember them no more. When you call us to follow you, our inadequacies confront us, our awe at your power overwhelms us; and we want to tell you to find someone worthier. Help us to hear the gentle voice of Jesus saying, "Do not be afraid; from now on you are with me." Guide us so that we know where to let down our nets. Give us your Spirit of caring and send us to join the others fishing in your waters, bringing people home to your love. We remember with thanksgiving all our brothers and sisters in the faith whose testimony through the generations has handed down to us the good news of Jesus Christ, who died for our sins, was buried, and was raised on the third day in accordance with the scriptures. In his name we pray. Amen. (Blair G. Meeks)

SERMON BRIEFS

LOOK, LISTEN, AND LEARN

ISAIAH 6:1-8 (9-13)

I. The Scene Isaiah Saw

Readers of the Bible have always been impressed by the scene Isaiah saw, but they often remember John 1:18, "No one has ever seen God." Is there a contradiction here? Not at all. Notice that Isaiah does not describe God. He describes the throne, but he never describes the One who sits on the throne. He describes the robe, but he never describes the One who wears the robe. He describes the winged creatures, but he never describes the One attended by the winged creatures. He describes the room but he never describes the One whose presence fills the room. This impressive description tells us that God is never to be taken lightly. God must be approached with great reverence and deep humility. God is not "the man upstairs." God is "the Lord God Almighty!"

Notice also the timing of the vision. It was "in the year that king Uzziah died." Uzziah had been a good king. "He did what was right in the eyes of the Lord" (2 Chronicles 26:4 NIV). But would his son Jotham do the same?

Many times good kings were succeeded by evil kings. It was at a time of uncertainty that Isaiah received his vision of heaven. In another time of uncertainty, when the Roman Empire was disintegrating, Augustine wrote his book *The City of God!*

II. The Song Isaiah Heard

The song Isaiah heard is the same song John heard! The song that echoes through the Old Testament echoes also through the New. Eight hundred years after Isaiah's vision they were still singing that song (Revelation 4:8). And when *we've* been here ten thousand years, *we* will be singing that song. What does it mean—this threefold emphasis on the holiness of God? It means that we serve a God who can be trusted. Contemplate for just one moment what it would be like if God were evil? Who would dare to pray? Suppose you pray for rain and there is a flood and your house is swept away, and in the background you hear the cackle of Divine laughter, "You got what you asked for!" But God is not evil and we are not afraid to pray. Of course to speak of the character of God is to reflect on our own. How can we who are not holy come into the presence of a God who is holy? Isaiah faced that difficulty, and so do we. It is only by invitation that we come into the Divine presence, and it is only after we have experienced spiritual cleansing.

III. The Assignment Isaiah Received

It was an awesome assignment. He was to go on God's behalf. He was to be a Divine ambassador delivering God's message, not his own. He was reluctant to go for he was not worthy. It was an unwelcome assignment for it was not good news. Here our assignment differs from his. We have the privilege of delivering good news. Like Isaiah, we go on God's behalf. We, too, are Divine ambassadors (2 Corinthians 5:20). The message we take is not our own, but God's. And sometimes, like Isaiah, we are reluctant to go. We feel unworthy. But we should go gladly, for our news is good news. (Robert C. Shannon)

67

RESURRECTION REALITY

1 CORINTHIANS 15:1-11

In this text, Paul confronts the Corinthians with the centrality of the Resurrection for faith. The divisions apparent in Corinth must not have been around the substance of faith. The faith, says Paul, is based on the death of Jesus and his resurrection. This *is* the good news. However, the grace, operative in the climactic gift of the Christ for the sins of the world, is the challenge. Can this miracle be believed?

Clearly, for Paul, the issue of witnesses is paramount to the verification of this unbelievable occurrence, so he enumerates those who attest the resurrection as reality, including himself in the number. The good news Paul has shared is also what he received: *Christ has died, Christ is risen*. His self-inclusion as a witness highlights the significance of this text—a sinner who persecuted the church, Paul now is a dedicated follower of the Way. His story illumines the power of the resurrection. He has been transformed from an enemy of Jesus to his most fierce and incessant disciples.

Can you name those who are witnesses to the resurrection reality? My home church brings to mind the names of several who were certain that Jesus was raised from the dead. The quiet dignity of Marie Marshall who recognized my call to preach when I was but a lad, laid before me the resurrection hope. The vocal affirmations of Milton Byard and Abner Davis, men who survived the sin sick malady of racism by the sheer pride birthed in the womb of their faith heritage, told me of how wonderful it was to know Jesus is risen. The love and care of Virginia Davis and Bernice Martin, church members who took great pride in my gifts and sent "care" packages to encourage me in college, assured me of the fundamental reality they knew through the resurrection of the Christ.

Who, in your life, saw Jesus and assured you that he lives? Was it someone in your growing years? Your young adult years? In your times of doubt and disillusionment, who pointed out that there is power beyond any destructive doubt or force imaginable? These are the believers who demonstrated the vitality of Christian faith.

Still, there is no substitute for the your own testimony. Each of us needs to know this power for ourselves. If we are not convinced of the impact and potency of resurrection in our own lives, we cannot, with integrity, persuade others of its relevance in their lives. What has the Christ event meant in your life? The difference that it has made for you, as with Paul, is a prodigious contribution to your faith journey. If others are to believe, then we ought to first believe. Are you convinced? Has the Resurrection made a soul changing difference in your life? Like Paul, we must each be certain of the resurrection reality in our own faith journey! (Vance P. Ross)

THE KEY TO HOPE

LUKE 5:1-11

Sometimes a knock at the door is a welcome sound, but not always. Somehow I knew this was no ordinary knock. Walking to the door, I found a church member sobbing the kind of sobs that only tragedy could bring.

Two years earlier, my friend Al had kissed his seven-year-old daughter goodnight as he had tucked her into bed. About three hours later, little Jennifer had awakened her parents to tell them she didn't feel well. Al and his wife found Jennifer had a mild fever. They gave her some medicine, put her back to bed, and kissed her goodnight a second time. Six hours later Al went in to awaken Jennifer, only to discover that his precious daughter, the joy of his life, had died in her sleep.

For two years, Al and his wife had been trying to get their lives back together, but most days it didn't work. This was one of those days. Now Al was at my door, begging me to help him find some hope in what seemed to be a hopeless world.

It's hard to have hope in the midst of despair. When your life is filled with depression, anxiety, and crisis, hope can seem a cruel illusion.

Such was certainly true of the story presented in Luke 5:1-11. Verse one tells us, "the crowd was pressing in on [Jesus] to hear the word of God." Why? Because they were desperate. Their nation was occupied by an oppressive foreign army. Unreasonable Roman taxation was crushing. Hunger was rampant, the death penalty was commonplace, and public beatings were a daily occurrence. The Hebrews wanted deliverance. They wanted to know God had not abandoned them. In short, they wanted *hope.* So they turned to this new rabbi who spoke "as one with authority," praying he would have the answers in a time of despair.

Like those people by the lake and the fishermen who would become Jesus' first disciples, everyone needs hope. Without hope, life is heart wrenching and meaningless. Nevertheless, hope often seems fleeting because far too often we grasp at false hope rather than accepting a hope that lasts. Yet, such is not surprising since we are taught from childhood a false picture of hope. Therefore, if we are going to receive and ultimately embody true hope, we must start by identifying what hope *is not!*

I.   True hope is not wishful thinking. It is natural for us to have wishes, and there is nothing wrong with wishing. However, we must remember that most of our wishes are simply perceptions of what we *think* would make us happy, and life rarely marches to the drumbeat of our self-centered wishes. Face it: most of our wishes are the products of selfishness. We are far more likely to wish for wealth and position than for the opportunity of humble service and sacrifice.

II.   True hope is not profound longing. Longing is simply wishful thinking taken to the extreme. In fact, longing is perhaps what substitutes for prayer in many circles. We beg God for our longings while rarely asking, "Will true peace be mine if my longings are realized? Will anything or anyone be honored by the fruit of my longings?" The Hebrews longed for the kingdom of God, but they longed for a kingdom where *they* would be the rulers and the Romans would be their slaves. They wanted to hear God's Word, *provided* God's Word confirmed their longings and their prejudices. Sound familiar?

III.   True hope is not optimism. True hope can *produce* optimism, but optimism cannot produce true hope. Optimism without true hope born from God's grace is simply a positive affirmation without a foundation for belief. Optimism without a basis is false hope. Like wishing and longing, it is based solely on *us* and on our limited capacity to produce what we *think* will make us happy.

So, what is true hope? True hope is found in Christ. Jesus produced boatloads of fish where fish had not been found in order to show his would-be disciples that God was the God of the impossible! God can empower us with the miraculous. He cannot only birth great expectations, but he can bring them to life. He can heal the brokenness, the anger, and the hatred in people. He can change the bruised and the battered into a force for salvation and world deliverance. And perhaps most important to our modern world, Jesus can kindle a vision of a never ending tomorrow that is so real, so true, that it brings confidence to both the joyous and the brokenhearted that God is in control! Heaven is real, it's forever, and we are safe within the everlasting arms.

True hope is what was born to those first disciples and to my friend Al, and true hope is what can be born to us, for the best is yet to come. (Tommy McDearis)

FEBRUARY 11, 2001

❧

Sixth Sunday After the Epiphany

Worship Theme: We are called to proclaim God's reign and to live in the light of the resurrection so that others may know God's love through us.

Readings: Jeremiah 17:5-10; 1 Corinthians 15:12-20; Luke 6:17-26

Call to Worship (Psalm 1):

Leader:	Happy are those who do not follow the advice of the wicked, or take the path that sinners tread;
People:	**but their delight is in the law of the LORD, and on his law they meditate day and night.**
Leader:	They are like trees planted by streams of water, which yield their fruit in its season, and their leaves do not wither.
People:	**In all that they do, they prosper. The wicked are not so, but are like chaff that the wind drives away.**
Leader:	Therefore the wicked will not stand in the judgment, nor sinners in the congregation of the righteous;
People:	**for the LORD watches over the way of the righteous, but the way of the wicked will perish.**

Pastoral Prayer:

Precious Lord in whom we trust, when we find ourselves in a wilderness of uncertainty, you encourage us to put down roots and find your streams of living waters. You test our minds and search our hearts, and yet you calm our fears. O God, you have promised to give the poor a kingdom and the hungry a filling feast: Help us to remember that your reign begins now and that we are your disciples, serving those in need. You have promised the grieving that they will know laughter, and the ridiculed and outcast that you have for them a place of refuge: Give us grace to bring your comfort and embrace to hurting hearts. Make us rich in your kindness and fill us with your joy that others may know your love through us. We thank you, God, that even when death's shadow seems to rule, we know your power for life and proclaim with joy Christ's resurrection, in whose name we pray. Amen. (Blair G. Meeks)

SERMON BRIEFS

CHOOSING THE RIGHT FOUNDATION

JEREMIAH 17:5-10

These verses from Jeremiah are simple wisdom sayings that squarely reflect his thought and preaching. In these verses, Jeremiah boiled human existence down to its most fundamental level, emphasizing the need for humanity to trust in God. The crisis which humanity faced then, and the crisis we still face today, results from our unwillingness to place our trust in God. Most ancient wisdom sayings sought to illustrate the truth of this age-old crisis by showing the consequences experienced by those who chose wrongly.

I have recently taken up gardening as a hobby, and one of the first lessons I learned was that the difference between a plant flourishing and a plant struggling to survive often lies in the soil. A gardener cannot simply dig a hole, pull the plant out of its container, and place it in the ground. Only the heartiest plants can withstand that kind of treatment. The plants that bloom and produce fruit are the ones with which the gardener spends some time and effort with in the initial stages of planting. If the gardener will loosen the soil, the roots will be able to stretch out and provide a firm foundation for the plant. If fertilizer, nutrients, and peat moss are added to the soil, the environment will be welcoming, and the needed sustenance will be provided to the plant during long, hot summer days. Plants that do not have this extra care are more susceptible to drought, weak roots, and all types of disease. The soil does make all the difference.

Jeremiah knew from watching the world around him that the soil made all the difference. His message to the nation of Israel was that the foundational environment they chose for their lives would have very real consequences for their daily lives. As Emil Brunner so eloquently stated, "there is nothing said about sin which means anything other than the act of turning away from God. But . . . this act is conceived as one which determines man's *whole* existence" (*Man in Revolt*, in *The Interpreter's Bible*, Volume 5 [New York: Pierce and Washabaugh, 1956], p. 953).

Jeremiah makes use of the analogy of two plants in different environments to show the importance of trusting in God rather than humanity. The shrub planted in the desert is much like a life lived trusting in our own strength and the strength of other humans. A life lived by trusting in our human strength is a life lived on the edge. There are some situations that we believe we can handle by using our own strength and resources, but soon we find ourselves wondering whether what we have will be enough to carry us through the long haul. Like a shrub in the desert, we fail to do anything but subsist. Deep in our hearts we know that if hot, scorching trials come, we will be unable to withstand their punishment.

Yet, Jeremiah tells us there is another way. Trusting in God is like having an endless reservoir from which to draw. Even when life is dry and unpromising, we will not be afraid. God's foundation is secure and nourishing. We will prosper and bear fruit, even in the worst of times. A foundation that lies securely in the strength and presence of God is one that finds nothing lacking.

Jeremiah reminds us that the choices we make now will matter in the difficult times of life. It's not a matter of wondering if the difficult times will come, but rather what resources we will have to draw upon when they arrive. It's a matter of loosening the soil, strengthening the roots, and choosing the right One in whom to place our trust. (Wendy Joyner)

BELIEVING IN "COMEBACKS"!

1 CORINTHIANS 15:12-20

Our resurrection hope for Christians comes through the resurrection reality of Jesus. The philosophical argument raised by Paul in this text is a rational attempt to refute those who despise the impossibility of resurrection—killing the hope of those newfound to this faith. He does so by appealing to the illogic of agreeing that Christ was resurrected, but his followers could not be. If Jesus was a man, and we can believe in his resurrection, it follows that the power that raised him can also raise his followers.

What do we believe about the power of God in Jesus? Is this power a "very present help" or was it a one-time effort now 2000 years old? The potency of the living God remains an essential question for Christians and nonbelievers, for new disciples and longtime adherents. The capacity and prerogative of God in Jesus is always a query of importance, especially in this postmodern era.

People have a need to believe in "comebacks!" Can victory still be pulled from the jaws of defeat? Is it possible to raise the *Titanic* to "Love Boat" status? Will God meet us today with the same power proclaimed by Scripture? These are questions that will not go away.

Many literary sources, read through faithful, faith-filled eyes, demonstrate God's comeback tendency. The lives of significant personalities such as Helen Keller and Abraham Lincoln declare that God resurrects us from formidable obstacles. The abolition of slavery, the defeat of Nazi Germany, the destruction of apartheid, and the withering of Communism broadcast decisively that truth crushed to earth may rise again.

Still, in the twenty-first century, a belief in bodily resurrection seems ignorant and miseducated at best, deceitful and mean at worst. The question now becomes: What limits will we place on God?

In *The Gospel of Good Success*, Kirbyjon Caldwell tells a wonderful resurrection story, the comeback of a very significant person in his life. He proclaims, without apology, that God can do all things, and he reminds us that God is in the resurrection business—even for people like you and me.

Paul understands God as omnipotent, limitless except in God's own choosing. God can interrupt time and space to do anything that God wishes. This is the absolute trust Paul wants to convey—a trust for which he has given his life. And yet, God's limitless power demands an answer. Where have you seen this power at work in your life? With your family? In the congregation? Community? Around the globe?

Traveling to the Soviet Union some 15 years ago, I was struck by the age of the churches there. Predating the conversion of Constantine, the church lived in the midst of a government and a system that was bent on destroying religion. Men and women constantly heard that their faith would be crushed, the church destroyed, and their people murdered.

Today there is no Soviet Union, but the church of Jesus the Christ lives in Moscow and St. Petersburg, in Tbilisi and Yerevan. But not only that, slaughtered men and women have witnesses who keep their testimonies alive. Their faith in the throes of persecution lives on in their progeny. Their stories are still being told.

Resurrection is true, for people and for our faith. But its totality is at issue here. As did the apostle Paul, we cannot ignore the implications of what we believe. Ultimately the question that is raised is this: Is there something impossible for God? If there is, then our faith is in vain, our religion bankrupt, and our preaching empty. But if there is nothing impossible for God, *that* is good news to be shared. Glory Hallelujah! (Vance P. Ross)

TO CHOOSE

LUKE 6:17-26

In her fine sermon, "Making Choices," Janice W. Hearn recalls one of the great stories of the movie industry that concerned the making of the animated classic *Snow White*. When that movie was being made, an army of animators spent over two hundred days making a four-and-a-half-minute segment where the dwarfs made soup for Snow White and practically destroyed the kitchen in the process. According to everyone who saw it, it was an enormously funny sequence. In fact, it is said that Walt Disney laughed out loud when he screened it. So it is not hard to imagine how shocked the animators were when Disney had the segment cut from the film because he said it interrupted the flow of the story.

Some people would probably call that investment a waste of time and resources. Nevertheless, Walt Disney had to choose what would go and what would stay in order to make the movie the best it could be. And given that the movie became a masterpiece of the film industry, one would have to say that Disney chose well.

Such is the case in Luke 6:17-26. This is a lesson on choosing. It is a lesson on deciding what should go and what should stay if we are going to have the life God intends for God's people.

This passage of scripture is called the Lukan Beatitudes, but unfortunately, this version of the Beatitudes is seldom read. In truth, Matthew's version is far more popular. Matthew lists nine blessings and no woes. Luke lists only four blessings and he includes four woes in contrast to each blessing. Matthew's version sounds romantic; Luke's version is stark. Matthew's version is comforting; Luke's is curt. Therefore, it is more pleasing to read Matthew's version of this passage. Nevertheless, it is important for us to avoid passing over the Lukan Beatitudes since Luke's version offers a lesson not explicitly found in the Matthean version. Unlike Matthew's rendition of the Beatitudes, Luke's version shows Jesus presenting us with a direct lesson on *choosing*.

I.   When we think about heaven and earth, we normally think of these as being two distinctly different places. Earth, with its struggles, is occupied by humanity. Heaven, a place of peace and joy, is the domain of God. However, the New Testament says that when Jesus came, the kingdom of heaven became *present* with us. But unfortunately, the kingdom of earth did not disappear when the kingdom of heaven came to be with us through Christ. Therefore, we still live with the tainted values of *this* world and we are still influenced by them.

II. Perhaps a better way to look at this issue is to see heaven and earth as two bodies of water existing side by side. The water of the world is perhaps a swamp. It has no obvious boundaries. It is constantly fed by secular values and our more carnal ways of thinking, yet it has no flow. Therefore, it becomes dark, stagnant, and teeming with danger. On the other hand, the water of heaven is like a clear mountain river that is fed by the love and grace of God. It flows with life and majesty. It is pure, generous, and life giving.

III.   In the Lukan Beatitudes, Jesus notes that we have to choose which body of water beside which we want to be planted. If you choose to be planted beside the waters of earth, then anything goes. In this bog, nothing is more important than *our wishes* and *our desires.* We simply live for the here and now since nothing is more important than *me, my, and mine.* However, if we choose to be planted beside the river of heaven, then choices are required as to what can stay and what must go from our lives. We must decide what is truly important. We must decide what is of *ultimate value* in life. In other words, who and what will we trust with our futures?

IV.   In Luke 6:17-26, Jesus draws a stark contrast between the things of this world and the values of the kingdom of heaven. By including the woes, he notes that the things our world trusts and values are perishable. They look delightful on the surface, but choosing them can drag us into a swamp filled with harm and destruction. However, Christ's message is that we do not have to make the wrong choices. By choosing to be planted beside the river of heaven, we can be nourished by the living waters of Jesus Christ. To choose Christ is to choose to know the truth. It is to be set free from merely existing for ourselves. It is to be set free to flow in the rhythm of God's eternal love. (Tommy McDearis)

For more on the theme of choosing, see *Lectionary Homiletics*, February, 1995, pp. 19-20.

FEBRUARY 18, 2001

❧

Seventh Sunday After the Epiphany

Worship Theme: God's assurance of life in Christ Jesus empowers us to love the unlovable and to give to the ungrateful in Jesus' name.

Readings: Genesis 45:3-11, 15; 1 Corinthians 15:35-38, 42-50; Luke 6:27-38

Call to Worship (Psalm 37:4-8, 39):

Leader: Take delight in the LORD,
and he will give you the desires of your heart.

People: **Commit your way to the LORD;
trust in him, and he will act.**

Leader: He will make your vindication shine like the light,
and the justice of your cause like the noonday.

People: **Be still before the LORD, and wait patiently for him;
do not fret over those who prosper in their way,
over those who carry out evil devices.**

Leader: Refrain from anger, and forsake wrath.
Do not fret—it leads only to evil.

People: **The salvation of the righteous is from the LORD,
he is their refuge in the time of trouble.**

Pastoral Prayer:
Merciful God, by your power of resurrection you assure us of life, now and when we are raised to your glory: May our joy in

79

your promise empower us to bring hope to those whose survival is threatened by famine, homelessness, conflict, and despair. Because we are your children, O God, help us to remember the kindness of Joseph, whose brothers sold him into slavery, and to be kind to the ungrateful. Teach us to love those who do not love us back, to give to those who cannot respond, to lend to those who have no will to repay, for you are kind and full of mercy, and we long to live in your image. In your perfect love, free us from all fears and comfort us with your promise that we will be raised imperishable, bearing the image of Christ, the man of heaven. In the name of your life-giving Son we pray. Amen. (Blair G. Meeks)

SERMON BRIEFS

DEFINED BY THE MERCY OF GOD

GENESIS 45:3-11, 15

We are invariably shaped by the evil things people do to us. That much is beyond our control. Once in a while, we hope not often, someone does something profoundly evil to us. That sin shapes us. But must it define us? Our present text is one of many in Scripture that suggests we have an alternative, the mercy of God.

I. Defined by Sin

The sins of others exert powerful force in our lives, especially when the sinner is someone close to us. Those sins threaten to define us, to become the dominant factor in our identity. An example of this from classic literature is Hamlet. The murder of his father utterly consumes him. That wrong and its effect on Hamlet define his character. Ultimately it leads to his ruin. Of course Hamlet is merely a figure in a play, an exaggerated character well crafted to keep the audience interested. But isn't it the part of us we see in him that fascinates us?

I have known too many people defined by the sins of others. I do not seek to criticize because most of them had perfectly understandable cause: abusive parents or spouses, betrayal in marriage, children taken from them through the violence of others. I do not criticize, but I would offer hope.

One thing I hope to never preach is easy forgiveness. Forgiveness does not come easily, and perhaps even our ability to forgive can be beyond our control. It may come to us as a gift of God's mercy. But it must come. The beauty and power of forgiveness is that it ends the destructive power of sin. Until you are able to forgive, that sin someone has done to you continues to work in your life. This is why forgiveness is as important to the victim as to the perpetrator—perhaps more so. In forgiving you gain freedom forever from the wrong that has hurt you.

II. Defined by the Mercy of God

Sin will not define us if we are instead defiined by the mercy of God. Joseph is such a figure. His jealous brothers had sold him as a slave. Life had been hard on Joseph. Falsely accused, he spent years in prison. How often in those years did he dream of revenge? At last his opportunity comes. Through God's providence he has become an important man. Now his brothers unknowingly step into his jurisdiction. He has them where he wants them. And what does he do?

The answer tells us not only the fate of his brothers, it tells us who Joseph is. And we find that he is not defined by their sin. Joseph has recognized the hand of God upon his life. This mercy is what will define him.

Joseph also gains two additional gifts of God's mercy. The relationship between him and his brothers is restored, and he emerges from his suffering with a sense of its meaning. These gifts too do not come easily, if they come at all. A restored relationship may not always be practical or desirable. Time had passed for Joseph, and his brothers were not in a position to do him further harm. That is not always the case for us. When relationships can be restored, however, we experience the mercy of God.

Above all else we may desire a sense that our suffering means something. As Joseph looks back over a long life, he can see God at work, even in and through his suffering. We cannot always make sense of our suffering. Hopefully time and our faith can help us set it into a greater perspective. Whenever that happens, we again experience the mercy of God.

If someone has wronged you horribly, if you think you can never forgive, do not despair. That sin does not have to define you. The mercy of God can set you free. (David Mauldin)

THE IMMORTAL GIFT

1 CORINTHIANS 15:35-38, 42-50

In this scripture text, Paul lays it all down. The resurrected body is of God's doing: the miracle accomplished by God is not only in the gift of new life. It is also in the redemption of the body that receives new life. Crucial to this understanding is the idea that immortality is not given to the finite. The perishable must be transformed to something more, something better. The Kingdom shall be inherited but not by those who remain the same. The resurrection miracle continues in the change wrought over us.

"Just As I Am, Without One Plea" has been a favored hymn for generations because it speaks to the joy felt by those who receive the redemptive love of God in Jesus. Persons are invited, regardless of state or position, to come to God through Jesus for salvation. The crucified and Resurrected One brings for them an escape from the dread of their existence. They, and we, can be accepted.

Just As I Am does not mean just as I will stay. The God who redeems us not only moves us *from* something, but moves us *to* something. The expectation is that we will grow into all that God has made us to be. We are no longer enslaved to the old self. The sin of our existence has been cast aside as a matter of imprisonment. We are freed to live in the hope and power of a God who specializes in redemption.

But what should we make of those who claim to follow Jesus? Many claim to follow, but are they different—flesh and blood cannot inherit the kingdom; that is to say, to be beholden to the vices and trappings of this life is to fail to follow Jesus. Pop music star Madonna wrote a song in the 1980s called "Material Girl" that epitomizes all that is perishable, that persons crave in this culture—cars, diamonds, fame, money, power, pleasure. None of these in and of themselves are evil. However, when we become possessed by them we fall victim to "flesh and blood."

We cannot ignore, in our capitalist, economic society, the perishable temptations of a Wall Street, Internet, or a "Benjamin" (colloquialism for $500 bills) mad culture. Paul says that there is something more in the reality of resurrection—that the immortal gift through Jesus can become flesh and real.

My daughter Alyssa and her friends repeat this rhyme during the Christmas season years ago: "What shall I give him poor as I am? If I were a shepherd I'd give him a lamb. If I were a wise man, I'd do my part. What shall I give Him? I'll give him my heart." In this resurrection challenge, we are asked to give God our hearts in Jesus. We believe the heart, mind, body and soul shall be made to inherit the kingdom of God, imperishable and readied for all that the Reign of God shall be. (Vance P. Ross)

CHOOSING A RADICAL LIFE

LUKE 6:27-38

There is a story that has circulated for years that is perhaps fiction, but it is still a marvelous story of choosing the right priorities.

According to the story, in the late nineteenth century there was an English family who traveled to Scotland for a holiday. Upon their arrival, the young son ran away by himself to a farm pond. Being a bit mischievious, the boy took off his clothes and jumped into the water. Shortly afterward he was seized by vicious cramps so debilitating, he could do nothing but scream for help. Fortunately, another boy was nearby working in the field. Hearing the desperate cries, the boy dove into the water and he pulled the drowning boy from the pond.

When the English boy's father heard what had happened, he went to the young lad who had saved his son. After some conversation, the Englishman asked the Scottish youth what he wanted to do when he grew up. The boy said, "I suppose I will be a farmer like my father." The Englishman said, "Is that what you want to do?" The boy replied, "No, sir. I would like to be a physician, but my family is too poor to send me to school." Then the Englishman said, "Do not worry about the money. Make your plans to study medicine and I will see to the cost."

Years later while visiting the troops in North Africa, Prime Minister Winston Churchill became seriously ill with pneumonia. Only a short time before, Sir Alexander Fleming had discovered a new wonder drug called penicillin. The British High Command flew Dr. Fleming to Africa to give the drug to the ailing Prime Minister. When he did, he saved Churchill's life for the second time, for it was the boy Alexander Fleming who had pulled the boy Winston Churchill from that farm pond over sixty years earlier.

Is this a true story? Who knows. However, it is a fine illustration of a recurring theme in Luke's Gospel: *there is a profound relationship between radical living and the blessings of God.*

In Luke's version of the Sermon on the Mount, Jesus notes that radical living will always bring a sense of blessing. In other words:

I.   Life is *life* by the choices we make. The *life* God intends for humanity is found not by traveling the road well traveled, but by traveling a road seldom trod by human foot. It is found by choosing a *radical relationship.* Only Christ can enable us to transcend the limitations we so often site as the mere hazards of being human. We can transcend our sinful nature and our negative emotions. "Dog eat dog" does not have to be the rule of existence. We *can* have a miraculous relationship that enables us to see that *life* is not found by spiraling downward to the lowest common denominator.

II. True blessing is found as we discover that *there is something we can be, but will never be, apart from Christ.* Every person is unique, which means there is something we can do in God's service that no one else can do just as we can do it. Therefore, we will never be *truly alive* until we are doing it. Part of our blessing is to discover our *unique* purpose for existing on this earth, and then living out that purpose as a *steward of life.*

III.   The word *steward* comes from an ancient Hebrew word meaning *caregiver.* A caregiver for God was a person who lived and displayed the blessing of *radical joy.* And what is *joy?* Joy is not happiness. Happiness is often dictated by outside circumstances. Joy, however, is finding that nothing can separate us from the love of God. Joy is accepting that we are unconditionally accepted by God. Therefore, a true *steward* is one who joyfully celebrates an eternal relationship with a God who loves us even when our behavior paints us as *God's* enemy . . . with a God who has turned the other cheek when we have struck God with our sinful hand . . . with a God whose constant prayers and beckoning spirit remain steady even when we have cursed *God.*

IV.   God has indeed blessed those who have cursed God. A steward of life is one who chooses to follow God's radical call by passing along God's radical blessing. We model after the one who set the standards in his dealings with us. How? By treating the world around us as God has treated us. Our lives are changed by that blessing. More lives will be changed as they experience that blessing through us. God gave us mercy and love long before we knew it. God treated us as friends—as family—before we recognized our place at God's table. Now Christ calls us to raise the bar of daily living from that which proclaims, "Do it to others before they do it to you," to "Do unto others as you would have them do unto you." For after all, that is what God has done for us: "that while we were yet sinners, Christ died for us."

How different might the world be— *might it see Christ*—if we treated the world with the same radical blessing that we have received from our radical God? (Tommy McDearis)

FEBRUARY 25, 2001

❦

Transfiguration Sunday

Worship Theme: God allows us to glimpse the majesty and glory of the divine Son and then leads us to lives of service accompanied by this same beloved Son.

Readings: Exodus 34:29-35; 2 Corinthians 3:12–4:2; Luke 9:28-36 (37-43)

Call to Worship (Psalm 99:1-5, 9):

Leader: The LORD is king; let the peoples tremble!
He sits enthroned upon the cherubim; let the earth quake!

People: **The LORD is great in Zion; exalted over all the peoples.
Let them praise your great and awesome name.
Holy is he!**

Leader: Mighty Ruler, lover of justice, you have established equity;
you have executed justice and righteousness in Jacob.

People: **Extol the LORD our God; worship at his footstool.
Holy is he!**

Leader: Extol the LORD our God, and worship at God's holy mountain;
for the LORD our God is holy.

Pastoral Prayer:

God of truth, you lead us to the mountaintop in prayer to see the glory of your Son revealed: Grant that when we come away, our faces are changed, our purpose is renewed, and our ministry is confirmed. We confess that sometimes when we wait for you, we become weighed down and muddled; free us from our longing to keep you in a dwelling we have made. Help us, O God, not to lose heart in our ministry. Teach us to rejoice in your freedom and to claim for ourselves the freedom that comes from the Spirit of the Lord. We thank you, God, for Jesus' willingness to come down, to engage in remembered acts of mercy, and finally to accomplish in Jerusalem the dawning of our deliverance from sin and death. We pray in Jesus' name, through whose power we are being transformed daily to life in your glorious image. Amen. (Blair G. Meeks)

SERMON BRIEFS

A GLIMPSE OF GLORY

EXODUS 34:29-35

Transfiguration Sunday is perhaps the most obscure holy day that our church celebrates. On any other holy day you can ask a child, "What are we celebrating?" The answer you get will probably include a Bible story and something about the meaning of the event. But what about today? Most adults, even our ministers, would be challenged by the question. We are familiar with the Gospel accounts of the transfiguration. We know the story, but what does it mean? What are the gospels, in their own particular way, trying to tell us about Jesus?

I. Moses, the Clue

I believe the best way to unravel the transfiguration is to turn back in our Bibles to Exodus. There we find Moses in circumstances similar to the transfiguration of Jesus. The parallels between these traditions warrant reflection. Both occur on a

87

mountain. In both stories an overshadowing cloud signals the presence of God. In both instances the divine glory is revealed and results in someone shining: Moses' face shines and, according to Luke 9, "the appearance of [Jesus'] face changed, and his clothes became dazzling white." There is one key verbal connection between the Gospels and the Septuagint rendering of Exodus 34: Jesus' disciples see his glory *(doxa)*; Moses' face shone (an intransitive use of *doxazo*).

These parallels, along with the tendency of the Gospels to define Jesus vis-à-vis Old Testament figures, lead me to conclude that the transfiguration tells us about Jesus what Exodus tells us about Moses. *The transfiguration accounts are constructed to call our minds back to Moses, then lead us to conclude something similar, yet grander, about Jesus.*

II. Moses, the Mediator

Our text in Exodus concludes an exciting run of events for Moses. As chapter 32 opens, Moses is atop Mount Sinai while the people grow impatient. They commit a terrible sin by worshiping a golden calf. God's anger burns hot against the people, and Moses intercedes desperately on their behalf. Moses has found favor with God, and his plea is successful. Then God commands Moses to break camp and continue toward the promised land. God warns, however, that God will not accompany the people: "You are a stiff-necked people; if for a single moment I should go up among you, I would consume you" (33:5). Moses again engages God and persuades God to accompany the people: "My presence will go with you, and I will give you rest" (33:14). Finally, Moses asks to see the glory of the Lord. Incredibly, God's answer is favorable. Moses is allowed to see God's passing glory, even if not fully. When he comes down from the mountain, his face is shining.

What does this tell us about Jesus? The most important answer is that Jesus is a mediator. Just as Moses interceded on behalf of the people, so too does Jesus. Just as Moses represented God in the giving of the law, so too does Jesus speak for the Father. Just as Moses reflected the glory of God, so too does Jesus, though the New Testament stresses that Jesus himself shares in that glory. The Israelites found God's glory frightening and dangerous, and yet it was life to them. Moses pleaded, "If your presence will not go, do not carry us up" (33:15). His shining face was evidence that God would be with God's people and lead them to rest. The transfiguration suggests that Jesus is the presence of God and that he will lead us to rest.

So what are we celebrating? The inscrutable mystery of God. The wonder of a God so transcendent that even our most precise descriptions are metaphor. We celebrate the majesty and glory of God . . . and the hope that a glimpse of God might be shown to us. (David Mauldin)

I CAN SEE CLEARLY NOW

2 CORINTHIANS 3:12–4:2

We have before us a passage that is in many ways very strange. It speaks of veils, and it speaks of Moses' shining face and the Old Testament law. What does this have to do with us today? At first glance it seems like it has little to say, but the first glance would be deceiving. In the midst of this strange passage, we encounter some great encouragement for Christian boldness, hope, and courage. In verse 12 Paul says, "Since we have such a hope, we are very bold" (RSV). In chapter 4 verse 1 he says, "We do not lose heart." What is it that will enable us to have that dynamic? It's all a matter of what we can see.

I. The Manifestation of Christ's Presence (v. 16)

Paul says there has been a barrier between people and the Word of God. The veil between them has kept them from seeing clearly what God wants to tell them. That veil may be there to cover our own inadequacy in living up to what we read in the law. That veil discourages us from understanding the true nature of God. Only Christ can take away that veil.

In verse 16, Paul says, "But whenever anyone turns to the Lord, the veil is taken away" (NIV). That means that we can now see Christ clearly. There are no barriers. Jesus is the perfect embodiment of the law. This immediate presence of Christ is surely an encouragement to us. Also encouraging to us are . . .

II. Reflections of Christ's Glory (v. 18)

Who are the reflections of Christ's glory? We are. We are like the moon to Jesus' sun. We don't generate the light, but we do pass it on in a dark world. We "all reflect the Lord's glory" (NIV). Perhaps you have heard the story of the boy who attended a church that had stained-glass windows depicting the saints. When asked the meaning of the word saint, he said, "They are people the light shines through." We don't have to be Christ, we only have to reflect him, and that is enough. We are also encouraged by . . .

III. The Transformation of Christ (v. 18)

In verse 18, Paul says we are, "Being transformed into his likeness with ever-increasing glory." While we may not see it, if we are sensitive to the leading of Christ, if we abide in his word, if we are sensitive to his spirit, we will more and more bear his image in the world. A bearded friend of mine and I were once eating in a fast-food restaurant, and a little girl came up to him and asked, "Are you Jesus?" He was quite embarrassed of course and replied, "No ma'am, but I do love him." She was, of course, thinking of a physical resemblance to Jesus that she had seen in a picture. But in our behaviors and attitudes, we should look like him.

Several years ago a certain kind of picture became quite popular. The picture, at first glance, looked like visual gibberish, almost like an impressionistic piece of art. However, the more you looked at the picture, you were able to see interesting three-dimensional pictures. Some of the pictures were quite complex and beautiful. Once we saw it, we couldn't understand why we couldn't see it earlier. Once we saw it, we could not "un-see" it. When we really look, we can clearly see Christ in his essence. We can see his light shining through us, and we can see him transform us into his likeness. (J. Michael Shannon)

MOUNTAINTOPS

LUKE 9:28-36 (37-43)

The longing for someone or some experience can prod us to efforts and attention we cannot otherwise muster. The arrival any moment of a loved one returning gives energy for preparation and attentiveness that keeps us looking every few minutes to the point of arrival. And then when they get there—ahhh, such a moment of completion.

I. You Don't Just "Happen By" a Mountaintop

The climb to the top of a mountain requires a similar effort and close attention. Arriving means a mixture of collapse from the strain and breathtaking pleasure at the view! Scripturally, mountaintops have meant encounters with God that were also mixed emotionally. Frightening and awesome, corrective and empowering are characteristics of these events.

Jesus has come to this place in daily walks of faith and obedience to God. His invitation to the disciples means that they too have the view of the mountaintop but the requirements of trust as well. They stayed awake and saw, and even heard, the full presence of God. It changed them as much as it changed Jesus.

If we continue to be open and awake to God in prayer and contemplation, we too will experience the wonder of the divine in human form. The transfiguration of Jesus is the gift of knowing him as human *and* God.

II. Mountaintops Enable One to Face the Valleys with Hope

Jesus "who would soon fulfill God's purposes in Jerusalem" knew what lay before him. The disciples knew it too, and that was all they could see: a dreaded outcome that would best be avoided.

Too often *all* that we can see is the darkness of life. Our eyes become accustomed to the dark. We futilely resign ourselves to thinking that darkness is all there is. It is then that we do not even recognize the valley. Jack Nicholson's character in the movie *As Good As It Gets* has accepted that perspective in his life of isolation and bitterness. It is unexpected love that lifts him to see that unhappiness is only *part* of life, not all of it.

The hope one experiences on the mountaintop tempts one to avoid ever returning to the valley. "Let's build three booths here" is a chorus we could join with the disciples. Martin Luther King's famous lines about being on the top of the mountain were followed by his bold return to martyrdom in the valley, but he had the confidence of knowing why he was there when he returned.

"Listen" to my Son, says the voice of God; don't isolate yourself. Remove the obstacles that keep you from listening to Jesus. It is the reason for the disciplines of Lent.

III. The High Experiences Are Sustained Without Staying There

The high moments of our lives continue to live in us with simple symbols that recall them. Sweet memories and inside stories of a family require only a word and everyone laughs: they bespeak of intimacy and belonging. The symbols of our faith can have that same sustaining power if they reflect such an intimacy with God. The cross, the Lord's Prayer, the ritual of worship can be points of reliving the mountaintop of being in God's presence, but only if we have been there and come down. Letting our faith freeze at the point of those high moments means the relationship is only a dead memory, like a shed decaying on some forlorn crest of a mountain. (Kay Gray)

REFLECTIONS

❧

MARCH

Reflection Verse: "Mary took a pound of costly perfume made of pure nard, anointed Jesus' feet, and wiped them with her hair. The house was filled with the fragrance of the perfume" (John 12:3).

She enters the room, her eyes on Christ, in her hands the exquisite jar of perfume. As you see her move to him and kneel at his feet and pour onto him her lavish gift, what name would you give to her role in that room? A sister, grateful to have her brother back? The most discerning disciple in the house? A prophet? A paradigm for personal devotion and extravagant sacrifice? Mary of Bethany is all of these. But the nature of her gift and the way she gave it makes her one thing more. Whether she means to or not, she functions here—powerfully—as a leader in worship.

It's a personal gift she brings to him, a most personal and intimate gift. But it's no private act of devotion. She gives it in the presence of a gathering of his followers. The house is filled with its fragrance; so are the nostrils of everyone there. Her gift is for Christ; but it changes the room, penetrates everyone in it.

What if you and I were to think of what we bring to worship in those terms? The prayers we offer, the gestures we make, the sermons we preach—in the context of worship, these are never just services performed for the people. They are our personal, embodied offerings to God in the presence of the people. We come to worship every week with a jar in our hands and pour out its contents for Christ's sake. And the house will be filled with the smell of it. The people present will absorb the essence of our gift. It should prompt us to ask of all we offer in worship: Is it costly to us, or cheap? Fragrant or rank? Is it a generous outpouring of all we can bring, or a chintzy dribble?

The fact that the gift is for Christ's sake can sometimes mean that it's not what some people in the room would prefer. This was the case with Mary's gift; some didn't like it. When Judas cleared his throat to register his objection, he may have been speaking for others. His reasoning makes sense. It was a very large sum of potentially useful cash that she had spilled into puddles on the floor. She could have anointed Jesus amply without pouring out so much excess. Had she met the "WWJD" test here? He was on record as saying, "Sell what you have and give to the poor."

My hunch, though, is that some in the room were disturbed in a different way, and it's more to the point of what Jesus himself said of her gift. He said this anointing was for a burial.

Yes it was; and it's possible that some of them sensed it before he said it. In that culture, anointing anyone you wished to honor meant pouring fragrance on the head, literally the "royal treatment." Anointing of other parts of the body was reserved for the dead. And for the dead, whole jars of fragrance were used. She has covered him in roses for his funeral! We all have experienced how a scent in the air can startle long-forgotten memories and awaken deep feelings. The pungent smell of her poured-out parable curled its way deep into everyone's consciousness. Their nostrils were filled with it, their eyes burned with it. She had brought them all into the presence of death. They were breathing it with Jesus and with her.

That doesn't make her gift some kind of ghoulish object lesson for their benefit. Her gift was to him, and it was purely gorgeous—not only by virtue of its fragrance and extravagance, but because it bore to him the news that he all too rarely received, and had never received so movingly as this: that someone *knew* him. It's hard to believe he didn't fall into tears. She knew. She knew he had emptied her brother's grave to make room for himself. She had seen his tears in the cemetery, seen him shudder. She could see him already pouring himself out; so she beautifully answers his gift, as best she can, with a gift of her own in kind. And it's in the nature of such a gift that it pours into other people too.

Here's an invitation to be the kind of leader in worship that Mary of Bethany was, especially in this season. Take up your courage, and bring death into the room. There will be some present who do not want this. Like the disciples on that evening, they may think they have come for another satisfying dinner party in Jesus' honor. But you know something more is at work here and something more is wanted. You look at Christ, and see there is death in his eyes. You look at the people; death is there too, just behind their eyes. For the sake of Christ, offer your costliest gift to pour out a fitting and loving and deeply truthful response. Don't let us leave the party unreminded of his hard necessity, and of our own. But don't lecture us on the subject, please. You are giving a gift, after all, to Christ—a gift in reply to the costliest and loveliest of gifts. Let your words and gestures be an answering parable. The others in the house will take in the fragrance of it, and some will want to follow.

When the dinner party was over that night, who do you think was most changed by it all? I'd say it was Mary herself. Whatever lingering effect the fragrance had on the others, it lingered most with her. She had wiped his feet with her hair. Now she wore the fragrance of her gift and his. His death and her answer were on her. They hung beside and beneath her face, rising again and again to her remembrance, for who knows how long.

This is the cost and the beauty of our calling: in the presence of others to pour out offerings that echo the offering of Christ, and to do so in such a way that it gets unmistakably on us. (Paul D. Duke)

MARCH 4, 2001

❦

First Sunday in Lent

Worship Theme: The season of Lent calls us to remember the life-giving promises of our baptism and to give thanks for God's forgiveness and sustaining presence.

Readings: Deuteronomy 26:1-11; Romans 10:8b-13; Luke 4:1-13

Call to Worship (Psalm 91:1-2, 11-12, 15-16):

> *Leader:* You who live in the shelter of the Most High,
> who abide in the shadow of the Almighty,
> will say to the LORD, "My refuge and my fortress;
> my God, in whom I trust."

> *People:* **For he will command the angels concerning you
> to guard you in all your ways.**

> *Leader:* On their hands they will bear you up,
> so that you will not dash your foot against a stone.

> *People:* **Those who love me, I will deliver;
> I will protect those who know my name.**

> *Leader:* When they call to me, I will answer them;
> I will be with them in trouble,
> I will rescue them and honor them.

> *People:* **With long life I will satisfy them, and show them my salvation.**

Pastoral Prayer:

God of our wandering ancestors, you come to us with a mighty hand and an outstretched arm: We ask for your deliverance. We know that the powers of evil never withdraw for long but are there to confront us when we are most vulnerable. Remind us that we do not need bread made from the stone of oppression; teach us to feed others with the bread of freedom that strengthens body and spirit. Lead us to worship you alone, to give up longing for realms of possessions and position that consume us and turn us away from you. Your word, O God, is near to us, on our lips and in our hearts; teach us to trust in your protection, not to test you by our foolishness and superstition. We thank you for the bounty of your good earth and pray that, together with strangers and friends, we may join in offering you the work of our hands, for you are Lord of all and generous to all who call on you. We pray in the name of Jesus, whom you raised from the dead. Amen. (Blair G. Meeks)

SERMON BRIEFS

A COMMAND TO GET EXCITED ABOUT!

DEUTERONOMY 26:1-11

More than once I have been asked, "Why is the Christian life so hard?" It certainly can be, but here we are commanded to *celebrate*. At last, we have a commandment to get excited about!

"Then you, together with the Levites and the aliens who reside among you, shall celebrate with all the bounty that the LORD your God has given to you" (26:11). It's a party, and everyone is invited. This excitement balances somewhat the main point of the passage, obligated giving. The Israelites were to bring a portion of their crops for the support of the Levites and the needy. We Christians are aware of a certain obligation to support the work of the church and care for the needy. As long as we're giving, let's look deeper and see how to do it right. Let's not forget the celebration!

I. A Boldly Personal Confession

In this text, giving and celebrating are tied to remembering. Each Israelite who brought an offering presented it with a confession, "A wandering Aramean was my ancestor. . . ." (26:5). The worshiper goes on to recount God's mighty saving acts in Israel's history, but in a boldly personal way. *We* went down into Egypt. *We* cried to the Lord. The Lord brought *us* out of Egypt with a mighty hand and an outstretched arm. Never mind that these instructions were addressed to later generations, most of whom had never been to Egypt. This act of worship draws lines; it connects the dots between God's mighty acts and the life of the worshiper. They brought crops and gave thanks because God had set them free and given them land to farm. If God's arm had not stretched out, the worshiper would be in no position to give or to celebrate. God's great plans and gracious will had touched the life of every worshiper. This liturgy stated that plainly and personally.

We need to express our faith in such a boldly personal way. We need to connect the dots. I learned to do this from my mother. I was adopted under some highly unusual circumstances. The story is odd, but my mother saw God behind the events and told me all about it at a very early age. She first told me the story of Moses' unusual beginning. She then told me how God intervened in the birth of Samuel. And, yes, she even added the miraculous birth of Jesus. By the time she got to my story, it seemed to me the most natural thing in the world that God should work through strange circumstances in the birth of a child. I grew up believing that I mattered to God and that God had a hand on my life. That remains at the core of who I am to this day.

II. A Personal Challenge

In this special season, I challenge you to remember and celebrate in an intentional way: Write down your own liturgy. Connect the dots between God's mighty saving acts and your life. You may want to do this as a family. Begin with creation; let it remind you of the material blessings that sustain your life. Continue with the law and prophets, through whom God has spoken to you. Emphasize Jesus—his death for you and his resurrection, which is your hope. Mention specific blessings God has given you. This confession is personal, yet it should connect you with the faithful in every time and place. You might mention specifically this church.

Keep your liturgy fairly short. Write it on a note card and bring it to worship throughout Lent (if preached on Thanksgiving, substitute Advent). Pray it silently during the offertory as you bring your gift. (David Mauldin)

CALLING ON GOD IN TRUST

ROMANS 10:8*b*-13

This text from Romans gives us the opportunity for self-examination as we begin the season of Lent. The theme throughout the entire book of Romans is the good news of God's power to bring salvation to all who believe and trust; that is, to those who have faith. This portion of the letter of Romans speaks of basic beliefs of the Christian faith. Those who call on God in trust through Jesus Christ will be saved. It may be fitting for the beginning of Lent to examine these very basic beliefs and what meaning they have for our lives as we look toward Easter.

I. Basic Beliefs

Paul emphasizes throughout the letter the basic beliefs held by those who trust God. The first is that Jesus Christ is Lord. The second is God raised him from the dead. Verse 9 is a verse people often use in helping others come to a saving faith in Jesus Christ. To "confess with your lips" and "believe in your heart" show us that salvation and righteousness must have elements of both faith and confession. Paul emphasized that everything is rooted in God's graciousness. It has nothing to do with what we can do by ourselves. What does it mean to say Jesus is Lord? Do we confess with our lips (not just actions) the faith we claim in Jesus? What does it mean to "believe in your heart"? Why should we ask these questions?

II. Too Religious?

Throughout the book of Romans, Paul makes it clear that God has been faithful to God's promises. This was to be the completion of Israel's story. Paul even uses a verse from Deuteronomy 30:14 to emphasize that from the beginning God's Word was on their "lips" and in their "hearts." Israel's problem was that its people abandoned faith in the Giver of the law and took a more "religious" stance toward the law. They wanted to take their salvation into their own hands, make it a "do-it-yourself" project. They pushed aside God's trustworthiness and did not call on God in trust. What are things we are "religious" about today? How do we attempt to take our salvation into our own hands? What gets in the way of our putting total trust in God? Are there things we "worship" that are not in keeping with putting total trust in God?

III. Inclusiveness

"Everyone who calls on the name of the Lord shall be saved" (10:13). This may be the key verse for this portion of scripture. It is important to note that Paul believes that God intended salvation for all from the beginning of time. Within his theological argument, Paul is looking at the fact of Israel's rejection and the God whose salvation is for all who confess and believe. When we look at ourselves in self-examination, we may not like this text deep down. Our judgmental side may say there are other persons who profess Christian faith with whom I would rather not be with in heaven, but that is not our choice. Whether they be a different race, sexual orientation, religious conservatives or liberals, if they confess and believe they will be saved by the same Lord who "is generous to all who call on him," (10:12).

Another biblical story comparison that may be helpful would be the story of Jonah. Whether a person be Jew, Ninevite, Roman, American, African, Asian, or any other, God's trustworthiness is sufficient. Call on God in trust. (Marcia Thompson)

THE MAINTENANCE-FREE SOUL

LUKE 4:1-13

In recent years, I have become aware not only of our dependence on technology, but also our identification with the technology we own. A colleague laments, "my hard drive crashed this morning, so I can't do any work." The clerk taking catalogue orders over the phone advises, "Please call back later. We don't have power right now, so I have no idea what's in stock." My favorite, though, is the auto mechanic who addresses me as though I were my twelve-year-old car: "Didn't you feel your brakes getting mushy?" "What do you mean your oil light didn't go on?" "You need new shock absorbers."

They try to make you feel guilty because your car isn't maintenance free—as though sheer pigheadedness on your part made the master cylinder corrode inside. We live in denial of the truth: that the best cars need tune-ups, that hard-drives can wear out, that power shortages sometimes occur because of circumstances beyond human control. Everything in God's creation requires care and upkeep in order to be all that it is meant to be. Like our technology, the human soul is not maintenance free. More than the physical need for food and shelter, one needs discipline and opportunity for growth in order to fulfill God's purpose for that person. But how does one do maintenance work on a soul? What happens if it isn't done? Who does this work?

These questions are answered in the Gospel reading for the day: the story of Jesus' temptation in the wilderness. It begins with the words, "And Jesus, full of the Holy Spirit, returned from the Jordan and was led by the Spirit for forty days in the wilderness." In other words, before any of this ordeal began, Jesus was in tune with the Spirit of God, obedient to the leading of God. He didn't go away to fast in penitence for some sin. By our standards Jesus was in top spiritual condition, with no need for improvement. But in studying Luke 4 we find that even the most godly person who ever lived was subject to assaults from Satan. The strongest and most righteous person must draw near to God to have his/her strength and righteousness renewed. A servant of God must grow in order to continue serving God. Nobody has or has ever had a maintenance-free soul; not even our Lord and Savior.

The Lenten season is an invitation to walk in the wilderness with Jesus again: six weeks set aside to prepare each of us for Calvary and the Easter that follows. It is a forty-day period of "taking time out" as our Lord did, to take stock of our relationship with

God, to be disciplined by him, and to grow stronger through him. There are, of course, Christians who resist this invitation to engage in Lent's self-examination and discipline. Some simply don't like the serious, even somber nature of the season. Some have other priorities: making money or keeping up an image. Still others are afraid to admit their need for maintenance or growth, thinking it suggests their faith was not genuine in the first place.

A challenge to us during Lent is to proclaim to the world that we are not maintenance-free souls. We have a ministry to those who think real Christianity means there is no need for further growth, and we have a need, ourselves, to walk with Jesus these forty days that lead to a cross.

First, we have to admit to each other, the world, and God that we're still growing, still struggling, still in need of grace. In admitting our mistakes and failures, others can see God's forgiveness at work. In sharing our struggles, we are encouraged. Years ago, when I worked with a youth team doing street evangelism, I noticed that the testimonies with the most impact on passersby were not our success stories but the confessions: the stories of how God receives us in our brokenness and makes us whole. In automotive terms, nobody believes a car is really maintenance-free, but everyone wants to know of a good mechanic who's always available.

Second, we have a ministry to the supposedly maintenance-free Christians. It isn't our job to point out their shortcomings or cut them down to size. Instead, we should be examples to them: by the depth of our caring for one another and the sincerity of our devotion to Christ. We can be available to our brothers and sisters in Christ, be vulnerable, and leave the rest to the Holy Spirit. It was the Spirit who led Jesus into the wilderness, after all, and the Spirit who has brought us thus far in our own pilgrimage of faith. Only the Holy Spirit can convict a person of his or her weakness and need for growth.

Third, during Lent we ourselves need to go into the wilderness to fast and pray—not only because we ought to, but also because we need to do it. Through physical hunger we become more attuned to our spiritual hunger for God. We realize our total reliance on Christ for all our needs, and we find joy in knowing he satisfies our hungers. In the wilderness God's Spirit teaches us, making us wiser in discerning good from evil. The mark of a strong Christian isn't never feeling temptation, but seeing temptation for what it is, and resisting it.

The challenges and discipline of Lent prepare us to grapple with the crises of life, so that when real trials come, with God's help we are strong and ready to meet them. There's no such thing as a maintenance-free soul. Jesus demonstrated that during his forty days in the wilderness. But during Lent he invites us to walk with him through the time of testing, all the way to Calvary and beyond. (Carol M. Norén)

MARCH 11, 2001

❦

Second Sunday in Lent

Worship Theme: We seek God's blessing in our lives that we may be firm in the faith, allowing others to see in us God's mercy and righteousness.

Readings: Genesis 15:1-12, 17-18; Philippians 3:17–4:1; Luke 13:31-35

Call to Worship (Psalm 27:1, 4-5, 7-8, 13-14):

Leader: The LORD is my light and my salvation; whom shall I fear?
The LORD is the stronghold of my life; of whom shall I be afraid?

People: **One thing I asked of the LORD, that will I seek after:**
to live in the house of the LORD all the days of my life,
to behold the beauty of the LORD, and to inquire in his temple.

Leader: For he will hide me in his shelter in the day of trouble;
he will conceal me under the cover of his tent; he will set me high on a rock.

People: **Hear, O LORD, when I cry aloud, be gracious to me and answer me!**
"Come," my heart says, "seek his face!"
Your face, LORD, do I seek.

Leader: I believe that I shall see the goodness of the LORD in the land of the living.

People: **Wait for the LORD; be strong, and let your
heart take courage;
wait for the LORD!**

Pastoral Prayer:

O God, you are always ready to gather us under your wings like a
mother hen. Give our hearts courage to look into the terrifying darkness and count the stars, for there we will know your blessing. Teach
us to believe you as Abraham did, so that our faith will be reckoned
to us as righteousness. Make us bold to follow Jesus' path, minister-
ing to those in need even when we are bullied by the foxes of this
world. We long to seek your face, O God, to live in your house all
our days; remind us that your home is with mortals. Show us the way
to seek you where you live among the homeless, the hurting, the
imprisoned, and the dying, for you have promised to transform all
that is humiliated to the glory of Christ's body; in the name of Jesus
the Christ, who reigns with you and the Holy Spirit. Blessed is the
one who comes in the name of the Lord. Amen. (Blair G. Meeks)

SERMON BRIEFS

SUPER ORDINARY FAITH

GENESIS 15:1-12, 17-18

The Old Testament is about a people and their land, a land and
its people. Much more than we realize, and probably to a greater
degree than we are comfortable with, the Hebrew Scriptures are
about real estate. This is one passage among many that draw a
connection between this people and this land, a connection said
to be of divine origin. To us it speaks of practical concerns and
ordinary faith, yet it shows us that such ordinary faith transcends
practical concerns.

I. Super Faith

If you could dialogue with God, carry on a conversation back-
and-forth, what would you talk about? Abram wants to talk about

his heir, or rather his lack of one. God promises an heir and then moves the conversation to what God wants to talk about, land. As they talk, the promises are woven together, heirs for the land and land for the heirs. We might hope for a discussion of the meaning of life, the problem of evil, or other spiritual matters. But the big talk is about kids and land.

God promised, and Abram believed. Our text adds, "and the LORD reckoned it to him as righteousness" (15:6). Abram's great act of faith was trusting God with these seemingly simple, every-day concerns: children and land. Yet the results are profound: God declares Abram righteous. Simple trust makes Abram an example of faith for all times. When Paul wants to describe how faith in Jesus Christ unites us to God, he says that we are children of Abraham through faith. Although Abram and God seem to talk about mundane matters, something wonderful happens. God is bound to Abram through promise, and Abram is bound to God by faith.

II. Ordinary Faith

Sometimes the most basic, common things can be tremendous acts of faith: putting down roots, having a child. Jeremiah bought a field as a bold, prophetic act—God would restore Judah (Jeremiah 32). Many people are reluctant to bring a child into a world like this one. I understand their reservations. I wrestle with them myself from time to time. If I someday become a father, my trust in the goodness and providence of God will have allowed me to do that. I like to think that my faith is sufficient for the task of fatherhood. I know that without faith I could never, in good conscience, father a child.

Such a common thing, parenthood. Yet it requires superordinary faith. . . . Or is it just ordinary faith with super results? Sometimes the most profound act of faith can be getting up in the morning. Finding the courage to simply go on, to face practical concerns, may arouse in us the kind of faith that pleases God. Of course, this faith does not come from within; it is a gift from God. We learn to trust God, as Abram did. We hear God's promises: to be with us, to provide us a future. We hear and we trust.

Remember Jesus' words in the parable of the talents, "You have been trustworthy in a few things, I will put you in charge of many things" (Matthew 25:21). As we learn to trust God, the line between the mundane and the eternal begins to blur. God's promise is seamless: God claims us now and forever. Our trust in God over relatively common matters is the same faith that will cling to God when we face death. Through this faith our lives become oriented to God. Like Abram, we are bound to God by faith, as God is bound to us by promise.

Ordinary concerns. Ordinary faith. Superordinary results, thanks to the gracious will of God. (David Mauldin)

TO LIVE OR NOT TO LIVE AS A CHRISTIAN?

PHILIPPIANS 3:17–4:1

The great question facing every Christian involves the fundamental issue of integrity in life. It really comes down to Shakespeare's classic query: "To be or not to be?" It is that question which confronts life. While the Bard's question may be viewed by some as a theatrical commentary on the superficiality of life when contemplating death, it is in fact the basic question of meaning in life itself. That question is rooted in the genuineness and significance of a person's commitment to ultimate reality. Indeed, it is best represented in a human's *persona* or the projected image that a person actually epitomizes in life. This image, model, or example of the person in reality challenges others to accept or adopt it as their own model or *persona* for life. This challenge is the point that Paul is making here.

I. Copying the Best Model (3:17)

For some contemporary readers the challenge of Paul to copy or imitate him sounds like brash pride. But in the Hellenistic world the idea of imitation was the normal pattern of a teacher with learners. The pupils of the stoic teachers would follow their instructors through the marketplace and porches (*stoa*) of the city.

Similarly, Jesus told his disciples to follow him so that he could make them into his learners/disciples (*mathetai*). In this vein of thinking Paul believed himself to be an authentic model for others to copy. But his belief did not stem from his own pride. It came from his absolute conviction that he was copying the model of the self-giving Christ (2:5; 3:7-14).

II. Rejecting the Wrong Models (3:18-19)

The integrity of Paul demanded that he had to make it indelibly clear to his Christian friends that those who focused their basic commitments on earthly realities, such as money, material goods, power, and prestige, were in fact enemies of Christ. Moreover, he minced no words in condemning such a mind-set as being in danger of ultimate judgment. Such a message is hardly one that the twenty-first century's materialistically driven person wants to hear.

III. Gaining the Ultimate Reward for Integrity (3:20-21)

Paul was absolutely convinced that following the right model would guarantee citizenship in heaven. While some who live in the twenty-first century may think that Paul was a "pie-in-the-sky-by-and-by" dreamer, he was a realist about sin and yet absolutely convinced that when he died, he would be with Christ (2:21). He also believed, in contrast to Greek thinking, that he would not be a mere disembodied soul floating in eternal soulness. Instead, he was convinced that the powerful God who is ultimately in control of the universe could change his frail, mortal body into a glorious body prepared for its heavenly inheritance, having its own identifiability.

IV. Accepting the Present Challenge (4:1)

Because the world is not heaven, this life is not the place of divine reward. Living in an imperfect, rebellious world, therefore, requires faithfulness and courage from Christians. Accordingly, in a gentle spirit Paul called his friends to steadfastness in Christ. Can we do less for others, particularly wayward Christians? (Gerald L. Borchert)

AN OTHER-DIRECTED OR INNER-DIRECTED LIFE

LUKE 13:31-35

Where do you look for direction in life? Do you look for direction from others or from within yourself?

While Christians believe that Jesus is much more than a teacher, most people would agree that Jesus is one of the world's greatest teachers. In Luke 13 Jesus is portrayed as the unequaled teacher. His teaching methods demonstrate four marks of a great teacher: A greater teacher teaches what is relevant; a great teacher loves people and sees their full potential; a great teacher communicates one central truth; a great teacher enables the students to find inner direction.

Unfortunately, many of us are guilty of radar living. We aim our radar gun at others, trying to pick up on their moods and wishes. We try to fit in, make it, and be right with the crowd. A market analysis can tell us exactly what people want to hear.

I. Herod's Threat (vv. 31-33)

In Luke 13:31-35, it is clear that Jesus refused to be other-directed. When he was warned by some of the Pharisees that King Herod was out to get him, he replied that he would not allow the "sly fox" to set his agenda. Jesus wasn't going to change his plans. He refused to be intimidated or deterred by the threat of Herod. For three days, symbolic of the brief limited time of his public ministry, Jesus would cast out demons and perform miracles until his work was complete. Jesus refused to be trapped into trying to please others.

Robert Louis Stevenson wrote: "To know what you prefer instead of humbly saying, 'Amen' to what the world tells you ought to prefer, is to have kept your soul alive."

II. The People's Rejection (v. 34)

Finding direction from within oneself rather than from others also means that you and I must be willing to accept that there will always be people who will not accept the kingdom of God. Not everyone embraced Jesus and his message. Jesus agonized over the rejection. Jesus broke out in a lament for Jerusalem. Verse 34 is a sob of anguish, not an expression of anger. His compassionate heart was broken. The lament was not just for the Pharisees who had tried to provoke him. It was for the whole nation. The Holy City's unwillingness to accept Jesus as the Messiah broke not only Jesus' heart, but also his heavenly Father's heart. Whenever anyone rejects Jesus as the Messiah, they break the heart of God.

III. Jesus' Promise (v. 35)

Yet, in spite of the rejection, Jesus pressed on and promised that one day the streets of Jerusalem will be lined with people shouting, "Blessed is the one who comes in the name of the Lord." The promise partially came to pass with his triumphal entry on Palm Sunday, but it will be fully realized one day when every knee bows and every tongue confesses that Jesus Christ is Lord! Until that time comes, there is time to repent, to receive pardon for sin, and to welcome the reign of God in our lives. That offer will continue to be made following Jesus' death, resurrection, and ascension. It is an offer not only to Jerusalem, but to the entire world. (Bob Buchanan)

MARCH 18, 2001

❧

Third Sunday in Lent

Worship Theme: God provides refreshment for our spirits, water in dry places, food for the journey, and asks us to bring the comfort of God's presence to all who suffer.

Readings: Isaiah 55:1-9; 1 Corinthians 10:1-13; Luke 13:1-9

Call to Worship (Psalm 63:1-8):

Leader: O God, you are my God, I seek you,
my soul thirsts for you; my flesh faints for you,
as in a dry and weary land where there is no
water.
So I have looked upon you in the sanctuary,
beholding your power and glory.

People: **Because your steadfast love is better than
life,
my lips will praise you. So I will bless you as
long as I live;
I will lift up my hands and call on your
name.**

Leader: My soul is satisfied as with a rich feast,
and my mouth praises you with joyful lips
when I think of you on my bed,
and meditate on you in the watches of the night;

People: **for you have been my help,
and in the shadow of your wings I sing for
joy.
My soul clings to you; your right hand
upholds me.**

Pastoral Prayer:

God of life, your thoughts and ways are high above ours, and yet you are near to us and ready to be found. We wander in a dry and weary land, and yet you are calling us now to the refreshment of your waters. Teach us to listen so that we may live; show us the rich feast that is ours without money or price; guide us to share all that is necessary for the life of your children everywhere. When we hear of human calamities and natural disasters, O God, we wonder where you are. Hear our prayer for all who suffer; show them your presence and comfort them with your Spirit as you cared for your people in the desert. We confess that we have often failed to do what is right; we have complained, and we have put you to the test. Forgive us and nurture us like a gardener until we bear good fruit. We lift our hearts in praise and sing for joy in the shadow of your wings, through Christ our rock. Amen. (Blair G. Meeks)

SERMON BRIEFS

AN INVITATION TO GRACE

ISAIAH 55:1-9

This lection contains the first three of five strophes found in chapter 55. Note that they are filled with urgent imperatives: *come, buy, eat, incline, hear, seek*. Imperatives are almost never welcomed, except when one is in need of what he or she is commanded by invitation to receive. When I was a child, my mother used lots of imperatives in her conversations with us. "Take it," she would say. "Get ready!" "Go!" "Clean up!"

Although my mother used *imperatives* often, I have come to understand that her imperatives were loving words expressed in my interest and for the benefit of the rest of my family.

Notice that Yahweh's invitation by imperative is to those who are thirsty. They are offered fresh water. This serves as a reminder of a scorching heat wave we experienced one summer when the thermometer reached 100 degrees almost daily. A former bishop of an African country who was visiting America sent an e-mail saying, "It remains a wonder to me just how hot this continent can get." Of course, the weather doesn't have to be this hot for one to get thirsty. But it does make us crave water. This craving for water *literally* offers us opportunities for ministry, if we will accept the invitation.

A reporter of a well-known radio station interviewed a representative of the local rescue mission as he delivered bottled water to the city's homeless in their tents. Surely Isaiah's invitation for the thirsty to come and drink is a reminder that there are always persons who can be decently and respectfully offered what they do not have. It would be tempting to focus on the historical context of Isaiah's words. But, if one believes that we are experiencing the Living Word through these Scriptures, then let him or her loosen the imagination, mount up with the wings of the Spirit, and wait upon the Lord who will give the message for the moment. (Jim Clardy)

NO AUTOMATIC ARMOR

1 CORINTHIANS 10:1-13

In his compelling summary of this ironic juxtaposition, Paul points out how great blessings do not necessarily make people good. Despite their intimate experience of God's power, precious guidance, miraculous rescues, and providential, constant care, the majority of the Israelites could not remain faithful, even under the legendary leadership of Moses. The road to freedom and the promised land turns out not to be for the faint-hearted *or* the overconfident. Paul wants the Corinthian Christians to know that a people can be greatly blessed and *still* miserably disappoint and exasperate the God trying to save them.

Recounting this vivid lesson from their own history, Paul reminds them that *all* those pilgrim Israelites had that special baptism "into Moses in the cloud and in the sea" (10:2). Let Christians beware of any assumptions about baptismal privileges being automatic. *All* those people with Moses ate and drank "the same spiritual food" (10:3). Paul lifts up that "rock" from which they drank and shows us there the source of all living water from the beginning of time: "the rock was Christ" (10:4). Let Christians watch and pray, lest they presume that to commune with Christ's body and blood assures any automatic immunity to sin.

Be *aware*, Paul stresses, that thousands of Israelites did these incredible things that directly parallel Christian baptism and communion, wherein God through Moses poured out grace upon grace for them, but *nevertheless*, most of them still so displeased God that they were "struck down in the wilderness" (10:5).

Best not to presume or assume anything automatic from the privileged partaking of God's sacred presence and sacramental food. And food happens to be a big issue for these Corinthians who are just then being tempted to eat meat offered to idols. Paul is concerned with their insensitivity to how this could affect others' faith and their arrogance about their own faith's invulnerability.

Better not to be so oblivious of how easy it is to fall into temptation so that we actually desire those things that displease God and cause our own destruction. We can be so good at double-talking ourselves into the abyss of sanctification by "special privileges." We think we understand something correctly, so we can do the "wrong" thing for the "right" reasons, and so forth. Paul, like Jesus, was not legalistic, because he knew the demands and constraints of the law of *love*, in people sensitized by the Spirit, are so much *greater* than any laws on the books.

I. Just Deserts

My son, Nathaniel, told me years ago that it's easy to remember which one, dessert or desert, has two "s's": all you have to remember is that you want *two desserts*. So did the Israelites and without even one *desert*. But between slavery and the promised land there is always temptation in the desert, with a severe shortage of desserts.

Notice "sexual immorality" (10:8), lest anyone might be tempted to take it casually, caused 23,000 to fall in one day. Testing God caused many others to be destroyed by "serpents" (10:9). Why risk it?

Then what would you put next on the list of things so seriously evil and abhorrent to God as to cause the *destruction* of the prac-

114

titioners? Would "complaining" even be anywhere on your list? Paul has it, right up there in the top three on his! Note that "testing God" had a lot to do with "grumbling" too. So both numbers three and two on Paul's list are surprisingly close to things that many "Christians" do, without noticing perhaps that these are two of the top three examples of what ruined the Israelites! All those gifts and graces that *could have made them special*, did not immunize them against the ravages of temptation and sin. Just because God blesses you greatly, don't imagine that makes you invulnerable to sin, Paul says.

II. Always a Way Out

But Paul closes with words of assurance and encouragement. Just as all those most blessed have been vulnerable to sin anyway, so also do all of those tempted share the same commonality of testing. And God will not test anyone beyond what they are able to withstand. As we learn to trust this, we will ask God to show us that promised way out of every temptation and even so, we will find it.

My sister, Ava, just gave me a gold ring with *"Amor Vincit Omnia"* engraved on it, as a constant reminder that love can always find a way to remain loving, and that *is* the ultimate victory. (Kathleen Peterson)

THE SERIOUSNESS OF SIN OR THE SERIOUSNESS OF JESUS?

LUKE 13:1-9

I. Rate My Sin!

You and I have played the little game called Rate My Sin! It's a comparison of what we consider to be a "minor" sin versus those we know to be "major" sins. If it's a matter of not being completely honest, we rate ourselves against those whom we "know" to be major liars. Given the current coverage of national sinners, our sins pale in comparison or so we hope. And we close the game with the parting gift of "I'm not such a bad person anyway!"

It was this same game some wanted to play with Jesus. And they thought this game would be an easy one to win since the ones involved were Galileans, hometown folks! It seemed that Pilate had killed some rebellious Galileans who did not believe in paying tribute to Rome, and he intermingled their blood with the blood of animals offered to God in sacrifice both as an example and as a punishment to this act. The questioners want to know if perhaps their death was justified? In other words, did God send this punishment? Jesus answers that all sinners will "perish," if they do not repent. Jesus himself then brings up an incident that surely was on the mind of those around him—a tower that had collapsed and eighteen people were accidentally killed. The age-old question is still asked even today by some if only in silent thoughts, did those people die because they were evil or wicked? The seriousness of sin, Jesus explains, is that all that continue to be unrepentant will perish. Sin is serious in the eyes of God, and Jesus stressed this over and over. As illustrated in Genesis 4:7, sin has an animal-like quality like a predator, "lurking at the door; its desire is for you, but you must master it." Sadly, the Lord knew that people are better at being mastered by sin. But God also knew that was the reason for his being among them, to offer them a victory over sin. It is easy for the living to point at the already perished and ask if perhaps life isn't a reward for being better. Jesus answers that all who are sinners run the same risk of perishing if repentance is not sought.

II. Learn from the Fig Tree

Jesus told a parable of a man who buys a fig tree to plant in his vineyard. At the time when fig trees are to give fruit, he comes and finds none. And he waits one, two, and finally three years. It was then that the man furious with the lack of fruit orders the gardener to cut it down. In the opinion of the owner the fig tree was simply wasting soil. The gardener who obviously loved his work and the plants with which he worked, pleaded for one more year in which to work more closely with the tree. He promised to "dig around it and put manure on it." It is the view of the gardener that with attention merited by the tree, it would bear the fruit as expected. It is Jesus speaking of himself and the people of God. What they have been lacking has been the attention of a "gardener" that loves them. Jesus offers them this love. He also offers them new and powerful insights into God's teachings. He offers them a way to be fruitful. He offers them a way to life.

III. Repent or Perish

The seriousness of sin is that it leads to eternal death. Paul would later say that the "For the wages of sin is death, but the free gift of God is eternal life in Christ Jesus our Lord" (Romans 6:23). The seriousness of Jesus was that he meant what he said: we must repent of our sins or perish. The good news is that Jesus paid the price for our lives! (Eradio Valverde)

MARCH 25, 2001

❦

Fourth Sunday in Lent

Worship Theme: God joyfully welcomes those who return from the emptiness of broken ties and alienation; all in God's household are called to be ambassadors of reconciliation.

Readings: Joshua 5:9-12; 2 Corinthians 5:16-21; Luke 15:1-3, 11*b*-32

Call to Worship (Psalm 32:1-6, 11):

> *Leader:* Happy are those whose transgression is forgiven, whose sin is covered.

> *People:* **Happy are those to whom the LORD imputes no iniquity,
> and in whose spirit there is no deceit.**

> *Leader:* While I kept silence, my body wasted away through my groaning all day long.
> For day and night your hand was heavy upon me; my strength was dried up as by the heat of summer.

> *People:* **Then I acknowledged my sin to you, and I did not hide my iniquity;
> I said, "I will confess my transgressions to the LORD,"
> and you forgave the guilt of my sin.**

> *Leader:* Therefore let all who are faithful offer prayer to you; at a time of distress, the rush of mighty waters shall not reach them.

> *People:* **Be glad in the LORD and rejoice, O righteous, and shout for joy, all you upright in heart.**

Pastoral Prayer:

Faithful God, your care is always with us and you have made us your heirs. Open our hearts to rejoice with you at the feast of forgiveness. We were wrong, O Lord, when we presumed that we could live in a distant place where no one knows who our father is. Help us to see the emptiness of days lived counter to your generous love; bring us home again; embarrass us with your extravagant joy. Prepare us now for the coming celebration of Jesus' death and resurrection, and teach us the joy of living as Christ's new creation. God, you feed us with food from the land of promise. Give us grace to follow Jesus and welcome to our table those whom others shun. Make us worthy of your trust in us, and guide us with your Spirit to be your ambassadors of reconciliation, showing to the world the joy of everything made new in Christ Jesus our Lord. Amen. (Blair G. Meeks)

SERMON BRIEFS

A NEW BEGINNING

JOSHUA 5:9-12

All of this week's lessons speak of newness of life and are likely welcome in this fourth week of Lent. Themes of repentance and renunciation, needful as they are, can burden preacher and hearer alike. This week's lessons give us a different perspective: a foretaste of the Easter for which we are preparing. It is unfortunate that this brief passage from Joshua is so easy to overlook, coming with such familiar words from Paul and Luke. Our passage provides additional insight into new life that strengthens us during Lent.

I. The Passage

Our passage records a crucial moment in Israel's history. Moses has died, and the mantle of leadership has fallen now to Joshua. Under Moses, the children of Israel time and again turned from God, grumbled about their situation, and put God to the test. God punished them, gave them additional chances, and provided for their needs even as they wandered in the wilderness. Under Joshua they have crossed into the land of promise and are observing the first Passover there. A new day is at hand; and yet the promise is not fulfilled completely. These two facts give us a fertile tension within which to work and to locate our own experience.

Many ordeals lie ahead of the children of Israel before the land will finally be in their possession. Even the food they ate in that Passover recorded here was not their own. The manna, the tangible daily evidence of God's presence and provision, stopped the next day. So we are sure to understand, we are told again, it stopped "on that very day." Likewise, in our worship, Sundays are "in Lent," yet not "of Lent." On each Lord's day, we remember that we have entered the land of promise. We know, however, that Holy Week lies ahead, and with it Christ's passion in which we are called to enter. We do not know what trials and demands that may lie ahead. With the children of Israel who have entered the land of promise, yet still do not possess it, we will be called into "ventures

of which we cannot see the ending,

by paths yet untrodden,

through perils unknown"

(*Book of Common Worship* [Louisville: Westminster/John Knox Press, 1993], p. 501). A key question for our spiritual reflection during Lent is: "What will sustain us along the way to receive the promise?"

To sustain them in their condition of promised yet not realized fulfillment, the children of Israel had the sign of the covenant in which the land was promised—circumcision. During the time of the wilderness wandering, circumcision was not observed. We witness in our reading the resumption of the practice. Even as they lack the tangible evidence of God's presence, they will have the sign of the covenant. Because of the significance of this recovery, it might also be advisable to read verses 2-8.

II. Application

Liturgical scholar Philip H. Pfatteicher explains that the first six weeks of Lent are to be a time of renewal. The focus of this renewal is baptism (*Liturgical Spirituality* [Valley Forge: Trinity Press International, 1997], pp. 120-21).

Our Lenten preparation reminds us of our great promise of newness under the sign of the covenant. In and with, Christ we too have entered a new place of promise. We have a new leader. To sustain us in our faith, we have the sign of the covenant—our baptism. Lent is a time in which we do well to explore the meaning of baptism and our covenant with God. (Philip E. Thompson)

WHAT'S LOVE GOT TO DO WITH IT?

2 CORINTHIANS 5:16-21

Tina Turner once asked, "What's love got to do with it?" Her question had to do with romantic relationships. She called it a "secondhand emotion." The kind of love we will be talking about is of a different sort and there is nothing secondhand about it. We could still ask the question, "What's love got to do with it?" What does love contribute to the Christian life? Second Corinthians 5:16-21 follows up on a statement Paul made in verse 14 where he said, "For Christ's love compels us" (NIV). We can all agree that true love does compel us to exhibit new attitudes and behaviors. God's love compels us:

I. To See People from a New Perspective

Paul admits that at one time in his life he saw people from a worldly point of view (5:16). As a Pharisee of the Pharisees, he no doubt thought the Gentiles were unworthy of God's grace. Now in Christ, he sees Gentiles as brothers and sisters. Christ's love had compelled him to see Christ in a different way.

He also admits in verse 16 that he once regarded Christ from a worldly point of view. Paul had always been zealous for God. But he once regarded Christ no doubt as a mere human being. Someone to be despised or pitied, not someone to be emulated or worshiped. Paul is to the point in his life where it is Christ now who has given him meaning and purpose. In verse 17, Paul gives us the great declaration that if anyone is in Christ, he is a new creation.

II. Love Compels Us to Share the Good News with a Greater Urgency

Paul speaks of the importance of reconciliation through Christ and the fact that those who receive reconciliation then become ministers of reconciliation. It is not enough to receive the gospel; we must also share it. He describes himself as Christ's ambassador.

Ambassadors do not create their own message; they share the message of the one who sent them. Ambassadors are citizens of one country who must live in another country. Christians often feel that way. Ambassadors have to be sensitive to the cultures of another land if they wish to communicate with the people who live there. Ambassadors are willing to accept the risk that sometimes comes from representing one country in a society of another. All this is true of Christ's ambassadors as well.

For Paul this venture is no small thing. He says in verse 20, "We implore you on Christ's behalf: Be reconciled to God" (NIV). Those who have been reconciled must share the message of reconciliation with others. The whole matter is summed up in verse 21: "God made him who had no sin to be sin for us, so that in him we might become the righteousness of God" (NIV).

This leads us to consider the presence of Christ on a cross, which is the ultimate message of love. There is a story about a brother in a monastery who was assigned to preach. All the brothers came into the chapel and found the lights off. The brother who was supposed to preach lit a candle. He took that candle and held it up to the crucifix. There he illuminated the thorn crowned brow, the pierced hands and feet and after doing so for a few seconds he extinguished the candle and dismissed the audience. He said, that it was a sermon on the love of Christ. And so it was. (J. Michael Shannon)

RETURN FROM A DISTANT COUNTRY

LUKE 15:1-3, 11b-32

The parable of the prodigal son has many messages, each with its own redemptive relevance. Today, we are going to explore one that is often overlooked. The parable is, at least in part, a story about a decision that is made and then remade between two ways of life. That story reflects something of our own experience in a way that can teach us something we need to know.

I. Tempting Rumors from Afar

In the parable, a certain young man has grown up on a Galilean farm where hard work, moral discipline, religious tradition—and love—shaped daily life. He had benefited greatly from that lifestyle—but he didn't know it.

Not everyone lived that way. The young man on the farm kept hearing about the glamorous and self-indulgent lifestyle that was in vogue only a long day's walk away in the Greek cities of the Decapolis.

Recently, one of those Greek cities has been excavated. It was the city of Scythopolis. It boasted magnificent Grecian architecture, arenas for competitive sports, theaters for dramatizing Greek philosophy and culture, and in the center of town, right across from the city hall, an ornate brothel and the baths with their terraces where orgies of self-indulgence were held.

We can imagine that reports of this lifestyle must have made the farm boy's work seem like dull drudgery. Finally, he made a decision. He broke all sorts of Jewish traditions and asked his father to give him his inheritance early. He took the resources that generations of hard work had accumulated and left the world of hard work, moral discipline, religious tradition, and love. He moved into the life of material affluence and self-indulgence. The journey was not long in miles. But, in terms of ways of life, it was indeed a journey into a distant country.

Do you know any other people—or nations—that have made similar moves?

II. Discovery and Return

At first the glamorous, self-indulgent, lifestyle must have seemed exciting. But resources unreplenished soon ran out. Then the young man discovered just how shallow the relationships and the satisfactions were in this new way of life. He discovered what was missing from the way of materialism and self-indulgence. Love was missing.

The young man's life withered away. He pondered what he should do. What was lost was lost. But at least, in his father's house there was love. He felt sure that would still be there for him. He decided to trust that love and return to the life of hard work, moral discipline, religious tradition, and love.

He made a good decision. When will we?

III. A Sobering Thought

The young man in the story was fortunate. There was still a home there for him to return to. But homes and ways of life need maintenance. One cannot stay a prodigal too long without losing what hard work, moral discipline, religious tradition, and love can produce. Thomas Hart Benton painted a picture which he called "The Prodigal's Return." It shows a young man with a suit coat slung over his shoulder standing dejected before a house. He had returned to the family farm to find the house empty and dark and the fields overgrown from neglect. The life base from which he had gone forth had disintegrated in his absence, perhaps because he was absent.

We still have the opportunity to return and rebuild. Let's not wait too long to take it. (Jim Killen)

REFLECTIONS

❦

APRIL

Reflection Verse: "Mary Magdalene went and announced to the disciples, 'I have seen the Lord'; and she told them that he had said these things to her" (John 20:18).

She was the first, and we all stand behind her. Everyone since her who ever heard the news of Christ's Resurrection, first heard it second hand. But not her. She was the first to see him and the first to tell. The others who saw him that day had already heard it through her. Ever since, the news has been flowing down the centuries like a swelling river; but the start of it all was a clear little stream of words from Mary Magdalene's mouth.

Since this makes her more or less the first Christian preacher, we would do well to stand beside her for a while to learn what she teaches about our vocation and ourselves.

Isn't it something that the first proclaimer of Easter did it with red-rimmed eyes? Who knows what else was in her face when she told the eleven, "I have seen the Lord!" but her eyes were still swollen and bloodshot from hard crying. I have little doubt that many of you who read these words will identify with her here. While it's true that the news we preach is finally and supremely good, there are many losses along the way. The news follows our losses—*follows* them—which means we never really comprehend the news apart from comprehending the losses. What this suggests is that, in the end, the most effective preparation for proclaiming Resurrection may well be the anguish of personal, terrible grief. Or, in the words of Jesus, "Blessed are you who weep now; you shall laugh."

How did Mary come by such grief? By being faithful. By refusing, unlike so many other disciples, to flee the bloody scene of execution. She stood there facing that hideous death, and God only knows what it cost her. Even when his agony finally ended,

125

she stayed grimly with the fact of his death, following his corpse to its grave. And now in the dark on the third day she is back to attend to his death. You may call this her love, but you may also call it her courage. In her is not a trace of denial, not an ounce of escapism, nor any other kind of absenteeism from pain. More than anyone, she resolutely faces the wrenching horror of this loss, lets herself shudder in the chill of it, and is utterly undone by it. So she is the one in place to comprehend—and preach—Resurrection.

The deadliest occupational hazard we face is to preach what is not real to us. It's an understandable seduction. Not only do most of us have to get up every Sunday and say something about the deepest and highest of all realities, but we have to take our themes according to the calendar! How can we not, on some occasions at least, fall into talking away about news that we ourselves have neither touched nor tasted nor lately even longed for? Some of us are such effective little professionals in this regard that we're fooled by the eloquence of our own speech into not even noticing the incongruity. But something hidden in us knows it. In the soul such falsehoods accumulate in layers like silt. We are made shallow. More and more our speech is reduced to a spread of platitudes, not an honest, coursing depth. Something in the congregation knows it too.

Maybe it would be presumptuous to say that the way of Mary Magdalene is the only way for our own sense of Easter to become deeply real. But wouldn't it be a shame if hers were the path we most needed to take, and yet—because of dullness, or denial, or fear, or unfaithful busyness—refused to take it?

So why not ask yourself the following questions: What recent crucifixions have occurred in my world? Have I turned away from them or attended to them? Have I been refusing to face pain, death, and loss, in any of their forms? Have I sufficiently mourned what I need to mourn? Is it in any sense true that "They have taken away my Lord, and I do not know where they have laid him"? Are there still unwept tears in me, and if so, what keeps me from weeping now?

"Blessed are you who weep now . . . ."

And of course tears can blind us for a time. That's the great and tender joke of John 20. Mary Magdalene's eyes are so clouded with crying that she can't tell it's two angels, beside themselves with glee, asking her, "Woman, why do you weep?" And when the very one she's looking for stands at her elbow to ask the same rich question, she's sobbing so hard she doesn't know the voice—not until the voice makes clear that he knows her. But the deepest and best joke of all is that this woman who was brave enough to be ruined enough to mourn and mourn and mourn—hers was the first name called by the risen Christ. She who most faithfully faced what her world had lost, was found. And with all the rest that she found, she found her voice, and so started the great stream of Resurrection news.

How different it might be in many a church at Easter if the preacher, instead of delivering another proper sermon for the occasion, could arrive to say truthfully, beautifully, simply: "*I* have seen the Lord. *I* have." Likely as not, any who do so will do it with red-rimmed eyes. (Paul D. Duke)

APRIL 1, 2001

❦

Fifth Sunday in Lent

Worship Theme: God's people are created to offer lives of praise to God in thanksgiving for Jesus Christ and the new life given in his death and resurrection.

Readings: Isaiah 43:16-21; Philippians 3:4*b*-14; John 12:1-8

Call to Worship (Psalm 126):

>*Leader:* When the LORD restored our fortunes,
>   we were like those who dream.

>*People:* **Our mouth was filled with laughter,**
>   **and our tongue with shouts of joy;**
>   **then it was said among the nations,**
>   **"The LORD has done great things for them."**

>*Leader:* The LORD has done great things for us, and we rejoiced.
>   Restore our fortunes, O LORD, like the watercourses in the Negeb.

>*People:* **May those who sow in tears, reap with shouts of joy.**
>   **Those who go out weeping, bearing the seed for sowing,**
>   **shall come home with shouts of joy, carrying their sheaves.**

Pastoral Prayer:
O God, you formed us as a people so that we might declare your praise. Prepare us for Easter; keep us awake and ready for the new thing you are about to do. We give you thanks for your promise of

128

rivers in the desert and highways in the wilderness, for water when we are thirsty and a clear path when we are lost and tired. Help us to care daily for the poor, who confront our complacency by being always with us. Be present to those who are sick; and to all those who weep, give hope for your harvest of joy. Encourage us to forget what lies behind and press on toward your high calling in Christ. Teach us to be extravagant in our devotion to him so that our prayers may rise before you like the aroma of costly perfume. Guide us by your Spirit to know Christ and the power of his resurrection. In his name we pray. Amen. (Blair G. Meeks)

SERMON BRIEFS

HAVE YOU HAD A WILDERNESS EXPERIENCE?

ISAIAH 43:16-21

Have you ever had a wilderness experience? I do not mean an adventure in the outdoors. I mean a formational experience with God, a season in your life when theology became more practical than theoretical. I call it a *wilderness* experience because in scripture this kind of thing seems to happen in the wilderness. The exodus from Egypt was perhaps the original wilderness experience. In the wilderness Israel learned to be God's people. You might think also of David's years hiding from Saul, of John the Baptist going out into the wilderness to baptize, of Jesus' forty days of temptation, or of Paul's time in Arabia after his conversion (Galatians 1:17). Of course God is not limited geographically, so this kind of experience can happen anywhere. The tradition in scripture grows out of the exodus, so that the wilderness becomes the place where God's people are formed. Hence the name.

I. Exodus Revisited

In today's text the exiles are promised a new exodus. God is about to bring the people back from captivity in Babylon to freedom in Jerusalem. They face another long journey through expansive wilderness. The prophet cannot help seeing how much this will be like the original exodus. Our text is full of allusions to it: a way in the sea, chariot and army extinguished, water in the desert. God has done this kind of thing before. Why should the exiles hope? Because their God specializes in rescues and wilderness journeys.

For the prophet and the exiles, this new exodus was more than a trip home. Just as Israel had been formed in the wilderness, they would be re-formed as God's people. On the way from Egypt, God had given the law and made a covenant with Israel. The people had experienced God's power, anger, and mercy. In the process they had become God's people. Their wilderness experience had been formational. The prophet saw the same thing happening on the journey from Babylon.

II. A New Thing

The music was old, but the lyrics were new. The same word from God that called to mind the exodus also said, "Do not remember the former things." We are tempted to ask on behalf of the exiles, Is the exodus a pattern for understanding God's action in our lives or not? As soon as we ask that, however, we have our answer. Yes, this experience would be *like* the exodus, but it is a further work of God. God is acting in the present. The things of old help us understand how God is working, but God is doing something new.

This is true for us as well. As we read the scriptures, we find patterns by which to recognize and understand God's work in our lives. But God's word to us is still "I am about to do a new thing." And that is why I ask if you have had a wilderness experience. We stand in a great tradition of faith. We know God's mighty acts in history. Yet we are a part of that living, unfinished history. So we must be open to God's work among us.

And that is what this experience is: God's work. You cannot contrive it; you cannot go to this class or read that book to make it happen. At best you can be open to it, so that when the time comes, you do not miss God speaking. Because God is faithful, God's deeds look the same. But God is also dynamic and creative,

APRIL 1, 2001

so each work is new. May you discover this for yourself in your
own wilderness experience. (David Mauldin)

THE POWER OF PERSONAL TESTIMONY

PHILIPPIANS 3:4*b*-15

Some Christians say that they are unable to witness for Jesus.
But everyone who has experienced the transforming power of
God through Christ Jesus has a testimony. That testimony is significant and unique for every person. What is most significant,
however, is not one's life prior to confessing Jesus as Savior and
Lord. Ultimately important is what Christ means to a person as
the result of recognizing that transforming presence in his/her
life. Paul provides here a model for Christian testimonies. Following this model can provide a means for every person to
develop a testimony concerning Christ's impact on life.

I. Reflections on One's Life Prior to Christ (vv. 4*b*-6)

Prior to confessing Jesus, some people's lives are filled with
hate, immorality, cursing, and all types of crime. Other people's
lives remind one of pabulum—colorless, innocuous, and seemingly insignificant. Still others appear to be successful, dynamic,
and captivating. The latter category would be a picture of Paul.
He was, according to his own accounts here and in Galatians
1:13-14, a successful, zealous Jew with a first-class pedigree who
thought that God was smiling on him. But that background is
only the introduction to the story. It is not the primary element in
a testimony. Everyone's background story is different but it is
only an introduction to talking about the power of God in one's
life.

II. Transformation to a New Perspective (vv. 7-11)

Meeting God in Christ changes one's perspective on life.
Because of what Christ has done for us in his self-giving death
and powerful resurrection, the focus of our lives shifts from

131

ourselves to Christ. As a result, everything about our life looks different—even suffering and death. The significant becomes insignificant (Paul calls it *manure [dung]* in verse 8 KJV). The previously unrecognized way of Jesus then becomes crucial. Righteousness from God becomes the key to acceptance in life. Our testimonies, therefore, ought to highlight what God has done and continues to do in transforming our perspectives on life.

III. Resulting Adjustment of Life's Goals (vv. 12-15)

Based on a new perspective, new evaluations in life take place. God becomes the standard of judging achievement. Accomplishments are viewed as partial in the light of ultimate reality. The goal of meeting the calling of Jesus becomes the quest of life. To that ultimate quest Paul committed himself and called everyone else to follow. Testimonies are, accordingly, not merely reflections of our past lives or the story of our past transformation, but they are also assertions of what is becoming increasingly significant in our lives daily as we "press on" toward our goals in Christ Jesus our Lord. (Gerald L. Borchert)

A PURPOSEFUL ACT OF WORSHIP

JOHN 12:1-8

Around the globe, each Sunday, Christians of all brands gather for worship. They gather singing from hymnbooks or reading words of choruses off projector screens. They listen to reflective homilies or fiery sermons. Their worship may climax with the celebration of the Eucharist or a call to salvation. Although there are numbers of traditions and subtraditions within the context of Christian worship, God's criterion is simply that we worship in the spirit of truth. This text gives a tangible example of genuine worship.

I. Costly Worship (vv. 1-3)

The celebration for Passover was at hand. Jesus chose to celebrate with his friends at Bethany. Here was the place of what could arguably be his greatest miracle, raising Lazarus from the dead. Martha and Mary had a better understanding of Jesus' identity since that miracle. For them, he was the resurrection and the life, no questions or debate. For Mary, there still lingered an intense sense of gratitude woven into the complete awe surrounding the resurrection of her brother. She had grown to love this Christ, and words could not fully express her gratitude.

In the midst of those gathered, Mary made time to express her worship. She humbled herself before Jesus in the presence of onlookers. In fact, the real humility was that she worshiped in the presence of spectators. She would not hold back anything in her expression, regardless of their reaction. Reaching for that precious bottle of perfume saved for special occasions (and then it was to be used only sparingly), she poured it over the feet of her Lord. Taking an even more humble position, she unbound her hair (a taboo in the first century Near-Eastern culture) and wiped his feet.

This was not an act of worship that was without thought or given from rote habit. This was an expression that calculated the great cost of her pride, her prize possession, and her reputation. It was worth it. She had to express her devoted gratitude. Although it cost her dearly, she worshiped.

II. Rational Analysis of Worship (vv. 4-6)

This act would not go unnoticed. Judas, the crooked treasurer who stole right from the moneybag, gave particular attention. His rationalization sounded so reasonable. "Wait let's think this through. Why waste so much valuable commodity on an act of worship? Where are our values anyway? Don't we even care for the poor?" The words had an edge to them that questioned the integrity of Jesus for even allowing such an act to be done in his presence without rebuke.

But was that Judas' real intention? Not really. It seems that Mary's worship irritated him for reasons other than concern about stewardship for the poor. She worshiped in a costly manner. He followed to get what he could out of the endeavor. She bent low in humility to express her love. He demanded that Jesus fit with his agenda and goals. She poured out something valuable.

He stayed along while it was convenient. No, this act of worship created conviction for Judas that he did not want to face. There was an out for him though; he could rationalize her worship as a mindless act of spontaneity that just did not stand the test of good financial management.

III. Purpose in Worship (vv. 7-8)

Jesus sees through Judas' facade quite easily. The poor are not the issue. They are with us and we will always have an obligation to them as long as they are among us. The power of Mary's act was that it was intentional. From a divine perspective, she was preparing him for his burial. She did not know this perhaps, but the act was purposeful from God's viewpoint. God could use her pure expressions for God's purposes.

Worship has not changed through the centuries in regard to the purity and purposefulness of the act. It will cost us something in the way of pride, possessions, and even reputation. We will be tempted to rationalize it all away and keep our pride and possessions intact. But real worship will demand from us a priority list that keeps God at the top and our expressions of gratitude pure. However, such is the kind of worship that the Father seeks, and we can offer no less. (Joseph Byrd)

APRIL 8, 2001

❦

Passion/Palm Sunday

Worship Theme: Jesus, the obedient servant, rode a humble donkey and was lifted high on a cross, but God raised him from the dead and exalted his name above all others.

Readings: Isaiah 50:4-9a; Philippians 2:5-11; Luke 22:14–23:56

Call to Worship (Psalm 118:19-20, 25-29):

Leader: Open to me the gates of righteousness,
              that I may enter through them and give thanks to
              the LORD.
              This is the gate of the LORD; the righteous shall
              enter through it.

People: **Save us, we beseech you, O LORD!**
              O LORD, we beseech you, give us success!
              Blessed is the one who comes in the name of
              the LORD.
              We bless you from the house of the LORD.

Leader: The LORD is God, and he has given us light.
              Bind the festal procession with branches,
              up to the horns of the altar.

People: **You are my God and I will give thanks to**
              you;
              you are my God, I will extol you.
              O give thanks to the LORD, for he is good;
              for his steadfast love endures forever.

135

Pastoral Prayer:

God our Savior, you sent Jesus, your divine and royal son, to be both mortal and a servant that we might have life in abundance. Lift up our hearts to the one who was lifted up on the cross. Give us grace to know the Christ who was humbled and exalted. Teach us the astonishing love for the world that made your son weep over the city and offer his radical obedience for the healing of us all. We thank you for those who teach the ways of reconciliation, those who set their faces like flint and endure senseless wrongs; may they know your honor. We remember, O God, the sick and those who are dying; may we show them the comfort of your promises in this Holy Week of our Lord's passion. Guide us to the victory that comes by your hand, for peace and glory belong to you. Give us songs of praise to bless the one who comes in your name, and teach all tongues to confess that Jesus Christ is Lord. All glory and honor to God, through Christ and the Holy Spirit. Amen. (Blair G. Meeks)

SERMON BRIEFS

WANTON SPECULATION

ISAIAH 50:4-9*a*

Whenever we read Isaiah with reference to Jesus, I feel a desire to explain how we can do so. Chapters 40 through 55 of Isaiah were originally addressed to the Jewish people in exile. The image of the servant originally referred to the nation. The prophet's description of God's suffering servant so resonated with Jesus' first followers, though, that they turned to these texts for help understanding Jesus' death. Thus, a tradition of interpretation was born.

Reading Isaiah with reference to Jesus is legitimate, given proper introduction, because in a sense Jesus, as Messiah, stood for the nation. Its calling to be the servant of God and a light to the nations was his calling.

Given all the ways to read Isaiah, and there are a lot of them, I wonder how Jesus himself read it? Did it inspire him with confidence that he could win by losing? With wistful irony the prophet employs a psalm of lament to describe the vocation of God's suffering servant. We can see how this would have touched the hearts of the exiles. A psalm of lament was the only appropriate way to sing their song. Yet when the prophet sang, he told them God had elected them for a special purpose. Their suffering began to make sense within the larger scheme of that purpose. The band played a dirge while the singer sang of life.

Did the song touch Jesus' heart the same way? When he was struck in the face, did something in his mind go back to the prophet's message? When people spat on him, did he bear it with as much dignity as possible because he trusted that God would not let him be finally disgraced? As he was convicted and sentenced, did he still believe God would help him? Could he hear the prophet's words, however faintly, "He who vindicates me is near"? Most important, did Jesus not shirk the cross because he believed that through his death the purposes of God might be accomplished?

How we answer these questions does not really matter. For the most part our inquiries are wanton speculation. Who could know what Jesus thought? What does matter is God's marvelous way of turning humiliation into victory.

God did vindicate Jesus, who suffered in God's service. If you come back next Sunday you can hear about that. But today we focus on Jesus' suffering. Why? Because it was not only the power of resurrection that overcame hate, sin, and death. Jesus triumphed over his accusers when he did not curse them. He avoided disgrace when he set his face like flint against the fists and the spit that struck him. It took resurrection to make his victory apparent, and it took resurrection to show us that Jesus' death was for us. God's purpose was to save us; and because Jesus did not shirk the cross, his death accomplished that purpose.

Jesus not only offers us life in eternity, he teaches us how to live. In our text, trust in God allows the servant to endure suffering and humiliation. The servant obeys God no matter the cost. Jesus too was faithful to his mission, though it took him to the cross. The Father had sent him, and nothing could make him abandon his vocation. God asks for our ultimate allegiance. Our obedience may meet with opposition in this sinful world. The

One who vindicates us is near, however. So we cast our lot with Jesus, identify ourselves with him, continue his work, and share his message. We are not ashamed to worship as God this man, once nailed to a tree in disgrace. We recognize the victory in his defeat and the honor in his humiliation. His suffering deeply touches us, both because it is so horrible and because we are grateful. Yet the cross does not turn us away from him; it draws us to him. On this day especially, we remember his suffering. As we contemplate Jesus' death, the tune we sing is a dirge, but the words, they are life! (David Mauldin)

THE STRANGE PATTERN OF JESUS

PHILIPPIANS 2:5-11

Everywhere we look there are patterns and models. Successful movies like *Star Wars* and *Superman* have their sequels. Copyrights and patents try to protect new models, while sleuths seek out variants that will permit them to copy the originals. Drug manufacturers seek new formulas, and generic producers wait to undersell them. New videos and discs are advertised for high prices, while foreign pirates muscle in on these markets. Copying patterns, whether legal or illegal, is big business. Moreover, patterns are used for making a multitude of things from dresses to townhouses.

In the Hellenistic period it was believed that in the world of ideals there were archetypes for everything from wheels to horses to chairs, and those archetypes were copied in various ways throughout the phenomenal or actual world. It is, therefore, not surprising that Paul used such pattern-thinking to communicate the message of Jesus. But what he did with such pattern-thinking would have been strange and shocking to his readers. It seems no less strange to readers today who take their clues for success from Madison Avenue. Paul's pattern for success was rooted in a divine reversal that accomplished far more than mortals could imagine. To that pattern every Christian is called to copy and embody.

I. The Divine Example of Humility (vv. 5-7)

When Paul proposed to his readers to adopt the mind of Christ, he reminded them that Jesus had left the divine realm to come to earth. In doing so, the pattern he forged was not one of selfish grasping for prestige and power. Even though in his very nature he was every bit God, he gave that up to be born a human. While theologians have debated to what extent Jesus emptied himself of his divine nature, what is eminently clear is that he truly became human and was subject to pain, hunger, temptation, and the many other aspects of mortals, except for yielding to sin (cf. Heb. 4:15).

II. Jesus' Model of Obedience (v. 8)

Not only did Jesus exemplify humility, but the New Testament is explicit that although humanly speaking Jesus did not want to suffer the agony of crucifixion, he yielded obediently to the will of his Father and died the horrible death on the cross (cf. Luke 22:42; John 12:27; Hebrews 5-8). This death of Jesus for us we call the atonement for our sins (Romans 3:25; Hebrews 2:17; 1 Petet 1:18; 1 John 2:2; Revelation 5:9). While many theories of the atonement have been articulated by theologians, one fact remains absolutely clear: the New Testament writers declared that Jesus died for our sins and that we are to live in self-giving response toward others.

III. God's Judgment on This Pattern or Model (vv. 9-11)

The "therefore" of verse 9 thunders throughout all realms of reality that God has confirmed the servant pattern of Jesus. Moreover, God has endowed this Jesus with the preeminent name in all of creation so that all creatures will be duty bound, whether they like it or not, to acknowledge him as *kurios*/ Lord! God knew the implications of sending Jesus to the cross, and even though the power structures of this age have always thought that they would win (1 Corinthians 2:6-8), the ultimate victory and glory belongs to God. And all Christians should respond by praising the Lord for the ultimate victory that has been won in Christ. (Gerald L. Borchert)

PALM SUNDAY

LUKE 22:14–23:56

If your congregation participates in Holy Week services and gets a picture of the whole story of Jesus' death, then you may want to choose a portion of the Scripture to focus on for Palm Sunday. If your congregation does not have this opportunity, you may want to consider reading the whole text, dividing it in portions, using music between to interpret. This will enable the congregation to witness the last days of Jesus' life as the sermon.

I. The Last Supper and Foretelling of Betrayal (22:14-38)

Jesus eagerly breaks bread and shares the cup with the disciples. This kingdom meal takes place under the knowledge that Jesus is about to suffer, though the disciples do not fully understand. Instead of talking about the significance of the meal—"This is my body, which is given for you" or this cup is "the new covenant in my blood"—the disciples become preoccupied with questions of who will betray Jesus and who is the greatest. When we partake of the kingdom meal, do we understand the significance of the body and blood of Christ, or are we preoccupied with trivial matters and our own self-interests?

II. Gethsemane (22:39-53)

Jesus must have felt utterly alone in Gethsemane. He had been in prayer and had urged his disciples to join him. The disciples did not pray; Jesus found them "sleeping." They were so overwhelmed with their own grief and anxiety, they lost sight of the one whom they had chosen to follow. As soon as they were caught "sleeping," they were ready to draw swords and come to Jesus' rescue. A "so-called" disciple betrayed him with a kiss; not exactly the expected greeting for someone you have sold out. The chief priests and temple officials questioned him constantly throughout the week, yet they waited until "the cover of darkness" to come and arrest him. How many times are we caught "sleeping" only to try out of our own efforts to come to Jesus' rescue only to fail miserably?

III. Peter's Denial and Jesus Before Caiaphas (22:54-71)

Jesus is arrested and led away to the house of Caiaphas, the
high priest. Peter follows at a distance and sits by a fire in the
courtyard. Peter was courageous to follow Jesus to the place
where he was being held, but his courage would not be enough to
help him "testify" to know Jesus (cf. Luke 21:13). He denies him
three times, the cock crows, and Peter realizes his failure to be
faithful in the heat of the moment. When we are under pressure
or the possibility of suffering, are we faithful witnesses of Jesus?

IV. Jesus Before Pilate and Herod Antipas (23:1-25)

The temple assembly brings Jesus before Pilate. Pilate tries to
free Jesus because he does not see a basis for any accusation. Since
Jesus is from Galilee, Pilate sends him to Herod Antipas. Herod
and his men "mock" him and treat him with "contempt," but send
him back to Pilate. Pilate again finds no fault against Jesus, yet the
"mob mentality" rules the day. Pilate falls to pressure from the
mob. The crowds convince him to release a criminal and to kill an
innocent man. As Christians, do we stand alone through faith with
passion and conviction or fall to the pressure of the mob?

V. The Crucifixion (23:26-56)

Throughout the entire narrative of chapter 23, there is the
underlying question of Jesus' identity. Jesus is led away to be crucified with two other criminals. The various people throughout
the narrative must decide for themselves who Jesus is. There are
the women who followed weeping; the leaders who say "Save
yourself if you are the Messiah"; the soldiers mocking him, calling him "King of the Jews"; the criminals who hang there with
him—one who wants the Messiah to save him from physical
death and the other who seems to understand Jesus; the centu-
rion who declares Jesus' innocence; and righteous Joseph of
Arimathea who takes the body of Jesus for burial. How do we
identify Jesus? What kind of salvation are we looking for? (Marcia
T. Thompson)

APRIL 13, 2001

❧

Good Friday

Worship Theme: The church remembers Jesus' crucifixion, an unthinkable act of rejection, suffering, and humiliation, endured for love of the world. But Jesus on the cross is Christ our Victor; God's triumphant song of life sounds in the midst of death.

Readings: Isaiah 52:13–53:12; Hebrews 10:16-25; John 18:1–19:42

Call to Worship (Psalm 22:1, 3, 19, 25-27):

Leader: My God, my God, why have you forsaken me?
        Why are you so far from helping me?

People: **Yet you are holy;**
        enthroned on the praises of Israel.

Leader: But you, O LORD, do not be far away!
        O my help, come quickly to my aid!

People: **You will lead us to praise your name in the great congregation.**
        We will renew our promises before all who honor you.

Leader: The poor shall eat and be satisfied;
        those who seek him shall praise the LORD.
        May your hearts live forever!

People: **All the ends of the earth shall remember and turn to the LORD;**
        and all the families of the nations shall worship before him.

Pastoral Prayer:

God of our salvation, your Son was betrayed, denied, and hung high on a cross. Give us grace to look on the one whom Pilate delivered over to death, our King of Life. Give us courage to stand with Mary Magdalene at the foot of the cross, saying, "I was there when they crucified my Lord." Help us to raise our eyes while others hide their faces, that we may see in the Despised and Rejected One the glory of your promised victory over death. Guide us to proclaim your resurrection power to those who suffer as your Son suffered, to those who are acquainted with sorrow, to those who are counted as lost. We thank you, O God, that you have washed us with pure water; you have forgotten all our sins. Teach us to confess our unwavering hope, to join our voices in Christ's triumphant song, for you are the Faithful One who reigns with Christ and the Holy Spirit, one God forever and ever. Amen. (Blair G. Meeks)

SERMON BRIEFS

TWO PARADOXES

ISAIAH 52:13–53:12

Though scholars offer other explanations and possibilities for the words of Isaiah, the Christian Church has traditionally understood them as a prophecy of the life and death of Jesus. For a while, let's think about them as such. Immediately two paradoxes claim our attention.

I. Paradox One

He will be both *lifted* up and *exalted* (52:13). How so? How can the act of being lifted up bring exaltation? The cross was something used to hang rebellious slaves and bandits on. It was a place of embarrassment, shame and death. No exaltation here.

Nevertheless, if we continue to interpret this in the light of the church's traditional experience, we can affirm that "God highly exalted him and gave him a name that is above every name"

(Philippians 2:9). Jesus' suffering led to his exaltation. Can the church be exalted through suffering? Is the church a suffering servant? Is it possible?

During the past couple of years many churches and communities throughout Tennessee, and the nation, have been severely damaged or destroyed by tornadoes. God's people have suffered. People sometimes ask, "Why does God cause these things to happen?" But this poses the wrong question. Instead the question I would suggest is, "How does God work in spite of these things?"

One pastor of a church destroyed by a tornado said that exaltation had come through suffering. He observed that in his church people had focused truly on what the church is called to be. Loving cooperation, spiritual values as opposed to material ones, thinking of others first—these qualities have all been nourished through suffering.

It may be that there can be no exaltation without suffering. If so, then the true nature of servanthood has been revealed. Yes, it's paradoxical.

II. Paradox Two

People who *have not heard* from this servant *will be in contemplation* (52:15). How can one be contemplative about that which one is not aware of?

We're so tied to the normal empirical experience of truth. If we can't see it, feel it, touch it, taste it, or hear it, it's not real. So, how can someone contemplate what he or she has not experienced? Well, it's experience of a different nature. Wasn't this Jesus' argument when he said to Nicodemus, "The wind blows where it chooses . . ."? John Wesley spoke of *prevenient grace*, the grace available to use before we become aware of it. Maybe our definitions of experience are incomplete.

Spiritual matters are not to be judged solely on the basis of the normal categorizations. A young man from Africa University is coming to an American seminary for further study without any knowledge whatsoever of where tuition funds are coming from, but says, "The Lord will provide." The tuition funds don't exist

but there is contemplation of provision. This is the real nature of
faith. And, yes, it's paradoxical.

Look at the world around you. Is it possible for Jews and Arabs
to live together in peace? Can we conquer racism? Can the poor
of this world be filled with both food and hope? Not without the
contemplative approach which focuses on the impossibilities as
realities. It seems that such an approach is precisely the one
taken by the suffering servant of Isaiah's prophecy. (Jim Clardy)

THE WAY

HEBREWS 10:16-25

Christian faith is experienced in great paradoxes. Central in
our faith is the assertion that Jesus was at the same time fully
human and fully divine. Other assertions speak of God's love and
judgment, divine foreknowledge, and human freedom, and of
corporate, covenantal inclusiveness in salvation and personal
decision. Another paradox is the necessity of personal obedience
and the free gift of God's grace.

The church that the writer is addressing is a church that has
begun to cool off in its fervor for the faith. There is no longer the
sense of joyful abandonment to faith in Jesus which had earlier
characterized it. In order to help the congregation face the character of faith, the writer, in earlier chapters, contrasted the insti-
tutionalized religious practices of the Jewish temple with the
charismatic priesthood of Melchizedek and then identified Jesus
with the shadowy figure from Genesis. The contrast was intended
not only to portray Jesus as superior to the Jewish priests; it was
primarily given to counter the complacency of the congregation
to which Hebrews was written.

The new covenant of Jeremiah 31:33 fits in neatly with the
noninstitutional character of the priesthood of Jesus. The
covenant of the heart is "portable," not tied to religion, even the
"religion" of Jesus. Because of this freedom from institutionalism,
Christian faith escapes the dragging around of weight which
would contribute to the dullness of spirit which characterizes the
congregation to which Hebrews is written.

In verse 19, the writer moves from exposition of the point being made to a call for the readers to respond to it. Throughout Hebrews there has been an alteration of exposition and exhortation. As the purpose of Hebrews is being accomplished, each swing incorporates not only the section immediately preceding but also the whole of what has been developed.

"On the basis of what has been said," the writer asserts, "do these things." What has been said is a presentation of the work of Jesus seen through the lens of the Jewish sacrificial system. (There is an ambiguous apposition in verse 20. The preacher would do well to work through the problem in the commentaries but should not find it necessary to lay all "the skeleton" out before the congregation.) Jesus has made a new way possible; a way through the veil accomplished through his sacrificial death. Those who have accepted this way are challenged to walk in it. The benefits, responsibilities, and prerequisites of "the way" are the same. For one to claim to have access to the sanctuary but to hold back from it is to continue to live outside "the way."

Christians are urged to hold fast to "the way," here viewed as a confession of faith. One of the contributing factors to the cooling of the fervor in the church was the threat of persecution for the faith. Whether this is a challenge to be ready to make a "confession" of some formula which asserted one's allegiance to Jesus Christ or a call to the expression of one's personal faith is of little consequence. Either of the two alternatives demands that witness be borne in the face of threat.

Finally, Christians are commanded to maintain the community life that encourages and strengthens the church. The community of faith is not merely an assembly but it is at least that. When people have decided for whatever reason to "go it alone," the results are often disastrous both for the individual and for the church. The church is a grouping of people who encourage one another to live in the way. Living the Christian life is never an easy task. It is a joyous task but not an easy one. In order to be successful, Christians need one another.

For the writer of Hebrews, the separation sometimes made between faith and obedience is spurious. Because Christianity is a way of living, those who are Christian live in obedience to "the way." (Lee Gallman)

PETER, PILATE, OR JOSEPH AND NICODEMUS: WHICH ONE ARE YOU?

JOHN 18:1–19:42

Vivid, sharp images of people and place fill this long section of John's Gospel. Use your senses to hear and smell this important story of the arrest, crucifixion, and burial of Jesus. The passage begins in a garden in the Kidron Valley (18:1) and ends in a garden called Golgotha (19:41). The story of Jesus in John's Gospel begins to slow down considerably here. Up to this point, the reader has been clipping through events at a rapid speed. We have met people in the first twelve chapters and watched them interact with Jesus. We have seen Nicodemus secretly creeping in the dark. We have witnessed the conversation between Jesus and the woman from Samaria in the glaring blaze of a noonday sun. We have watched the faith of a government official whose son was deathly ill. We have heard the grumbling of the crowds who want to see a magician feed their hungry stomachs. We have seen the disciples struggle with Jesus' identity; we sadly watched the defection of some of those who could not bear the demands of Jesus' mission. A blind man has been given sight, and we feel as if we can see better as well.

And then the plot to kill Jesus is introduced in chapter 11, and the pace slows down. Narrative time is no longer counted in days and weeks, but hours and minutes. Jesus enters Jerusalem and we pause. We slow down. We breathe more slowly. Reading now becomes thick, like a spoon moving through a big molasses jar. Jesus is about to die, and we know it. Time is valuable. Travel time gives way to speaking time. Jesus walks less and speaks more. We hear lessons for life and death. We learn about Jesus' impending death from wheat seeds and heavenly houses. We watch Jesus prepare for death. He goes into deep prayer and then with sleepy, unconcerned disciples he enters a garden and is arrested. The next scenes take us from the garden to the court of the Jewish high priest, and Peter takes central stage. Then we travel to the Roman praetorium, where Pilate is the one to watch. Finally, we arrive in the garden, where Jesus will be crucified and buried; Nicodemus and Joseph of Arimathea are the ones to

147

view. Jesus is about to die. We watch those around him respond. Rejection, ambivalence, or steady faithfulness are the choices here. How do we respond?

The first response is Peter. Peter, eager to do the right thing yet always doing the wrong thing, strikes again—literally this time with his sword (18:10) As Jesus is arrested, Peter wants to start a war (for whose sake we will never know, but we have a good guess!). As Jesus is being interrogated by the Jewish high priest, Peter stays outside warm and cozy by the fire and denies that he ever knew this one inside. Three times Peter underscores that he is not associated with that one on the inside (18:15-18, 25-27). Satisfied with the temporary warmth of the charcoal fire, Peter lacks the courage and commitment to stand for Jesus and justice.

Pilate, on the other hand, does not have it so easy. The rules are not as clear. There is no warming fire and peer pressure from friends. Pilate, although accustomed to making quick, executive decisions, cannot quickly resolve this one; he physically and emotionally moves back and forth, back and forth, back and forth. Notice the presence of the English prepositions, *inside* and *outside*, that chronicle Pilate's movement. Pilate goes *out* (18:29); Pilate goes *in* (18:33); Pilate goes *out* (18:38); Pilate goes *out* again (19:4); Pilate goes *in* (19:9); Pilate finally goes *out* for the last time (19:13). This dramatic, physical movement of back and forth, back and forth illustrates Pilate's internal struggle. He wants to preserve Jesus' life. On the other hand, he wants to be a good leader. He wants to save this life; on the other hand, he does not want a mob insurrection. Pilate is torn. We agonize with his long decision-making process as well as the final outcome. Unlike Peter who quickly established his position with the sound of a clanking sword and a cock crowing, Pilate is not so sure. He wants to preserve Jesus' life. But like Peter, Pilate will give way to the pressure of the people and will decide to crucify this innocent man.

The irony rests in the decision making of the final characters in the story—Joseph of Arimathea and Nicodemus. Two secret disciples, known more for their lack of courage than for their public acknowledgment of Jesus (12:42), are the very ones who respond appropriately in this passage. In the next chapter, faithful Mary Magdalene will model the exemplar disciple; but in chapters 18 and 19 Peter and the others miss the mark, and Pilate is not so sure. Yet, these two Jewish leaders decide that it is better for them to declare themselves disciples of Jesus than to follow their peers in rejection. Thus, they choose to bear the responsibility for caring for Jesus' body and providing a place of burial. In performing these death rituals, they publicly identify with Jesus regardless of the cost. Joseph and Nicodemus, although slow to come to decision, are in the end the very ones who respond appropriately to the dying and rising Lord. Peter is relieved of the burden; Pilate remains anxious; but Joseph and Nicodemus have made their choice—they will follow Jesus even to death. (Linda McKinnish Bridges)

APRIL 15, 2001

❦

Easter Day

Worship Theme: God raised Jesus from the tomb and, by that resurrection power, promises that we may walk in abundant life now and be raised to live with Christ in God's glorious future.

Readings: Acts 10:34-43; 1 Corinthians 15:19-26; Luke 24:1-12

Call to Worship (Psalm 118:1-2, 15-17, 20-24):

Leader: O give thanks to the LORD, for he is good;
                  his steadfast love endures forever!

People: **There are glad songs of victory in the tents
                  of the righteous:
                  "The right hand of the LORD does valiantly;
                  the right hand of the LORD is exalted;
                  the right hand of the LORD does valiantly."**

Leader: I shall not die, but I shall live, and recount the
                  deeds of the LORD. . . .
                  I thank you that you have answered me and have
                  become my salvation.
                  The stone that the builders rejected has become
                  the chief cornerstone.

People: **This is the LORD's doing; it is marvelous in
                  our eyes.
                  This is the day that the LORD has made;
                  let us rejoice and be glad in it.**

Pastoral Prayer:

    God of life, you raised Jesus from the dead: Let our praise never cease and our joyous songs echo through all the world. Send us to declare the stories of Jesus who went about doing good and healing; teach us to proclaim the glorious message: "I have seen the Lord." Comfort those who grieve and those who are dying; give them hope in your promise that Christ will put death, his last enemy, under his feet. We give thanks that you bring all peoples to you through the lifting up of your Son Jesus Christ. Teach us to live together as one people, showing no partiality and proclaiming peace through Jesus Christ, who is Lord of all. Give us grace to eat and drink at the victory feast with the one who is our risen Lord; through Jesus Christ, the resurrection and the life, who reigns with you and the Holy Spirit, now and forever. Amen. (Blair G. Meeks)

SERMON BRIEFS

WHERE IT ALL COMES TOGETHER

ACTS 10:34-43

The Sundays from Easter to Pentecost provide a wonderful opportunity for preaching the book of Acts. We can gain fruit from the text by reflecting on why we give such attention to Acts during this time of the church year. Why do we take our first lesson during the Great Fifty Days from Acts and not the Hebrew Scriptures? The rationale frequently given focuses upon the content of the Acts lessons. We hear in them proclamation of that upon which all else in the Christian faith depends—the resurrection of Christ. We further witness the responses made to that proclamation, and so are ourselves urged to make response.

Given the strong theme of the gospel's universality, this is certainly a proper observation. In the resurrection, God vindicated Jesus and defeated the evil that opposed him. The resurrection thus unifies God's work in the earthly life of Jesus and proclamation of the risen Jesus as "Lord of all" (10:36).

The heritage of the Church sheds more light still on the practice for us. Reading Acts in Easter is no recent innovation, but it is quite ancient. It appears to have been well established by the latter half of the fourth century. The lectionaries of John

151

Chrysostom in the East and Augustine in the West reflect wide use of Acts. Chrysostom explained for his Constantinople congregation why Acts was preached during Easter:

> Just as we read the things about the cross on the day of the cross, . . . so also it is necessary for the apostolic wonders to be read on the days of the apostolic signs. . . . [T]he apostolic signs are a demonstration of the resurrection, and this book [of Acts] is a school of apostolic signs. That which especially confirms the resurrection of the Master is what the fathers legislated should be read immediately after the cross. . . . For this reason therefore, beloved, after the cross . . . we immediately read the signs of the apostles, so that we might have a sure and indisputable demonstration of the resurrection. ("Fourth Homily on the Beginning of Acts," quoted in Michael B. Compton, *Introducing the Acts of the Apostles: A Study of John Chrysostom's* On the Beginning of Acts, unpublished Ph.D. dissertation., University of Virginia, 1996, p. 70)

It is not simply the content, but the very fact of apostolic proclamation that is significant. According to the Gospel accounts, during Jesus' earthly ministry, the disciples were more often than not "good bad examples" of what followers of Jesus should be. Left in their hands, the Jesus movement would have surely succumbed to the first law of thermodynamics—losing energy and matter until it finally became inert. But it did not! By the logic of early Christian preaching, the fact that the apostles preached with such power and effect and continued to perform miracles such as Jesus had performed on earth ("doing good and healing all who were oppressed by the devil," v. 38) could mean but one thing. Just as Jesus' ministry was a demonstration that God was with him (v. 38), so the apostles' ministry was a demonstration that Jesus was risen and with them in power. Remember that the sermon in our lesson was preached by Peter to Gentiles! Only the resurrection of Christ could make possible such witness and testimony.

Both the ancient and the contemporary reasons for preaching Acts converge at one point. Whether you wish to focus upon the gospel and its claims throughout the ages, or upon the powerful works done in Jesus' name in and by the church, neither would even be an issue for us in the early twenty-first century apart from the resurrection. Reading Acts brings us to the essentials. (Philip E. Thompson)

THE ULTIMATE GRACE GIFT

1 CORINTHIANS 15:19-26

In this text there comes a final victory in Resurrection. It is the Resurrection of all Christians. This rising is not mere caprice, nor so-called Hellenistic wisdom; this is Fanny Crosby's "Blessed Assurance!" Jesus is ours precisely because of what God does through him in the Resurrection. New life for all who believe comes in this astonishing and totally believable notion. He lives, and because he lives we can live.

Out from this event *grace* leaps forward. We have neither earned by works nor merited by attitude this immortal opportunity—yet we have it. Jesus "pulls" us into the future through the inventive proficiency of our incredible God. We would do well here to focus on the load that Jesus gladly bears. As a responsible older sibling, Jesus endures our needs, being the weaker sisters and brothers that we are.

But how, then, do we respond to the one who has taken on our weight, our bodies, and burdens for our betterment? Where are the examples and what is a fitting response? The life and witness of Ella Baker, a civil rights pioneer and mentor, is a fitting example. Baker took on the likes of giants no less than Martin Luther King, Jr., in asserting the gifts, needs, and aspirations of women and youth during the controversial days of the 1960s. Her grassroots advocacy—within a movement for freedom—is hardly renowned, but is ripe for exploration of this resurrection theme. Who are the giants in your life and in your community who graciously "put the community" on their backs? Who are the leaders of your family, families in the community, the church, and of literature that demonstrate the heroic idea of offering new life to those who have lost life? We need to delve into the oral and written history of our community, and seek the wisdom of elders within our church to find other examples of resurrection.

For examples make the resurrection—life from death—a present reality for those who would dare disbelieve. Although we live in a culture that denies this reality, we need to commit to the idea of new life on a palatable level—a concept that unfortunately remains foreign even to some twenty-first-century church members. But our task is to make it real. Then, having illustrated the meaning of resurrection, we can seek to make evident that Jesus' resurrection is for others that came after him—not a miracle offered for him alone. When this has been done, the further responsibility is knowing the proper response. When believers and nonbelievers alike are confronted with the resurrection reality, when we accept it and believe it, the fitting response is *gratitude*. We ought to be thankful for what God has done for us in this fantastic and unbelievable event. Jesus died and rose for you and me. This free gift is an absolute blessing, an affirmation of our eternal significance. We ought to be grateful.

However, examining the notion of thanks is foreign these days. Gratitude is almost a non-issue for many people, but critical in this biblical context. However, investigating thanksgiving in our "for profit" culture demands some risk. We must be willing to prod ourselves, and others, to see how much we receive unmeritoriously. Many believe they only get what they deserve. But we must come to see how blessed we are without even knowing that we needed something, much less earning the gifts we receive.

By recognizing Jesus as the "first fruit" of the Resurrection, we accept that the Resurrection is not merely a "Divine Magic Show" for us. It is God's Ultimate Grace Gift. We ought to thankfully believe and receive the gift. (Vance P. Ross)

WHAT DO YOU EXPECT?

LUKE 24:1-12

In the Luke text for this Easter day, there is no appearance of the risen Lord. The appearance of the risen Lord happens on the Emmaus road (23:13-35). What we have in today's text is an empty tomb that is visited by the women, two men in dazzling clothes who proclaim that Jesus is risen, the disciples and Peter.

I. Go to the Tomb

Invite your congregants to the tomb on that first Easter morning. Go with the women to the tomb and watch from a distance.

Remember with the women how you have seen Jesus heal the sick, show compassion, eat with sinners, and bring hope to the hopeless. With the women, remember the dark side where the religious leaders constantly questioned his authority and his "Sonship." Remember with the women this last week of emotional upheaval. Jesus said he was to suffer and that trials would come our way. Jesus broke bread with us, was betrayed by a disciple, was arrested, crucified, and buried. Now the women have come to prepare his body with ointments for burial after the Sabbath. As the women get close they notice that the stone is rolled away from the front of the tomb. Inside there is no body. The women had seen the body placed in the tomb (23:55), so they must have had all kinds of questions racing through their minds. Suddenly two angels appear to them and proclaim that Jesus is risen. The angels ask them to remember how Jesus had said he would be crucified and on the third day he would rise. The women remember and return to the disciples to tell all that they had seen and heard only to meet disbelief. Peter decides to take a look for himself. Maybe he expects the angels to appear to him too. When he enters the tomb, he sees that the body is gone. He goes home amazed, but does not believe. Apparently, what Jesus had told the women and the disciples to expect about his suffering, death, and resurrection, they had forgotten, misunderstood, or could not believe. The expected became the unexpected. To move from grief to belief, from despair to hope is a tremendous leap.

What do we expect to see at the empty tomb? Are some full of grief over the death of a loved one? Are some grieving the loss of a friend, a job, or a miscarriage, a broken marriage? Is life full of despair or hope? Do we want to believe when it seems impossible? Where does belief come from?

II. Come to the Table

Luke is clear. Look what Peter says in Acts 10:41, and read the Emmaus story. They knew Jesus in the breaking of bread. Our best hope of coming to belief that really matters, that convinces us that everything has changed, is encountering the risen Lord around the Lord's table. In this meal, we share in the fellowship of his sufferings and the power of his resurrection. Is it automatic? For some it is. For others it is not. We come to the table bringing our loose ends and frayed edges; our achievements and failures; our joys and sorrows; our not-quite belief; our lives are placed under the promise of God that death is overcome. We have hope. We have eternal life in Jesus. We can participate in Christ's victory now because Jesus is alive and present with us today. (Marcia Thompson)

APRIL 22, 2001

❦

Second Sunday of Easter

Worship Theme: We know the risen Jesus through the testimony of those who were with him, who saw his wounds, and who passed to us his greeting of peace.

Readings: Acts 5:27-32; Revelation 1:4-8; John 20:19-31

Call to Worship (Psalm 150):

Leader: Praise the LORD!
Praise God in his sanctuary; and in the mighty firmament!
Praise him for his mighty deeds; praise him according to his surpassing greatness!

People: **Praise him; with trumpet sound; praise him with lute and harp,**
Praise him with tambourine and dance; praise him with strings and pipe,
Praise him with clanging cymbals; praise him with loud clashing cymbals!

Leader: Let everything that breathes praise the LORD!

People: **Praise the LORD!**

Pastoral Prayer:
   Almighty God, who is and who was, and who is to come, we thank you for Jesus Christ, the faithful witness, the firstborn of the dead, the ruler above all rulers. Love us, free us, make us your people. Give us courage to speak your truth, to rely on your authority, and to live in your Holy Spirit. We pray for those whose sadness confronts our joy, those who live in the shadow of death

157

and cannot see who you are. Teach them to know you as the God of sorrow and of gladness; send us to weep with them as Jesus wept with his friends, that by our touch they may know your presence. Guide those who work to resolve conflicts; grant that the whole earth may hear your greeting: "Peace be with you." Strengthen our faith that we may know you as our Lord and our God, who raised Jesus from the dead. In his name we pray. Amen. (Blair G. Meeks)

SERMON BRIEFS

THE BURDENS AND BLESSINGS OF BOLDNESS

ACTS 5:27-32

Our sermon text is centered in a cloud of confrontation, yet conviction in the power of the gospel of Jesus Christ. It details some of the concluding events of the initial movement of the Holy Spirit into a hurting and hostile world. It follows the miraculous and powerful event known as Pentecost.

To fully understand Acts 5:27-32, we must grasp the context of events intertwined in these verses and the preceding two chapters. Peter, John, and the apostles, "bold, uneducated, ordinary men" (4:13) now filled with the power of God within them, have been moved out by the Holy Spirit as witnesses of the resurrection of Jesus Christ. They've received the charge to proclaim repentance and forgiveness of sins to all who believe in his name. Through their actions, a lame man from birth is healed, and thousands believe in the Lord Jesus and are saved. It is a scene unlike any other, filled with excitement and enthusiasm, wonder and amazement, exhortation and encouragement. It is a penultimate picture of revival, redemption, restoration, and renewal. Yet within this community of jubilee is the air of tension and turmoil. There is the face-to-face confrontation between Peter and the apostles, and the priests of the Sanhedrin council. There is the dynamic of the miraculous power of God working through ordinary, uneducated men juxtaposed against the exposed powerlessness of people who were long believed to represent God. Through Peter and John, the Holy Spirit is liberating suffering souls. But through the priests comes an ugly picture of organized religion shuffling quickly to maintain its stature, even at the expense of suffering souls.

Peter and John are pressed with the decision as to whether to obey the movement of God through the Holy Spirit or obey the wishes of faithless men. The decision is obvious. We must obey God before human authority. Bold believers do just that. But as we do so, the text teaches us that there are burdens, yet blessings that come with the boldness of this decision.

First of all, through Peter and the apostles' bold decision we see that proclamation of the truth will bring problems from the opposition (v. 27). Peter and the apostles' mission of liberation disturbed the status quo, and the status quo reacted. There were imprisonments, threats, and ultimately floggings that Peter and the others endured for their actions. With proclamation comes persecution. It is one of the burdens that responsible and accountable believers must carry if we're committed to serving God before human authority.

Second, when we obey God before human authority, we must understand that our persecution may come from the most unlikely people. Peter and the apostles found their opposition coming from the people we'd assume would support, not challenge our position (vv. 27-28). Ironically, most of Jesus' controversial and problematic encounters in the Gospels came from those representing organized religion. Today's "council" and "high priest" of 5:27 are represented by various facets of the organized church, organized boards, and organized agencies that are filled with certain ordained clergy and empowered laity who, by their position, claim authority, yet by their actions reflect that they are lacking *the authority*. When others, particularly those "less educated," cause this reality to be exposed, there will be conflict. It is one of the burdens bold believers are called to carry.

Third, when we obey God before human authority, the powerless will seek to quiet the powerful. In 5:28, Peter and the others found again a command from powerless men to be silent—a charge previously articulated in chapter 4. The religious elite were suddenly the apostles' greatest enemies, determined to silence them from teaching. This behavior often occurs for two reasons: (1) many of those with perceived authority need to be liberated themselves, and are either in a state of denial or cover-up; and (2) no one, particularly those in positions of power likes to be exposed as having little, if any power themselves, or as having taught false or incomplete doctrine. When people are embarrassed and exposed, cover-up and a conspiracy of silence are natural human behaviors. It's one of the burdens of being bold for Jesus.

But finally, when we obey God before human authority, the power we have will ultimately prevail. God's Word will lead people to repentance and enable them to experience forgiveness of sins (v. 31). These are the blessings of boldness. There are many souls who will be saved, healed, rescued, and delivered by the power of God through our collective proclamation. Speak, be bold, and the Lord will bless mightily! (Joseph Daniels)

20/20 FORESIGHT

REVELATION 1:4-8

Faith Popcorn wrote: "You have to see the future to deal with the present." The writer of the Apocalypse would respond: "That is precisely what I mean." No other book of the Bible has suffered as much from its interpreters as the Revelation. G. K. Chesterton once wrote "though St. John the Evangelist saw many strange monsters in his vision, he saw no creature so wild as one of his own commentators" (*Orthodoxy*, [New York: John Lane Co., 1909] p. 29). Yet no other writing in the canon can bring us so near to the throne of God, nor move us to unbidden doxological worship as the Revelation. This ancient truth from God is our best guide to living the present with joyous confidence, anchored in a faith in the future victory of the church and her bridegroom.

I. Addressed to the Church

The Revelation is addressed to the seven churches that are in the province of Asia, the modern nation of Turkey. This address is rich in meaning for understanding the rest of the book. The Revelation is primarily a pastoral document, written to bring comfort and understanding to the people of the early church. It is intended to be interpreted for the benefit of the church, a reality that renders incomprehensible all of the attempts so popular with television evangelist-interpreters to relate its message to current events in piecemeal fashion. The message of the Revelation is repeated in such a way that all five senses of human beings and all the faculties of a rational person are engaged in affirming its central truth—that God, his Son, and the church will triumph over Satan, his followers, and all the forces of evil.

Through the use of the number seven, which signifies a divine sense of inclusion, we are also intended to be recipients of this letter. Like the early church, we are living in the "mean time" between the creation of the world and its redemption by God. The message of the entire Revelation, and not just one section of it, is meant for the edification of the church at all ages, until the Lord brings with him the end of time.

II. Blessed by the Trinity

"Grace and peace," a traditional greeting in the early church, began a blessing to the reader and the hearer (v. 3) from the source of all blessing, the Triune God. The writer describes the Father as present to the reader in all three tenses, the Ever-Present One, a title appropriate for the Father in the genre of Jewish apocalyptic. Though there is spirited debate among scholars, there seems to be some consensus that the unusual designation of the Holy Spirit as the "seven spirits before his throne" refers to the plenitude of the Spirit and may refer to Isaiah 11:2 in the LXX, in which there are seven characteristics attributed to the Spirit of the Lord. The Son is described as "the faithful witness" to strengthen a church under persecution; as "the firstborn from the dead" to emphasize his victory over death and his role as the first fruit of resurrection; and as "ruler over the kings of the earth" to assert his dominion even over the emperor who would demand worship from the faithful. Some interpreters categorize this description of Christ in terms of his offices of prophet, priest, and king.

III. Dedicated to Jesus Christ

Why does the writer utilize an atypical order in the blessing by the Trinity? So that he can follow with a doxology of praise to Jesus without interruption! The Apocalypse is frequently interrupted by spontaneous songs of praise to God, to Jesus (the Lamb), and to the Holy Spirit. In this instance, the doxology serves as a dedication of the entire book and as the statement of the central theme: that Jesus Christ is the focus of life present, past, and future. He saved us once and for all by his blood (past), he loves us (present), and he will return some day to take the redeemed to heaven (future). His purpose in "setting us free" was to allow us to be royal in service to God's kingdom and to loose us to serve each other as priests before God. The response of the writer is still our response: "Amen!"

IV. Authorized by God

The Revelation is the Word of God. It bears the imprimatur, the authorizing seal of God. The Revelation does not reveal anything new about God that is not present in the previous sixty-five books of the Bible, but is rather a comprehensive statement of the comprehensive salvation of the redeemed by a comprehensive God. God is over all creation (from A to Z), and present at all times (in all three tenses). Its message rings loudly in the words of Dietrich Bonhoeffer: "We live each day as if it were our last, and each day as if there was a great future because of Jesus Christ." (Mickey Kirkindoll)

FAITH THAT FACES FEAR

JOHN 20:19-31

Jesus has died. The disciples are afraid. Their personal fear overrides their grieving for the loss of their Teacher. For they could be next. Whatever Jesus had done, they had done too. They were guilty by association. They could hang just as easily as Jesus. So they remain hidden behind closed doors (v. 19). They are afraid of the religious leaders. And they stay hidden.

Jesus miraculously comes to them, walking through the closed
doors. He knows their fear and offers them consolation when he
says, "Peace be with you." Jesus shows them his hands and his
side, perhaps to prove his identity and the reality of his crucifixion. Again, he offers consolation to them.

The fear of the disciples is tangible. They know firsthand what
to expect if they were to ever be captured. They heard the
sounds of the death, the cries of the woman from Golgotha, the
defiance of the angry mob, the instability of the political leadership. If the Roman authorities did not kill them, then the religious leaders would certainly have their way, they must have
thought. Either way, they feared their own death. And that fear
was real.

Another kind of fear appears in this passage, although cloaked
as skepticism and doubt. Thomas, whose very name suggests
doubt, also exhibits fear. Thomas's fear, however, appears far less
noble to us than the fear of the disciples. Thomas, who was not
with the disciples when they first saw Jesus, does not believe
their report. His skepticism takes precedence and he retorts,
"Unless I see in his hands the print of the nails, and place my fin-
ger in the mark of the nails, and place my hand in his side, I will
not believe."

Eight days later, Thomas and the other disciples are still in hiding. And again Jesus comes to them. Jesus offers them consolation: "Peace be with you." Thomas, again, expresses his doubt.
Jesus, again, this time to Thomas, shows his hands and side.
Thomas finally accepts the Risen Lord and believes. We read
about the fear of the disciples, and we have sympathy. We read
about Thomas's skepticism, and we become judgmental. But what
if Thomas and the disciples are truly afraid; the disciples fear the
known (they can be assured that they will be killed) and Thomas
fears the unknown (how can he believe when he has not seen?).

Fear resides in all of us. We can be fearful of the known. If we
find ourselves in a raft with no paddle and about to drop into a
class six white water rapid, we have every right to be fearful. If
we are face-to-face with an angry bull in a pen with no protective
gear and are wearing red, we have every right to be afraid. Fear
comes from knowing the dangers and risks that are inherent in
the event.

The fear of the disciples can be understood. We can understand why they would want to stay locked up in a house for over
eight days for fear of their own death. They had followed Jesus.
They were identified with him. People knew their name. Crowds
had watched them assist Jesus feed the five thousand, heal the
sick, bring food to Jesus, secure transportation for Jesus' travels.
The names of the disciples were known by the crowds and could
easily be secured by the religious leaders. They were afraid of the
known.

Even though at first glance Thomas appears cocky and self-
reliant, the internal emotion is fear. We call it skepticism, or lack
of faith. We know people who do not rely on feelings or evaluations of others but want to be shown the numbers before they
will believe. "Just give me the facts," the doubting Thomas will
say. "I want to see it before I will believe it."

Although we often show compassion for the individual who
fears the known, we show disdain for the skeptic. We allow the
fearful one to have time to ponder the risks and insecurities of
risk. We even prepare for the fear. We take a guide with us down
the river to maneuver the rapids with us. We applaud the brave
matador in the bullpen. But to the skeptic, we offer no sympa-
thies. What if we understood skepticism as another form of fear?
What difference would that make in our relationships with one
another? What if we offered the same kind of consolation to
those who fear the known as well as those who fear the
unknown? Jesus did. Jesus asserts that the ideal faith response is
to believe without having to see. But for some of us, the road to
belief runs first through skepticism and doubt. God can use that
too. (Linda McKinnish Bridges)

APRIL 29, 2001

❦

Third Sunday of Easter

Worship Theme: We are fed by the risen Christ, and our love for him calls us to respond by feeding the hungry with food for the body and for the soul.

Readings: Acts 9:1-6 (7-20); Revelation 5:11-14; John 21:1-19

Call to Worship (Psalm 30:1-5, 11-12):

Leader:	I will extol you, O LORD, for you have drawn me up, and did not let my foes rejoice over me.
People:	**O LORD, my God, I cried to you for help, and you have healed me. O LORD, you brought up my soul from Sheol, restored me to life.**
Leader:	Sing praises to the LORD, O you faithful ones, and give thanks to his holy name. For his anger is but for a moment; his favor is for a lifetime.
People:	**Weeping may linger for the night, but joy comes with the morning.**
Leader:	You have turned my mourning into dancing; you have taken off my sackcloth and clothed me with joy, so that my soul may praise you and not be silent.
People:	**O LORD my God, I will give thanks to you forever.**

Pastoral Prayer:

God of earth and heaven, myriads of angels and thousands of earth's creatures will sing with full voice before your throne. Lift up our hearts that we might join in your praise and bring honor to the Lamb who was slain. God, you have made all things new through the death and resurrection of your Son; guide us in our new lives that we may not long for the old ways. Remind us not to rely on old habits or go back to old tasks as if we no longer expected Jesus to be with us. Give us instead the enthusiasm of Peter, who, in his eagerness to meet Jesus, jumped into the sea. Let us hear your steady voice calling us, smell the inviting aroma of the meal you prepare, and taste the goodness of your promises. Forgive us when we fail to comprehend the extent of what you ask us to do, and soothe our hurt feelings when we are misunderstood. We know that your lambs and sheep are to be fed, God; give us the compassion to feed victims of famine, disaster, and injustice, and to nourish each other in our hunger for your love. To you, O God, belong blessing and honor, glory and might, forever and ever. Amen. (Blair G. Meeks)

SERMON BRIEFS

A HARD NUT TO CRACK

ACTS 9:1-6 (7-20)

We first encounter Saul at the end of Acts 7 where he is giving approval to the stoning of Stephen. Saul specialized in persecuting Christians, particularly those of the church in Jerusalem. A devout Jew, who believed in and practiced the Mosaic law with zeal surpassing any other human being, Saul quickly emerged as the chief antagonist fighting against the movement of the Holy Spirit and the establishment of the church of Jesus Christ throughout the known world.

Many believers were dragged to prison by Saul and his evil motives. His antics spread throughout the land, causing the church in Jerusalem to become scattered. The proclamation of the good news of Jesus Christ continued, however, as the scattered went from place to place preaching and teaching the word (8:4).

As we reach chapter 9, we still find Saul breathing threats and murder against the people of the Way, the term used to describe Christians at the time (vv. 1-2). Now that the Jerusalem church had been scattered, Saul's next goal was to persecute Christians in Damascus. Saul was a hard nut to crack. No one or nothing was going to stand in his way of keeping Judaism pure and unchallenged by the Christian faith. But what we discover in the Acts 9 text is that Jesus will not allow human beings to persecute him or torment his people without reply. Jesus will take steps to change or transform anyone, particularly those representing his greatest enemies. Jesus has the power to crack the "hard nuts," those that by their actions rebel against, persecute, and torment Jesus and his believers.

In chapter 9:1-20, we're given an eyewitness account as to how Jesus cracks "hard nuts" like Saul. First of all, we discover that Jesus will stop rebels dead in their tracks and demand their attention. Through the light from heaven, Jesus overwhelmed Saul, knocked him to the ground, and then demanded an accounting as to why Saul was persecuting him. "It is hard for thee to kick against the pricks," Jesus tells him (v. 5 KJV). Indeed, when we rebel against Jesus, we ultimately bring pain on ourselves. Ananias and Sapphira are examples, as their account in Acts 5 so graphically details. Interestingly enough, Saul recognized who Jesus was, symbolized by his reply stating, "Who are you, Lord?" (v. 5). Oftentimes those who rebel the most against Jesus, are quite aware of Jesus and the power Jesus possesses. Saul's reference to Jesus as Lord, also symbolizes the authority Saul gives to him through this blinding encounter.

Second, we discover that Jesus transforms rebels by making them totally dependent on him. Jesus told Saul to get up and go to the city, where Saul would receive divine instructions. Eyes open, but seeing nothing, Saul was forced to depend on Jesus, through depending on others to get to Damascus.

Rebels are often blind to reality and need new vision to see how life is to be lived. People often think that we can be in control of our own situations and circumstances, without being responsible or accountable to anyone else. Jesus shows us that

167

dependence on him and interdependence with others enables us to accomplish God-given tasks and to experience the fullness of Christian love and godly relationships. Through three days of cleansing and emptying (v. 9), Jesus forced Saul to learn this.

Finally, Jesus transforms rebels by leading them to discover new vision and new life. Through Ananias (not of Acts 5), once a target of Saul's persecution, but now a vessel for delivering the Holy Spirit to Saul, Jesus changed Saul's life (vv. 15-16, 18-20). He removed the scales from Saul's eyes, had him baptized, and then commissioned him to preach the good news to the Gentiles.

All of us know "hard nuts," or have been rebels ourselves. The Jesus we serve is able to crack their rebellion, and change their lives for the good. He's done so for us. Glory to God! (Joseph Daniels)

WORTHY IS THE LAMB

REVELATION 5:11-14

The first four *Star Wars* movies have each ended in the same manner: the major characters receive the adulation of an enormous number of lesser and unnamed characters while grandiose music plays, and the film and its story comes to closure. But the close of the film is illusory, as the audience knows, for the next installment in the series awaits. In the Revelation to John, the setting is far different: the major character is a lowly Lamb, already bearing the wounds of his apparent defeat, and the music comes from the angels, beasts, elders, and people assembled before the Lamb. Amazed by the grace shown to mankind by the Lamb, and "lost in wonder, love and praise," the assemblage joins to praise the Lamb in a song of simple faith and complete confidence in the victory of the Lamb over death and evil.

I. Why Is the Lamb Worthy?

Implicit in the song of praise to the Lamb is that the Lamb is worthy of our worship. In one of many passages in the Revelation tinged with heart-rending poignancy, the first-person narrator weeps when he sees the scroll, which contains the final revelation from the Father, and realizes that no person ever born is pure and righteous enough to approach the Father's throne and to take the scroll. Yet the plans of God are thwarted and the mercy of God incomplete until the will of God is revealed in the reading of the scroll. An elder approaches and says that the great Lion of Judah is worthy to take and open the scroll and its seals. The narrator dries his tears and looks to see the Lion, who has revealed himself instead as a Lamb which has already been slaughtered. This reversal of images is among the most startling revelations in the scripture. The Lion who conquers is the Lamb who was slain!

The Lamb is worthy because he was sacrificed for our sins. This image, redolent with the images of Isaiah's "Suffering Servant," glorifies the ransom paid for us by the spotless Lamb of God. The Lamb's sacrifice on our behalf, and his holiness before God, give him the right to approve the throne and accept the scroll from God. Explicit in the new song of praise sung to the Lamb is his victory over evil and his power over forever. The suffering Christians of Asia Minor could take hope; the Lamb will reign over earth forever.

II. How Can We Express Our Worship of the Lamb?

The narrator "looks and hears" (a characteristic description of the overwhelming sensory experiences in heaven) a sound which seems to come from around the throne of God. He sees a great host of angels and uses a typical numerological hyperbole to describe the vastness of the sight and sound before him. So overwhelming, though, is the sight of the Lamb; and so captivating is the transformation of the Great Lion of Judah into the slaughtered Lamb of God, that the writer has eyes only for the Lamb. Even the throne of God and its attendants are no match for the glory of the Lamb. The number of angels is descriptive and imprecise intentionally, so that the Lamb is magnified in comparison. The worthy Lamb commands our undivided attention.

The song sung to the Lamb is a new kind of song, sung in full-throated unity by all who surround the throne. Some of the most unforgettable experiences of my life have come when I have heard the Atlanta Symphony Orchestra and chorus sing the great works of the sacred choral literature. Yet not even Bach, Beethoven, or Mozart has ever written a work that can compare with the song of the Lamb. Who the Lamb is and what he has done for us deserves our fullest praise.

The original readers and hearers of this song were Christians under the threat of persecution by the Roman emperor and provincial governors. The faithful faced trouble for the foreseeable future, but the triumph of the Lamb is announced before the battle is even joined. Nothing, and no one, will stand victorious before the Lamb. The Lamb is worthy of our complete confidence.

Augustine wrote: "Proud man would have died had not a lowly God found him." Worthy is the Lamb that was slain to take away the sin of the world. Amen. (Mickey Kirkindoll)

PETER'S RETURN

JOHN 21:1-19

The old adage sounds from the baseball field: "three strikes and you are out." But it does not apply to Peter, Jesus' disciple. One would think that a triple denial of Jesus, as recorded in John 18, would have eliminated him from the annals of the church. The story of Peter returns in chapter 21 in the same thrice-told manner—this time with the theme of redemption rather than denial. To deny Jesus is no trivial matter; but to be remembered as a faithful disciple who feeds sheep is remarkable!

First, the denial story. At the most conspicuous moment, when the spotlight is on Jesus and his followers, Peter denies any association with Jesus. No disarming statements of qualifications, such as "I heard him teach once or twice, but really never knew him well," or "I think that I have heard of this name, Jesus, from some of my family members." Peter bluntly denies that he has ever known Jesus. Warming his hands by the charcoal fire, Peter's heart and life become cold even though he stands close to the fire. He hears the maid's pointed question, "Are you one of this man's disciples?" And Peter says defiantly, without pause and reflection, "I am not." Two more questions, two more denials, and Peter still cannot find warmth—no comfort from the fire and none for his soul. The cock is crowing, the charcoal fire is waning, and Peter is so cold. The warmth of the fire subsides, and Peter, who had wanted to defend his special friend and teacher, Jesus, even go to war for him, now cannot even admit that he knows him. Peter is cold, very cold.

Peter quietly fades from the story in chapter 18. Peter may have even faded from the church's recorded memory were it not for the addition of John 21 to the narrative of the Fourth Gospel. Some Johannine scholars contend that John 21 was added last in a long history of composition by an ecclesiastical redactor, writing in the last decade of the first century, who wanted to strengthen the church. The church wanted to record Peter's redemption story. Peter's story of denial was not the final chapter of Peter's life. Peter would leave the fire of denial and jump into the waters of redemption, as recorded in the narrative to become one of the strong pillars of the church. And here as the Fourth Gospel is completed, the twin stories of denial and redemption, of sin and grace, are carefully repeated through the voice of Peter, Jesus' disciple.

In John 21 we read of another charcoal fire, but unlike the fire in chapter 18, this time Peter is getting warmer. Jesus and his disciples are eating, and Peter is given another chance to be a disciple. Jesus asks Peter three times, "Do you love me?" Three times he declares his love, and three times he is commissioned to feed sheep. Peter has been restored. Peter has returned to the church's story.

This balanced story, written in the 90s, may have been a way to honor Peter in his later years of life or perhaps even after his death. From the Acts account we know that he had become a giant leader in the Jerusalem church in the early 50s and 60s. Often at odds with Paul and the Gentile mission, Peter maintained a voice of leadership for the Jerusalem church. The church chose to honor his leadership, even though the church as reflected in John's Gospel was very different than the Jerusalem church reflected in Acts. Peter is remembered not for his three acts of denial. That is not the last word. Peter is remembered because of his love for Jesus and his willingness to feed the sheep. The last word is redemption.

Our story is the same. The way of faith is not a pristine path of completed higher righteousness. The story of the church refused a whitewashed antiseptic version of reality. The notion that one of God's chosen followers could decide to deny Jesus and still be involved in the church's story of redemption is not the kind of justice we understand. We know best the version, "If you are bad, you must pay, you cannot be used of God." The story of faith is just the opposite, "If you have been bad, God forgives, and God will use you." Denial and redemption are integral parts of the story of faith. (Linda McKinnish Bridges)

REFLECTIONS

MAY

Reflection Verse: " You will stretch out your hands, and someone else will fasten a belt around you and take you where you do
not wish to go" (John 21:18).

I can't think of a more poignant word spoken to anyone by
Christ than this final word he spoke to Peter. Especially haunting
is how these words come hand in hand with a call to pastoral
ministry. True, John quickly explains that these words were Jesus'
way of predicting Peter's particular martyrdom. But is that really
all there is to it? Jesus is calling someone to tend his sheep, then
immediately speaks of unwanted destinations. Is there a pastoral
minister anywhere who can't see a connection?

The odd thing is that up to this point on that morning by the
lake, Jesus had been handing Peter his freedom. The whole thing
happens under a rosy dawn sky, still in the glow of Easter. First
there is the business with the fish. Peter and his pals can't catch a
thing till Jesus tells them to work from the other side of their
boat, where they find extravagant success. Then there is what
gets called "the rehabilitation of Peter"—Peter in rehab—con-
ducted by Christ with such tender precision. First he fills Peter's
nostrils with the painfully reminiscent smell of charcoal smoke,
then administers the threefold question—"Do you love me? Do
you? Do you?"—to the man who had three times said, "I don't, I
don't, I don't." Then, when Peter has choked out his three broken responses, Christ bends to the raw heart of his friend and
applies a bright, new calling like a salve: "Take care of my sheep."
In all scripture I can't think of a kinder conversation. It's nothing
less than emancipation.

In a sense, ministry is all about freedom. We accept a glad call
to get over ourselves, to forsake the shallow subject of our own
failure for the deeper issue of our love, and in that freedom to

tend the flock for Christ's sake. Christ gives this liberation to us all as he gave it to Peter; and for most of us, making that shift from self-obsession to love-obsession will constitute a lifetime of learning to fish from the other side of the boat.

The shocking thing is how swiftly Christ shifts the conversation to what sounds like the very opposite of freedom. Up to this point, as I see the scene, Peter and Christ had been moving along the shore side by side, exchanging their words and bearing the great silences of unspeakable love between them. But now Jesus turns to look his friend in the eye as he says, "Very truly I tell you, when you were younger, you used to fasten your own belt and to go wherever you wished. But when you grow old, you will stretch out your hands, and someone else will fasten your belt around you and take you where you do not wish to go." Then, after what must have seemed an eternal silence, he says, "Follow me" (v. 19).

What kind of freedom is this, to stretch out your hands and be led where you don't want to go? And why mingle this dark work with a call to pastoral ministry?

Maybe we should say that the freedom of ministry takes two forms. The first is freedom's active way, the way of initiative. In this mode of ministry, we lead, we feed, we serve, we make pastoral choices. But there's another way of equal necessity and power. It is the passive way of ministry, the way of response to persons and events that act upon us, often painfully. Here our freedom takes a very different shape. It's not a freedom to choose the way, but a freedom to respond to a way pressed upon us.

Both freedoms were embodied in Jesus. He lived by stunning initiative in the active way: traveling, teaching, confronting, touching, healing. He was the master of his own verbs. But then he entered the passive way, the Passion way (both words share the same root). Now all the verbs went to others, while he received, absorbed, and bore what they laid on him and what God trusted him to carry.

This line of thinking is dangerous, of course. Too many of us are already given to confusing ourselves with the Messiah, too easily posing as saviors or seeing ourselves as victims and martyrs. We should run from all forms of ministerial masochism.

But the fact remains that pastoral ministry will mean, again and again, being led where you don't want to go. It happens in a thousand unwanted interruptions, in the conflicts and calls for help that derail your own agenda. It happens when people you dearly love suffer and die looking to you for strength you don't have. It happens when your best efforts are rejected or misunderstood. It happens when any task is set before you that you'd run from if you could but you can't and still be faithful. To care for the sheep, again and again, you stretch out your hands.

It's as if we're never free to feed those to whom we will not grant their lead. It's as if ministry finally happens best when we are managing least. And our freedom to love is purest and strongest when we are most fully out of our own small hands.

This calling will lead you where you don't want to go. When it does, you can rage against it if you need to. You can lament it, grieve it, beat your fist against the wall. The One we follow did that faithfully too. But perhaps you also can bear it, with the knowledge that this, too, is your freedom in Christ.

His final, most freeing word is, "Follow me."

Stretch out your hands. (Paul D. Duke)

MAY 6, 2001

❦

Fourth Sunday of Easter

Worship Theme: We know the voice of Jesus the Good Shepherd; we are sheltered by his hands, given abundant life, and assured a place in his reign of glory.

Readings: Acts 9:36-43; Revelation 7:9-17; John 10:22-30

Call to Worship (Psalm 23):

Leader: The LORD is my shepherd, I shall not want.
He makes me lie down in green pastures,
he leads me beside still waters; he restores my soul.

People: **He leads me in right paths
for his name's sake.
Even though I walk through the darkest valley,
I fear no evil; for you are with me;
your rod and your staff—they comfort me.**

Leader: You prepare a table before me in the presence of my enemies;
you anoint my head with oil; my cup overflows.

People: **Surely goodness and mercy shall follow me
all the days of my life,
and I shall dwell in the house of the LORD
my whole life long.**

Pastoral Prayer:

God our Shepherd, we hear our Savior's voice; he knows us by name and no one can snatch us from his hand. Give us courage to follow him through every adversity and accept his offer of abundant life. Teach us acts of kindness; show us the way of your servant Dorcas whose good works enlivened her community. Be with us in the darkest valleys; guide us to springs of water, and wipe every tear from our eye. Come to those who are lonely and those who search for home; abide with them and with us; shelter us from all harm. Strengthen this congregation and all who call on your name. We offer you our songs of praise that we might join the great multitude from every race and nation before your throne. Blessing and glory, wisdom and power be to our God forever and ever, through Christ who is the shepherd and the Lamb. Amen. (Blair G. Meeks)

SERMON BRIEFS

HE STILL WORKS MIRACLES

ACTS 9:36-43

The story of Tabitha in Acts 9:36-43 is yet another powerful testimony of the resurrection power of Jesus Christ working through the world after the experience of Pentecost. Tabitha, in Aramaic, or Dorcas, in the Greek (both meaning, "gazelle"), is a well-known and well-liked woman in the seaport town called Joppa. She was a disciple of the Lord, known for her devotion to doing good works and performing charity for many (v. 36).

As the story goes, Tabitha unexplainably becomes ill and dies. The disciples of that area, hearing that the apostle Peter was in the nearby town of Lydda, a place where rabbis studied and trained, summoned him to come at once to respond to Tabitha's situation. Upon hearing the news, the apostle departs for Joppa. He then performs the miraculous act of raising Dorcas from the dead, leading many to believe in the Lord.

Tabitha's story parallels closely the Lukan account of the raising of Jairus' daughter (Luke 8:41-42, 49-56) and reminds us of miracles performed by Elijah and Elisha in the Old Testament (1 Kings 17:17-24; 2 Kings 4:32-37). It is a remarkable reminder to us that when we call on the risen Christ in the presence of the Holy Spirit to be with us, power to overcome the greatest of obstacles is in our midst. For he still works miracles. But there are some other powerful reminders within this text that encourage and uplift us.

First of all, we can see through this wonderful drama that no longer is the resurrection power of Jesus limited to Jesus alone. It is available to all who believe. While the Lukan account reveals Jesus raising Jairus's daughter, the greater revelation of Acts 9:36-43 for men and women today is that through Peter, Jesus shows us that his resurrection power can be instilled in anyone whom Jesus chooses. Jesus told his disciples that those who believe in him will also do the works that he did, and greater works than he did they would do (John 14:12). The power to perform divine miracles is present in the lives of human beings as Jesus, through the Holy Spirit, activates it. Paul speaks of this in his expose on the gifts of the Spirit (1 Corinthians 12:10-11).

Second, we can see through this amazing account the power of prayer. The power detailed in verse 40 cannot and should not be overlooked. It was through prayer to God that Peter performed the miracle. While the widows and others stood around Tabitha weeping and lamenting her death, and mourning her loss through showing some of the clothing she'd made, Peter got down to business. While crying is healthy, natural, and a necessity in times like these, there is also a time when the people of God must approach God for the power to overcome trying situations. We find that power in prayer. Kirbyjon Caldwell, pastor of Windsor Village United Methodist Church in Houston, Texas, says in his book, *The Gospel of Good Success*, that prayer is the most underutilized asset we have (New York: Simon and Schuster, 1999). Peter knelt down and prayed! Through his prayer, the power of God was revealed in his midst (v. 40).

Finally, we must lift up the greatness of 9:41 as well. Many people along the Christian journey stumble and fall due to the temptations of sin, let alone the realities of the unexpected. Unexpected deaths, unseen crises, unplanned catastrophes and the like are a fact of life in our world. People may not die, like Tabitha, but may still be in need of restoration and renewal—the ability to experience new life through the resurrection power of Jesus. Like Peter, we need to extend a helping hand, and take time to help others rise up through the strength the Holy Spirit provides. Then we need to show them alive, so that the entire world can testify to the goodness of God and proclaim that yes, God still works miracles! (Joseph Daniels)

THE ESCALATOR TO WORSHIP

REVELATION 7:9-17

Martin Marty wrote that an amen is like an escalator, moving people to a new stage. The Hebrew word *amen* plays a central role in this reading, providing both beginning and ending punctuation for a song of praise to God from a multitude of the faithful. Much of the commentary on this passage concentrates on the nature of the crowd of 144,000 described at the first of the chapter and the dissimilarities of that group with the unnumbered multitude described in verse 9. It seems that the author arranged this chapter to emphasize the similarities, and not the differences, in these two groups. Both are faithful to God, the kind of disciples who can comprehend the will of God and respond by saying "Amen."

I. Jesus Is God's Amen to the World

Isaiah describes the covenant God of Israel as the God of "Amen" (Isaiah 65:16 NKJV). In the letter to the church in Laodicea (3:14 NKJV), Jesus is described as the "Amen." In each of these cases, the word *amen* is transliterated from Hebrew rather than translated, for there was no Greek word to adequately substitute for *amen*. From the time of the Septuagint on, Christians of all times and languages have appropriated this essential word into their own vocabulary. In our time, *amen* takes the sense of "Count me in!" or "I'm down with that." It connotes a recognition of the otherness of God and a willingness of the responder to submit to the will of God. Welton Gaddy captures this by saying that amen is a response of the total life.

II. Amen Connects Us to God

Like the sound made by two modems when connecting to the Internet, the word "amen" is both our identification and our password into the presence of the Savior. This presence has "out-of-this-world" benefits: Jesus himself provides nourishment, protection, and tender care giving. His strength is perfectly complete, as symbolized by its sevenfold description, abundant in its availability, and eternal in its duration. To say "amen" to God is to make an offering of yourself and your will to his service.

III. Amen Means Saying "Yes" to God

No person can offer to Jesus more than he has offered to us, but no worshiper dare offer less than a life fully devoted to God. Sometimes people come to worship with the expectation that they will "receive a blessing" or "be fed by the sermon." No other attitude could be less Christian. We all come to worship before the living God, and it is arrogant to enter the presence of God with the assumption that God exists primarily to fulfill "my" needs. We come to worship to recognize the blessing of living in relationship to a loving God. For no matter how many promises God has made, they are "Yes" in Christ. And so through him the "Amen" is spoken by us to the glory of God (2 Corinthians 1:20 NIV).

IV. Amen Is the Last Word in Worship

Other writers have used the word *epeuphemei,* meaning "shout in applause" to express the early church's use of *amen* in worship. The Revelation points the hearer to the truth that all of the promises of Christ will be fulfilled by God in the future, but also that the fulfillment is present in Christ today.

Handel's *Messiah* is one of the most-beloved pieces of music in the Western world. If asked, however, most persons would assume that the "Hallelujah!" chorus would be the last chorus in the work. Instead, "Worthy Is the Lamb" is the final chorus, and its ending is a magnificent, multifold "Amen."

After two-plus hours, the final word that Handel has to say on this subject comes down to this crowning ending, which resolves into an escalator-like series of modulations that lift the singer and the hearer alike into the presence of God. Amen! (Mickey Kirkindoll)

GOLD CARD MEMBERSHIP

JOHN 10:22-30

Each day, new credit card offers are delivered at thousands of houses across the United States. They tout the benefits and perks of being a member. It sounds too good to be true. Of course they wait until you respond before the conditions of membership are revealed. They play to our God-given need to belong. God placed that need in us, so that we would look for membership in God's kingdom.

I. Disingenuous Questions (vv. 22-24)

During the festive atmosphere of the Feast of Dedication, certain enemies of Jesus had an agenda that went beyond celebration. Cloaking their intentions in honest inquiry, they ask him to reveal if he is the promised Messiah. They assert that he was playing coy with them, keeping them in suspense. "Tell us plainly . . ." was their mantra. They wanted no doubts about his claims and demanded empirical evidence supporting his claim.

Actually, they were saying, "submit to our criteria." Tell us your answer in the language in which we desire. It is easy to miss in this text, but they were setting themselves up as the judges and determiners of truth veiled in the guise of a quest for knowledge. The truth is, the world is no different today, although a bit more technological and certainly more arrogant about our generation's purported intellectual sophistication. The mantra today? "Bring God here under our microscope, and we will tell you if there is proof enough to validate God's existence. But God must submit to our criteria." One modern theologian noted however, that we do not possess the criteria as humanity to judge divine character. Jesus, an ancient theologian, made the same point in the next two verses.

II. The Sad Truth of Human Inability and the Hope of Faith (vv. 25-26)

Jesus retorts that he already made this truth plain to them, but they refused to believe. The issue was not the lack of evidence, but their refusal to accept evidence into the equation of their belief system. The evidence was there; the miracles spoke for themselves as signs pointing to the true identity of Jesus. They would not be persuaded because they would not believe. They did not believe because they were not sheep under Jesus' care.

Faith is the litmus test for true believers in Christ. It is not solely a rational decision to follow the truth of Christ, which is still scoffed at by infidels as foolishness. Faith is the agency into God's kingdom, and without it, it is impossible to please God. It sounds unfriendly to say, but without faith to look beyond our rational abilities, one simply cannot gain membership into the flock. With faith, however, we see God through whom all things are possible and know that we are not alone or forsaken.

III. Being the Sheep of Jesus (vv. 27-30)

The distinguishing mark of the sheep of Jesus is that they listen to his voice; he knows them and they follow him. When non-believers read his words, they are but ancient poetry in a religious book. To those who believe, his words and actions are the power of God for salvation. One must be careful not to look exclusively at the "ministry" produced from everyone who claims to be his "sheep." The issue is if he "knows" them. In fact, Jesus elsewhere notes that some may claim to heal the sick and cast out demons but can fail to be known by him. Jesus says that those who love him will keep his commands; that is, they will follow him.

His sheep are given eternal life that cannot be taken from them. The Father gives them to Jesus, and no power can subvert his divine action. There is no fear for the sheep of Jesus that

182

believe and are known by him. They are not given a spirit of fear but a Spirit of power, love, and self-discipline. These sheep can trample upon snakes and scorpions, but nothing will harm them. What joy to be in the flock! This is abundant life. This is the kingdom of God "gold card membership." (Joseph Byrd)

MAY 13, 2001

❧

Fifth Sunday of Easter

Worship Theme: God creates a new way of life and invites us to take part. Are we ready to open our lives to God's new creation and our hearts to love for one another?

Readings: Acts 11:1-18; Revelation 21:1-6; John 13:31-35

Call to Worship (Psalm 148:1-2, 5, 7-12, 14*b*):

Leader:	Praise the LORD! Praise the LORD from the heavens; praise him from the heights! Praise him, all his angels; praise him, all his host!
People:	**Let them praise the name of the LORD, for he commanded and they were created.**
Leader:	Praise the LORD from the earth, you sea monsters and all deeps, fire and hail, snow and frost, stormy wind fulfilling his command!
People:	**Mountains and all hills, fruit trees and all cedars! Wild animals and all cattle, creeping things and flying birds!**
Leader:	Kings of the earth and all peoples, princes and all rulers of the earth! Young men and women alike, old and young together!
People:	**Praise the LORD!**

Pastoral Prayer:

Creator God, you promise a new heaven and a new earth. Open our hearts to the new thing that you are doing even now, in the midst of the old and worn out. Let us see, as Peter did, that our old biases are made obsolete by your outstretched arms. Free us from our fondness for "the way things used to be" and move us instead toward the new work of the Spirit. Teach us to offer others your embrace, that we may never in our pride be a hindrance to the transforming power of your love. Comfort all who face unasked for change. When our lives are in disarray, may we know that you yourself, God, have chosen to make your home with us, to dwell among us and make us your peoples. Calm our fears; let us hear your voice assuring us that the chaos of the sea will be no more; death will be no more. We come before you in thanksgiving, ready to drink with our Lord from the spring of the water of life; in Jesus' name. Amen. (Blair G. Meeks)

SERMON BRIEFS

GOD'S SPIRIT AT WORK

ACTS 11:1-18

I. The Work of God's Spirit Then

This passage from the book of Acts is Peter's explanation of the baptism of the Gentiles. In order to understand Peter's argument, we must look at the previous chapter (10:44-48). While Peter was preaching, the Holy Spirit was poured out on the Gentiles who were then baptized. Peter recognized the work of God's Spirit among the Gentiles and was himself converted to the idea that it was not necessary to be a Jew to be a Christian.

Peter had to defend his association with and baptism of the Gentiles because word reached Jerusalem that the Gentiles had been baptized. Peter's defense was before obvious opponents of such openness, "the circumcision party." "The circumcision party" were Jewish Christians who believed that the Gentiles could be saved only if they observed the circumcision ritual. Only in such way could Gentiles be on equal footing with the Jewish Christians.

Peter told the Jewish Christians about a vision of a great sheet coming down with all types of four-legged animals. Peter was told to kill and eat animals a devout Jew would have considered unclean. Being a devout Jew, Peter refused more than once. Then Peter heard a voice from heaven say, "What God has made clean, you must not call profane" (v. 9b). Puzzled by this, Peter was led by the Spirit to a Gentile family in Caesarea. The lesson of the vision suddenly became clear in the application. The giving of the Holy Spirit to the Gentiles was God's work. They were acceptable to God without ritual prerequisite. Peter even remembered the words of Jesus, "John baptized with water, but you will be baptized with the Holy Spirit" (v. 16). (These words are found in some form in all four Gospels: Matthew 3:11, Mark 1:8, Luke 3:16, and John 1:33.) Baptism of the Spirit was given to the Gentiles by God, not Peter. Peter's argument concluded by asking who he was to "hinder" the work of God. The Gentiles were to be recognized and treated as brothers and sisters in Christ. God said so in the sending of the Holy Spirit.

II. The Work of God's Spirit Now

As a youth, I remember our church having a big discussion about "open membership" (accepting persons who had not received immersion baptism as believers into full membership in a Baptist church). Many Baptist churches did not even discuss this subject, but our college town church, with its diversity, found it an issue needing attention. Many people attending our church belonged to other denominations not represented in the area. Prior to the discussion, persons requesting membership into the church who were not immersed were given "associate" membership, meaning that they could participate in some aspects of church life, but not all. They were not really, fully "in." I could not understand how our church would not accept everyone on equal terms into membership. I was astounded at the ones who argued against accepting those whose baptism had been other than Baptist. These folks were often the most mission oriented. It did not make sense to separate people of faith by the time and method of baptism. They all proclaimed Jesus Christ as Lord. Eventually, our church did vote for open membership.

In the church today, is everybody on equal footing? Does ethnicity, social status, or age make a difference in how people are recognized and treated in the church? Are all recognized and treated as brothers and/or sisters in Christ? Is God's Spirit at work among people recognized, and is God glorified and praised? God's love has been poured out through God's Spirit for all who believe. It is beyond anything we could do. We only need to accept the Spirit's amazing movements and praise God. (Marcia Thompson)

A NEW CITY WITH AN OLD NAME

REVELATION 21:1-6

Many people seem to think going to heaven will be like going on a vacation to a place where the weather is pleasant and the people are better. The closing vision in the Apocalypse is of a new city coming down from heaven to earth, bringing with it the completion of God's purpose for us and for his earthly creation. Of all of the visions in this book, this is perhaps the strangest. Shouldn't heaven be in a garden like Eden or like the "paradise" promised to the thief on the cross?

I. Cities in Scripture

Cities in the biblical record deserve their bad reputation. The first city, Enoch, was founded by Cain, who murdered his brother. The second recorded city was at Babel, still a symbol for man's grasping greed and ambition to replace God with human might. Add Sodom and Gomorrah to the list, and it becomes even more difficult to imagine God in a city. Babylon, the stand-in for Rome in the Apocalypse, is described as a whore—someone who uses and is used by others for material gain. Even Jerusalem, founded by David, rejected both God and Jesus. How then should heaven be a city, new or not?

II. The Dwelling Places of God in Scripture

God's dwelling places in the scripture were portable (the Ark and the Tabernacle), multiple (Shiloh and Jerusalem), and destroyed (the Temple, twice). The religious importance of the Temple made it susceptible to abuse by those prostituting themselves after religious power. God provided many places for expressing the desire to be in close relationship with the faithful, and sinful man fouled them all with a religion devoid of faith. In the creation of the heavenly city, God provided a final dwelling place with God's people, saying, "It is done!" thereby echoing the completion of God's judgment and the completion of God's earthly life (Revelation 16:17). The new Jerusalem is wonderful beyond all comprehension, so much so that the writer could only describe it in terms of what it was not: a place with no death, crying, mourning, nor pain.

III. "I Am Making All Things New!"

God made the church new. In yet another stunning image the church is described as a bride adorned for her husband. It is difficult for those most involved in the life of the church to conceive of her in quite these terms, yet God reserves any introduction to the splendors of heaven until after the bride is introduced. The place of honor on the day that we first see the new Jerusalem is given to the church!

God makes an old city new. Just as he creates a new being from sinful man, God creates a new kind of city from the old. In the ultimate urban renewal project, God creates a new Jerusalem, not by renovating buildings, but by renewing the hearts of women and men. If God can rehabilitate the city to be suitable for dwelling, is there any city or any person beyond God's transforming power?

God makes our relationship with God new. While we live on this earth, our relationship to God is as variable as our faith is fickle. We are all Gomer and Mary, Judas and John, in our relationship to God. Only God's love is constant. In heaven, God reveals the final plan for God's relationship to us, the completion of God's presence with us. As Jesus once "tabernacled with us," so God now tabernacles with us finally, completely, and permanently. He himself will wipe away our tears of sorrow and of joy, and we will be completed (Philippians 1:6) as he intended. God will fulfill the promise of Isaiah 66:13: "As a mother comforts her child, so I will comfort you; you will be comforted in Jerusalem." (Mickey Kirkindoll)

SAYING FAREWELL, HONORING OUR HERO

JOHN 13:31-35

Moving to the end of my sermon notes of my two hundred seventh funeral, I scanned my listeners before I asked, "What will they say about you or about me when it is our turn to lay here?" I was really asking, "how do we really make a difference?" I think I have read every card and heard every attempted comforting expression during the previous two hundred six funerals. How do we really honor a loved one who has passed away? Could it be that when we say "farewell," we should honor that person by living our lives differently because of their influence on us? When we are eulogized, the greatest expression about our life will be manifested in the lives of the people that walk away from our grave living life differently because they knew us. Jesus was preparing the disciples to say farewell. They would honor him through their obedient lives after he was gone.

I. Farewells Are Tough (vv. 31-33)

It is not easy to say good-bye. As the senior pastor, I had to push the youth group toward the plane and to say final good-byes to family as they headed out to a week of mission work. It makes you feel like "the bad guy," separating families. Farewells are tough. They were just as tough on the disciples of Jesus. Some would wander in denial. Others would attempt to wrestle with the reasoning behind his insistence on leaving. Yet others would sit numb trying to cope with the fact that he was going.

It was not as if Jesus' departure did not have a higher and more important purpose than the empty feeling left in the stomachs of

189

the disciples. He was necessarily going to be glorified and in the process bring glory to the Father. This was the very purpose in his coming to begin with. This necessary act would exclude his closest friends of three years; yet, it was for their sakes that he would leave. Higher purposes always trump the empty feeling of a friend leaving.

II. Real Honor Is More Than Words (vv. 34-35)

How can we tell who a Christian is? Is there a Bible knowledge test that we can administer to people so that they prove their proficiency in doctrine? Are there certain acts of charity that they must fulfill to gain acceptance? No, Jesus is quite clear here. Everyone knows who the disciples of Jesus are because they love one another. This is a quality that goes beyond the occasional luncheon. Jesus lays out a command that his followers will love each other as he loves them.

A true expression of honor to Jesus is to keep his commands and allow our lives to conform to his teaching. Here is a primary command, "love one another." It is interesting that when we fail to love a brother or sister because of race or denomination, we attempt to explain it with what we perceive is a justifiable reason. However, the truth is that such an act is dishonoring our Lord and disobeying a direct command from him. It is a denial of our relationship with him in that we do not show the fruit of being part of his vine. No one will know we are his disciples, because we do not reflect his character.

In order for our faith to be more than "lip-service" we must appropriate the words of Jesus in our everyday living. To truly honor our hero, we must try each day to live like him. Otherwise our lips will honor him, but our hearts will be far from him. We wait to greet the Lord at his return. It is a different context for us today compared to the disciples, but we still demonstrate honor for the Lord in the same manner. We must love one another. (Joseph Byrd)

MAY 20, 2001

❦

Sixth Sunday of Easter

Worship Theme: We are reminded by the Holy Spirit of all that Jesus said and did so that we may truly love him. We receive the peace of Christ that calms our fears.

Readings: Acts 16:9-15; Revelation 21:10, 22–22:5, John 14:23-29

Call to Worship (Psalm 67):

Leader:	May God be gracious to us and bless us and make his face to shine upon us, that your way may be known upon earth, your saving power among all nations.
People:	**Let the peoples praise you, O God; let all the peoples praise you.**
Leader:	Let the nations be glad and sing for joy, for you judge the peoples with equity and guide the nations upon earth.
People:	**Let the peoples praise you, O God; let all the peoples praise you.**
Leader:	The earth has yielded its increase; God, our God, has blessed us.
People:	**May God continue to bless us; let all the ends of the earth revere him.**

Pastoral Prayer:

God of the fearful and troubled, you give us courage by revealing our home in the promise of your own future: Show us the city that needs no sun or moon but takes its light from you in all your glory; show us the sacred place where our praise of you knows no bounds of space or time. We thank you for the present joy of the home you make with us now. Give us patience to be taught by your Holy Spirit and to remember all that Jesus said and did. Open our ears to the voices that call us in their need that we may come to them in your name: free them from want; calm their fears; rescue them from oppression. Teach us your gracious hospitality that we, like Lydia, may welcome your servants into our churches and homes. We pray for the healing of the nations; may those who have been excluded from the world's homes know the balm of the tree of life. Thank you for the gift of peace received through your Son Jesus Christ, in whose name we pray. Amen. (Blair G. Meeks)

SERMON BRIEFS

WHO NEEDS THE GOOD NEWS?

ACTS 16:9-15

The text begins with Paul's vision (v. 9) that instructs him to carry the good news to Macedonia. This would be the first Christian missionary trip to Europe. It may also be seen as the beginning of the gospel being spread to all nations as Jesus commissioned his disciples, which Luke recorded in Luke 24:47-49. Luke began the book of Acts with Jesus ascension and statement to the disciples that they would carry the good news "to the ends of the earth" (Acts 1:8).

It is important to note a change in person just before our text. The third person plural ("they") with which chapter 16 begins suddenly changes to first person plural ("we") in verse 10. Luke has joined Paul and Silas, and so was an eyewitness to the work in Macedonia. Paul, Silas, and Luke make their way to Philippi, which was a Roman colony in Macedonia. On the Sabbath day they came to a riverside, which was a place of prayer. Paul spoke to the women that gathered there (v. 13). The first convert was Lydia, a woman of wealth since she was "a dealer in purple cloth"

(v. 14). From Thyatira, she was a religious, godly, and prayerful woman, even a "worshiper of God" (v. 14). Still, she needed salvation; still she needed Christ. We are told: "The Lord opened her heart" and she believed the good news that Paul spoke that day. She and her household were baptized. Lydia even tested Paul's confidence in her belief by inviting them to stay with her. Paul, Silas, and Luke stayed, and Lydia provided hospitality to her missionary guests.

Most often when we think of the work of missionaries or speak of evangelism, we imagine their work to be directed toward people who are "utter heathens"—those who do not know God at all. Or we may think of people who are outcasts of society who have family problems, drinking problems, or drug problems as the ones to whom ministry is directed. Our text presents us with a population that often is ignored. There are many religious people out there who are prayerful and upright, who have a sense of God, but are still not acquainted with Jesus Christ. They are still, from a Christian perspective, in need of salvation.

I remember a girl who lived in our neighborhood for two or three years during my preteen years. She was my age and went to my school. I remember her spirit as being kind and gentle. She was very moral and upright, and my first thought was that she was a Christian. When I invited her to my church, I learned she was from another faith—the Baha'i faith. I was impressed by how loving and upright this girl was. She was religious, yet she still needed Christ. Sometimes if we do not ask, we do not know if people know Christ.

Another theme that one could consider is the prominent place of women in the history of the church. The centrality of women is key to Luke in both his Gospel and in Acts. The first convert in Europe is a woman, Lydia. She then becomes a supporter, backer, even an underwriter, of the Christian mission. Those who do not see women as full and equal participants in the church need to understand their spiritual heritage. Women throughout the ages have been the backbone of the missions effort. Look back at your missionary tradition and find those faithful women who inspire us to carry on the missionary effort to spread the good news to others today.

Finally, consider Lydia's hospitality. The work of missions and evangelism is too often identified only with "going out" to others. A needed balance would be provided by focusing upon the evangelistic work of "welcoming in" in hospitality. (Marcia T. Thompson)

DON'T YOU LOVE IT WHEN A PLAN COMES TOGETHER

REVELATION 21:10, 22–22:5

In amazement or surprise, people observe something coming together in perfect harmony and as planned, and they remark: "Don't you love it when a plan comes together?" The scripture for today in the Revelation to John is perfectly suitable for that remark, for in it God reveals the extent of his plan for mankind's eternal future. Ray Summers, a great exegete of the past generation, wrote: "In symbol, God says: 'Heaven is a place of perfect fellowship, perfect perfection, perfect provision of needs, and perfect service to God' " (*Worthy Is the Lamb* [Nashville: Broadman, 1951]).

I. Perfect Fellowship

God's eternal city will have twelve gates to provide perfect, in the sense of unclogged, access to the city. This is in sharp contrast to the walled cities of human antiquity, which would have only one wall in order to make the city more defensible. With no need for human defenses, the gates to the city are always open, as is the throne of God. The redeemed will know no gridlock, no personal identification numbers, no padlocks in heaven; for access to the God of all creation will be forever possible. The redeemed will see God clearly, and be clearly seen, fulfilling the promise of 1 Corinthians 13:12: "Now we see but a poor reflection as in a mirror; then we shall see face to face. Now I am known in part; then I shall know fully, even as I am fully known" (NIV). To live these words will not produce the same acute discomfort as to read them now, for we will have been perfected by God as planned from the beginning (Philippians 1:6).

II. Perfect Protection

Heaven will be a place of perfect protection by God for the redeemed. For the original readers of these words, persecuted to the point of death by the authorities, these words must have given immeasurable comfort. To the inhabitants of the new millennium, this promise produces the same comfort, for we are living in dangerous times. The walls of the heavenly city are described as either two hundred feet thick or two hundred feet high. In either case, such walls are convincing that safety is complete within their boundaries. There is light enough to see by, as well, with no dark alleys or the valleys of dark shadows to fear, for the Lord is the light of the city, fulfilling God's promise to us. Even the composition of the gates is a clue to the completeness of God's plan for the city, for each was composed of a single pearl, signifying that the suffering of our earlier lives is redeemed in the heavenly city. God transforms even the sorrows of the past in order to provide a brighter and more beautiful future!

III. Perfect Provision

The Revelation does not contain a blueprint of heaven, but instead provides a catalog of heaven's delights to tease us and to whet our appetite for a future that exceeds the descriptive powers of human speech. A garden will provide all our need for food or sustenance. The fruit from the garden will not require the sweat of our brows, but will appear at the necessary intervals to provide our needs. The river through the center of the golden street will contain the water of life, fulfilling the promise of a water that provides eternal slaking of our thirsts (John 4:13). The leaves of the tree of life, which we last encountered in the Garden of Eden before the fall, are for "the healing of the nations" (v. 2). What healing can this describe? Perhaps it is the healing of the differences that have divided the people of the world into warring nations, a "tower of Babel" in reverse.

IV. Perfect Service

What will we do in heaven? The scripture only states cryptically that "his servants will serve him." The only hint provided to us is that we shall see God's face. We will not be hampered in our service to God by inaccurate or inadequate visions of God, nor will we lack the light to see the outcome of our service to God. Perhaps it is best to leave speculation aside at this point and to simply trust that God's plan for the service of the redeemed is as perfect as God's plan for their fellowship, their protection, and their provision. F. F. Bruce commented on these verses by writing that to see God is like simultaneously being with and knowing and rejoicing in God. (Mickey Kirkindoll)

AN UNQUESTIONED ANSWER

JOHN 14:23-29

During the early days of my first unit of Clinical Pastoral Education (CPE), I was asked to draw a picture of the "warmest" place in my house. I drew our den.

As it happened, the backdoor of our homeplace opened in from the driveway and onto that room. Anyone entering the house came through there. In its corners sat three chairs— thrones, really—to which my dad, my mom, and my grandmother, Memie, ascended each evening after work and dinner and chores. Those in the den were surrounded by our clan's triumvirate. To the untrained eye, Dad appeared to be reading. Mom appeared to be watching TV. Memie appeared to be sewing. Veterans knew better. The elders were holding court. And if being beset in such a fashion could be unnerving on occasion—especially to guilty adolescent males—it could also prove a wonderful toddy against the outside's cold.

Really interesting stuff seemed always to be taking place within the triangle: our best talks, our best scraps, our best tears and laughter. And if strangers to the triangle didn't always understand at first, they would come to see the triangle itself as a kind of entrance into the depth of our family's life.

Later in CPE, I would learn how "triangled" communications

could be dysfunctional and really unhealthy. Surely, ours was that way at times. But stability, and "warmth," also depends on such a configuration.

We have just such a configuration in our text for today—a triangle, if you will, of Father, Son, and Holy Spirit; a door, an entrance, into the depth of the Christian family's life.

It is not necessarily into the inner life of God. Not here anyway, for, as scholars are quick to remind us, when in John's Gospel talk turns to the unity of Father, Son, and Holy Spirit—as it does in the "farewell discourses" of chapters 14 through 17—the unity is not ontological as much as it is teleological. That is, Jesus here is describing the unified purposes to which Father, Son, and Spirit are dedicated, and perhaps even the evidence of that unified purpose in the church. God's will, Jesus' word, the Spirit's teaching and motivating: this is the "triangle," the homeplace, into which all the faithful enter, and which they themselves evidence.

The point at which our lection begins disguises the fact that Jesus' pronouncement in these verses is an answer to a question put by Judas (not Iscariot) in 14:22. Jesus' word might be described, then, as an "unquestioned answer." Amazingly, John 14:22 is excised altogether from the Revised Common Lectionary! And that when Judas's is such a good question!

Judas asks, "How is it that you will reveal yourself to us and not to the world?" Judas has at least a nascent understanding of the crisis looming at Jesus' departure. That is, since Jesus' presence has been the very revelation of God among them—Judas's faith is "incarnational"—and Jesus is leaving—the Incarnation is about to end—how will they (and we) come to experience God?

Jesus' answer, to strangers to the triangle, is inscrutable. But to those at home there it makes perfect sense. He is going away, but they will know his peace. He is no longer with them, but the Holy Spirit will remind them of all he said. When they obey, they will experience the love of Jesus and know that Jesus is in fact present. They will be without him, but they will rejoice.

In other words, "within the triangle" is where all the best stuff takes place. It is there that one feels the warmth of God's promises, remembers and receives the best of Jesus' teachings, and feels the most at home (v. 23). And all who enter the church will enter at this door. (Thomas Steagald)

MAY 27, 2001

❧

Seventh Sunday of Easter

Worship Theme: God loved Jesus before the world began and loves us with the same unending love. Our love for one another shows that we are one with Christ.

Readings: Acts 16:16-34; Revelation 22:12-14, 16-17, 20-21; John 17:20-26

Call to Worship (Psalm 97:1, 4, 6, 9-12):

> *Leader:* The LORD is king! Let the earth rejoice;
> let the many coastlands be glad!
> His lightnings light up the world;
> the earth sees and trembles.

> *People:* **The heavens proclaim his righteousness;**
> **and all the peoples behold his glory.**
> **For you, O LORD, are most high over all the earth;**
> **you are exalted far above all gods.**

> *Leader:* The LORD loves those who hate evil;
> he guards the lives of his faithful;
> he rescues them from the hand of the wicked.

> *People:* **Light dawns for the righteous,**
> **and joy for the upright in heart.**
> **Rejoice in the LORD, O you righteous,**
> **and give thanks to his holy name!**

Pastoral Prayer:

God, giver of glory, you loved your Son Jesus Christ before the foundation of the world. We thank you for loving us as you have loved him. We pray for your church throughout the world, that we may be one as you are one with Christ. Give us the grace to love one another, to show to those around us by our wholeness that we are yours. God, you promise joy to the upright and salvation to those who believe. Strengthen our households in faith that they may affirm your justice and mercy. We pray for children everywhere: children who are ill, homeless, or hungry; children who are exploited by those who should care for them; children whose houses are full but whose hearts are empty. May they know you as a loving parent and find in us the kindness of your touch. We pray for the coming again in glory of Jesus Christ, the beginning and the end, the bright morning star. The grace of the Lord be with all the saints. Amen. (Blair G. Meeks)

SERMON BRIEFS

THE KEY TO SALVATION

ACTS 16:16-34

This text is a continuation of Paul's and Silas's journey in Philippi. The previous week's lesson from Acts tells of the beginning of the church's spread into Europe through the belief and baptism of Lydia and her household. This text can be examined in three portions.

I. Who Is Enslaved? (vv. 16-18)

The key word to examine in this portion of the text is the word "slave." The slave girl was used by men for monetary gain because she was possessed by a demon. She was a slave first to the "spirit" which possessed her. She was only secondarily a slave to the men who used her to satisfy their own greed. It is interesting to note how the demon within her spoke about Paul and Silas. In verse 17, the demon says, "These men are slaves of the Most High God, who proclaim to you a way of salvation." The evil spirit called Paul and Silas "slaves," but they were slaves to a higher power, God, that even the demon recognized. The girl who was a slave to the demon was used as a fortune-teller. Here the demon knows and speaks a truth that is very powerful, but its own power would soon be shown to be broken. Paul and Silas, slaves of God, proclaim the salvation in which all lesser powers have been overcome.

The slave girl needed to be freed from the demon within and from the men that used her for their financial gain. The men, too, were in need of evil to be taken from within. They were not possessed by a vocal spirit like the girl they exploited, but they were "possessed" with the desire for wealth at the expense of another human being. That too is enslavement to a power less than God. There are many things that enslave us. Demands that draw our attention away from focusing on Jesus in whom we find salvation. What enslaves you and others in the congregation? What are the "demons" within that are against the spread of the good news of salvation in Jesus?

II. There Is Always Opposition to the Truth (vv. 19-24)

Because Paul and Silas had released the girl from slavery to the demon within and the men without, they found themselves in trouble with the authorities. The owners seeing that they no longer had "power" over the girl realized that their financial advantage had come to an abrupt end. These men took Paul and Silas before the rulers and called them Jewish troublemakers. The charges against them are not clear, but the rulers probably had them beaten and thrown into prison to keep order (v. 22). The men did not like the opposition that caused them to lose their profit, which was an easy way to make money by exploiting another person.

Paul and Silas, in freeing the slave girl from the evil spirit, fought for freedom and truth in setting her free. Those who fight for the rights of others to bring about God's intention for creation can always expect opposition in many forms. Sometimes the opposition comes from powers such as the state, which are "legitimate" but yet fallen and less than God. Are we in our institutional participation the "opposition," or are we ready to speak a word of salvation even if it means risking all for Jesus' sake?

201

III. Believe (vv. 25-34)

This text ends with the familiar story of Paul and Silas in jail singing and praying. A great earthquake comes and opens all the prison doors. The jailer who is in charge considers suicide, fearing that all the prisoners will leave. He needs to be saved from himself. Paul intercedes and assures the jailer that all of the prisoners are still there. The jailer recognized the power of God and wants to know how to be saved. This question leads to the key verse for the whole text, "Believe in the Lord Jesus, and you will be saved" (v. 31). This is the good news of salvation that is relevant for all times. (Marcia T. Thompson)

THE STILL POINT OF THE TURNING WORLD

REVELATION 22:12-14, 16-17, 20-21

The language of the Apocalypse is poet's language—simile and metaphor, hiddenness and mystery. Only in poet's language is it possible to come to the end of this revelation from God, at once hidden and clear. The content of this revelation is clear: Jesus Christ redeemed, redeems, and will redeem mankind by his death on the cross and his resurrection from the dead. What remains suggested but abstract is the "how" of this trinity of redemption.

I. The Redemption of the Past

In chapter 22:12 (NIV), Jesus says, "My reward is with me, and I will give to everyone according to what he has done," echoing what Paul wrote in Romans 2:6 that God "will give to each person according to what he has done." One of the persistent themes of the Revelation is that Jesus will reward the overcomers for their perseverance in the face of persecution. This reward will satisfy the cry for satisfaction by the martyrs (6:10), and set into right relationship with God the justice done on earth. What kind of reward will he bring? How will he distribute this reward? How will he decide what kind of reward each will receive? We explode with questions, all of which die stillborn on our lips with the realization that this reward will come after the judgment and after the redeemed are taken into the heavenly city for the banquet of the Lamb. What reward besides these do we desire? Is there a greater reward in heaven than to be in attendance to the God of all creation and to his Son? The desire to experience the delight of the Lord is sweet enough to motivate service to him and sacrifice for him even now.

II. The Redemption of Now

"I am coming soon" is a powerful incentive to live today with an urgency born of the assurance of judgment for all men. Our message is life giving and timely, so we must be about the work of the Lord while it is still day.

"I am coming soon" is a powerful corrective to the apathy and indifference of lukewarm churches and ministers. We hold in our hands the mystery of life. We dare not hoard it as misers or allow it to fall fallow in our laziness.

Time is neither a spiral nor a timeline. "Chronos" time is redeemed in the "chairos" time of the cross. T. S. Eliot wrote in "Burnt Norton":

> Time present and time past
> Are both perhaps present in time future,
> And time future contained in time past.
> If all time is eternally present
> All time is unredeemable.

Jesus Christ, "the still point of the turning world," is the redemption of now from the futility of spiral and the tyranny of the timeline. In the words of Dietrich Bonhoeffer, martyred at Flossenburg: "We live each day as if it were our last and each day as if there were to be a great future." In Jesus Christ, the Lamb of God, both are present in each day that we live.

III. The Redemption of Time

"Come, Lord Jesus!" are the words introducing the Eucharist in many Christian traditions. How fitting, how perfect is God's choreography to lead us to the end of the Revelation at the beginning of the Lord's Supper. We are not left to thirst after an unimaginable and unattainable future, but are led to the table of Jesus Christ, wherein past, present, and future are redeemed by the grace of God and the redemption of Christ. The Revelation leads us to explore our beginning and our end, so that

> We shall not cease from exploration
> And the end of all our exploring
> Will be to arrive where we started
> And know the place for the first time.
> (T.S. Eliot)

(Mickey Kirkindoll)

EXTRAORDINARY ORDINARINESS

JOHN 17:20-26

Gaudete Sunday is the Third Sunday of Advent. It provides a joyful break from fasting and penitence.

As far as I know, the Seventh Sunday of Easter has no name, but I think we need a break about that time just the same. After all, we have been blowing our trumpets hard and loud for six weeks. The Easter Morning fanfare began a crescendo composed to hold through the Great Fifty Days.

The next week is the firefall of Pentecost. We will burst out, fortissimo, in "Happy Birthday to the Church." The week after that is Trinity Sunday, the apogee of our springtime jubilation, when from heaven's rafters, as it were, will peal our most distinctive anthem, the most characteristic of Christian refrains: the Trinity.

We will have sung, we will have danced, we will have done it up big. So why not take today, before we begin the final kick of this liturgical marathon, and slow down a little—pause—to listen. Why not quiet down a little—so that we can hear a prayer drop— from the lips of the Savior.

We aren't turning out the lights, exactly; the party ain't over. But today let's take a break, take a breath, and listen.

In our lesson for today Jesus is praying for those he loved. He didn't just call them and teach them; he didn't just empower them and reprimand them; he loved them. The depth of that love, evidenced both when he washed their feet and fed them the meal, is evidenced yet once more here in his prayer for them. His prayer concludes the "farewell discourse" of John 14–17.

Over the last several weeks we have noted how these chapters summarize Jesus' relation to God, Jesus' relation to the disciples, and the relation of the disciples to God through the Spirit. We have noted the "covenant atmosphere" permeating the Last Supper, and Jesus' pledge to fulfill for his part all that God has asked him to do—even if the disciples would prove, at first anyway, unable to fulfill their part of the bargain.

Jesus' obedience to God will take him away from the disciples. Of that he is sure. And he is sure, too, that his death is imminent. He has precious little time left, and he will spend it praying for his friends.

It is a humbling picture, really, Jesus praying for his friends. He prays that there will be a unity among all his disciples—those first ones and those that believe through their testimony, those of who have believed through them and the next generations, too. He prays that all his disciples will be one, unified in the same ways Jesus and God are one: one in purpose, one in will, one in covenantal commitment. Jesus' prayer claims the promise of God on behalf of all who will claim Christ as Lord.

What happens if we take time to listen, quiet ourselves? We overhear Jesus' prayer for us. We, too, are his friends. We, too, this very generation of believers, were somehow on his mind. And so he lets us hear his prayer, perhaps as a way of encouraging us to work for that which only God can give.

A few Sundays hence, according to our liturgical calendar, we will be entering "ordinary time." No major festivals till the fall. Just Sunday by Sunday, routine worship—if worship can ever be called routine. Still, it is the ordinariness of most time that makes other times extraordinary; it is the extraordinariness of some times that makes ordinary time welcome. Today's lessons remind us of what makes ordinary time so extraordinary. For Scripture says that Jesus ever intercedes for us. Standing at the Father's right hand, he ordinarily has the Father's ear on behalf of his friends. He regularly prays for us. What an extraordinary notion! (Thomas Steagald)

REFLECTIONS

❦

JUNE

Reflection Verse: "Then [God] said to me, 'Prophesy to these bones, and say to them: O dry bones, hear the word of the LORD. Thus says the Lord GOD to these bones: I will cause breath to enter you, and you shall live' " (Ezekiel 37:4-5).

The rabbis used to debate the character of the account of Ezekiel in the valley of dry bones. Was it a vision? Did an actual miracle occur? If so, what was the nature of the miracle? The Talmud records one of these debates. One rabbi said, "The dead that were raised by Ezekiel stood up, praised the Lord and died again." Another said, "No, they went home and got married and had children . . . and my grandfather was one of them." A third rabbi said, "All this was a true parable." "Really?" said another. "How is that possible? If it was true it wasn't a parable; if it was a parable it wasn't true." The answer came back, "It was truly a parable."

Maybe the story is all of these. It is true, and it is a parable, and it happened to our grandparents. What would be nice is if something much like it would happen to us.

See the scene: a grim valley, the site of a great slaughter. Thousands had screamed and died here. Now vultures and jackals and the elements have done their work. Skeletal remains have been dragged about, picked clean, and bleached white. The valley is littered with human leg bones, arms bones, rib cages, and skulls grinning. Lizards and scorpions scuttle through the bones. Over it all stands a man weeping. These are the bones of his people. So many have died, and the rest were dragged into exile. The bones represent not just the death of these thousands, but the death of his community and his nation. In a way they're his bones too. Standing among these acres of bones, Ezekiel's brain is burning with a question that seems to have come from God: "Mortal, can these bones live?" He replies, "O Lord God, you know" (v. 3).

It seems to me this reply could be spoken in more than one possible tone. The tone you give it may reflect how hopeful or despondent you are. So imagine this: You are standing over a field of dead hopes or dead dreams or a dead community, and God puts the question to you, "Can these bones live?" Now how do you say your line? Is your face lifted with expectant eyes, your voice rising to a confident exclamation point? "Lord God, you know!" Or is it more like shaking a bowed head and heaving a sigh, a sad voice trailing into ellipsis: "Lord God, you know . . . ." Or could these words be more like a shrug? Or a fist?

Whatever tone is taken, the striking thing is what we could call the abdication in this reply. When we are asked, "Can these bones live?" we are up against a question that we cannot answer. Staring into the unlit abyss of death, we cannot know who or what will be restored, or how, or when. Some deaths are final. A dream can die and never be reborn. A relationship can end and never be recovered. A community can perish, never to rise again. It's naive to sing over the bones, "Yes, they will live!" But equally, it's premature to answer, "No they won't." If God is God, who can say? Abraham Joshua Heschel said that all despair is presumptuous. When you stand in a valley of communal or personal wreckage, and your mind turns to the question of ultimate outcomes, be reminded of what you cannot know. The wisest and truest conclusion will always be open and God-ward: "Lord God, you know."

The God who knows is also free enough to invite our help. "Prophesy to these bones!" says the Almighty to Ezekiel. Now there's a daunting call: preaching to skeletal remains. Is it possible you feel like you've been there, done that?

There may be much that we don't know; but by divine command, there are things we can do. It may seem to you that what you do can't possibly make a difference—absurd as preaching to a boneyard. But you don't know! The Word is not from you but through you; and since the Beginning, the Word has specialized in creating wonders. Ezekiel, knowing how much he doesn't know, leaps right in and does the absurd, as directed. And while still in the middle of his sermon to the footbones, the anklebones, the shinbones, and so forth, "there was a noise"—all over the valley a rattling and knocking and clicking as bone snapped into bone. Then sinews appeared, then muscles, organs, skin, and hair.

Ezekiel's response is not recorded. My response would be to pass out.

Still, it's not enough. This was a miracle of restructuring. All the parts have been assembled, but nothing works. It happens often in the church. We work organizational wonders that result in a much-improved morgue. Something more is wanted. "Prophesy to the breath!" says God (v. 9). Call to the *ruach*, the breath God blew into Adam's nostrils, cry for the wind of God to blow here. Ezekiel did it. The Breath came. Chests began to rise and fall; the spark returned to thousands of eyes; "and they lived, and stood on their feet, a vast multitude" (v. 10).

All these themes feel familiar in this season of the church year. On the mount of Ascension, when the disciples asked Jesus, "Is this the time when you will restore the kingdom?" his answer was: "It is not for you to know." They were given a command; they gathered together and prayed. The breath came. They stood and they lived and made such a noise that bystanders thought they were drunk. They weren't. They were just "wondrously" alive.

It really did happen to your grandparents. Could it happen to your community? To your deepest-buried hopes and dreams? To you? The Lord God knows. In the meantime, why not do what is commanded? Absurd as it may seem, as you are directed, speak life to what has died in others and in yourself, and pray for the Breath. (Paul D. Duke)

JUNE 3, 2001

❧

Day of Pentecost

Worship Theme: God's Holy Spirit anoints us and empowers us to do God's work. All who are led by the Spirit are joined together as children of God.

Readings: Acts 2:1-21; Romans 8:14-17; John 14:8-17 (25-27)

Call to Worship (Psalm 104:24, 30-34, 35*b*):

> *Leader:* O LORD, how manifold are your works!
> In wisdom you have made them all;
> the earth is full of your creatures.
> When you send forth your spirit, they are created;
> and you renew the face of the ground.

> *People:* **May the glory of the LORD endure forever;**
> **may the Lord rejoice in his works—**
> **who looks on the earth and it trembles,**
> **who touches the mountains and they smoke.**

> *Leader:* I will sing to the LORD as long as I live;
> I will sing praise to my God while I have being.
> May my meditation be pleasing to him,
> for I rejoice in the LORD.

> *People:* **Bless the LORD, O my soul. Praise the LORD!**

Pastoral Prayer:

God of wind and fire, you promise that those who are led by the Spirit are children of God and that they, like Jesus, will call you "Abba! Father!" Breathe into us the new life of our risen and ascended Lord; make us your sons and daughters. As your Spirit anointed Jesus to heal the sick and proclaim good news to the oppressed, empower us by that Spirit to bring comfort to those who suffer, release to the captives, food and drink to those who hunger and thirst. Fill us with the Spirit's fresh winds that we may be united in the joy of your presence with peoples from every nation under heaven. Kindle in us the fire of your love and make us eager to keep your commandments. May the Spirit of truth abide in us and bind us with Christ in his suffering love, so that we may be glorified with him who reigns with you and the Holy Spirit, now and forever. Amen. (Blair G. Meeks)

SERMON BRIEFS

LANGUAGE AND REVOLUTION AT PENTECOST

ACTS 2:1-21

This familiar, often-preached story of Pentecost, traces an important transition in the life of the church. The passage marks the transition from a quiet group of people traveling around following a teacher and healer, the son of God, Jesus Christ, to a visible movement built on memories of the great leader, attended with great numbers and energy. The followers had gathered in one place. People living in the Diaspora had come from all over to celebrate the Jewish holiday. The streets were crowded. Many had their own interpreters to translate the sacred Hebrew, heard on the streets of Jerusalem, into their own language.

Many preachers will focus on the magnificent signs accompanying the coming of the Holy Spirit. The tongues of fire and the speaking in tongues will be preached as important points in the beginnings of the church. This focus is not in error, but it may ignore the larger Lukan picture. This is not the initial debut of the Holy Spirit; the Spirit has been moving on the face of the earth since the early days of creation. The signs of supernatural fire and ecstatic speech can also belong to the stories of magicians and street vendors. The turning point comes in Peter's sermon when Luke announces a new beginning in the life of the people of God.

Peter preaches something new, something old. From the prophet Joel, Peter establishes a new beginning in the tradition, which in reality is a refurbishment of the old: "In the last days it will be, God declares, that I will pour out my Spirit upon all flesh. . . ." (v. 17). Life will be different because sons and daughters will prophesy, the young men will have visions, and the old men will dream dreams (v. 17). Pentecost not only marked the presence of the Holy Spirit in the life of the newly formed people of faith, but also marked a radical beginning; a beginning that changed the face of religion yet maintained the symbols of the old era.

Alfred North Whitehead writes that any lasting revolution will revere the sacred symbols of the past all the while ruthlessly revising them. The symbols of the past for the Jesus movement-now-becoming-organized-church were rooted in the ancient Jewish symbols of the prophetic tradition and Hebrew language. Prophet Joel was remembered in these early moments of the church's new life. This ancient religious tradition was not eliminated. The religious energy of Jerusalem and the sacred festival celebrated fifty days after Passover (Pentecost) were to be used to inaugurate the new tradition we now call Christianity. The old symbols were not excised but were folded into the new.

"Revere the old, but ruthlessly revise" is the mantra for change. The revision occurs when the multitudes can hear in their own language. Imagine Peter, standing with the eleven, on the streets of Jerusalem, in the middle of the great feast of Pentecost preaching to crowds of locals and visitors. Languages other than Hebrew are represented. The Parthians, Medes, Elamites, Mesopotamians, Cappadocians, Asians, Egyptians, and many more are standing there, one moment not understanding anything that is being said, having to rely on their own personal translator. Then in the next moment of miracle, the visitors hear and understand, even while the Galileans are speaking in their own tongue.

The speech can be recognized in each language represented as Pentecost. What a miracle! This is not speech formed in the middle of an ecstatic experience, that we usually label *glossalia*. These are languages, dialects from all parts of the known world. In their own syntax, with their own inflected or noninflected language systems, in their own noun base and verbal structures, with their own language specific semantic fields, the good news is heard. This is the greatest miracle of transformation.

The church began that day with the presence of the Holy Spirit, accompanied with some fantastic displays of fire. But the greatest miracle is that the transformation evoked the presence of ancient prophet Joel and then was translated into foreign languages. The powerful gospel has the energy to reshape the old traditions; to give impetus to change; to translate the message into unknown language systems, foreign to sacred Hebrew. The good news is resilient and powerful, able to reshape and reform, yes, even culture and language.

We should not be surprised when the Spirit of God nudges us to reform the old structures. In that moment of change and reformation, we can learn from the lessons of Pentecost: Have reverence for the symbols of the past, and at the same time, ruthlessly revise them. New language forms (representing new cultural patterns) will help shape the previous religious tradition into a new experience of grace and power. And the church will continue! (Linda McKinnish Bridges)

PENTECOSTAL POWER

ROMANS 8:14-17

How do we make sense of the gift of the Spirit that we celebrate at Pentecost? While the Gospel lesson promises the Spirit and our Acts lesson reports the Spirit's coming, this lesson offers an opportunity to reflect on what it means for us that the Spirit has come. Calvin wrote:

> Until our minds become intent upon the Spirit, Christ, . . . lies idle because we coldly contemplate him as outside ourselves— indeed, far from us. . . . But he unites himself to us by the Spirit alone. (*Institutes of the Christian Religion*, vol. 1, Ford Lewis Battles, trans. [Philadelphia: The Westminster Press, 1960], p. 541)

At Pentecost, the whole mystery of God's redeeming work "comes home" for every believer and for the church. Our lesson provides a balanced treatment of this.

We risk distorting Paul's message, however, if we fail to keep his apocalyptic worldview in mind as we work with this lesson. Apocalyptic vision sees a sharp division between the present fallen age, and the redeemed age which will be brought about through God's decisive intervention. Paul came to believe that through Christ, God has already intervened decisively to inaugurate the age of salvation. While the new age is not yet complete, and will not be until the parousia of Christ, it is really present in the midst of the old. The Holy Spirit is the guarantee of this (2 Corinthians 1:21-22; Ephesians 1:13-14). In our lesson Paul discusses the redeemed age under the image of the family of God. In preaching, it is important to remember this because Paul's emphasis is not upon our status as children of God, but upon what God has done to make us God's children.

In the decisive victory that God has won in Christ, we, who are in Christ, have been liberated from the powers of the old age. It would be dangerous for two reasons, however, to stop at this point. First, it will be obvious to many sitting in the pews this Pentecost Sunday that the powers of the old age still have plenty of fight left in them. They seem not even to be aware that they have been defeated. If they are aware, they do not act like it. Careless proclamation of victory rings hollow when there are still devastating illnesses, addictive behaviors that radiate hurt in wide circles, tragic occurrences that appear to be merely random, estrangements in once vital relationships.

Second, to stop at the victory is not true to Paul himself. Paul quickly notes that we are not simply set free from the old age, but taken, "adopted," into the new. In the age of redemption, God is near, so intimately so that we may call on God as "Abba" ("Papa" or "Daddy"). We are given a stake in the new age and are made heirs in the family of God. Yet if we are brought into the family of God, we will also face the consequences. The fallen age, though defeated, remains in full rebellion against God. This rebellion will also be directed against those of God's family. Suffering can be a sign that we have broken with the old age, because we are now allied with the enemy of the fallen powers.

This itself does not give easy answer to the problem of suffering. No such answer exists. Note, however, that here and elsewhere Paul does not resolve suffering prematurely by moving to the resurrection. Rather, he moves from the victory to the suffering that it will entail while the victory awaits consummation (cf. Philippians 3:8-10). In the verses following this lesson, Paul connects this suffering anticipation to the whole of creation (vv. 18-25). This would argue strongly against translating *eiper* in verse 17 as "if, in fact." This could imply that by suffering we earn adoption. As in Romans 3:30 and 8:9, the better translation is "since." Since Christ suffered for us, we suffer with Christ. We conclude our profession of the mystery of faith "Christ will come again!" To hold this profession in the midst of suffering is to know the power of Pentecost. (Philip E. Thompson)

I AM (NOT) SATISFIED

JOHN 14:8-17 (25-27)

The Nicene Creed spends the most of its time describing the "one Lord, Jesus Christ." While four lines, total, are given to God the Father, and five lines are given to the Holy Spirit, eight lines are devoted to Jesus' pre-existent divinity alone, while another seven lines detail the Resurrection, the Ascension, the Final Judgment, and Christ's everlasting kingdom. Sandwiched in between these affirmations of Christ's divinity are four lines detailing his true humanity—specifically his birth, suffering, and death.

For the more historically minded of my theological generation, this "slighting" of Jesus' humanity seemed typical, and not only of the creeds. "Ideological taint" (otherwise known as faith) infected the Gospels, too, and especially the Gospel of John. The Jesus of John seemed too "cosmic" or "ethereal" to reveal very much of value regarding Jesus' real humanity.

Accordingly, if one were trying to touch the hem of Jesus' actual garment, as it were, and one had to read a Gospel at all, better to read Mark.

In Mark, of course, you do see compelling aspects of Jesus' humanity: his anger; his frustrations; his amazement at the disciples' lack of faith. You see his inabilities, even, when faced with unbelief (Mark 6:5). This, while a casual reading of John revealed

Jesus to be always in control. More God than human. More Greek than Hebrew. Impassive, almost.

But John's Jesus is much more complex than that caricature. There is real humanity, here. After all, where in all the Gospel narrative do you see Jesus' tears? Only in John. Where does Jesus say to the twelve, "Are you going to leave me too?" Only in John.

In John, Jesus does act powerfully. But the careful reader of John will find there great moments of humanity and moments of great humanity. Poignancy, almost. As we see in our lesson for today.

Raymond E. Brown has noted what he calls the "covenant atmosphere" of John 14–17—the Farewell Discourse—and specifically of the Last Supper (*The Gospel According to John XIII–XXI* [Anchor Bible 29A. New York: Doubleday, 1970], 631). Typically, Jesus summarizes the nature of his relationship to God and to the disciples, and the disciples' ongoing relationship to God through him and in him by virtue of the Advocate.

And he commissions them, too. Even if the disciples will all fall away, Jesus will be faithful. He reminds them in advance of their covenant obligations, and promises that they will, in fact, fulfill them.

The theological material reaches its climax in 14:6-7: "I am the way, and the truth, and the life. No one comes to the Father except through me. If you know me, you will know my Father also. From now on you do know him and have seen him."

And just then, Philip says, "Lord, show us the Father, and we will be satisfied." As if to say he's not satisfied. As if to say he has not seen the Father. Which ways, of course, that he hasn't really seen Jesus, either.

All this time Philip has been with Jesus. He was one of the first disciples. He was one of Jesus' first "evangelists." And here at the last, he is confessing that he has not really seen Jesus at all. "Have I been with you all this time, Philip, and you still do not know me?" Jesus asks (v. 9). Still you don't understand? Still you are not satisfied? What have you been looking at? What have you been looking for?

And do you hear the amazement in Jesus' reply? The incredulity? The very human pain in verse 9: How can you even say such a thing?

The spiritual writers often tell us that in a real sense, God has only Godself to give us. Jesus has given himself to the disciples and the people, and still Philip is not satisfied. Perhaps Philip has been looking for what Jesus isn't willing to give. Perhaps Philip is a lot like us. (Thomas Steagald)

JUNE 10, 2001

❧

Trinity Sunday

Worship Theme: We know God as a community of love. God loves us through the gift of the only Son Jesus Christ, empowers us through the Spirit, and invites us to join their threefold embrace of life.

Readings: Proverbs 8:1-4, 22-31; Romans 5:1-5; John 16:12-15

Call to Worship (Psalm 8:1, 3-9):

Leader: O LORD, our Sovereign,
how majestic is your name in all the earth!
You have set your glory above the heavens.

People: **When I look at your heavens, the work of your fingers,
the moon and the stars that you have established;
what are human beings that you are mindful of them,
mortals that you care for them?
Yet you have made them a little lower than God,
and crowned them with glory and honor.**

Leader: You have given them dominion over the works of your hands;
you have put all things under their feet,
all sheep and oxen, and also the beasts of the field,
the birds of the air, and the fish of the sea. . . .

People: **O LORD, our Sovereign,
how majestic is your name in all the earth!**

218

Pastoral Prayer:

God of power and might, your Spirit hovered over creation, and your Word, like an artist, played at your side, rejoicing in the work of your hands. Enfold us your creatures into your divine embrace. Bring us into your glorious dance that we may live, move, and have our being in you. Pour your love into our hearts through the Holy Spirit; grant us grace to know all that you gave to your Son Jesus Christ as the Spirit of truth declares it to us. Teach us acts of justice and kindness that we may extend your community of love to the outcasts and those who hunger for your presence. Give endurance to those who suffer, character to those who are weak, and hope to those who are disappointed that they may live forever in company with you and all the saints. We look to you for life, God our Parent, Savior, and Advocate; we praise you for your glory, Father, Son, and Holy Spirit. Amen. (Blair G. Meeks)

SERMON BRIEFS

GOD'S AMANUENSIS, PLAYMATE OF ETERNITY

PROVERBS 8:1-4, 22-31

Last spring, a weekly news magazine graced the racks of supermarket checkout lanes. On the cover was a photograph of Italian superstar actress Sophia Loren. The headline proclaimed: "Sophia: Still Sexy at 65!"

In the beginning was the Word. Or was it *sophia*, Wisdom, who in this portion of Proverbs reminds us of a playful feminine partner of the Most High? She is that invisible matrix (*matrix*, "womb") which maintains the interconnectedness of all things. Where Jesus is the Lord of the Dance, she *is* the Dance.

In Wisdom are the original blueprints of all things. Woodworkers—professional and amateur (in the best sense of the word), alike—know of the importance of having plans from which to work. A table leg might be too short, or a chair may not "feel" right if a design plan isn't followed. Contractors comply with strict guidelines so their buildings won't collapse after years of wear and tear. Wisdom is required, even in the act of creation. What God has made cannot function without *sophia*.

Wisdom may well be the *genio ignoto* (unknown genius) behind the 80-20 rule. The 80-20 rule states: "The greater part of any activity draws on but a small fraction of resources" (Hugh Kenner, *Mazes: Essays by Hugh Kenner* [Athens, Ga.: University of Georgia Press, 1995], p. 22).

Professor Hugh Kenner of the University of Georgia says that if 20 percent of the contents of your office are piled on your desk, then 80 percent of your needs can be satisfied by what is immediately to hand. Computer programmers find the 80-20 rule a commonly observed standard. Creativity, you see, is a messy business. A photograph of artist Francis Bacon standing in his studio depicts the usual collection of brushes, jars of linseed oil, paint rags, easels, palettes, and canvases (both blank and "in progress"). But along the chair rail along the studio's perimeter, on boards placed over steam radiators, on window sills, even on the walls are smudges, blotches, and daubs of paint where Bacon has been mixing colors to achieve the proper effects for his acclaimed psychologically dark masterpieces.

I confess a passion for the 80-20 rule in my office at home. While books are placed neatly on shelves like objects of reverence in a shrine, as I work on a project or a sermon, the paper piles up on the desk, and books and notes begin spreading into the room like cultures of mold in petrie dishes. Essayist John Boe suffers the same thing:

> For me writing has always involved an immense relationship between the order in the room and the order on the page. . . . as the piece I'm working on gets more ordered, the room gets, with each successive draft, more disordered. When I'm finally done, clutching a few neat pages, my study looks like a bomb hit it. ("Messiness Is Next to Goddessness" in *Life Itself* [Wilmette: Chiron Publications, 1994], p. 6)

Creativity is a messy business. Those of you who have given birth can attest to that. While we celebrate in the beginning was the Word with God and in reality God, we forget, or ignore, that feminine aspect of God, which brings life to the order that the Word brought out of chaos. The Word brings order—God's order—into (or back into) our lives. Wisdom brings *life*. It is because of Wisdom that food is so good, that life is so full, that there is creativity, fertility, sexuality, unpredictability, adventure— on goes the list. While we do not read it often enough, the book of Proverbs reminds us that Wisdom wants us to create and enjoy the fruits of life. We are not called to fashion perfection in our lives but to make lives of fullness and wholeness. Wisdom teaches us how. Remember when Jennifer Anniston, star of the TV sit-com *Friends* used to do the public service announcement on the importance of education for kids? What was it she said? "Knowledge is sexy." So is Wisdom. (Eric Killinger)

REAL LIFE

ROMANS 5:1-5

Trinity Sunday can prove difficult for preaching. It is the only Sunday of the liturgical calendar commemorating a doctrine rather than an event in Christ's life. Trinity is our transition into "ordinary time." Beginning this Sunday, we turn from our long engagement with the history of God's saving work in Christ to ponder our life in the world in light of God's work: our life in the Triune God. Trinity—the doctrine and the Sunday—gathers all of this up. It gives signal declaration to the divine mystery and proclaims that we have a place in it. Thus, we come to a time not for abstract speculation about Christian dogma, but for speaking of real life in the gracious mystery of God.

The liturgical transition finds a parallel in this lesson. Having discussed the universal human bondage to sin and God's intervention in Christ, Paul here turns to take up the consequences of God's action in the lives of human beings. He addresses two concrete aspects of this life made possible in and by God: peace and hope. Neither of these is a subjective state. Peace is neither a feeling of peacefulness nor serene detachment. Hope is neither a human wish nor desire for what we perceive to be our good. Rather, peace is the proper ordering of our relation with God, even if the fullness of this relation lies ahead. Hope is trustful confidence in God that the relation will be consummated (we will share the glory of God, v. 2).

How does this connect to "real life"? Are we not simply replacing theological speculation with speculation of another sort? Paul turns in verse 3 to the theme of suffering. There is the stuff of real life! How may we think of suffering in spiritual terms? How may we boast in it? Writers of the early church cautioned that, indeed, suffering is not an end in itself in which we are to rejoice. Yet suffering can become the arena of redemption, of peace and hope with God.

It is not so automatically, however. Suffering and adversity can be strong temptations to fall back upon our own resources, to make our own way, achieve our own peace. W. H. Auden reflected this temptation using the Roman Empire as its symbol:

> True, the Western seas are still infested with pirates,
> And the rising power of the Barbarian in the North
> Is giving some cause for uneasiness; but we are fully
> Alive to these dangers; we are rapidly arming; and both
> Will be taken care of in due course: then, united
> In a sense of common advantage and common right,
> Our great Empire shall be secure for a thousand years.
> (W. H. Auden, *Collected Longer Poems* [New York:
> Random House, 1969], p. 163)

This temptation will lead us away from God and from God's peace. John Calvin cautioned that "[p]eace with God is contrasted with every form of intoxicated security of the flesh" (Quoted in Karl Barth, *The Epistle to the Romans*, trans. Edwyn C. Hoskyns [London: Oxford University Press, 1968], p. 151). Where is this peace to be found?

Our lesson needs to be considered in connection to Romans 4:13-25 and so to the figure of Abraham. He was one who was acquainted with adversity, often the result of his own actions! In 4:18, Paul tells his readers that Abraham hoped against hope. How did he do this? Whether he intended it or not, after his own schemes had come to naught, he found himself waiting upon God and God alone. The God who came to Abraham has also come to us, Paul tells us; justifying us in Christ, pouring love into our hearts by the Holy Spirit, bringing us into the triune life of

God. We have this peace with God and its attendant hope. We can wait upon God and God alone, therefore, and so resist the temptation to meet life's problems by our own strength. God will come to us in redemptive ways in the midst of our suffering. Waiting upon God we properly enter life in "ordinary time." (Philip E. Thompson)

DETAILS TO FOLLOW

JOHN 16:12-15

We will take aim toward the beach later this summer. That's something we have tried to do most summers, even when we didn't have money for some necessities. W. B. Yeats once said, "I made a poem out of a mouthful of air. . . ." Likewise, we made lasting memories out of an empty checkbook.

The waves scared my son when he was a little guy, but he loved the pools that formed back up the beach from a receding tide. He loved how the dying waves would crawl up to where he sat— the surf's last gasp—and expire before splashing him.

I would sit with him sometimes. Sometimes I would try to urge him a little closer to the action and promise to hold him if the water came too fast. Eventually, after several summers, he came to want to ride my back into the shallow surf, like his older sister.

From the start she loved the surge and current. She wanted to challenge the breakers—but only if it wasn't too deep, and only if I'd hold her. So I would take her to where the ocean could beat on us a little. We'd bob and dip, corks on the salt. Every now and then I'd take her out toward deeper water, to get us a little more in the path of the ocean's power. And its peace too: you have to get beyond the first obvious turbulence (those first breakers) to experience how an ocean can be pacific.

He was drawn to the ocean, but wanted it only in small, manageable doses. She was drawn to the surf, but wanted it only in the shallows. Both wanted the ocean, but they wanted the ocean to come to them on their terms.

I am thinking of the ocean today because it is, of all days, Trinity Sunday. Today we name and acknowledge and praise the full-

223

ness of God as we Christians have come to know God. God the Father. God the Son. God the Holy Spirit. Three persons and yet mysteriously One. One God, a unity of essence, yet mysteriously a triad of mutually related distinctions.

The Trinity is the most complex and confusing of Christian doctrines, and yet it is the simplest and most practical of our doctrines too. It is so daunting, in a way, that many preachers never touch it. And yet it is so wonderfully uncomplicated, in another. It makes me think of the beach, this Trinity Sunday, and of Jesus' words here in John.

How?

Jesus said, "I still have many things to say to you, but you cannot bear them now. When the Spirit of truth comes, he will guide you into all the truth. . . ." (vv. 12-13). There is, in other words, more to know than we now know. Details will follow. They will not be altogether new things, for the Spirit learns from the Son and the Son learns from the Father, and what we hear is from the Father. But there is yet more to be heard than we have heard.

The Trinity is our doctrine of God's fullness. It is a reminder that what we know of God is never all there is to God.

Harry Emerson Fosdick used to say that when one goes to the beach and walks in the surf, what you feel is all ocean. But it's not all the ocean. There is more to the ocean than what one can experience at the shore, but what one experiences at the shore is a reliable sample.

And the same with God. What we have experienced of God is all God. But what we have experienced is not all of God. And the Trinity is our guide, telling us that while we begin to know God as God comes to us on our terms—as a human, in our need—we will never experience the fullness of God until we go to God and allow God to have us on God's terms. I believe Jesus would call that "life in the Spirit." (Thomas Steagald)

JUNE 17, 2001

❦

Second Sunday After Pentecost

Worship Theme: Jesus loved us and gave himself for us; therefore, we offer hospitality to Jesus and show others by our lives that Christ is living in us.

Readings: 1 Kings 21:1-21*a*; Galatians 2:15-21; Luke 7:36–8:3

Call to Worship (Psalm 5:1-4, 7-8):

Leader: Give ear to my words, O LORD;
give heed to my sighing.
Listen to the sound of my cry,
my King and my God, for to you I pray.

People: **O LORD, in the morning you hear my voice;
in the morning I plead my case to you, and
watch.
For you are not a God who delights in
wickedness;
evil will not sojourn with you.**

Leader: But I, through the abundance of your steadfast
love,
will enter your house,
I will bow down toward your holy temple
in awe of you.

People: **Lead me, O LORD, in your righteousness
because of my enemies;
make your way straight before me.**

Pastoral Prayer:
   Faithful God, your Son Jesus Christ loved us and gave himself for us. Give us grace to live by faith in him alone. We give thanks

for farmers and pray that they and their families may have protection against the loss of their land and livelihood. Renew the earth they till and safeguard it from harm. Teach us all to treasure the place you have given us and to remain faithful to you. Forgive us for judging others while allowing pride to mask our own failings. In your mercy, teach us the truth about ourselves that we may respond to your forgiveness with astonishing gestures of love. We thank you for the freedom to leave behind our need for status and accomplishments and to give ourselves completely to the saving grace that comes from your hand. Restore us and let our light shine so that others may see Christ living in us. In his name we pray. Amen. (Blair G. Meeks)

SERMON BRIEFS

TAKING SIDES

1 KINGS 21:1-21*a*

I. Pitfalls

We must be careful to avoid two things in preaching this, one of the more important narratives from the Elijah material. On one hand, the temptation is clearly present to enter into the text's own lampooning of the wicked characters. It would be too easy to depict childish, pouting Ahab and calculating Jezebel as resembling the characters Boris Badenov and Natasha Fatale in the old "Rocky and Bullwinkle" cartoons.

On the other hand, proclamation from this lection may be paralyzed if we dwell upon what seems to be an intolerable impasse. Why does the word come to Elijah only after Naboth has been killed? Why could not the Lord have spoken to Elijah in time to intervene on behalf of Naboth? As legitimate as these questions may be, they may steer us away from more basic issues.

II. Two Approaches

I suggest two ways in which this vividly told story may be preached, each corresponding to a pitfall. The first centers upon human beings' relation to God. In his refusal to sell his vineyard, Naboth showed himself to be faithful to God. He paid a price for his faithfulness. The land was of utmost importance in Israel's covenant relation with God. God provided rules concerning the way in which property was to change hands. It was to be kept within the family, testifying to God's abiding faithfulness. Even in times of great crisis, faithful citizens of Israel maintained this provision (cf. Jeremiah 32:6-15). Naboth refused, even when approached by the king himself, to violate God's laws. His faithfulness to the land paralleled his faithfulness to God.

Ahab and Jezebel were likewise unfaithful. There is clearly an element of melodrama in this narrative. Yet the royal couple are more than mere foils to Naboth, or to Elijah, who rushes in at the height of the drama. They are not only wicked, but have power to order the death of one who frustrates their desires. James D. Newsome notes that Ahab and Jezebel are more than just bad people in high places. They represent an oppressive social order wherein power structures and systems deprive ordinary citizens of what we today would call their "rights" (*Texts For Preaching*, Year C [Louisville: Westminster/John Knox Press, 1994], pp. 382-84).

I would avoid language about "rights." It obscures the fact that the primary offense is not against Naboth, but against God and God's command. Certainly, it *is* an offense against Naboth, but the offense against him is derived from the more fundamental offense against God. Naboth is an innocent victim of oppression, but he is more than that as well. He is a martyr.

The second approach to preaching this lesson, one that resonates with the other lections, centers on God's relation to humanity. Quite simply, it is to point out that God takes sides and that God does not side with the wicked. Elijah is instructed to confront Ahab and speak concerning Ahab's end. Sin has definite consequences in this narrative, and we do not find here the problem of wicked persons who never seem to be found out. Ahab and Jezebel's ability to "get away with murder" proves finally to be illusory. Ahab offered to buy the vineyard and was refused. In taking it by treacherous means he "sold himself" and bought a terrible lot (in another sense!). God takes sides. Elijah was on God's side, and Ahab recognized as much (v. 20). Our call is to follow Naboth in faithfulness and to follow Elijah in taking the side God takes. (Philip E. Thompson)

THE GREATEST THINGS

GALATIANS 2:15-21

The word "great" has almost lost its meaning. Sometimes we say great when we mean average. There are only a few things that deserve the title great. The greatest truths taught in Galatians do indeed live up to the true meaning of the word great because they deal with life and death issues and the very essence of God himself. It speaks of a love nearly unfathomable.

I. Mankind's Greatest Need

Paul speaks in this chapter of man's greatest need, which is justification. That is a word we don't commonly use, but it speaks of being set free from the condemnation of sin. In verse 16 he notes that we are not justified by observing the law. We can try to keep the Ten Commandments and all of God's laws, but we will never keep them perfectly. In verse 17, he says it is evident that we are sinners. This is consistent with what Paul said elsewhere that all have sinned and fallen short of the glory of God. If we are at enmity with God, we are in a sorry state of affairs. Surely it is man's greatest need to find forgiveness, grace, and justification.

II. Mankind's Greatest Gift

But, Paul also tells us about man's greatest gift. The greatest gift we have received is the grace made possible through Jesus Christ. We are not saved by the law or our own good deeds, but in chapter 15 we are told by our *faith* in Jesus Christ. His death was allowed to count for our own. Verse 20 tells us that we have been, "crucified with Christ." We also no longer live, but he lives in us. It has been said that the greatest love is one that lays down his life for his or her friends. Jesus taught that, but he himself showed a greater love. He laid down his life for his enemies.

III. Mankind's Greatest Tragedy

This message also tells us of man's greatest tragedy. The greatest tragedy is to reject this wonderful offer of grace. In verse 21, Paul says, "I do not set aside the grace of God, for if righteousness could be gained through the law, Christ died for nothing." How tragic to have received the greatest gift ever offered and yet not open the gift or refuse it altogether.

IV. Mankind's Greatest Opportunity

This passage also tells us of man's greatest opportunity. If justification with God is our greatest need, then experiencing that justification is surely our greatest opportunity. It is the chance we have to live clean before God in this life and to be prepared to live forever with him in eternal bliss. We live on earth, hopeful about our future. We approach death with reassurance. We also have the opportunity to share this good news with others.

Many pilgrims make their way to see the famous passion play in Oberammergau, Germany. While many have heard of the play, some do not know the story. The Plague was a horrid and fearful disease that spread across Europe. The people of Oberammergau prayed they might be spared. They vowed that if they were spared they would put on a play to honor Christ every ten years until the end of time. They have kept their vow. Jesus has spared us from the greatest disease known to mankind—a spiritual disease called sin. That great work is worthy of our remembrance and honor, for it is truly the greatest thing that ever happened to us. (J. Michael Shannon)

FINDING A HEALTHY FAITH

LUKE 7:36–8:3

Several years ago, a father came to my office to talk about the problems of his fourteen-year-old daughter. For years she had struggled in school. Now he knew why. She was severely learning disabled. A strong IQ coupled with dyslexia and a diminished long-term memory had joined to form a pained and frustrated child. As a result, the young lady was acting out her anger. Sexual promiscuity, alcohol abuse, and near physical combat with her parents were commonplace.

Her father was brokenhearted. Such was understandable. However, he was also guilt ridden. Why? The painful answer was almost more than he could bear to share. Two years before her birth, John had an affair with a woman at work. Now he was certain God was punishing his daughter for his sins. When I asked him why he believed such a thing, he responded, "Because it's biblical: 'The sins of the father will be visited on his offspring to the third and fourth generations.' The Bible says it. That's the end of it. This is all my fault."

As we continued to talk, I realized this man's religious history had been long on legalism and wrath, but woefully short on grace. The result was a deep-seated but burdensome religiosity that bore little resemblance to the teachings of Christ.

When one reviews Luke 7:36–8:3, the usual tendency is to focus on the grateful and loving behavior of the redeemed woman. This is quite legitimate. This woman's life had been transformed by Christ, and the result was a thankful and giving heart. Nevertheless, the portion of this story that is often overlooked is the reaction of the Pharisee. Furthermore, when the Pharisee does receive attention, he is usually painted as cold and callous. As a result, the characterizations given the Pharisee are often as venomous as the Pharisee's words regarding the woman. This is why we should look at the distinctions between the healthy faith of Christ and the ailing religion of the Pharisee.

I. Why Did the Pharisee Respond As He Did?

One could argue that it was because he had no compassion. However, like the father who came to my office, most people develop their religious beliefs through personal history. Few study the character of God. In the Pharisee's case, his training centered on the Law of Moses and on the cumbersome instructions of the scribal law. These provided little incentive for compassion. By law, the sinful woman was not allowed to touch a man, and particularly a rabbi, since doing so would render him publicly disgraced and ritually unclean. Therefore, the Pharisee's indignant response was in keeping with his religious tradition. He did not lack compassion. He lacked the truth. Nevertheless, when compared to the words and actions of Christ, the Pharisee's response revealed a sick religion colored by merciless attitudes and vitriol. Neither of these was found in Christ.

II. Most of Us Are Susceptible to Unhealthy Religion

One need not be insecure or paranoid to be lured into a sick faith system. Many of us are tempted to accept teachings that confirm our prejudices, our traditions, and our preconceived notions. This is why many otherwise kind, white southerners so readily accepted preaching that affirmed slavery and racial segregation. Such teachings violate the entire Christ event, but many people embrace sick religion because it often makes them comfortable with their *sin!* Such was the Pharisee, and such are we.

III. So, If Sick Religion Is Based on Rigid Rules, Laws, and Judgments that Provide a Measurable, Though Often Spurious, Structure for Life, What Are the Signs of a Healthy Faith?

I believe there are at least *four tests* for determining the presence of a healthy faith. Taken *together,* these tests can guide us to a healthier walk with God.

(1) Does my faith liberate or incarcerate my spirit? Does it call me to examine my sin, my life, and my relationship with God in such a way that I feel released from guilt and pain once I have met God's grace and love?

(2) Does my faith breed compassion, love, and forgiveness for others? Does it make me more open, trusting, and caring? Sick religion builds barriers of distrust, pessimism, cynicism, paranoia, and judgment. Healthy faith is healing and unifying.

(3) Does my faith help me to understand why people act, feel, or believe as they do? Unhealthy religion condemns what it does not understand and it calls it evil. Healthy faith

says, "Why do they act as they do and how can my faith speak to their needs?"
(4) Does my faith compel me to share my life, my possessions, and my love for Christ with others? Is my faith so joyous and life-giving that I wish for others to experience it?

Christ liberated the women in our story. He struck the chains of sin and a paralyzing religion to involve them in a faith that brought tears of joy and acts of celebration. May such be so for us. (Tommy McDearis)

JUNE 24, 2001

❧

Third Sunday After Pentecost

Worship Theme: If we listen for God's quiet voice and answer the call to declare what God has done for us, God will feed us with the Bread of Life and prepare us for the journey.

Readings: 1 Kings 19:1-15*a*; Galatians 3:23-29; Luke 8:26-39

Call to Worship (Psalm 42:1-2, 4, 8, 11):

Leader: As a deer longs for flowing streams,
so my soul longs for you, O God.
My soul thirsts for God, for the living God.
When shall I come and behold the face of God?

People: **These things I remember, as I pour out my soul:**
how I went with the throng,
and led them in procession to the house of God,
with glad shouts and songs of thanksgiving.
a multitude of pilgrims keeping festival.

Leader: By day the Lord commands his steadfast love,
and at night his song is with me,
a prayer to the God of my life.

People: **Why are you cast down, O my soul,**
and why are you disquieted within me?
Hope in God; for I shall again praise him,
my help and my God.

233

Pastoral Prayer:

God of the prophets, your mighty deeds put pretense and falsehood to shame; you need no earthquake, wind, or fire to announce your presence. Make us ready to hear your faintest whisper. You ask us what we are doing here, and we confess that we sometimes lose sight of the answer. Give us a clear mission and a bold spirit that we may declare what God has done for us and work for your reign of joy. Be with those who are depressed; hear their prayer for comfort and hope. Give assurance to the disappointed and confidence to the uncertain. Heal those who are sick and restore us all to new life in your Spirit. We thank you for the new clothes of freedom in Christ Jesus that we received at our baptism. We thank you for breaking the bonds of slavery, for release from old compulsions and entanglements, for your welcome of the world's unwelcome ones. Teach us to live in Christ, no longer separated by labels that limit and exclude. Feed us now with the Bread of Life and prepare us for the journey, O Lord God of hosts. Amen. (Blair G. Meeks)

SERMON BRIEFS

SEEKING A NEW WORD

1 KINGS 19:1-15*a*

I. In Trouble for Being Faithful

This lesson's familiar story is perhaps misunderstood in all its familiarity. We find help viewing the narrative in its larger setting. Just as last week Naboth was killed for his faithfulness, here Elijah himself faces the same prospect. (You may wish to note that this effect is due to the Lectionary assigning the stories out of order.) Our lesson picks up Elijah's story immediately following what looks like triumph. He won the contest on Mount Carmel with the priests of Baal. The long, devastating drought has ended. For his faithfulness, however, Elijah finds himself targeted for murder by Jezebel. The triumph of God has brought to a head the animosity of the royal court toward God's prophet. We are thus invited to ask with Elijah, "Where do we turn when faithfulness brings trouble?" and, "What do we expect?"

II. First Inclinations

Elijah's response to his plight strikes resonant chords in the experiences of many persons of faith. Faith is risky and may have difficult consequences. We may see our own lives as individuals and communities reflected in some way in Elijah's. Our responses may also be similar. Since fight appears not to have worked, Elijah flees—to the most remote area possible in the land of God. He doubts himself—his words in verse 4 may be rendered, "I am not as good as my ancestors." Elijah feels himself unable to provide the kind of leadership Moses and Joshua had provided. He attempts to retreat into the past, the "good old days." Elijah is often portrayed as analogous to Moses. Here he recapitulates Moses' wilderness trek, returning to Horeb (Sinai), a place of certainty and revelation. As Moses had received a word and even encountered God in the aftermath of the golden calf incident, perhaps he too would receive direction and assurance. Finally, Elijah feels isolated and abandoned, if not by God then certainly by other people (v. 9).

III. God's Responses

The Lectionary omits verses 5 through 7, but they are important and should be included. In the depths of Elijah's despair, God proves faithful and gives provision for the journey to encounter. Even in the hard times, Elijah is able to proceed upon the strength given by God alone. We have here acknowledgment of the legitimacy of retreat. If retreat is legitimate, however, it is not sufficient. When Elijah reaches his destination, God's word to him carries the sting of a rebuke. John Gray translates it, "What is your business here, Elijah?" (*The Old Testament Library: I & II Kings* [Philadelphia: The Westminster Press, 1970], p. 406).

Against this background, God's well-known final response to Elijah in this story takes place. Be warned—the matter is made, not clearer, but more perplexing. Popular interpretation makes of this a powerful encounter with God, not unlike that of Moses.

God's response does indeed begin as though Elijah is about to receive a special insight. He gets all the "special effects" of a theophany. But, to paraphrase, the Lord was not in the special effects. Then there is silence (consult a good critical commentary regarding how the phrase is to be translated), and Elijah covers his face. He expects God to come. Then God simply repeats the previous question, Elijah repeats the previous answer; and God says, "Go, return on your way. . . ." (v. 15).

IV. The Lesson

No direct answer is given to Elijah; no clear insight, no unambiguous revelation. He receives a command. There is no new way to be prematurely grasped and no option of merely returning to the old. Elijah, and we with him, are told to continue on, obedient to God, trusting in God's provision for us along the way. (Philip E. Thompson)

B.C. OR A.D.

GALATIANS 3:23-29

We have traditionally marked our calendars, B.C. and A.D. This is a tribute to the effect Jesus has had on history. We can mark the difference between the time "before Christ," and "the year of our Lord." But, we can also mark our individual lives B.C. and A.D. Jesus should have made a radical difference in our lives. As a tribute of the difference he has made in our lives, we can mark our personal histories with Jesus as the watershed.

I. Our Lives B.C. (What We Were) (vv. 23-25)

What was our state prior to becoming a Christian? Paul says we were prisoners in verse 23. We were prisoners held by the law, "Locked up until faith should be revealed" (v. 23 NIV). We were prisoners under a harsh taskmaster. All analogies have limits. We should not misunderstand Paul. The law had its place in the plan of God. It's not that the law was all bad, it's just that in and of itself, the law gave us no hope. The law only showed us how bad we were. There is no good news in that.

Paul also says that before Christ, we were students. Verse 24 says the law was put in charge to lead us to Christ. That word describes what would today be called a tutor, or teacher. The law was a teacher, but a harsh teacher. It taught us what good behavior looked like, but it gave us no real power to live the commandments, nor promise of grace for the breaking of them. The main lesson learned was how bad we were.

II. Us A.D. (What We Are) (vv. 26-29)

Paul does not leave us in despair. He points out that in Christ our whole life has changed. He gives us three encouraging word pictures.

First, we are called Sons of God. That means we relate to God in a new way. We are considered his sons and daughters—his children. That is a lot better than being a prisoner, or a student.

He also says that we are brothers and sisters to each other. In verse 28, he reminds us that there is no longer "Jew nor Greek, slave nor free, male nor female, for you are all one in Christ Jesus" (NIV). Not only do we relate to God in a different way, but also due to Jesus, we relate to each other in a different way. This must be. If we had the same parent and elder brother, then we are brothers and sisters to each other.

We are also according to Paul heirs to the promise of Abraham in verse 29. Not only do we relate to God differently and to each other differently, we relate to history differently. While Gentiles may not have been literal inheritors of Abraham's promise, through faith in Christ, we do inherit that promise. Why? Because only in Christ could Abraham have blessed all the peoples of the world. It is considered quite an honor to be an heir. If we were heirs of a great financial fortune, we would consider ourselves blessed indeed. But, we are something far greater. We are heirs of a spiritual fortune.

A woman who was greatly troubled, frightened, pregnant, and unmarried came to a church and found acceptance. After a time she came to a place of decision. She gave her life to Christ and submitted to Christian baptism. She said to her preacher that time, "Now I know why they call it being born again." She had a B.C. to A.D. experience. (J. Michael Shannon)

COSTUMED OR CLOTHED IN CHRIST?

LUKE 8:26-39

I. Clothes Make the Person?

One of the false claims of the culture is that our being is shaped by the covering we wear. Certainly there is a minor connection in feeling good about oneself when the clothes are well fitting, not out of style, nicely matched and appropriate for the occasion. Ordinarily, though, it is the being, the person, who selects the clothes and not the other way around.

In Jesus' encounter of this Gerasene Demoniac, there are no clothes! His "costume" is ripped from him by his own terror and panic. He is naked. He is totally vulnerable and scarcely seems to notice or care that he has no protection. We may be thankful to have had little experience having this kind of encounter with persons; we assume most of them are locked away. But that really isn't true; they live among us and perhaps even in our own skins.

The clothing of "the possessed" may in fact be extra layers rather than nudity. It may stem from depression or guilt or a deep sense of unworthiness. It is apparent perhaps not in wild and crazy behavior such as this man, but in excessive crying or in making foolish choices that only increase the isolation. The outward appearance may be sanity, but the defensive behavior and being overly guarded is a kind of clothing that reflects a person as cut off from the "right mind" and wholeness, as this poor individual.

II. Where Did the Gerasene Lose His Clothes?

We can imagine that just as he ripped off the chains with which authorities had attempted to restrain him, he also tore off his clothes. Was it a sense of having no identity that drove him to such extremes? Whatever the form of a person's mental distress, it is almost always the case that the person has lost a sense of being a person of value. The loss of identity, of being a nobody, happens sometimes because of circumstances life has given us and sometimes by an accumulating of consequences of our own making. Whatever the origin, the demons drive us to destroy ourselves, ripping away any dignity or self-worth remaining.

The tragedy is that others find such persons untouchable. These people are avoided because they need so much, give such confusing signals, and stir up the demons in other people. We know that troubles and confusion are not contagious, yet our behavior indicates we might "catch it."

Jesus did not have such fears of contact with the diseased. He went without fear to this man, as he went to any person whose life was fragmented. He went with love. He went with the confidence of one having the authority of God. And he went with healing and mercy. The demons were driven out and the man was clothed in his right mind.

III. Going-Home Clothes

When the man who had suffered isolation and confusion was freed of his demons, he begged to stay with Jesus. There were many who found healing and salvation with Jesus and they DID go with the Master. This man was different. Did he need to experience "wearing" salvation? Did he need to have some further understanding and experience of being a whole person? Perhaps. The Gospel writer indicates that Jesus might have sent him back to be a witness.

The truth for all of us who have times of great brokenness and a naked feeling about our lives, is that Jesus claims us—clothes us in baptism as children of God. This man did not need to continue in the physical presence of Jesus to retain his recovery. He only had to remember that Jesus has power over the demons. He needed to tell that to others so he wouldn't forget. Being in Christ is not a costume to be worn on Sundays and other special occasions, it is a robe of joy and freedom and wholeness for all of our days. (Kay Gray)

REFLECTIONS

❦

JULY

Reflection Verses: "A thorn was given me in the flesh. . . . Three times I appealed to the Lord about this, that it would leave me, but he said to me, 'My grace is sufficient for you, for power is made perfect in weakness. . . .'" Therefore I am content with weaknesses, insults, hardships, persecutions, and calamities for the sake of Christ, for whenever I am weak, then I am strong" (2 Corinthians 12:7-10).

No one knows what Paul's "thorn" was. He gives no description, just an allusion; his readers apparently knew what it was. Scholars and amateurs have tried cutting and pasting clues from his letters, but it's hard to diagnose a patient who's been dead for nineteen centuries. I have seen it suggested that he had ophthalmia or some other affliction of the eyes, or that it was epilepsy or malaria or migraines or Malta Fever or a speech impediment or a nervous disorder or chronic depression or homosexuality or—I'm not making this up—a bad marriage. I don't recommend listing all these options from the pulpit. Personally, I'm glad he never said what his thorn was. This way we can all nod and say, "I know exactly what he means."

But he named it a thorn; so, whatever it was, it must have galled him like a thorn. It was something sharp and stinging in him, lodged deep into the sinews of his life. It was a constant, painful presence, embarrassing, agitating, maddening.

He did with his thorn what most of us would do, he begged to be rid of it. On three painful occasions he begs God to take this horrid thing out of his life. But all three times, when he gets up from his prayers—and still the next day, and still the next—there it still is, this unbudging, sharply hurtful thing.

He stopped asking. Was it because, in the middle of his third try, he heard a voice giving God's answer? Or, more likely, did

240

that answer form slowly in his mind over the course of time, gradually emerging and ripening like fruit? Regardless, the answer he got turned out to be a word that he often offered to others. This time it was for him: *charis*, grace. "My grace is suffi- cient for you." At first blush, we might take this answer to mean something like: "So what if you've got a thorn in your flesh? You've got my huge grace on your life, don't you? My grace has saved you, set you free, promised you a place in the life to come. Don't sweat your thorn! It's a needle in a haystack of blessings. My grace is enough."

But as the answer keeps emerging, clearly the word *grace* here means something much more pointed, as pointed as a thorn— "for power is made perfect in weakness." "Oh," says Paul, and begins to see: his wound was more than a trial that grace would get him through, but an opening through which grace would flow with new force.

Some fairly sick interpretations can be made of this, so let's be quick to say what's not going on here. None of us is God's victim. God does not inflict pain. Pain doesn't happen for some purpose of making us better people. Suffering remains a dark and bloody mystery. We may rightly call it senseless. What's more, suffering itself is certainly no virtue, and can just as easily leave us more twisted instead of more gracious. Suffering can make us whiners "Poor, poor me!" It can make us liars—"Oh, I'm just fine!" It can make us cynics, climbing our pile of misery to throw rocks at the world. It can make us more self-centered, cradling our pain and using it to get what we want. It can freeze our hearts into ice, make us so angry and scared that we tighten into a fist. I heard it in an old song: the blues can make you bad; hardship can make you hard. For all these reasons, let's don't get sentimental over anyone's suffering. No romancing the thorn!

But having said this, here are some unsentimental facts of my own experience. The people who have spoken to me the word I was most hungry to hear had found their word on the far side of some terrible silence in their lives. The people who have been for me the most profound bearers of the presence of God had met the presence in their own anguish. The greatest spiritual powers and healing powers I have known came from people in whom some deep cut of pain had become a kind of chalice.

To be human can be so embarrassing. To be flawed and weak can be maddening. Ministers in particular are notorious for wishing they were perfect, and at times even striking the pose. But the joke is on us. The flaws, weaknesses, and wounds that we keep regretting and trying to cover up may turn out to be our best credentials, our most useful assets. By them, we can become men and women more available to the weaknesses and wounds of others. By them, we could quit applying for God's position—as it's already filled—and join grateful hands with the human race. We can learn the beauty of trust, the urgency of kindness, and the freedom of beggars.

By the end of our text, Paul is trailing into laughter. "So I will boast all the more gladly of my weaknesses, so that the power of Christ may dwell in me. . . . for whenever I am weak, then I am strong" (vv. 9-10).

Some weaknesses are worse than others, of course. If you bear a "weakness" that is more like a bleeding wound, you may be in no position to join in Paul's laughter. If this is the case, my first wish for you is that you will be relieved of your thorn, freed up to get on with your life less burdened by personal pain. My second wish is that if you are to keep whatever galls you—for a little while longer or for the duration—that Christ will fill your wound like a vessel that bears a strong and lovely grace for others, and for you. (Paul D. Duke)

JULY 1, 2001

❦

Fourth Sunday After Pentecost

Worship Theme: God shows us the power of our call, the steadfastness that means leaving behind all encumbrances, the joy of God's friendship, and the freedom of belonging to God.

Readings: 2 Kings 2:1-2, 6-14; Galatians 5:1, 13-25; Luke 9:51-62

Call to Worship (Psalm 77:11-15, 19-20):

Leader: I will call to mind the deeds of the LORD;
              I will remember your wonders of old.

People: **I will meditate on all your work,
              and muse on your mighty deeds.
              Your way, O God, is holy.
              What god is so great as our God?**

Leader: You are the God who works wonders;
              you have displayed your might among the
              peoples.
              With your strong arm you redeemed your people,
              the descendants of Jacob and Joseph.

People: **Your way was through the sea,
              your path, through the mighty waters;
              yet your footprints were unseen.
              You led your people like a flock
              by the hand of Moses and Aaron.**

Pastoral Prayer:
    Consecrating God, your prophet Elisha was like a wind that blows free, confronting corrupt rulers and empowering the oppressed. Grant us his spirit of audacity and vitality; give us the capacity to bring newness where minds are closed. Lord in your

mercy, comfort those who have nowhere to lay their heads; give promise to those who have been rejected; remember the children for whom no one accepts responsibility. God, we want to be disciples, but we have too much to do and we are discouraged. Give us discernment to see that what we thought were pressing duties fade when you call us to follow Jesus. We confess that we sometimes get caught up in the problems and pleasures of our families and fail to bring hope to the whole family of God. Show us the power of your call, the steadfastness that comes from leaving behind all encumbrances, the joy of traveling with you, the breadth of your freedom that captivates us completely. Teach us to live by the Spirit in generosity and peace, loving one another, for we belong to Jesus Christ, who was crucified and raised again to reign with you and the Holy Spirit. Amen. (Blair G. Meeks)

SERMON BRIEFS

STRENGTH FOR TODAY AND HOPE FOR TOMORROW

2 KINGS 2:1-2, 6-14

When I was in seminary, professors lamented that we have seen no great theologian arise of the stature of Barth, Tillich, and Niebuhrs. If there were such persons in the church today, it was implied, perhaps mainline Protestantism would not be suffering such decline in numbers and prestige. This challenging lesson speaks to all who long for leaders such as the former generations enjoyed. I suggest that the key is not to focus on Elijah or the strange symbolism of his assumption. We need to keep our eye rather on Elisha and the way in which he and Elijah themselves function on a symbolic level.

I. An Elisha Story

John Gray has noted that the Elijah stories are characterized by the lone prophet receiving the religious-moral Word of the

Lord. Elisha stories, by contrast, are marked by the presence of the community of prophets and miraculous elements. By these criteria, our lesson belongs not in the Elijah cycle, but the Elisha cycle (John Gray, *The Old Testament Library: I & II Kings* [Philadelphia: The Westminster Press, 1970], p. 466). This shifts our attention from Elijah, as he prepares to leave this world, to Elisha as he approaches the loss of his spiritual father.

Given this shift in focus, it is better to include verses 3 through 5 and 15 through 18, which the Lectionary omits. The issue is succession. Who will take Elijah's place? Elisha knows the time is approaching when the question will have to be answered. He is understandably anxious, not wanting even to talk about it (v. 5). He is not simply trying to savor every second with Elijah, though. He is staying close because he hopes that he will receive the blessing that will enable him to carry on as the successor. Like persons of every "new generation," he wants to rise to the occasion when the time comes, while being somewhat nervous at the same time. His request for the double share of the spirit, the power of God that Elijah bears, makes sense in this light. Elisha is motivated not by greed or a desire to be greater than Elijah. He asks for the portion due to the eldest son (cf. Gray, p. 475). He is stating his hope that he will be the successor. Elijah responds that it is not ultimately his to decide that matter; yet he does not foreclose the possibility either.

II. Symbolism

Elijah and Elisha serve as symbols of realities beyond the immediate context. They bring to mind another crucial time in Israel when one leader passed from the scene and a new leader arose. Elijah is often depicted in ways similar to Moses. Here we find Elijah and Elisha traveling in reverse a route almost identical to that of the children of Israel and Joshua. The implication is quite clear. As God provided for leadership after Moses, so now God will provide a leader after Elijah. The parallel between verses 13 through 14 and Joshua 3:14-17 leave little question. Elisha is the true successor of Elijah as Joshua was of Moses.

III. God Is Faithful

Elisha's crossing the Jordan raises a problem. The NRSV translation makes his heartwrenching question difficult to understand. Many Greek manuscripts insert "and it was not divided" after Elisha first struck the water. This may have been the original reading. The water divides on the second strike. From this we may conclude that God is indeed faithful in raising up new leaders, and will not abandon the people. Yet for each new generation questions remain even in the midst of assurance. These questions are not to lead to despair, though; but are to drive new leaders to persist in their turning to and seeking after God. (Philip E. Thompson)

DISCOVERING FREEDOM

GALATIANS 5:1, 13-25

The great statue that stands at the entrance to the harbor of New York is a striking symbol of the United States—commitment to liberty. But for many Americans the idea of responsibility is sadly divorced from the concept of freedom. Such is hardly the case with the apostle Paul, who in 1 Corinthians 6:12 warned his deviant followers that liberty in Christ did not mean that Christians were free to do anything they desired. For such an attitude would actually be the beginning of a slavery to the lower nature.

Here in Galatians, which has often been called the Magna Carta of Christian Freedom, Paul sets out the major parameters of Christian liberty.

I. Paul's Declaration of Freedom (v. 1)

Like a thunderbolt unleashed in the midst of his letter, Paul announced to his rebellious followers that Christian commitment must be to freedom and not to the way of bondage or slavery. Therefore, they are commanded to "stand up" clearly for the Christian way. They are staunchly forbidden to reenter the jungle snares of endless rules and regulations as a means for finding purpose to life and acceptance with God.

II. The Basis for Christian Freedom (v. 13-15)

Discovering the true nature of freedom necessitates under-standing the driving motivation of true Christianity. Its basic motivation is not self-centeredness and self-fulfillment (flesh = *sarx*). Rather, the true foundation to Christian freedom is love *(agape)*, and it is evidenced in "serving" others. Amazing as it may seem, Paul's thesis is that true freedom is to be found in a self-giving servitude *(douleuete)*. That is not the way we usually define freedom in our world. But it is the way of Jesus who came to serve and obey the will of his Father (cf. Matthew 20:28; John 5:30, 12:49-50).

III. The Two Ways of Living and the Resource for the Life of Freedom (vv. 13-25)

Later in Romans 7 and 8 Paul, in a more developed manner, would identify two basic ways of living, articulate the difficulties that Christians encounter throughout life, and challenge them to abandon the old way and follow the new way by relying on the resources of the Divine Spirit. So here in a briefer manner Paul spelled out the alternative ways for the Galatians and called them to rely on the Spirit.

Using a pattern of listing vices and virtues which were familiar in the Hellenistic world, Paul introduced this section with the familiar Jewish concept of the "walk" derived from the rabbinic concept of adhering to the correct way. But because he recog-nized that authentic walking in the way of God could not be done in one's own strength, he exhorted Christians to abandon the way of the self (flesh) and rely on the resource of the Spirit (vv. 15, 18, 25). The results of fleshly activity or the way of the self he termed "works" (v. 19); but the product of the Spirit he called God-given "fruit" (v. 22).

Let us all open our lives to true freedom through the leading of the Spirit so that our lives may be genuinely productive and reflect the nature of Christ and not the passions of the flesh. (Gerald L. Borchert)

"FIT" FOR THE KINGDOM

LUKE 9:51-62

Chippy, a prized parakeet, was accidentally sucked up in the vacuum cleaner by his deligent owner. She loved him and hastily removed him—she washed him vigorously to clean and revive him—she blew him dry with the hairdryer. He lived, but Chippy doesn't sing much anymore!

I. Too Often the Urgent Becomes the Most Important

Going through the hard times of life, like poor Chippy, we can get focused on the crisis, or preventing one, as the highest priority in life. Jesus teaches that he must be first, or we are not following him as Lord (Highest Priority) of our life.

Some of the matters that feel urgent are not deserving of first place in our lives.

(1) Getting revenge when we are rejected is not most important (call down fire on this village);
(2) Having a "place" is not (a place to lay our head, a place of our own, a place to worship God called the Temple or our local church building);
(3) Burying the dead, dealing with losses, are not so important as to become first place in our lives—they must be faced but only in the context of being part of life, all of which is in the hands of the King; and
(4) Saying farewell, looking back, is not a priority—keeping on with Christ is more important than that.

II. Jesus Gives Order to Priorities So We Remain Rooted in the Kingdom

None of these seemingly harsh demands is to indicate that our individual story is of no importance. Rather, when put next to following Christ, they become occasions for recognizing the kingdom of God.

(1) When rejected, we have the chance to really celebrate being claimed and loved by God who never rejects us; remembering that leaves no time for revenge.

(2) Might it be that Jesus' comment about having no place to lay his head is really an expression of gratitude? The care and storage and moving of all that accompanies a place to lay one's head is not a burden he must face!

(3) The experience of confronting the death of a loved one is a place to rejoice in the resurrection, not become caught up in funeral planning. It is true of "little deaths" as well; the losses that can become our whole identity needn't be (for example, the divorced man is still more of a person than just one who has experienced the death of his marriage).

(4) The reluctance to move ahead without looking back calls into question our commitments. The only vow that makes Jesus Lord of our lives is total surrender to him.

III. Being "Fit" for the Kingdom of God Does Not Mean Earning It

Citizenship in God's kingdom is God's gift declared and sealed in our baptism: the Ruler of the kingdom is our DAD. Fitness for it is like being physically fit to run the Boston marathon or mentally fit for the test you will take to get a license.

Fitness means obedience and discipline in order to experience something beyond the present feelings of the moment. The experiences of anger over injustice or gratitude for one's home or sorrow over one's losses are momentary emotions in our faith journeys, but they are not the kingdom of God.

Fitness means living a balanced life. Physically it means balancing health and exercise. Mental fitness requires a balance of full attention with resting our minds. Fitness in the Kingdom life is a balance of: prayer and action—of earnest searching and waiting—of community sharing and private reflection—of focusing on others and attending to our own confession and personal needs.

It is not always fun to work at fitness, but the gift of the Kingdom fully known in being fit, makes us sing, even when times are as hard as they were for Chippy. (Kay Gray)

JULY 8, 2001

❦

Fifth Sunday After Pentecost

Worship Theme: Affirming with Paul that what really matters is the change God has wrought in the cross of Jesus, we join the fellowship of those who are sent to declare the wonders of God's love.

Readings: 2 Kings 5:1-14; Galatians 6:(1-6) 7-16; Luke 10:1-11, 16-20

Call to Worship (Psalm 30:1-2, 4-5, 10-12):

> *Leader:* I will extol you, O LORD, for you have drawn me up,
> and did not let my foes rejoice over me.
> O LORD my God, I cried to you for help,
> and you have healed me.

> *People:* **Sing praises to the LORD, O you his faithful ones,**
> **and give thanks to his holy name,**
> **For his anger is but for a moment;**
> **his favor is for a lifetime.**

> *Leader:* Weeping may linger for the night,
> but joy comes with the morning.

> *People:* **"Hear, O LORD, and be gracious to me!**
> **O LORD, be my helper!"**

> *Leader:* You have turned my mourning into dancing;
> you have taken off my sackcloth
> and clothed me with joy,
> so that my soul may praise you and not be silent.

People: **O LORD my God, I will give thanks to you forever.**

Pastoral Prayer:

God our healer, Naaman the general learned of your power from a young girl held captive in his home. Give us courage to declare your works even in alien and intimidating places so that your name will be praised in all the earth. We pray for more workers in your fields, for companionship in the task of bringing your healing love to the world. Grant us the power of your Spirit when we confront the forces of evil; send your peace to the homes we visit; and grant us joy when we come together again. We pray for those who feel they have failed you; help us to restore them with gentleness to this community. Teach us to show with lives of mercy that nothing matters except the change you have wrought in the cross of Jesus. We thank you, God, that we have bathed in the river of life and that your redeeming grace has entered our lives, making us a new creation in Christ Jesus, in whose name we pray. Amen. (Blair G. Meeks)

SERMON BRIEFS

GOD'S SCANDALOUS INCLUSIVENESS

2 KINGS 5:1-14

From time to time, it is good for us to give attention to the scandals, literally "stumbling blocks," of God's work. God is not bound to our categories. The story of Naaman makes this clear, offering an opportunity to examine the matter from multiple angles. The situation will prove to defy simplification, speaking of God's complex involvement with the world.

I. God's Inclusiveness

One angle got Jesus into trouble when he pointed it out: God is inclusive where God's people tend to be exclusive (Luke 4:27). There is no "us—them" in the eyes of God (cf. Amos 9:7; Acts

10). This lesson is presented concretely to readers in the person of Naaman, who is immediately identified as not being an Israelite. Not only is Naaman one of "them," he is the commander of an army that opposed Israel. The tension is heightened by information that it was God who had given victory to the Arameans through him. Since his wife's servant was a captive Israelite girl, Naaman's God-given victory was in part over Israel.

The scandal of inclusiveness goes deeper, and soon is directed toward Naaman, and with him all persons of "power." Normal human relations of power are inverted throughout this narrative. Though he has prestige, Naaman is unable to heal himself of a dreaded disease. He never was the source of his accomplishments. He did not win the victories; God did through him. The illusion of human power is seen as Naaman must place his hope for healing in the words of two unnamed women, his wife and her captive serving girl. He must turn not only to women, and to a servant, but to an enemy. Later, pride would have prevented him from receiving the healing he desired; but unnamed menial servants once again intervene.

This brings us to another aspect of the scandal: God's demands on us have a way of placing a question mark over self-opinion. When Naaman arrives at Elisha's, he quickly receives three offenses. First, he expects a personal audience with the prophet. He has to talk to the secretary. Second, Naaman wants an automatic cure. He is given a task. Third, the task offends *Naaman's* notions of "us—them." He is told to wash in the Jordan, a river he deemed inferior to any number of rivers "back home." The least Elisha could have done was give Naaman a task that would allow him to show how brave and heroic he was. This treatment was obviously beneath him. He almost had nothing to do with it.

II. God's Exclusiveness

Important verses have been left out by the Lectionary. Within the assigned parameters, this seems to be one miracle story among several in the Elisha cycle. The more important point comes with the inclusion of verses 15 through 19. Just as Naaman's flesh becomes like that of a child, so does his heart. He comes to understand the exclusive place of Israel's God. This exclusivity is underscored by the personal absence of Elisha until verse 15. Elisha does nothing. The work of healing is God's. Elisha is even called "the man of God" rather than "the prophet." If the work is God's alone, then God can make any demand on anyone. Obedience to the command is key to the cure.

III. Application

Many of us, individuals and churches, long for renewal. For all our power, resources, and reputation, we cannot bring it about ourselves. In waiting for sudden infusion by the Holy Spirit or demands from God that will allow us to play the hero and so bring new life, how often do we miss the lowly requests? How often do we listen to whoever of God's "them" that may be in our orbit (liberals, conservatives, rich, poor) and so become open to God directing us toward our healing? (Philip E. Thompson)

DOERS AND NOT JUST THINKERS!

GALATIANS 6:1-16

People in Paul's time, just like people of all generations, were normally identified as either thinkers or doers, people of ideas or people of action. (Note Paul's distinction even between Jews and Greeks in 1 Corinthians 1:22.) Although the agnostic Ashley Montagu was heard to say that Paul was as great a thinker as Plato or Aristotle, it is crucial to understand that Paul was both a thinker and a doer. His goal, therefore, was to have Christians think clearly and live authentically. Accordingly, his letters are models of harmony between thinking and doing. So, after delivering a vigorous scolding to his Galatian followers for doctrinal deviations and having refreshed their memories as to the correct teaching concerning the nature of the gospel, Paul turned in the last chapter to make it eminently clear that correct thinking about Jesus and faith should lead to authentic living if one is to fulfill the law of Christ (v. 2).

But this law of Christ is not merely some replacement for the old set of rules and regulations that were endlessly developed by the rabbis out of the written Torah (3:24). This law of Christ was a new way of living under the guidance of the Spirit (5:16, 18) and one that was to be focused on love for others (5:14).

In 6:1 Paul announced the beginning of his paraenetic section or life-oriented exhortation by the use of *adephoi* (brother, or more appropriately rendered "Dear Friends" as in the NLT). Then he supported his advice by four uses of *gar* in verses 3, 5, 7 and 9 as the basis for his advice. And he closes his counsel by reminding his followers that the foundation of all true thinking and doing is the cross of Christ (v. 14).

I. Authentic Living Is Directed to Others (vv. 1-10)

Restoring sinning colleagues in Christ and helping those burdened by pains and the hurts of the world should be a significant focus for Christians who have been called to the way of love (5:14). But Paul went beyond mere altruism here to remind his readers in various ways that they are themselves merely human and are subject to deception (v. 3), boasting (v. 4), responsibility (v. 5), answerable to God's evaluation (v. 7), and they will be recipients of whatever reward is their due. Accordingly, their entire pattern of life ought to be focused on what is "good" (v. 10), the very theme of God's creative work in Genesis 1.

II. The Christian Motivation for Life (vv. 11-16)

In coming to the conclusion of this vivid epistle, Paul minced no words in clearly defining the fundamental motivating pattern for Christian living. Rejecting Galatian human efforts to gain status with God through adherence to law and circumcision, Paul took the pen from his amanuensis (secretary), and in no uncertain fashion articulated the fundamental thesis of the gospel: namely, that any gaining of status with God is not the result of human effort but the result of the self-giving death of Jesus Christ on the cross. Therefore, all praise and glory belongs to God (v. 14; cf. 1 Corinthians 1:28-30). (Gerald L. Borchert)

SENT TO HARVEST

LUKE 10:1-11, 16-20

I. Like a Bargain Shopper the Day After Christmas

One would not think of heading out to the mall, ripe with drastic markdowns, carrying armloads of packages setting out. The expectancy of "good pickings" in a sale means setting out armed only with a sturdy, empty shopping bag!

1) The aim of Jesus' mission for the seventy is reaping the benefits of a victory won. It is God's victory over sin in Jesus which they could not fully understand, yet they believed completely in him; they trusted he was right behind them; they no doubt remembered that even as they went as "lambs among wolves," Jesus had promised to be the Good Shepherd. With that awareness of authority and protection, what is the inconvenience of having no luggage or simple comforts like sandals?

2) The promise of a plentiful harvest keeps one focused, centered, and undistracted. The life of Kingdom seekers is such. Our lives are characterized by stress, harassment, disconnection. Isn't all of that a consequence of the failure to be centered in God?

II. Satan Has Fallen; the Demons CAN Be Put to Submission

The power of evil yet remains. The joy of the disciples is evidence of their surprise in having had the power over demons in their efforts. The experience of harvesting, though fraught with hardship or at least discomfort, is so rich that only joy remains.

However, even in harvesting for the Lord, the demons still exist. They will not harm you, Jesus promises as we continue to participate in the harvest, but they remain. "Do not rejoice . . . that the spirits submit to you, but rejoice that your names are written in heaven," may be a warning against pride or arrogance in having participated in the Lord's work (v. 20).

III. The Harvesting Is Done in Pairs

The work of the Kingdom is not to be done alone. Jesus taught that our prayers were to be "when two or more are gathered in my name." Why?

(1) With at least one other, there is the continual possibility of accountability. Admitting error or blind spots or confusion is more likely when there is another there to admit it to. Another can question us, point out discrepancies, give feedback.

(2) An automatic opportunity for encouragement exists when one has a partner in obedience. To think that harvesting, rich and abundant as it is, will always be easy is to omit the reading of several verses here! The discomforts of sleeping in someone else's bed, having no say-so about what's for supper, can capture one in grumbling or bitterness. The focus on those troubles, rather than the positives, is a temptation that a simple word of encouragement can overcome.

(3) It would be wonderful if serving Christ were always a matter of clear-cut choices: all dichotomies are false, a friend constantly reminds me. The mixture of life can make it very difficult to know God's will. A companion who knows us, knows our gifts and weaknesses, knows something of the same path we have walked, can be a great help in discernment.

Personal experience of Christ and his calling in our life is very important in our journey. We cannot share with others what we have not experienced for ourselves. That means there is an individual aspect to our faith walk. There are aspects unique to us that no one else can exactly replicate. But what an opportunity for demons to invade if we keep to ourselves in our spirituality. The call to go in pairs is the reminder of our need to balance individual time with shared time in the community of faith. (Kay Gray)

JULY 15, 2001

❦

Sixth Sunday After Pentecost

Worship Theme: God asks us to know strangers as our neighbors, to help them in their pain, and to confront injustice wherever it causes neglect and harm.

Readings: Amos 7:7-17; Colossians 1:1-14; Luke 10:25-37

Call to Worship (Psalm 82):

Leader:	God has taken his place in the divine council; in the midst of the gods he holds judgment; "How long will you judge unjustly and show partiality to the wicked?
People:	**"Give justice to the weak and the orphan; maintain the right of the lowly and the destitute. Rescue the weak and the needy; deliver them from the hand of the wicked."**
Leader:	They have neither knowledge nor understanding, they walk around in darkness; all the foundations of the earth are shaken. I say, You are gods, children of the Most High, nevertheless, you shall die like mortals, and fall like any prince."
People:	**Rise up, O God, judge the earth; for all the nations belong to you!**

Pastoral Prayer:

God our advocate and judge, your prophet Amos exposed the abuses of the rich who preyed on the poor; he rebuked the leaders who put their own interests before God's. Give us courage to confront injustice in our society and to open our communities to the abundant life you offer to all. God, you measure us and know our failings, and yet we know that you make life in your household possible for us. We offer you joyful thanks, for you give us the patience to endure everything, and you make us strong with the strength that comes of your glorious power. We pray for the safety of all who travel, and we thank you for the hospitality of those who have welcomed us along the way. Teach us, O God, to know our neighbors, to call them by name, and to offer them our mercy when they are distressed. Grant us grace to lead lives worthy of the Lord, fully pleasing to you, that we may share in the inheritance of the saints in the light. We ask these things in the name of your beloved Son, in whom we have redemption and the forgiveness of sins. Amen. (Blair G. Meeks)

SERMON BRIEFS

AN EXASPERATED GOD

AMOS 7:7-17

The Hebrew word that is translated "plumb line" in this passage of Amos has caused centuries of Bible translators to scratch their heads at its intended meaning. The word is really akin to our word for "tin," but such a meaning did not seem to make sense in the context of Amos' vision. A wall of tin? (See *The New Interpreter's Bible, Volume VII* [Nashville: Abingdon Press, 1996], p. 406).

It was a wordplay that does not translate well; a word that sounded like "sigh," as in God's exasperation with human folly. The idea of "plumb line," though very different from the original meaning, also conveys the idea that we are far from God's design for us. We go about our lives, off-center, off-balance, and offbeat. We have ignored the path of God. God sighs in exasperation through a shepherd-prophet and says, "I will never again pass them by . . ." (v. 8). Grace is not cheap, and there are consequences for ignoring the plan of God.

I. Grace Is Freeing, but Not Cheap

There is such irony in the idea of grace—God's unconditional love for us all. Grace is free, but not cheap. Grace is liberating, yet compels us to be yoked to Christ. Grace frees us from obligation, yet consumes us with the desire to be obedient to God. Indeed, answering the call to discipleship is our response to God's unmerited love for us.

We may not like the idea of God feeling exasperated, but consider the message it conveys. The imagery is Amos', and the wordplay is priceless. Call it a pun in Hebrew, if you will, but substitute "sighing" or "sigh" for "plumb line" and then *listen* to the meaning. It is meant to be a harsh, prophetic judgment of the people who are relying on their own success rather than trusting in God. God is saying, "I will not ignore this." There is a cost for disobedience just as there is a cost for obedience. We may think we create our own reality, but God is always at work in the larger scope of life.

II. Obedience to God Is Not Popular

The temptation in life is to live off-center. We are drawn to the unbalance of unbridled prosperity, hording, and consumerism, while ignoring the needy and the call of God. Those who follow God *appear* to live off-center, according to society's standards. They certainly answer a different beat, hear a different drummer, but the rhythm is actually the beat of life as it is meant to be. Those who are centered in God have discovered a joy that no other lifestyle can replace.

I love eating the middle of an Oreo cookie, twisting apart the cookie exterior and getting to the "good stuff" in the center. It is a metaphor for discovering God at the center of our lives. We can be on the conservative right or we can vibrate with the liberal left, but life in the center is a life in tune with God. Amos listened, was centered in God, then left his sheep and the simplicity of his life behind for the complexity, ridicule, and rigor of a prophetic calling to a wayward kingdom. He was confronted by the high priest and threatened by the power of the king, but he remained faithful to his calling. Such obedience is the mark of greatness, in prophets of old and in disciples today.

III. For Christians, Christ Is the Plumb Line

Christ stands as measure and model of what it means to love. Love is not a feeling. Love does not pass away. Love endures, believes, hopes, affirms, strengthens, accepts, empowers, and transforms. This is the love of Christ, and this is the standard; the plumb line for how we are to live and celebrate life. We are not called to die upon a cross; we are called to live the love of Christ so that others encounter the savior through us.

Ours is the Easter faith. There is hope through redemption, love in reconciliation, peace in forgiveness. There is real strength in being centered in Christ. Amos knew it, great women and men discover it, and wise folks today can still see the light and follow, if they so choose. (Gary G. Kindley)

PRAYERS IN THE FELLOWSHIP

COLOSSIANS 1:1-14

After the uniform salutation in the opening two verses of this text, Paul focuses upon two aspects of prayer that are offered on behalf of the believers at Colossae. He prays giving thanks for them, and he also prays interceding for them.

I. Prayer of Thanksgiving (vv. 3-8)

Thanksgiving is directed to God (the Father of the Lord Jesus Christ). That may seem to be a simple point and would need no reflective attention. However, directing our thanksgiving to God underscores our faith that God is the source of all good gifts and benefits. The prayer of thanksgiving then is an expression of faith as well as a demonstration of a grateful attitude.

The cause for offering thanksgiving is the news of the spiritual lives of the believers at Colossae. They were noted for their *faith in Christ* and for their *love for all the saints*. Our lives lived out in faithful discipleship will influence others and give them cause for rejoicing. Those who move ahead faithfully in Christ through the difficulties of life are celebrated here as heroes. Paul goes even further in describing the process of their spiritual fruit. These believers heard and understood the grace of God in all its truth. This grace, the gospel, was fruitful "all over the world." That is, it proved to change the lives of those who received it.

The gospel of God's grace had been bearing fruit in the lives of the Colossians as well. The positive response to the gospel results in hope for the believer. Hope is nested in the promise of God for now and for the future. Hope rings clear in dark hours for those who have embraced the gospel of God's grace. There is a qualitative difference for believers in the midst of what seems to the natural eye to be a hopeless situation. Believers are not hopeless because their hope does not originate in the abilities of humanity, but in the power and love of God.

Faith and love flows freely from this hope. When one puts trust in God, faith becomes dynamic and living, uncontrolled by external circumstances. Faith that flows from hope created by the gospel is that faith which sees beyond the natural realm and finds God at work in all circumstances. Love for believers is also a natural result flowing from one's hope in Jesus Christ. We reach beyond our own limited means and circumstances to express God's love as we have received it.

This kind of spiritually mature behavior inspires thanksgiving for Paul and his companions. For the fellowship of believers today we also need such heroes of faith who set a spiritual cadence for us to follow.

II. Prayer of Intercession (vv. 9-14)

The inspiration that evokes thanksgiving from Paul in his prayers for the Colossians also evokes his petitions and intercession. The request is that God would fill the believers with knowledge of spiritual wisdom and understanding. This request is made so that they would continue to bear fruit in their lives that inspired the prayers of thanksgiving. Paul intercedes for the Colossians to receive strength that they could continue living out the faith in which they had been walking.

The Colossians, like Paul, had been rescued from the domination of darkness and brought into the kingdom of God through redemption through Jesus Christ. Here the discussion returns to the gospel that brings hope. In fact, the gospel of God's grace stands at the center of the prayer of thanksgiving and the intercessory prayers. The gospel is the initial cause and the goal of pressing forward. Perhaps the New Testament directive that we are to pray in Jesus' name demonstrates the centrality of the gospel in our prayers. (Joseph Byrd)

NEW DEFINITIONS FOR LIVING

LUKE 10:25-37

We are introduced to a "lawyer" here. He was not like the characters in John Grisham's novels. He was an expert in the Jewish religious law. He is thus an expert witness.

The lawyer was going to expose Jesus—his ignorance, his arrogance, his true status. But Jesus turned the tables on him. The conversation took a new direction, one that the lawyer didn't expect.

In the conversation Jesus indicated that the lawyer, and others who thought like him, needed to rethink their positions. They needed some new definitions for living.

What words did they need to redefine? What new definitions did they need?

I. A New Definition of Neighbor

The first two men introduced in the parable are religious leaders. While we are shocked at their behavior toward the man who was robbed, Jesus' hearers were not shocked. Leviticus 21:1-5 explains their hesitation to touch a dead body. They would become ceremonially unclean, and may have been on their way to conduct a religious service so they needed to remain clean.

Jesus' hearers were shocked about the introduction of the third man in the story—a Samaritan. Jews and Samaritans came from a similar heritage, but had diverged into two separate groups several centuries earlier. The Jewish/Samaritan conflict is highlighted in Luke 9:52-56.

Jesus introduced a new element into people's thinking by asking a simple question. Given the circumstances, who is a neighbor? Proverbs 27:10c (NIV) says, "Better a neighbor nearby than a brother far away."

A minister reported that an old woman shuffled into the subway wearing only ragged clothes to protect her from the bitter Chicago winter wind. Her white, cracked, bony hands clutched a worn shawl tightly around her. The minister watched with wonder and pity. At the next stop, an energetic young man strode confidently onto the train. His clothes were sharp.

He too saw the woman's silent misery. Three stops later, as the train slowed, he glided by her to the other door and disappeared into the tunnel.

On the woman's lap lay his brown leather gloves.

The minister said, "I don't know if he was a believer in Christ or not. But I do know this: He saw her need and responded with compassion—while I just sat there. It never occurred to me to give her my gloves. That young man showed compassion in a way I'll never forget" (from *Our Daily Bread*, February 6, 1997).

II. A New Definition of Myself

Part of what Jesus was trying to do was to get people to open their eyes about their own responses to others. He challenged his listeners to put themselves into the parable. How do I respond when faced with a situation that challenges my steady, ingrained life? What happens when I see someone in need and can't find an "official" way to help? What are my responsibilities as an individual?

Shortly before the opening of the new *Star Wars* movie, people waited in line for weeks just to get tickets. Would they put out that kind of effort into helping someone else? The parable gets under our skin and pushes us out of our comfortable ruts.

People say, "I am only one individual. What can I do?" The Samaritan was one individual, and look what he did.

III. A New Definition of Religion

Many people's definition of religion is something like this: an archaic system of folkways and mores dominated by a series of "do's" and "don'ts," primarily "don'ts." Many people's solution to behavior they dislike is to say, "Don't do that. That's a sin."

But religion can cave in on itself and become a burden rather than a joy. We live by the grace of God, not by our own merit. Grace means that we see ourselves in relation to others as brothers and sisters. On one occasion Jesus quoted from the prophet Hosea who said of God, "I desire mercy and not sacrifice" (Matthew 12:7). God's intention is that religion will liberate us for loving service to others, not be a ball and chain we drag around like prisoners. So Jesus gave the lawyer something to think about. Who is a neighbor? Who am I? What is religious duty?

A little boy named Jesse fell down a well in Memphis in 1999 and was trapped for several hours. People had several options for dealing with Jesse's situation:

(1) The courts could have posted a sign at the well and ordered a fine for anyone falling into the well;

(2) The chamber of commerce could have drafted Jesse as part of their marketing strategy;

(3) The ministerial alliance could have preached powerful sermons on the evils of faulty well construction.

But what did Jesse need? Someone to pull him out of the well! Go and do likewise. (Don M. Aycock)

JULY 22, 2001

❦

Seventh Sunday After Pentecost

Worship Theme: We are distracted about many things, and we long for the joy of sharing a meal with Jesus, the calm of his voice teaching us, the peace of Christ in our midst.

Readings: Amos 8:1-12; Colossians 1:15-28; Luke 10:38-42

Call to Worship (Psalm 52:1-3, 6-9):

Leader: Why do you boast, O mighty one, of mischief done against the godly?
All day long you are plotting destruction.
Your tongue is like a sharp razor, you worker of treachery.
You love evil more than good,
and lying more than speaking the truth.

People: **The righteous will see, and fear,
and will laugh at the evildoer, saying,
"See the one who would not take refuge in God,
but trusted in abundant riches,
and sought refuge in wealth!"**

Leader: But I am like a green olive tree
in the house of God.
I trust in the steadfast love of God forever and ever.

People: **I will thank you forever,
because of what you have done.
In the presence of the faithful
I will proclaim your name, for it is good.**

Pastoral Prayer:

Ever-present God, you were made visible through Jesus Christ, in whom your fullness was pleased to dwell. Grant that, through Christ, we may bring your peace to a world that is distracted about many things and your reconciliation to all who are hostile and estranged. Sometimes in the clutter of our lives, we hurry our prayer and praise as if we had better things to do, and yet we are starved for your words. Show us the joy of hearing and doing. Teach us, like Martha, to be generous with our homes and tables and, like Mary, to be hospitable to your teachings. God, you desire life for every creature under heaven; we ask your blessing on the earth and all its inhabitants. You call us to remember the needy who are trampled on by indifference and greed; teach us the compassion of your Son who came to bring the poor good news. We pray in the name of Jesus, the head of the church, the hope of our glory. Amen. (Blair G. Meeks)

SERMON BRIEFS

TRAMPLING UPON THE NEEDY

AMOS 8:1-12

In these verses Amos challenges Israel at the point of its compassion. While keeping the letter of the Law, they ignore the greater spirit of it, especially as it has to do with caring for those who cannot care for themselves.

"You who trample upon the needy," he says, "and bring the poor of the land to an end. . . . [You] deal deceitfully with false balances, that we may buy the poor for silver and the needy for a pair of sandals. . . . " (vv. 4-6 RSV). Israel disrespects the Sabbath (indicated in verses 5 and 6) but even more profoundly disrespects people. And each of those issues indicates a fundamental disrespect for God.

Jesus touched upon this same theme when he said: "Just as you did it to one of the least of these who are members of my family, you did it to me" (Matthew 25:40). How we deal with the poor to a great extent determines how we feel about Christ.

Sometimes our response to the poor includes derision. Sometimes we respond by taking advantage of the disadvantaged. Sometimes our response is judgmental ("They are lazy abusers of the system."). Sometimes our response is simply a kind of benign neglect. On occasion, there is a blending of all those responses, even among those of us who know better.

Shortly after arriving at my current post as senior minister of a large downtown church, I was visited in my office by a street person. I quickly jumped to a predictable assumption about his intent. Ours is a forty-two-hundred-member congregation in the middle of a city. All the needy know who we are and where we are and assume our pockets are deep. Certainly, I guessed, he felt that there is a new guy at the helm of this ecclesiastical gold mine. The new minister doesn't know him or his routine yet. Strike while the iron is hot.

I gave him a few minutes to do what users always do—to tell me his story (his religious background, his bumps in the road, his history of being the innocent victim) and then to make his appeal for funds. He was a bit more long-winded than most, and I was busy. So midway through his speech, I interrupted, "Let's get to the point," I said. "There must be some reason you came here." He answered quietly: "Yes, there is. I know you are new at this church. It's a big place with lots of responsibilities. I just wanted to stop by and see what I could do to help you get started." He had come not to receive but to give—not with hands outstretched to take but rather to offer. "I just wanted to stop by and see what I could do to help you get started."

"You always have the poor with you" (Mark 14:7), said Jesus. As Christians, this passage from Amos should remind us that our actions *and* attitudes toward those poor reflect our basic posture toward Christ. Do we help or ignore? Do we serve or deride? Do we love or judge? Amos accused Israel of trampling upon the needy. Jesus calls us to love them. There really is no middle ground. (Michael B. Brown)

FOUR FACES OF REDEMPTION

COLOSSIANS 1:15-28

We lose some of our wonder and awe as we mature in the Christian faith. Somehow, we begin to believe that we have arrived and that we have figured it all out. The mystery of redemption is gone. Our text here calls us back to that childlike wonder as we view our faith and redemption. Christ is demonstrated with two varying roles as the mediator of our salvation. Believers are portrayed as sinners saved by grace and as thankful servants.

I. Christ as Creator and Redeemer (vv. 15-20)

These verses, thought to be a hymn by scholars, reflect the majesty and glory of Jesus Christ. Paul desires there to be no mistake among the Colossian believers. Jesus Christ completely reflects the glory of God the Father and the fullness of God dwelt in him. This was no up and coming rabbi who taught a good set of principles by which one could live his or her life. Jesus is ascribed with the divine act of creation of all things (in heaven and in earth) for his own pleasure.

He is not an abstract creator however. Jesus Christ is intimately involved with his creatures, leading them as their head and setting the way for them to follow even in the hope of resurrection. He becomes their mediator, reconciling his creatures to himself through his own blood shed on the cross. Here is the wonder of the first two faces of redemption: without provocation and motivated by his own pure love, Jesus Christ redeems his creatures from their rebellion against him.

The creatures did not respond according to the nature that Jesus gave them when he created them. His creatures chose to rebel against him and the nature he gave them. To restore fellowship, reconciliation was required—a reconciliation that only he could accomplish. So in due season, Jesus Christ the supreme and sovereign creator became the crucified savior and redeemed his rebel creation.

II. The Redeemed and the Servants (vv. 21-28)

All believers were at one time estranged from and hostile toward God. Humans do not care to look at themselves in such a self-deprecating way, but we must face reality. The evil deeds emerging from our behavior testified of our estrangement and hostility. In truth, our behavior reflected our rebellion. Paul reminded the Colossians of this truth in verse 21. But there is hope, and Paul reminded the Colossian believers of that hope as well as their prior rebellion.

Now we live in the reconciliation accomplished by the death of Christ's fleshly body. Life in that state means that he presents us as holy, blameless, and free of accusation. As long as one lives in this state of reconciliation, that is, the gospel, moving ahead securely established and steadfast in faith, one reaps the benefits of such a gospel.

Paul was so overwhelmed at the power of this gospel that he dedicated his life to the call to live as a servant to the Lord and the gospel. He makes himself an example to the Colossian believers as a servant in that he rejoices in suffering for their sake. There is nothing to dissuade him, nothing to distract him. He is obsessed with proclaiming the mystery that has been revealed in Jesus Christ. For Paul, it is worth all of his struggles and his work.

Maybe there are too many distractions today. Too many activities to take our time. Perhaps we are too intellectual to become so enamored with God's work of redemption in Jesus Christ. Yet, to those being saved, the message of the cross of Jesus Christ, the gospel, is the power of God. Maybe we are too active, too intellectual, and too distracted. Perhaps, we should rediscover the wonder of redemption. (Joseph Byrd)

A NEW LOOK AT AN OLD PROBLEM

LUKE 10:38-42

Jesus and his traveling companions arrived in their friends' home. Their hosts immediately began the preparations to receive them and feed them. This domestic story seems familiar. We all know the chaotic frenzy of hosting people and feeling the pressure to make certain everything is perfect.

Can't you just see the fussy, harried look on Martha's face? She gave Jesus a gentle rebuke: "Do not you care that my sister has left me to do all the work by myself?" Jesus turned the occasion into a teaching opportunity for Martha and for us. This narrative helps us take a new look at an old problem. That problem is this: how can we serve God while living in a world like ours?

I. Distractions

To serve God in a world like ours, we need to deal with distractions. Martha was distracted by her idea of hospitality. When we try to study, pray, or serve, sometimes we get pulled in many different directions by the distractions within us and around us.

Sometimes our distractions are simple boredom, and we do things in an attempt to relieve that boredom. One such man was Larry Walters. In 1982, he floated three miles above Southern California in a lawn chair rigged with forty-two helium-filled weather balloons. Walters, then a thirty-three-year-old North Hollywood truck driver, had no aviation experience but had always wanted to fly. Armed with a two-way radio, a parachute, a pellet gun and some jugs of water for ballast, he expected to rise gracefully into the sky from his girlfriend's backyard in San Pedro, California, then shoot the balloons down to make a gentle landing. When the mooring was cut, however, Walters shot up into the sky unexpectedly, soon reaching the sixteen-thousand-foot level. He passed a few private planes on the way up and was spotted by baffled jetliner pilots. The dizzy balloonist managed to shoot out about ten of the weather balloons before his gun fell overboard ninety minutes into the flight. His craft then drifted back to earth. The balloons eventually became entangled in power lines near Long Beach Airport, and Walters was able to hop down from the lawn chair into the waiting arms of the law.

Not everyone goes to such heights, though. In our anxiety to serve the Lord, we must learn to deal creatively with distractions to our spiritual life.

II. Devotions

Turning from distractions to devotions is not always easy. But Jesus helped Martha learn that sitting at his feet to learn is more important than cleaning the house or cooking the meal.

Spiritual guides down through the centuries have dealt with the transition from daily life to the devotional. That transition is not "either/or" but is "both/and." Fortunately we are not forced into choosing only daily life or only the life of devotion to God. We need to eat to survive, but we remember that we do not live by bread alone. We are made for communion with God.

III. Decisions

Moving from distractions to devotions requires decisions. Jesus said to Martha's complaint, "Only one thing is needed." What did he mean? He meant that the time comes to grab opportunities when they present themselves. Neither Mary nor Martha would have the opportunity to learn from Jesus much longer. He was on his way to Jerusalem and would die there.

Jesus challenged Martha to decide to accept what was offered to her. The sisters could clean the house another time. For now, the chance to learn from Jesus is there.

For us, these lessons help us learn to be here today—to seize this moment of worship and decide to let the distractions of life go by for a time. When we take a new look at an old problem, we see the need to move from distraction to devotion. What will you decide to do? (Don M. Aycock)

JULY 29, 2001

❧

Eighth Sunday After Pentecost

Worship Theme: By our baptism we are made children of the living God and given the confidence that God, who raised Jesus from the dead, will bring us to life in Jesus' presence.

Readings: Hosea 1:2-10; Colossians 2:6-15 (16-19); Luke 11:1-13

Call to Worship (Psalm 85:8-13):

> *Leader:* Let me hear what God the LORD will speak,
> for he will speak peace to his people,
> to the faithful, to those who turn to him in their
> hearts.

> *People:* **Surely salvation is at hand for those who fear**
> **him,**
> **and his glory may dwell in our land.**

> *Leader:* Steadfast love and faithfulness will meet;
> righteousness and peace will kiss each other.

> *People:* **Faithfulness will spring up from the ground,**
> **and righteousness will look down from the sky.**

> *Leader:* The LORD will give what is good,
> and our land will yield its increase.

> *People:* **Righteousness will go before him,**
> **and will make a path for his steps.**

Pastoral Prayer:

Gracious God, you bring light in the midst of despair. Remember your promises and speak peace to us. Grant us grace to live where your love and faithfulness meet so that we may give our children names of hope. Forgive us for surrendering to anxiety and distress when we can live our lives in Christ. If we are confused by noisy ideologies, remind us that we are rooted and built up in Christ. If we see that nations are in disarray, assure us that you have placed Christ at the head of every ruler and authority. We come to you abounding in thanksgiving, for you have said that by our baptism we will be raised with Christ and are even now alive together with him. Give the hungry bread enough for this day's needs, and tomorrow we will ask the same. We ask for what is good; we seek your righteousness; we knock at the door, confident of your embrace, for we are children of the living God whose power raised Jesus from the dead. Amen. (Blair G. Meeks)

SERMON BRIEFS

"HOW IS THIS OUR STORY?"

HOSEA 1:2-10

Every week when I lead a Bible study in my local church, I ask the same question at the end of the lesson. When I have read and commented on the text for the day, I inquire of those present: "How is this our story?" That question poses a dilemma for the reader of Hosea 1. We hope that this is not our story. We don't want to identify with Hosea or Gomer, or even Israel or Judah, at least not at this point in their history. The strangeness of the text reverberates against our sensibilities: that God would instruct a prophet to marry an unfaithful woman—a whore—to symbolize the unfaithfulness of God's people. We want to view ourselves as faithful and holy, not sinful and broken.

I. It Is a Story About How We Avoid Hearing the Truth

Some years ago three students in the junior class of the local high school where I served committed suicide within an eleven-month period. Those tragic deaths in a small town propelled the parents and leaders of the community into action. We called a

273

counselor from another city whose name was recommended to us as a good resource. Her community had been in the national spotlight for having a teen suicide rate that was several times the national average. The therapist's cynical comment to us was both riveting and convicting. "Only three deaths?" she inquired after we explained why we were calling, her voice thick with sarcasm. "We had to lose five teenagers before this community woke up and decided to do something about it!"

We do not like bad news. We do not like to think that some of the compelling, condemning texts of scripture apply to us. We do not want to believe that Hosea is our story, too.

II. It Is a Story About Our Own Arrogant Independence

We can actually believe that we are successful people by our own hand. Indeed, we can work hard and accomplish much, but we would not have life itself apart from God and the gracious acts of others. All of us, even those abandoned at birth, owe our very existence to others who cared for us, helped us to this point, and who pointed us in the direction of God.

I can say for certain that the less grateful and the more self-centered we are, the more unlikely it is that we will be a good giver. It is a gift to be able to give, and it comes from cultivating a grateful heart that recognizes the Giver of all gifts. The more independent we are, the less we depend upon God. The less we depend upon God, the less grateful and humble we become. We become like Israel, hardened to God's calling, disobedient to God's ways, and turned inward toward our own desires.

III. It Is a Story That Offers Hope

God does not leave us hanging, wondering, or guessing when it comes to hope. Life may be a mystery, but there is always hope when we place our trust in God and repent of our sin. Consider verse 10:

> Yet the number of the people of Israel shall be like the sand of the sea, which can be neither measured nor numbered; and in the place where it was said to them, "You are not my people," it shall be said to them, "Children of the living God."

It is a message of hope that follows this passage of consequence. God is rendering judgment, but God's judgment is always tempered with grace. When Anglican Archbishop Desmond Tutu met with the Council of Bishops of the United Methodist Church in May of 1999, he told them that God doesn't love us because we are lovable. "We are lovable because God loves us" (*Newscope,* May 14, 1999). Thanks be to God for such a gift! We are loved and forgiven. We are chosen and claimed. What a difference it is to live free rather than fearful. (Gary G. Kindley)

PRACTICAL AND THEOLOGICAL DIMENSIONS OF LIBERTY

COLOSSIANS 2:6-15 (16-19)

The New Testament teaches a life of discipline for believers but rejects legalism. At times this distinction is difficult to make, and confusion sets in causing some to emphasize the rejection of legalism over the anticipation that believers will live a life of holiness or vice versa. Often, such overemphasis of one side is at the exclusion of the other. Here, Paul is warning the Colossian believers not to fall under the condemnation of another who is judging them legalistically (vv. 16-19). The judgments of the supposed legalists apparently focused upon outward observance of rituals and maintenance of strange doctrines as their criteria. Paul argues the believer's identity and liberty are established in relationship to Jesus Christ.

I. Practical Issues: Which Compass for Life? (vv. 6-8)

Paul warns that believers are not to be "taken captive" through shallow and empty philosophy. Such philosophy is based upon human tradition and the basic principles of this world. What sets our worldview and life perspective? If we succumb to the intellectualism of our day, we should not be so naïve as to believe that such arrogance is a product of our age of technology. As Paul corrects the first century believers so we must receive the correction if our life compass is set by human rationale.

Instead Paul encourages that as believers received Jesus Christ as Lord, they are to continue to live in him. That is, the Christian life is determined by the standards that Christ sets for his disciples. The believer is rooted and built up in Christ. That is, Jesus Christ is the beginning and continuation of guidance for the believer. It is crucial for believers to recognize their identity flows from Christ and not from the evaluations of people around them.

II. Theological Issues: Identification with Jesus Christ (vv. 9-15)

Is Christ really sufficient to guide the modern life in our advanced world of technology and industry? In combating heresy among the believers at Colossae, Paul begins to give a theological description of the sufficiency of Christ. Primarily, the fullness of deity dwells in Christ bodily, who is the head over every power and authority. In Christ, then, is Divine authority that is sovereign and trans-rational.

This is not just an abstract thought for Paul. He notes that believers are in this omnipotent Christ (symbolized by spiritual circumcision and the act of baptism). The reality of this identification is made clear when we recognize that before Christ, we were dead in our sins. But the power of this Savior is that he has made us alive and has forgiven our sins. He then disarmed the powers and authorities nailing the condemning code to the cross. This is the new birth, the redemption of humanity, and salvation expounded.

If we can identify with the death and resurrection of Christ through baptism and receive his gracious gift of salvation for the most ultimate quandary of life, that is, eternity, is it reasonable to question his sufficiency to guide our lives? Comparing the influence of Christ to deceptive philosophy, is there any reason to give human rationale the primary place as our life compass?

Perhaps, we have not changed much from the days of high school when peer pressure determined what we liked or what we did not like. Now as adults we see that succumbing to that peer pressure was a sign of immaturity. Equally so, if we give in to the reality of spiritual peer pressure of legalists, we demonstrate our immaturity and lack of recognition of our identity in Jesus Christ. We surrender our inheritance of liberty for less than a bowl of

Jacob's lentil stew. If Christ saves us, he will guide us in the practical matters of life and we need not worry with the condemnation of others. (Joseph Byrd)

THE PRAYER TEMPLATE

LUKE 11:1-13 (NIV)

The disciples watched Jesus live and pray. His life and prayer seemed to be a seamless robe rather than two distinct things. They wanted that for themselves, so they asked Jesus to teach them to pray as he did.

He gave a template for prayer. When we place this template over prayer, we know we are in the ballpark. Let us examine each aspect of this prayer to see what Jesus meant.

"Father"

Jesus spoke in Aramaic, a language similar to Hebrew. He spoke of God as Abba, which is a personal term similar to our term "Daddy." This term expresses our relationship to God. God is not only the eternal Lord of the universe, but also the Father of Jesus and of his followers.

This is a personal term of address. Christians may reach out to God with the realization that God is our Heavenly Father who cares for us.

"Hallowed be your name"

This part of Jesus' model prayer teaches us that God's name is separate from all other names. It is holy, which is the meaning of the word hallowed. In the Bible a person's name referred to his whole character. God's name is hallowed when his nature and purpose are known and reverenced. People should show reverence for God.

"Your kingdom come"

God's kingdom is God's rule in the hearts and lives of people. To pray this part of the prayer is to pledge yourself to join God's effort to extend that rule to everyone. This prayer is sincere when we want others to know the Lordship of God.

"Give us each our daily bread"

God's care for people includes their total welfare. The needs of the body are important as are the needs of the soul. Jesus taught that God is interested in our everyday needs. This includes food, certainly, but also all of our basic needs.

We may properly pray for all matters in our daily lives including our home, our job, our health, our relationships with other people, and our deepest physical and emotional needs. Jesus taught that we can pray about everything that makes up daily life, which means God invites our prayers regarding our hurts, our hang-ups, our sexual desires, our loneliness, and anything else we may wish to share with and need assistance with. In short, we may rightly pray about everything that touches our lives.

C. S. Lewis pondered the mystery of Jesus' teaching people to pray like this.

Lewis wrote, "Can we believe that God ever really modifies His action in response to the suggestions of men? For infinite wisdom does not need telling what is best, and infinite goodness needs no urging to do it. But neither does God need any of those things that are done by his finite agents, whether living or inanimate. He could, if He chose, repair our bodies miraculously without food; or give us food without the aid of farmers, bakers, or butchers; or knowledge without the aid of learned men; or convert the heathen without missionaries. Instead, He allows soils and weather and animals and the muscles, minds, and wills of men to cooperate with His will" ("Does Prayer Really Change Things?" *Faith*, Feb.-Mar. 1989, p. 9).

"Forgive us our sins, for we also forgive everyone who sins against us"

Jesus made this a matter of importance. Forgiveness opens the door to relationships, both with God and with other people.

"Lead us not into temptation"

This part of Jesus' prayer has troubled many people. Does God actually tempt us? The word *temptation* in the original language is *peirasmos*. It can mean both "temptation" and "trial." No, God does not "tempt" people with evil enticement. Jesus meant that we should pray about the trials that come into our lives. His phrase "do not lead us into temptation" means "do not let us fall into a trial so difficult that we will fail." The issue is testing.

Jesus offered a model—a template—for our prayer. Let us follow that leading. Amen. (Don M. Aycock)

REFLECTIONS

♥

AUGUST

Reflection Verses: "Where you go, I will go; where you lodge I will lodge. . . . Call me Mara, for the Almighty has dealt bitterly with me" (Ruth 1:16, 20).

Meditating on the situations of Naomi and Ruth on the road to Bethlehem, you may identify with either character, or perhaps with both. If you are in a dark season of your own grief, you identify with Naomi. If you are busy trying to be of help to grief-stricken people, you identify with Ruth, though you will not forget that she must bear her own grief too.

Let's begin with Naomi. She is the picture of stark bereavement. By the time we first hear her speak, she has suffered three devastations. She has been led away, weeping, from three horrible graves. Her only two children and her husband are lost to her now, all three cut down in premature death. No one remains for her. She is crushingly alone.

To lose so much is to find your identity radically altered. The face gazing back from the mirror is a stranger. Naomi knew it in a name change. On her arrival back in Bethlehem, she announced to her friends, "Call me no longer Naomi," *Pleasant;* "call me Mara," *Bitter,* "for the Almighty has dealt bitterly with me."

If you've been where she is, you don't blame her for this. You don't add to her burden the insufferable weight of pious truisms and advice. She has told the first truth of an utter grief. It is our truth too, if cruelty and unjust suffering have struck down our loved ones or ourselves. In such devastation perhaps nothing else can be true until we have told this truth: that the Almighty *has* dealt bitterly with us, and we *are* bitter.

This is surely why Naomi is in no position to appreciate the early kindnesses of Ruth. Three times the older woman has told her daughter-in-law to go away. Orpah got the message after the second dismissal; but Ruth is relentless, stubborn as a burr on the side of a sock. Her promise comes out as a poem, a piling on of no less than six ways she'll be sticking with Naomi to the bitter end. The Hebrew word for such a stubborn love is *hesed*, the same word used of God's lovingkindness, and a word used more than once of Ruth. But Naomi seems unimpressed. She shows no gratitude. All we are told is that "When Naomi saw that she was determined to go with her, she said no more to her" (v. 18). It has the feel of a groaning resignation, a miffed silence, a glare shot from sullen eyes with unmistakable meaning: "Suit-yourself-but-stay-out-of-my-way."

The silence continues all the way back to Bethlehem, where Naomi declares that her name is now Bitter, since God has dealt bitterly with her. No matter that, in fact, God had been walking silently beside her the whole way home in the person of her dogged daughter-in-law. Commentaries on the book of Ruth often observe that in this very human story, little of the action is ascribed to God. The Divine is in the shadows, unnamed, speaking and working through the kindness of the human characters. In a real sense, through Ruth, it was God vowing to Naomi, "Where you go, I will go; where you lodge, I will lodge." A young woman's refusal to abandon her was the embodiment of the same Divine refusal. The *hesed* of Ruth was the *hesed* of God. And the grieving old woman cannot possibly know it, not yet. Naomi is numb, shrouded in thick shadow. That is the way of grief.

It suggests, at the very least, that when grief overtakes us, we may do ourselves a favor by showing some patience toward our pain. We who mourn are on a long path. It will take as long as it takes. If good gifts given to us along the way do not lift our spirits, nothing useful will be added by self-flagellation. Perhaps there is a kind of wisdom in Naomi's silence toward the gift given to her by Ruth. Silence in grief can be a way of waiting. Knowing that in such times the gifts of God may well be indiscernible to us, we can keep slogging through, open to the prospect that in time we may look back and see how the road behind us was lined with tender mercies.

As for Ruth, her position is not unlike ours who live beneath the calling to comfort those who grieve. Like us, she does not exercise her care from any pain-free position. Her own wounds are bleeding as she ministers to Naomi. The older woman seems oblivious to this. It is possible that both women are oblivious to the fact that the out-flowing kindness of Ruth has its secret source largely in her own grief, her own need. Unavoidably, that's how it is with most of us "caregivers." How can it be otherwise?

But notice especially the patience of Ruth—not just her plucky patience in refusing to go away, but her patience as well with the unresponsive silence of Naomi. She had given the best gift she had. She had abandoned her own security and offered her very life to the grief-stricken woman beside her; and from all outward appearances, it made no difference at all. Days later, she would hear Naomi publicly declaring her bitterness, as if Ruth's gift had made no sweet difference. Ruth embodies the powerlessness of all who love the grieving. We cannot deliver them. We can only stay stubbornly beside them, and wait, and watch, and leave the rest to time and to God.

Ruth invites us to be patient with the grieving, as Naomi invites us to be patient with ourselves. And the story itself reminds us that God inhabits the shadows where we can see neither the seeds of our own healing, nor the effects of our ministry. The story ends with Naomi and Ruth dancing at a wedding feast, then cooing over a baby. So it will be. Those who keep walking the long road of grief, giving and receiving kindness on the way, will arrive at last at a feast and a birth, astonished by the fruit of seeds planted and grown in the dark. (Paul D. Duke)

AUGUST 5, 2001

❦

Ninth Sunday After Pentecost

Worship Theme: Our life is a gift from God, and our joy comes not from accumulating possessions, but from the peace of mind of being rich toward God.

Readings: Hosea 11:1-11; Colossians 3:1-11; Luke 12:13-21

Call to Worship (Psalm 107:2-9):

Leader: Let the redeemed of the LORD say so,
those he redeemed them from trouble
and gathered in from the lands,
from the east and from the west,
from the north and from the south.

People: **Some wandered in desert wastes,**
finding no way to an inhabited town;
hungry and thirsty,
their soul fainted within them.

Leader: Then they cried to the LORD in their trouble,
and he delivered them from their distress;
he led them by a straight way,
until they reached an inhabited town.

People: **Let them thank the LORD for his steadfast love**
for his wonderful works to humankind.
For he satisfies the thirsty, and the hungry
he fills with good things.

Pastoral Prayer:
Holy God, you have held us in your arms and taught us to walk. When we turn away from you, your anger stops us like a lion's roar, yet you cannot give us up; we are the children of your

warm and tender compassion. Remind us of the healing that comes from your forgiveness. Teach us to use our energies for the common good. Forgive us for failing to question why some define their lives by an abundance of possessions while others struggle to find what is needed to survive the day. We thank you for the joy that comes, not from full storehouses, but from having Jesus as our friend. And we thank you for the peace of mind that comes from being rich toward God. Strengthen our resolve to give up whatever in us fails to reflect your glory, and teach us to set our minds on your grace. Renew us in the image of our creator that we may share with you a likeness that transcends race and class. Our life, O God, is a gift from you; keep it safe with Christ, so that when he is revealed, we will be revealed with him in glory; in the name of Christ who is all in all. Amen. (Blair G. Meeks)

SERMON BRIEFS

"A NEW DEFINITION OF HOLY"

HOSEA 11:1-11

How do you describe the nature of God to someone who does not know God? How do you define what it is to be "holy"? The eleventh chapter of Hosea gives us a glimpse of the true nature of holiness: to demonstrate grace and compassion in the face of ingratitude. The lesson of Hosea is not that holiness is found in rules, moralistic thinking, or an air of piety. Hosea pronounces what God clearly demonstrates: love is the heart of true holiness.

I. God Is Holy Because of Love

Holiness is more than piety and morality—it is righteousness that is rooted in love. The love of God has conceived creation, invoked the incarnation, and redeemed through the resurrection. God's love has catapulted the Christ into history such that history itself unfolds around the human response to Christ's passion. A life of holiness is a life that reflects the divine love, serves in pure humility, and acts in order to share the same love that has so changed itself. Love that is pure and selfless is a sign of the holy.

Consider the young mother of a three-year-old son. She learned that she was pregnant, and encouraged her son to help him prepare for his new baby sister. He would sing to his mother's tummy to welcome the new life that would soon emerge. When the mother went into labor there were complications. The infant was born in serious condition and not expected to recover. The newborn's brother insisted on going to the hospital to sing to the child, but it was against hospital rules.

Plans for bringing the baby home changed into making plans for her funeral. The three-year-old sibling begged to see his sister. "I want to sing to her," he insisted. The mother took her young son by the hand and led him to the scrub room. Donning a surgical mask and an oversized gown, he entered the neonatal unit where his sister was tended by machines and nurses. Over loud protests from the charge nurse, the little boy sang in a pure, angelic voice, "You are my sunshine, my only sunshine, you make me happy when skies are gray. . . ." The dying infant's pulse rate responded, and she calmed to the steady, familiar voice. He kept on singing and the baby lulled into a restful, healing sleep. She fully recovered and was dismissed from the hospital *the next day!* For family and hospital staff, it was indeed a miracle. The mother called it a miracle of God's love! Holiness begins with love.

II. God's Compassion Is Greater Than God's Anger

The metaphor of God as parent and Israel as the child opens this chapter. It is only the warmth and tenderness of God that keeps the fierce anger of the Divine from being executed (v. 8). Jesus got angry and demonstrated righteous indignation. Christians often do not handle that idea very well. We think of anger as negative or even sinful, and certainly it can be. Righteous indignation is different. God is responding to the infidelity of Israel, yet God responds with compassion.

Resistance demands a response. "The more I called them the more they went from me; they kept sacrificing to the Baals, and offering incense to idols" (v. 2). God responds because of Israel's resistance and disobedience, but God's compassion remains greater than the fierceness of the Creator's anger.

III. God's Righteous Judgment Is Done in the Name of Love

How many times have we heard someone say, "I am acting in your best interest"? What they usually mean is, "I am acting in what *I* think is your best interest." God is the one who truly does act in our interest. God's judgment upon the chosen people was out of love, as a parent teaches a child the danger of fire or the consequence of disobedience. Life itself can be an unrelenting teacher, but some persons are unwilling to learn. There can be misery in immorality, and we do not need to experience the misery when we obey God's call to live moral lives. God's ways are not meant as handcuffs or punishing rules, but life-giving truths, teachings, and insights.

A popular talk show host was asked if it was ever acceptable to lie. Her response was, "If the lie is done in the best interest of the one to whom it is told, and is done for selfless reasons." If we lie to cover our own necks, that does not meet the standard. If we withhold information in order to protect someone from mental anguish, inappropriate information, or something harmful to him or her, without consideration of our own benefit, then a lie may be justified. Selfless, unconditional love is the motive. Love is the heart of holiness. (Gary G. Kindley)

THE NATURE OF THE BELIEVER

COLOSSIANS 3:1-11

Legalism could be defined as the imposition of one's convictions upon another that does not share those convictions. Some have clung to the New Testament rejection of legalism to avoid the admonitions for believers to live in holiness. This text, written by the greatest scriptural expositor of grace in the New Testament, calls believers to live according to the principles of holiness before God. This text makes a clear distinction between behavior before redemption and behavior after one has been redeemed.

I. The Fruit (vv. 1-4)

It is a cliché but the truth is apple trees can only bear apples, not oranges or pears. The fruit in the believer's life is her or his behavior and lifestyle. The way we act is a reflection of who we are. Paul insists that since we identify with Christ, being raised in him, our thoughts and deeds should reflect that nature. Our minds should have a perspective of eternity, not immediacy. As our lives are now hidden with Christ in God, we can be sure he will take care of the future. It is unthinkable to believe that we can so closely identify with Christ, who is our life, and not have a nature change that transforms our thinking and our behavior. It is not human evaluation of hypocrisy that we should fear, it is the evaluation of the sovereign God who looks for branches bearing fruit as the vine (cf. John 15:1-8).

II. The New Nature (vv. 5-11)

Believers are to put to death those things in their lives that belong to their earthly nature. To do this we must move beyond "denial," that is, denial that we have any earthly nature. It may make some uncomfortable today to read Paul's list of vices to be put to death, but it was not more uncomfortable for the believers at Colossae. The earthly nature includes sexual immorality, impurity, lust, evil desires, and greed (defined as idolatry). These sins are softened by societies that demand freedom from all boundaries of behavior. Carnal society rationalizes such matters, pointing to universality of such behavioral tendencies. The next move is to vilify those who hold to standards of conduct. All this strategy may work in easing the dysfunctional conscience of modern society, but it does nothing in regard to the demands of God's Word relating to the behavior of Christian believers.

As unacceptable as the modern world may find this, Paul says this is the fruit of the unbeliever's life. These were parts of the lives of individuals before they found Christ, but after the transformation of Christ, believers are to rid themselves of earthly behaviors. Paul gives us a second list of behaviors to discard, including anger, rage, malice, slander, and filthy language. From outward acts, we move here to an even more defined list of matters of our speech. Even to the point that we are not to lie to each other as we now live in the new nature. We are to put on the new nature that reflects our Creator and our Redeemer.

These matters of holiness are matters of character. They influences how we relate to others. They really provide a set of tools to examine ourselves to determine if we are living in the new nature that reflects Christ or the old nature that reflects the world. We will often avoid such self-examination at all costs. But is that biblical? 1 Corinthians 13:5 exhorts us to examine (test) ourselves to see if we are in the faith. Interestingly, if we are busy looking inward and putting to death the old nature, we find little time to become judgmental toward others. When we ignore our need for self-examination, we have plenty of time to remove specks from our brothers' and sisters' eyes. (Joseph Byrd)

YOUR MONEY OR YOUR LIFE!

LUKE 12:13-21

The old Jack Benny radio program had a sketch of Jack being robbed at gunpoint. Jack Benny was reported to be the tightest man alive. In the sketch the robber says to Jack, "Hey bud, your money or your life." He got no reply. He said, "Hey, I said your money or your life." Jack replied, "Don't rush me. I'm thinking it over."

We laugh at that idea, but Jesus' parable makes us stop and think it over. The materialism of this era is well known. Many people live in order to accumulate more and more. But is it worthwhile? The parable of the rich fool makes us take a moment and reflect on the culture of consumerism.

I. Possessions Can Own Us If We Aren't Careful

Why did the farmer think he had to use his large crop for himself? Selfishness becomes a habit. We do things without even considering other ways of thinking.

A story is told of a Russian czar who came upon a lonely sentry standing at attention in a secluded corner of the palace garden.

"What are your guarding," asked the czar. "I don't know. The captain ordered me to this post," the sentry replied.

The czar called the captain. His answer: "Written regulations specify a guard was to be assigned to that area." The czar ordered a search to find out why.

The archives finally yielded the reason. Years before, Catherine the Great had planted a rose bush in that corner. She ordered a sentry to protect it for that evening.

One hundred years later, sentries were still guarding the now barren spot.

Let's not let our possessions own us without even thinking about it.

II. Sharing Our Possessions Is the Gospel Hope

Why did Jesus tell this parable? A man had asked him to tell his brother to divide the inheritance with him. Jesus did not respond directly. He simply asked who had appointed him as judge in such matters. Then he said, "Watch out! Be on your guard against all kinds of greed." Then he told the parable.

The possessive spirit of the farmer ruined him. It can ruin us, too.

ABC news presented a special on greed with reporter John Stossel. The program began with a look at the Biltmore estate in North Carolina. Stossel pointed out the house is a gargantuan— 250 rooms. Yet it was all built for just one man to live in. The dining room is as high as a five-story building. The dining table seats 64. The reporter said, "I guess when you're this rich, you make friends pretty easily. From here, you can take in the millions of dollars of art on the walls—Renoirs and Whistlers, Renaissance tapestries. Very beautiful, but isn't this greedy? Who needs a $100 million house?" ("Greed with John Stossel: Not Everyone Agrees That Greed Is Bad." Feb. 3, 1998).

But a giving spirit can be our liberation. For example, a man spoke with the Lord about heaven and hell. The Lord said to the man, "Come, I will show you hell." They entered a room where a group of people sat around a huge pot of stew. Everyone was famished—desperate and starving. Each held a spoon that reached the pot, but each spoon had a handle so much longer than each person's own arm that it could not be used to get the stew into each person's mouth. The suffering was terrible.

"Come, now I will show you heaven," the Lord said after a while. They entered another room, identical to the first—the pot of stew, the group of people, the same long-handled spoons. But there everyone was happy and well nourished.

"I don't understand," said the man. "Why are they happy here when they were miserable in the other room and everything was the same?"

The Lord smiled, "Ah, it is simple," he said. "Here they have learned to feed each other."

The old question is still real: your money or your life? Which do you choose? (Don M. Aycock)

AUGUST 12, 2001

❧

Tenth Sunday After Pentecost

Worship Theme: God's great pleasure is to give us the kingdom. Are we ready, relying on faith as our ancestors did, to let go all that holds us back from accepting the gift?

Readings: Isaiah 1:1, 10-20; Hebrews 11:1-3, 8-16; Luke 12:32-40

Call to Worship (Psalm 50:1, 3-8, 23):

Leader:	The mighty one, God the LORD, speaks and summons the earth from the rising of the sun to its setting.
People:	**Our God comes and does not keep silence, before him is a devouring fire, and a mighty tempest all around him.** **He calls to the heavens above and to the earth, that he may judge his people:** **"Gather to me my faithful ones,** **who made a covenant with me by sacrifice!"** **The heavens declare his righteousness, for God himself is judge.**
Leader:	"Hear, O my people, and I will speak, O Israel, I will testify against you. I am God, your God. Not for your sacrifices, do I rebuke you; your burnt offerings are continually before me.
People:	**"Those who bring thanksgiving as their sacrifice honor me;** **to those who go the right way** **I will show the salvation of God."**

291

Pastoral Prayer:

God of Abraham and Sarah, when you call us, we don't always know where we are going; we become like aliens in search of a homeland. Let us remember that we are your flock; let us hear Jesus' voice, saying, "Do not be afraid." When we are no longer at ease with the way things are, be for us the architect of the new city; lay the sturdy foundation; build our home where you reign that we may put our treasure and our hearts there. Your great pleasure, O God, is to give us the kingdom. Grant us grace to let go all that holds us back from coming through the door. Grant us the faith of our ancestors, who, though they were "as good as dead," opened themselves to your gift of life and became a channel of blessing for the generations. We worship you, God, with good intentions but sometimes with distracted minds. Argue with us until we come before you ready to be washed and freed for your service. Teach us to praise you by seeking justice, rescuing the oppressed, and pleading for the weak. Then you will find us dressed for action, lamps lit, prepared for the sudden coming of the Son of Man, in whose name we pray. Amen. (Blair G. Meeks)

SERMON BRIEFS

IT TAKES TWO TO TRANSFORM

ISAIAH 1:1, 10-20

Here, given expression by one of the great prophets, is a dream of life transition and change in vocation. Burnt offerings and sacrifice are no longer pleasing to God. It is as though God has undergone a remarkable "change" of God's own, from a tribal warrior deity to concerned parent, judge, and advocate, empowered and self-cleansed. And now, it is time for the people of Judah and Jerusalem to do likewise.

The people face what a number of social anthropologists have called a liminal state. That is, they stand at the threshold of something but encounter feelings of dislocation, almost like being in limbo. We live in a world of liminality, too. In fact, the only constant, other than the living and loving presence of God in the world's instability and lack of consistent reference points, is *change*. As Christians, we say, "Jesus Christ is the same yesterday, today and forever," but it doesn't mean God is by necessity static. We are the ones in need of change, not God, for God is always in the process of making and doing a new thing.

This is a step in the direction toward transformation. The traditions of the people of Judah and Jerusalem will no longer be viable, for God is demanding, indeed creating, something new. The people's spiritual life—if one can call it that, for they have lived with what William James termed in 1902 *varieties* of religious experience—is decaying, clouded with the fire and smoke of meaningless burnt offerings. Judah and Jerusalem, the crown and its jewel of the Middle East, are no more alive than Sodom and Gomorrah of ancient history.

God sits over them like a judge and advocate. God has pleaded the Almighty's case, and now desires argument from the plaintiff. But then there is quite a turn in the entire proceedings. God is in a re-creative mood, an attitude which has been from the beginning with God, and which continues even in this new millennium. And what God proclaims next in this dreamy vision of Isaiah's is astounding:

> Though your sins are like scarlet,
>   they shall be like snow;
> though they are red like crimson,
>   they shall become like wool.
> (v. 18)

God is full of forgiveness, and it is that lovingkindness that initiates the transformation of a stubborn and stiff-necked people.

But this transforming love of God is a kind of dance. It requires something of us, as well. We must be open to the winds of change as they blow from the breath of God. We must be willing to change and be obedient to God's plan of transformation. Our refusal can only lead to death and emptiness.

Traveling in France last spring, we were fascinated by how severe the vine growers and gardeners prune their vines and trees. Sycamore trees, in particular, looked like stubs on their trunks. Vines in the wine-producing regions of the Loire Valley were no longer recognizable as vines. But every year, each plant grows more foliage or grapes than the preceding span. Jesus spoke once of his being the true vine and God his Father, the vinedresser. Jesus was certainly pruned severely, nailed to a cross reserved for common criminals. But he came back with a fuller, more wholesome life than we could possibly imagine. And that new life shines in and upon us.

I sometimes wonder if the process of pruning us, of preparing us for the Kingdom is somehow therapeutic for God. Certainly God looks forward to lopping off with a vengeance the stuff that has built up in us over the years. Wouldn't it be funny to think that Wisdom popped up now and again to say, "Haven't you done enough?" or "Shouldn't you stop now?" or simply, "Stop it, stop it, stop it!" Wisdom may indeed have more sympathy for things with roots.

John Boe has friends who have a marvelous poster with a line by poet Pablo Neruda on it. The line reads: *"I'd like to do to you what Spring does to the cherry trees"* (John Boe, "A Time to Be Born" in *Life Itself* [Wilmette: Chiron Publications, 1994], p. 155).

Wouldn't you like to bloom right here where you're planted, to bud and blossom with life? Stick around. God is about to do something new with you, too. (Eric Killinger)

THE RELATIONSHIP OF FAITH

HEBREWS 11:1-3, 8-16

The starting point for human knowledge of divine actions is the act of God in Jesus. That final revelatory action is given to us in a concrete historical setting, first century of the Common Era. God, however, was active in the life of God's people long before then. One of the tasks of the early church was to rethink the story of God's acts in the life of Israel in the light of the completeness of the Word, which became flesh in Jesus.

When the writer of Hebrews imagines to the very beginning, the knowledge of the creative power of God stands as a witness to the continuity of the place of faith. We know of God's speaking the world into existence by our faith relationship with God. In the act of creation, the world of sense and sound came into being from the void, the nothing.

Faith is not a "thing" that can be possessed (or not). For someone to claim that she or he has no faith is not to have lost something but to assert a disengagement from a relationship. The claim to be a person of faith is to claim participation in a relationship. Faith is a relationship that can be understood only through experiencing it in our own lives. It is possible to observe the effect of faith in the lives of others. We can say, "Here is a person with faith in God; look at what faith did in her life."

The relationship of faith in God changes the life of the one who is in that relationship with God. Faith does not lead to good works; faith and works are inseparable. Because of the nature of God, faith in God is also hope and love.

Thus in this passage, beginning with Abraham and Sarah, there is a focus upon people of faith. They are not "examples" to illustrate a definition previously given; they are the human side of the faith relationship, a relationship that we can know only through observation of their actions.

Because of the relationship to God, initiated by God, Abraham and Sarah became risk-takers. The acts of faith (obedience) of Abraham and Sarah included their leaving home, their living as strangers in a land promised to them by God, their anticipation of the city designed and built by God, and their waiting for the coming of Isaac. Each act of obedience was at the same time an act of hope and love. At each crisis point in their lives, Abraham and Sarah had to choose between the safer probabilities and the riskier possibilities. Their story is not one of consistent faithfulness. Over and over again, Abraham and Sarah chose the probable over the possible. God did not let them "get away with it." Before their story ended, Abraham and Sarah demonstrated their grasp of how fully they were committed to their relationship of faith.

The "pay-off" for Abraham and Sarah was only partial; they lived on the land in tents, without being at home in it; the only cities they saw in the promised land belonged to others; Sarah saw only one descendant, Isaac. Yet Sarah and Abraham were people of faith.

The church to which Hebrews is written is a church that had

lost its zeal. The faith of the people had begun to waiver. "Faith" had become a way of speaking about a cluster of assertions individuals could make about events of the past. As the time interval between the historical Jesus and the present church became greater, the skepticism regarding those events and the doubts about their relevancy to the lives of the people also increased. "Church" became for them an institution.

The writer of Hebrews wanted those who read this correspondence to hear once again the stories of faith so that their faith might be strengthened. The alternation between the presentation of principles and the call to the church to live by them throughout Hebrews has the intention of spurring the church to renewal. In this regard, Hebrews is thoroughly pastoral. (Lee Gallman)

THERE'S NO NEED TO FEAR, JESUS IS NEAR!

LUKE 12:32-40

I. God's Steady Message: Do Not Be Afraid

A constant message from Jesus and angels at critical times in the lives of the believers was a simple, yet powerful one, "Do not be afraid." During the violent storm as he came to comfort them as he walked on water, Jesus calls to them with the same message, "do not be afraid." Again, as Jesus prepared his disciples for his death in John 14:1, Jesus says their hearts were not to be troubled. He knew that fear would not serve a good purpose in their lives, especially with what lay ahead in their ministry. At the empty tomb the women and the disciples heard angels share the same message. In the Upper Room, while in fear after the crucifixion and while awaiting whatever that was to follow, the risen Lord appears and shares the same message, "Do not be afraid." There is nothing too theologically profound about it. Jesus means what he says, "Do not be afraid."

Fear can ruin our attitude especially before a big undertaking or challenge, possibly destroying any hope of a positive outcome. Fear can even paralyze one's life. The patient who goes in for emergency surgery needs to hear and believe that message. A member of a church in the emergency room, already on a gurney to be taken to immediate heart surgery, told the pastor, "There's no need to fear, Jesus is here!" He had no fear for he knew the Lord was present with him during that critical time in his life. The surgery went well and the man fully recovered. Those who enter with much fear do so with a greater risk on their lives for the stress they are placing on themselves.

II. Place Your Heart on the Eternal Things

In this particular passage, the Lord is sharing with the disciples the need to be confident that God was on their side and theirs was the victory in all they had been assigned. The message was that they were now "Kingdom" residents and they should possess a "Kingdom" mind-set. Their attitude and their drive was to now set their sights on God's Realm while doing what God expected from them there and then. As radical as it sounds to hear Jesus tell his disciples to "sell their possessions, and give alms," Jesus is speaking of the way possessions sometimes possess us. For one to be committed to God and God's work, one must dispossess earthly things that can distract. Denis Waitley, noted author of leadership books, in recapping a commencement speech by actor Edward James Olmos, said, "If you chase money, it may catch you—and if it catches you, you'll forever be its slave" ("Chase Your Passion (Not Your Pension)," *Priorities*, June 1999, p. 11). Jesus knew this way back then. How wonderful for it to read, "If you chase God, God will catch you—and if God catches you, you'll forever be God's!"

III. Jesus Is Near!

Jesus promises that he will return. He does not specify the day or the hour, only that believers should be ready. In what he has already shared Jesus expects a readiness in dress, in attitude, in hope, and in action. In other words, every aspect of the believer's life should reflect a belief and a readiness for Jesus' return. Now, this is not to say that one must give up on this world and to sit and wait for the Lord's return. And God forbid those who think that we ourselves must hurry up that return. Jesus has stated there is much work to be done and it must be done, but in a manner that indicates our readiness. What's the reward? It is in what is a radical reversal of roles. Those that are ready, the Lord says, will be served by the master at the table. A great reward for faithful service! (Eradio Valverde)

AUGUST 19, 2001

❦

Eleventh Sunday After Pentecost

Worship Theme: We live in times we do not understand, yet we give our fears to God and are surrounded by that great cloud of witnesses, our parents in the faith whose story gives us courage.

Readings: Isaiah 5:1-7; Hebrews 11:29–12:2; Luke 12:49-56

Call to Worship (Psalm 80:1-2, 8-11, 14-15, 18 -19):

Leader:	Give ear, O Shepherd of Israel, you who lead Joseph like a flock! You who are enthroned upon the cherubim, shine forth. . . . Stir up your might, and come to save us!
People:	**You brought a vine out of Egypt; you drove out the nations and planted it. You cleared the ground for it; it took deep root and filled the land.**
Leader:	The mountains were covered with its shade, the mighty cedars with its branches; it sent out its branches to the sea, and its shoots to the River.
People:	**Turn again, O God of hosts; look down from heaven, and see; have regard for this vine, the stock that your right hand planted.**
Leader:	Then we will never turn back from you; give us life, and we will call on your name.
People:	**Restore us, O LORD God of hosts; let your face shine, that we may be saved.**

Pastoral Prayer:

God our hope and help, we do not dare to come alone to you; we cannot find our voice in isolation. But now we come, attended by that great cloud of witnesses, our parents in the faith whose story makes us bold. We live in times we cannot interpret; fear and chaos rule. O God, you weep for this world that proffers bloodshed though you expect justice; you hear our anguished cries though you seek our righteousness. Show us your reign of light where all else is shadows. Show us the signs of your presence where we believed we were forsaken. We pray for victims of violence, for prisoners, for the sick, for the dying, and for those who mourn. Lord in your mercy, bring your healing balm; let your face shine on us in hope; teach us to set aside every weight and look to the joy that is set before us. In the name of Jesus, the pioneer and perfecter of our faith, who endured the cross, disregarding its shame, and who sits at your right hand. Amen. (Blair G. Meeks)

SERMON BRIEFS

A SERMON IN SONG

ISAIAH 5:1-7

We often hear a sermon in a song. Sometimes we hear a song in a sermon.

I. Here Is a Familiar Picture

The vine was familiar to Israel. It was a familiar part of their landscape. You could see vineyards in most any direction. It was familiar in their history. Remember that the spies who went into Canaan came back carrying an enormous cluster of grapes. Today the symbol of the modern state of Israel is drawn from that. Their logo shows two men with a stick on their shoulders carrying one enormous cluster of grapes! It was familiar in their architecture. A great cluster of golden grapes adorned the front of the temple.

Isaiah does a superb job of taking a familiar picture and giving it a symbolic spiritual meaning. He does well what Jesus did better than anyone else—welding abstract truth to concrete image.

II. Here Is an Instructive Picture

No one would argue with the course of action the keeper of the vineyard takes. No one would have suggested a sensible alternative. He had given the vineyard every chance, every opportunity to produce. Now it must be destroyed. The lesson is so plain. God's people have been given opportunities and privileges accorded to no other nation. They should have responded with a high moral ethic characterized by justice and by righteousness. God is not unjust. God's expectation of God's people is based on their unique advantages. But they have disappointed God, and one should not be surprised if God's course of action is the same as that of the keeper of the vineyard.

III. Here Is a Picture Jesus Used

Jesus used this picture more than once. His parable of the tenants in Matthew 21:33-44 is a reflection of this picture and of this song. God tries to teach us in so many ways: in song, picture, and parable! This picture is also the background for the allegory of John chapter 15 where Jesus says, "I am the vine, you are the branches."

How skillfully Jesus used the concrete to teach the abstract, the familiar to teach the unfamiliar. How skillfully he wove together Hebrew Scripture, the scenes of daily life, and everyday common sense.

IV. Here Is a Picture Both Lovely and Ugly

We are touched by the loving care the husbandman lavishes on the vineyard. We are moved by the desolation that comes to the failed vineyard. The verses following this text repeat the word "woe" six times (verses 8, 11, 18, 20, 21, 22 NIV). The verses following *that* are a picture of judgment one does not like to view or contemplate.

301

What was a national picture in Isaiah is a personal picture in Matthew and John. We may be able to do little to bring a nation back to justice and righteousness, but we can make certain our own lives are characterized by justice and righteousness. Thomas Carlyle said that to make a better world you should make a better you. "Then," he said, " at least there will be one less rascal." (Robert C. Shannon)

REMEMBERING WHO YOU ARE

HEBREWS 11:29–12:2

One of the memories of my youth was being told, "Remember who you are." It was a comment my mother would share as I left the house to go with the guys. It was her way of saying, "Bill, remember you are a child of God and our child." It was a way of saying, "Remember to do the things that reflect all that has been shared with you." She wanted me to remember the times each day when prayers of thanks were offered to God for food; the times when the stories of the Bible were shared in ways that helped me know how God had been with people in good times and bad times: guiding, sustaining and calling them to act in responsible ways; and the times when I had come to know of the faith journeys of members in my family and extended family. "Remember who you are" was a reminder that I needed because it helped me remember that what I did was part of the faith story of our family and the ways our family was related to the greater family of all of God's people.

I am certain my mother and father knew that if I remembered these things, it would make a difference in what I did. The truth of the matter is it worked. I count this as one of the blessings that has made a significant difference in my life, even though I said many times, "I know, Mom," as I brushed it aside.

My parents were interested in my possessing a faith that was rooted in God's faithfulness to me, to us, and my response to God that reflected my acknowledgment of a responsibility for living a life worthy of God's call and claim upon my life.

The writer of Hebrews 11:29–12:2 recounts God's relationship with Moses and through Moses with the Hebrew people. The faith of his parents, his sensitivity to all that made that faith real for him, his sensitivity to what was going on with the Hebrew people, his awareness of God's call, and his response in gathering and leading the Hebrew people to and through the Red Sea provide the basis for remembering the other persons of faith recounted in this text who overcame one obstacle after another.

Faith is seen over and over as more than a belief about God. It was the confidence to act upon God's faithfulness to the people who had been called to be a special people. Seeing how those who had acted in faith in the past becomes the basis for acting now in ways that express confidence in God's faithfulness. Remembering in this way gives courage, hope, and promise.

God's faithfulness remembered calls us to take a new look at who we are in this ongoing heritage of God's people. We are persons who are in a community of believers who have acted in faith. We stand in that great tradition of people whose trust in God's faithfulness enabled them to endure and pass through the most trying circumstances: being beaten, scoffed at, tortured, imprisoned, stoned, oppressed, mistreated. In times meant to turn them away from their relationships with God, they remained faithful to God's purposes being accomplished through them. The writer of Hebrews knew these people had experienced the agony and the affirmation. They remembered God's faithfulness in the past, knew God's steadfastness in the present, and trusted in God's guidance for the future. They knew who they were and whose they were and what that meant for their future. We are called to do the same.

The writer of Hebrews, likewise, says such remembering gives us the courage to change and to get rid of all that stands in the way of our relationships with God. Clearing that which deters our faithfulness to God opens the flow of the assurance that produces endurance. The Christian has that assurance as a follower of Jesus Christ, who endured the cross so that he could be at the right hand of God forever, pleading for us with God. Remembering this, we can redouble our efforts in remaining steadfast in our relationships with God, overcoming handicaps, enduring the trying moments of life, and following where Christ takes us.

When we keep in mind God's faithfulness, we remember who

and whose we are. Such remembering is reflected in our faithful responses throughout life. (William Miller)

DID JESUS SUFFER FROM STRESS?

LUKE 12:49-56

The gospel will always be "good news" to those who receive and believe it. The message from God was a complete message of love and compassion for humanity. But what about those who couldn't care less about such a message? As difficult as it may be to believe, we live surrounded by people who would prefer their children to follow other pursuits than those of God. Two startling incidents have stayed with me these many years. While a campus minister at what is now the University of Texas-Pan American, I had a young man in a Bible class that gave his heart to the Lord. He decided to become active in our campus ministry program, but his mother would not give him permission to attend "'things of the church." He had to lie and tell her he was going to a dance in order to get her permission. While a pastor and talking with members of the pastor-parish relations committee I posed the question, "What would you tell your son or daughter if he or she felt the call into ministry?" One woman without hesitation and without thinking said, "God forbid!" It's to this environment that Jesus refers about "fire" coming to the earth, followed by "divisions." The fire is a passion of God's Holy Spirit bringing people to abundant life in Christian service. As was evidenced in Acts 2, the coming of the person of the Holy Spirit came in the form of fire. Those who received it without hesitation began to share in words immediately understood by all, the wonders of God's presence on the earth. The "baptism" to which Jesus refers is the suffering that he would undergo for the sake of the world. This was causing him great stress as it would to most humans to know that one must suffer great physical pain and endure a painful death such as that by crucifixion.

It is so ironic that the peace that Jesus brought for all would be seen as a removal of peace by some. The peace in the heart of a son or daughter answering a call into ministry causes great pain in the heart of a mother who knows, sadly, from firsthand and personal experience, just how much ministers sometimes suffer because of church members. A prominent businessman at a luncheon announcing his decision to give away a significant amount of money to his alma mater caused great division within his family, for this money was coming out of what his children believed to be their rightful inheritance. The man, once one to find great joy in drinking, had had a life-changing and life-saving experience through his faith. One of his children asked him why he was giving so much money. When he replied that it brought him great joy, the child pointedly asked why he didn't go back to drinking. The peace of a new life in Christ was the lack of peace in one who didn't understand or accept.

The bottom line is this: following Christ has never been easy. To truly believe and accept Jesus' Lordship on our lives involves a costly commitment. There is nothing inexpensive about being a disciple. For that very reason Jesus talked about the man who would build a tower must first sit and count the cost (Luke. 14:28). Jesus' further stress was with the righteous of his day. They knew they had simply lived a life of dos and don'ts and hadn't internalized the grace of God. Their attempts to be religious were just that, attempts. They had failed both God and God's people. Have we been faithful in completely accepting and living the wonderful gift of God? (Eradio Valverde)

AUGUST 26, 2001

❦

Twelfth Sunday After Pentecost

Worship Theme: Jesus kept the Sabbath as a day of praising God, freeing, healing, making whole. How can we recover the Sabbath as a day that blesses all creation?

Readings: Jeremiah 1:4-10; Hebrews 12:18-29; Luke 13:10-17

Call to Worship (Psalm 71:1-6):

Leader: In you, O LORD, I take refuge;
let me never be put to shame.
In your righteousness deliver me and rescue me;
incline your ear to me and save me.

People: **Be to me a rock of refuge,
a strong fortress, to save me,
for you are my rock and my fortress.**

Leader: Rescue me, O my God, from the hand of the wicked,
from the grasp of the unjust and cruel.

People: **For you, O LORD, are my hope,
my trust, O LORD, from my youth.
Upon you I have leaned from my birth;
it was you who took me from my mother's womb.
I will praise you without ceasing.**

Pastoral Prayer:

God of Sinai and of Zion, we come to you with reverence and awe, giving thanks and offering ourselves as an acceptable worship, acknowledging your hand in all things. We thank you for the gift of rest and for Jesus' Sabbath work of freeing, healing, making whole. Bless all creation with your Sabbath: renew the earth, refresh your people, free us from the bondage of debt, make the wounded whole. Be with our youth who wait for your call. Hear them in their uncertainty; assure them that you looked on them with compassion before they left their mothers' womb. Teach us to be your voice to the young, to find and nurture in them your gifts that they may grow strong in faith and serve you their whole life long. You are our hope, O Lord; we lean on you, for you invite us to your mountain and offer us the kingdom than cannot be shaken; in the name of Jesus. Amen. (Blair G. Meeks)

SERMON BRIEFS

A SPECIAL VOCATION

JEREMIAH 1:4-10

The most dramatic call story I have heard from a living person belongs to a guy I studied with in seminary. He said God spoke directly to him. The account goes something like this: My friend was in church one Sunday witnessing a baptism. At some point, he heard a voice, which he did not recognize right away as God's. The voice said something like, "You are mine. I have a special job for you." He stayed for a while after the service, praying. He realized God had spoken to him, and he interpreted the message as God calling him to the ministry of Word and Sacrament. No one questioned his story, because being good theologians, we realized that this was exactly what one would expect God to say, especially at a baptism. The last I heard, he had not heard an audible voice from God again. That initial experience, however, did sustain him through some difficult times.

Our text recounts the call of Jeremiah, and it naturally turns our thoughts toward God's call and our vocation. I suspect that not many of us have had an experience like Jeremiah's. My friend's story is still the best I have heard, and it seems weak next to Jeremiah's. Jeremiah was one of the great Old Testament prophets, and he has a call worthy of one. His story puts him in a league with Isaiah, who had a vision of God in the Temple, and Ezekiel, who was by the river Chebar when the heavens were opened so that he saw visions of God. If Jeremiah's call lacks anything in special effects, it makes up for it in content. Only the words at Jesus' baptism, "This is my beloved son," are stronger than those found here.

Jeremiah is told that God claimed him before he was born. "Before I formed you in the womb I knew you" (v. 5). Known before he could know, Jeremiah was consecrated as a prophet to the nations. Here we see the sovereignty of God, who knows what cannot be known and who speaks and makes it so.

We might think that would settle the matter, but Jeremiah apparently recognized the gravity of his situation. God's prophet to the nations is not necessarily a good job, and he wanted a way out if one was to be had. So Jeremiah pleads that he cannot speak well and that he is only a boy. God simply reassures Jeremiah and promises to be with him. In the final scene, the Lord reaches out and touches Jeremiah on the mouth. God has acted and settled the matter.

If you could experience something like that, would you want to? An experience like that would inspire a lot of confidence. You would be tougher than any crowd or situation you might encounter. You would also carry some pretty strong guarantees from God. On the other hand, a vocation like that tends to be all-consuming. You probably wouldn't have much of a life outside propheting. What do you think? Would you want such an experience? Consider carefully, balance the certainty you would have against the fact that people won't like you or believe you. Jeremiah is promised in verse 19, "They will fight against you; but they shall not prevail." These are his own people. What do you say?

Of course you don't have a choice. If God wants to issue you such a call, you probably won't have any more say than Jeremiah did. But don't hold your breath for anything so dramatic. We do not expect this kind of thing to happen to people, including ourselves; and yet we believe that God calls us. Is your call any less real for being less dramatic? Is your vocation unimportant because you have not been appointed over nations? Your vocation is special because it is yours. God has called you to faith and service. How will you respond? (David Mauldin)

UNSHAKEN!

HEBREWS 12:18-29

Life is filled with many moments that shock us and challenge the faith and resources of our lives: separation from those we love and count on; loss due to mobility, position, health, death, beliefs, ridicule, persecution, depleted financial resources, and so forth. Some people are so shaken by these events that they lose their bearings, and life becomes a "free-fall," just hoping to survive the "big splash." Some are shaken in such a way that they wander about trying all sorts of things to regain some normalcy in their lives. Some experience this shock and challenge to life without losing their focus. There is that "something" which bears them up, and one senses that he or she is in touch with that which keeps them unshaken in the midst of shaky surroundings.

The writer of Hebrews draws the contrast between what is temporary and can be destroyed and what lasts and is unshaken. It is the contrast between the old and the new; between the giving of the law on Mount Sinai and the new relationship with God mediated through Jesus Christ.

The old way is built on the sheer awesomeness and majesty of God. The people were so terrified of hearing God's voice for themselves that they asked Moses to go for them: God speaking and Moses responding. The emphasis of the writer is on the "otherness" of God, God's aloofness and the individual's terror before God. It made persons afraid to be open to God, and they became absorbed in the words and awe of God.

The new way is described quite differently. It is a crescendo of coming to Mount Zion with joy, all the things we can anticipate: a new creation that has none of the transitions of the life we know, with its mysteries, fear, loss, and separation; a place where the assembly of all God's people is to be found; a state of being where the awe of God as judge is met with the assurance of God's love and mercy to overcome fears; a culmination of a journey in which the goal of living the faith is affirmed; a relationship initiated by Jesus Christ who brings persons into a new state of being with God. Jesus has made the unapproachable approachable. Jesus, whose death was an expression of divine love, breaks down barriers and establishes new ways of living in his Spirit. We can be friends with God. We are not shaken.

Once again, the writer contrasts the old and the new. He draws a contrast between Moses who was the one who brought to the people the law God had given him and Jesus who was the embodiment of the Word. Jesus was God's voice and being among us. The law of Moses got persons bogged down in obeying the law to escape punishment and abandonment. Jesus is the one who brings us into relationships with God, which remain when all other things are changed. It is unshaken by the events of life.

This is the basis for affirmation in the midst of so much that would undo us in life. It gives us reason to worship God, to serve God with joy and love, and to do all we can to be open to God and grow in our relationships with God. It is a reminder that if we are true to God we gain everything, and if we forget God in life we lose everything. (William Miller)

THAT'S NOT IN THE ORDER OF WORSHIP!

LUKE 13:10-17

Some ministers would sooner die than to find themselves without an order of worship. Some congregations would find themselves lost and confused if they did not have printed in front of them the order of worship. It's incredible how most ministers will not forget to take up an offering or how a choir director will not allow the anthem to be skipped in consideration of the time. And God have mercy on those who try to bring in a last-minute change or "surprise" to the church, like an out-of-town former member who loves to sing or the great-grandbaby of the oldest member who is in town for only this Sunday and would love to have the child baptized!

What about the woman who for eighteen years has suffered an ailment that has kept her from standing straight? What does one do with such a surprise visit to the church? A woman whose walk draws the stares and glares of those who consider her a freak? It was she who interrupted the teaching of Jesus. It was the Sabbath, and Jesus was teaching. While most teachers would have considered a latecomer a terrible interruption and distraction, the Master considered it an opportunity to teach about changing hearts and attitudes about God and the worship of God. Jesus knew that in her body and in her spirit she had been a prisoner for all of those eighteen years. Everyday was a painful day of trying to live life to its fullest. Painful in body and spirit. Jesus called her over and declared her freedom from this affliction. He laid hands on her and she was able to stand up completely straight. Her response was to glorify God. God had set her free, and so God deserved her praise. Those who loved this woman would have rejoiced at this major victory in her life. But there was the leader of the synagogue who did not find a healing service listed in the order of worship for that Sabbath. Neither was his outburst, but that did not stop him from crying out with his displeasure. He tried to get the crowd to agree with him that Jesus had six days in which to heal, but he had blasphemed God by healing on the sacred day.

Jesus reminds them of how they care for their animals on the Sabbath in violation of Sabbath law. Did they consider their animals' lives more worthy of their care and attention than this woman's health? Was she not a daughter of Abraham? Was not God allowed to have a victory over Satan on the Sabbath? The crowd agreed and celebrated the victory in the body of this woman. The true question was of where in God's eyes do people rank versus traditions and laws? Had the Jews become slaves to their ritual rather than servants of God? The answer was sadly, yes. Jesus comes to remind them of the importance and value of people over empty rituals. Jesus came to show the openness of God's realm to all rather than an elite club for a select few. Who was truly "bent" in this story? Who had their eyes upward toward heaven while others watched only their feet and the ground on which they trod? One cannot help wondering if this leader of the synagogue was not the same one who when his daughter died risked all to bring her back to life. Was the lesson made complete with his daughter's death? The lesson was that sometimes God works outside rituals and traditions to bring wonderful surprises and blessings. (Eradio Valverde)

311

REFLECTIONS

❧

SEPTEMBER

Reflection Verse: "Let the words of my mouth and the medita-tion of my heart be acceptable to you, O LORD, my rock and my redeemer" (Psalm 19:14).

For many preachers all over the world, these words—with the slight twist of changing "my heart" to "our hearts"—have become a kind of weekly prayed preamble to the sermon. So these words constitute a doorway into the room of sacred speech, a doorway low enough to require the bowing of the head.

They are the final words of Psalm 19, and the whole gorgeous poem pours down into that verse like a funnel. C. S. Lewis called Psalm 19 "the greatest poem in the Psalter and one of the great-est lyrics in the world" (*Reflections on the Psalms* [New York: Harcourt, Brace, Jovanovich, 1958], p. 63). It even has a color. Psalm 19 is golden; it paints a picture of the shining sun, then the luster of fine gold, then the dripping of honey from the honey-comb.

It begins in the skies, "the heavens are telling the glory of God" (v. 1). The skies have their language for crying sanctity and splen-dor over all creation. It's mysterious language—no words per se—but even so, "their voice goes out through all the earth" (v. 4).

From the skies the psalm descends into Torah. The Word in the heavens condenses into words of sacred text. Scripture, according to Psalm 19, has powers as gleaming and warm as the sun: it revives the soul, makes wise the simple, rejoices the heart, enlightens the eyes. The ordinances of God are "more to be desired than gold . . . sweeter also than honey, and drippings of the honeycomb" (v. 10). Here the golden Word has found its thrilling way onto the tongue.

From the tongue the Word descends into the hidden places of the life. The Psalmist understands that behind the surface of a human life are unperceivable sins, roaches, and rats nesting in the woodwork. "Who can detect their errors? Clear me from hidden faults." As with the sun, from whose heat "nothing is hid," and as with the honeycomb, whose drippings fall into the dark hollow of the tree, the Word can reach and transform all secret places of the heart.

So the movement of the psalm is downward, from the skies to the book to the mouth to the heart. And the whole of it is a testament to the vast and intimate reach of Sacred Word and of its capacity to alter all in its touch.

Which brings us back to the last verse. "Let the words of my mouth and the meditation of my heart. . . ." Here, too, the movement is downward, from mouth to heart. The order may seem odd to us. I think I would have written it the other way. Don't the words of my mouth proceed from the meditations of my heart? Shouldn't my spirit be addressed before my speech? But the psalm is consistent with itself: Word and words exert enormous power over all. Our language may lead our lives.

This is sobering news for men and women whose vocation requires a frequent offering of public words concerning the sacred. Our language has more power than we may like to think. Human lives can be altered by it, for better or worse. Our own lives can be altered by it too.

Imagine Language and Experience in an ongoing dance. It's very true that sometimes Experience leads Language in the dance. Experience glides with Language in his arms and shows her what stories to tell, what lessons and feelings to express. But then Language takes Experience in her arms to lead. She whispers in his ear the name of new things to see, and until she names them, he doesn't see them. She speaks of longing for new destinations, and suddenly he wants to follow her there. She sings new music for Experience to move by.

Those who "use" language most may believe in it least. It is still epidemic in the church that preachers defile the hour of worship by tossing off careless sermons, ugly with unconsidered speech, meandering, self-serving, lazy, and dull. Don't you hope Jesus didn't have preachers on his mind when he said, "It is what comes out of a person's mouth that defiles" (Matthew 15:11); or "I tell you, on the day of judgment you will have to give account

313

for every careless word you utter" (Matthew 12:36). I would like to hope that he winked, but I'm not counting on it.

Over the course of any minister's life, there are certain recommitments to be made, sacred vows to be renewed. One such vow that may need renewing—or perhaps even taking for the first time—concerns our stewardship of speech. If words matter so much, why not make our words a worthier offering? Why not work to rid our speech of excess noise and haphazard pronouncements that say both too much and far too little of the human and the Holy? Not that we'll ever come close to getting it right. We're trying to say what can never fully be said. But humans were made to aim higher than they can hit, and we get to do this every Sunday, in public! We get to do it in behalf of people we love, and in behalf of God. We also get to offer such words in hospital rooms, funeral homes, at kitchen tables, and in our own homes. What if, in all these opportunities to speak, we proceeded as if a word could warm like the sun, could enrich like gold, could satisfy like drippings from the honeycomb?

"Let the words of my mouth and the meditation of my heart be acceptable to you, O Lord, my rock and my redeemer." I am tempted to suggest that you meditate on these things. But perhaps instead of meditating any further, we should set a good word on our tongues and taste it, sweeter than honey. You choose the word, and speak it well. (Paul D. Duke)

SEPTEMBER 2, 2001

❦

Thirteenth Sunday After Pentecost

Worship Theme: All are welcome at Jesus' table; those who come in lowliness are given the highest place, and by his grace we too open our hearts in hospitality to strangers.

Readings: Jeremiah 2:4-13; Hebrews 13:1-8, 15-16; Luke 14:1, 7-14

Call to Worship: (Psalm 81:1, 10-13, 16):

Leader: Sing aloud to God our strength;
           shout for joy to the God of Jacob.

People: **I am the LORD your God,**
           who brought you up out of the land of Egypt.
           Open your mouth wide and I will fill it.

Leader: "But my people did not listen to my voice;
           Israel would not submit to me.
           So I gave them over to their stubborn hearts, to
           follow their own counsels.

People: **O that my people would listen to me,**
           that Israel would walk in my ways!

Leader: I would feed you with the finest of the wheat,
           and with honey from the rock I would satisfy you."

People: **Sing aloud to God our strength;**
           shout for joy to the God of Jacob.

Pastoral Prayer:
    Lord our God, you are the one who brought us out of the land of bondage and led us through the forsaken country. We offer to

you our sacrifice of praise. Guide us now to the joy of your presence. Give us courage to quit our futile attempts to dig our own wells. Let us come instead to you, the source of our being, the fountain of life, the river of living water. Forgive us, God, when we shock the heavens by our disregard for the gift of your glory; guide us by your Spirit to reflect your image in lives of doing what is good and sharing what we have. We come to your table knowing that also present are those whose deepest needs alone can bring them to your mercy. Grant us your hospitality that we may touch the sick with your healing grace, pray for prisoners as though we were in prison with them, welcome strangers as we would welcome your heavenly messengers, and love each other as you first loved us. We pray in the confidence that the Lord is our helper and in the name of Jesus Christ, the same yesterday and today and forever. Amen. (Blair G. Meeks)

SERMON BRIEFS

WHERE IS THE LORD?

JEREMIAH 2:4-13

From time to time religious people need to take stock of their lives and their religious practice, lest what they do becomes a game or empty ritual. Our text reminds us to consider carefully what we are doing. Where is the Lord? And how often do we ask ourselves that question?

Last week we heard the exciting call of that great prophet Jeremiah. Today we witness the beginning of his preaching. Disaster will quickly fall upon the people, and they have no one to blame but themselves. That is the message he is taking on the road. In today's text, he wants to be clear that the destruction of the nation grows out of their idolatry. God has not abandoned them; they have abandoned God.

I am not preaching destruction. And I am not accusing anyone here of idolatry. Imperfect though we may be, we are hardly guilty of out-and-out worship of false gods. Nevertheless, this passage may help us. I doubt the people of Jeremiah's day set out to be idolaters. It seems they made a poor compromise here and there. Perhaps they grew complacent. They failed to examine themselves or to heed any warnings until it was too late. We should examine ourselves, particularly our religious practices, to see whether our zeal and sincerity are worthy of the One True God.

Twice the Lord, through Jeremiah, faults the people for not asking, "Where is the Lord?" In verse 6 the people forget to ask, and in verse 8 the priests forget. God practically says, "I was there for the asking. Why didn't you look for me?" As important as the presence of God is in the life of the believer and in the life of a faith community, we should be asking ourselves this question: Where is the Lord? Perhaps we fail to find God because we fail to seek. God can seem elusive in the modern world, but maybe our quest is simpler than we first imagined.

God also faults the people for making a bad exchange. In verse five, the ancestors went far from God and went after worthless things. In verse 11, the nation has exchanged its glory for something that does not profit. And in verse 13, God's people have forsaken God, the fountain of living water, and dug for themselves cracked cisterns that can hold no water. What they have done is not simply wrong, it is foolish. They have exchanged good for bad, something valuable for something worthless.

We know that compromise is a normal part of life. We make exchanges every day. We give a little time to make a little money. We exert ourselves in exercise for the payoff of healthy bodies. We choose one kind of song in worship over another. There is nothing wrong with any of this. We are finite creatures. Life is about give and take. Our passage merely reminds us to make wise choices. God has blessed us richly. We have tremendous opportunity. Will we exchange it for something worthwhile? Above all, God has called us by name, claimed us in the water of baptism, and made us God's own. For what could we ever exchange that and come out the better? The Christian life can be a challenge, but I wonder how much of it is simply treasuring the right things appropriately.

Finally, this scripture postulates that worshiping something worthless makes one worthless, and worshiping something futile makes one's own life futile. Might the corollary also hold true?

The worship of something meaningful makes one's life meaning-ful. The worship of the authentic God makes one's life authentic.

These things are worth considering. And we do well to ask our-selves: Where is the Lord? (David Mauldin)

LIVING OUR WORSHIP

HEBREWS 13:1-8, 15-16

Worship each Sunday can easily become an end in itself. It can be something we do because it is the good and right thing to do. As we leave, we can quickly leave behind us all the meaning, loyalty, commitment, and focus for life that has been a part of our worship.

Having completed a call for the reverence and worship of God that results in a lasting relationship with God, the writer of Hebrews turns to the very practical side of worship. We are con-fronted with a litany of very practical matters, which indicate how we live out our lives in reverence to God, who has called us into a holy relationship through Jesus Christ.

Verses 15 and 16 give us the key to understanding verses 1 through 8. In living a thankful life, we will offer to God deeds of kindness to those around us. These are the kinds of sacrifices God has created us to share because they reflect the life of the one who offered himself completely to restore our relationships with God.

Those deeds of kindness fall under the umbrella of sisterly, broth-erly love. The call in these words would have been heard by Chris-tians who were struggling with the essentials of the faith. In those days, as in our day, there were vehement discussions that erupted into discord over what their faith was, what people should believe, and how they should come to faith. It also resulted in harsh words being spoken and warnings issued; uncaring attitudes prevailed. It was essential to call persons back to a faith that was true to Jesus Christ. We know also that when attitudes become critical, filled with faultfinding, when harsh and bitter words are spoken, and there is insensitivity to one another, Christian love is destroyed.

In such times, faith without the love of Christ becomes empty and meaningless. With that umbrella thought in mind, the writer

318

of Hebrews turned to the specifics of how Christian love is expressed. There is the feeling that we are hearing again emphases that Jesus shared in the parable of the last Judgment (Matthew 25:31-46). According to the writer of Hebrews, we may do all the things that appear to be right and good, but ultimately Christian love is measured by specific attitudes and actions.

The first was hospitality. It fits with the Jewish tradition that lists those things recognized as important in passing into the world to come. It was even more important for Christians in a hostile culture. Since many Christians were slaves and had no home, and preachers and missionaries moved from one Christian community to another, it was essential to open one's home and share one's table with strangers. In so doing, the writer reminds the Christian community that you may be unaware that you are entertaining angels.

The second was remembering those in prison, those suffering from ill treatment, or those who were ill. Christians often landed in prison for their faith, for their indebtedness, or for being in the wrong place at a given time. Remembering meant staying in touch, doing what could be done to win their freedom, and praying for them as they went to their deaths. It was identifying with what was happening to a fellow Christian and bringing to him or her the presence of the community that embodies the reality of Christ's love and grace alive and well.

The third dealt with fidelity in the marriage and family relationships. Christians brought to their relationships in life purity reflective of the fidelity they were to have with God. It said to the world around them that Christians are true to the commitments they make to one another and to God.

The fourth dealt with freedom from allowing money to become a primary end in life. The pursuit of wealth was seen for what it does to the person. It blinds one to the presence and help of God, brings him or her to rely on self, numbs the desire to reach out, care for others, and live in community with one another.

The fifth dealt with initiating the faith we have come to know in Jesus Christ who "is the same yesterday, today and forever." This is especially true of all who would be leaders in the church. It is Jesus Christ who was God's living word among people. The Spirit of Christ alive in individuals enables the world to see the truth, the way, and the life that is eternal.

Worship becomes real in the actions of life, which help us see the true and living God in life. (William Miller)

"MIND YOUR MANNERS"

LUKE 14:1, 7-14

Sabbath Day hospitality was a significant part of Jewish life. Banquets and other mealtimes provided a casual atmosphere for philosophers and teachers to impart their wisdom. There was nothing unusual about Jesus being invited to a home for a meal after the weekly synagogue service. Most of the time the host was probably sincere, wanting to learn more of God's truth. Unfortunately, there were several occasions when Jesus was invited to dine only so his enemies could watch him and find something to criticize. That was precisely the case in Luke 14. According to verse 1, Jesus is invited to eat in the house of a leading Pharisee only so the guests could watch him closely and catch him violating some Sabbath rule.

However, Jesus turned the occasion into a teachable moment. The fourteenth chapter of Luke is four distinct units of material that do not depend on each other for meaning, yet the conversation occurs "around the table" and teaches us to "mind our manners." Today's text focuses only on the second and third units.

I. A Lesson for Guests (vv. 7-11)

Starting with verse 7, Jesus reverses the usual rules governing social situations. Through the parable that follows he says that humility is more important than being esteemed. When you go to a party, don't push and shove your way to the head table. Take the less prestigious seat and let your host elevate you.

Jesus' lesson to guests can easily be wasted. The human ego is quite clever and capable of converting the instruction about humility into a new strategy for self-exaltation. Jesus does not offer a divinely approved way for an individual to get what he or she wants. Taking the low seat because one is humble is one thing; taking the low seat as a way to move up is another. Jesus was not giving the disciples a "gimmick" that guaranteed promotion. The entire lesson becomes a cartoon if there is a mad, competitive rush for the lowest place, with ears bent toward the host, waiting for the call to ascend.

Albert Einstein said, "try not to become a man of success, but try to become a man of value." Humility is a fundamental grace and value in the Christian, yet it is elusive. If you know you have it, you have lost it!

II. A Lesson for Hosts (vv. 12-14)

Jesus turns his attention to the hosts in verse 12. He suggests we invite those people to our parties who are unable to invite us back. There is to be no thought of reciprocity. The usual law of life is to use our invitations and our social clout to acquire friends and prestige. We want to put in our debt those who can enhance our social and business status.

The second lesson warns against generosity and gifts with strings attached. Since God is host of us all, we as hosts should behave as guests, making no claims, setting no conditions, and expecting nothing in return. The church is constitutionally committed to the care of the poor and the disabled (verse 13). Jesus was not calling on Christians to provide for the needs of the poor and the disabled; he simply says, "Invite them to dinner." This is the New Testament understanding of hospitality. The word "hospitality" literally means, "love of a stranger." Christian hospitality is more than having each other over on Friday evenings. It involves welcoming those who are in no position to host us in return. The text doesn't speak of sending food to anyone. The text speaks of host and guest sitting down at the table together. The clear sign of genuine acceptance, of recognizing one another as equals, of cementing fellowship, is breaking bread together.

In Luke 14:7-14, Jesus reminds those who gather at the table of the Lord to operate under a different set of guidelines than those that motivate the world. In the church, in our meals, and in all our meetings, the first are to be last and the last first, and the lowest and the least are treated as the greatest and the highest. (Bob Buchanan)

SEPTEMBER 9, 2001

❦

Fourteenth Sunday After Pentecost

Worship Theme: God the potter takes us up and remolds us into a new image, asking us to love the newly created family of God that includes strangers and the forsaken ones.

Readings: Jeremiah 18:1-11; Philemon 1-21; Luke 14:25-33

Call to Worship (Psalm 139:1-4, 13-14, 17-18):

Leader: O LORD, you have searched me and known me.
You know when I sit down and when I rise up;
you discern my thoughts from far away

People: **You search out my path and my lying down,
and are acquainted with all my ways.
Even before a word is on my tongue,
O LORD, you know it completely.**

Leader: For it was you who formed my inward parts;
you knit me together in my mother's womb.
I praise you, for I am fearfully and wonderfully made.
Wonderful are your works; I know that very well.

People: **How weighty to me are your thoughts, O God!
How vast is the sum of them!
I try to count them—they are more than the sand;
I come to the end—I am still with you.**

Pastoral Prayer:
   God, you are a potter of artistry and persistence; we are astonished at your willingness to take us up again and make us new.

Smooth the muddled clay of our lives and shape us till we reveal our Maker's beauty. We want to follow you unconditionally, God, but we confess your words are hard for us. You encourage us to "build and plant," but you warn that you are ready to "pluck up and break down." You invite us to be your children, but you tell us to love our family only by loving your kingdom first. Show us how to be disciples, to carry your cross, to finish what we start, to give up all that holds us back. Recast us in your new mold of freedom so that we are no longer slaves to constraints against our calling but unloosed for service in your name. Give us grace to love the new family you create of all who are lonely and forgotten that we may embrace with them once more those we hold so dear. Send us now, empowered by the joy and encouragement we receive from each other, to share the faith and do the good that we can do for Christ, in whose name we pray. Amen. (Blair G. Meeks)

SERMON BRIEFS

STARTING FROM SCRATCH?

JEREMIAH 18:1-11

The image of God as potter is one of the most familiar images in all of scripture and one of central importance to the prophet Jeremiah. Part of the power in this image lies in its simplicity and straightforwardness. However, the reader who pays close attention to this passage will not find easy comfort in the image of God as potter. Rather than seeing God as the gentle artisan who simply creates beautiful pottery, here we see God struggling to make something useful out of clay that is not always malleable. Jeremiah holds the knowledge of God's providence and power in tension with human choice and freedom.

At the potter's house, Jeremiah sees acted out before him a picture of Israel's relationship with Yahweh—"the vessel he was making of clay was spoiled in the potter's hand, and he reworked it into another vessel, as seemed good to him" (v. 4). The word of the Lord speaks, asking "Can I not do with you, O house of

Israel, just as this potter has done?" (v. 6). The answer, of course, is "yes," the Lord as sovereign creator can do as the Creator pleases with the nation, even if it means starting from scratch.

The problem with this image however, is that it leaves the prophet struggling with the role of humanity within the will of God. Is there no hope for a disobedient nation? Are we simply held captive at the whim of a capricious God? Is the final shape we take the result of predestination? The answer is "no," for even in God's sovereignty, there is room for human response. Yahweh says that "If that nation, concerning which I have spoken, turns from its evil, I will change my mind about the disaster that I intended to bring on it" (v. 8).

The call is for the people of God to turn from their sinfulness and seek once again to be obedient to God's will. This image of turning is central within the passage, especially in verses 8 and 11, as seen by the usage of the verb *shub,* to turn. One scholar notes that "its central core meaning is having moved in a particular direction, to move thereupon in the opposite direction, the implication being (unless there is evidence to the contrary) that one will arrive again at the initial point of departure — hence to return, to come all the way back to the place or person one has left" (*The Broadman Bible Commentary,* [Atlanta: John Knox Press, 1988] Volume 6, p. 11).

God the potter is all powerful *as well as* all loving. Even in this oracle of judgment, there is a word of hope. God the potter wills the very best for the nations that seek God's face and listen to God's voice. Jeremiah calls the people to return to Yahweh. He encourages them to be the kind of clay that is soft and pliable in the hands of the master, and that word sounds through *our* lives even today. What kind of clay will the divine potter find in the stuff of our lives? Are our lives ready to be shaped by the Spirit, or are they rocky and hard, filled with lumps and grit? Can we truly begin again with a clean heart that is open to God? Can we turn back towards God and listen anew for God's voice? As R. E. Clements writes, "divine justice does not exclude the possibility of human repentance. Rather it demands and expects it!" (*Interpretation: A Bible Commentary for Teaching and Preaching, Jeremiah,* [Louisville: John Knox Press, 1999] p. 113). We can, and indeed, must start from scratch. (Wendy Joyner)

FREEDOM THROUGH CHRIST

PHILEMON 1-21

Onesimus, the runaway slave was, like Paul, a prisoner of Jesus Christ. He came to the realization that in order to be a slave of Christ, he would also have to submit again to the yoke of slavery. We are familiar with the defiant songs of freedom coming from our own history of enslavement of other humans:

"Oh, freedom; Oh, freedom, Oh, freedom all over me. . . . An' befo' I'd be a slave, I'll be buried in my grave, An' go home to my Lord an' be free."

No one has authority to call for the death to self that Onesimus was asked to accept. Aristotle had said that some people are born to be slaves. Even if one accepts that rather dubious declaration, Onesimus was not born to be a slave. He had escaped the clutches of slavery. How could Paul ever ask such a sacrifice from an escaped slave?

From Paul, Onesimus learned about the Savior who called upon his followers to deny self and take up the cross. He heard Paul speak about the mind of Christ who did not hold on to the basic expectations of "the pursuit of happiness" but "humbled himself and became obedient unto death, even death on the cross." Onesimus may have come to accept a very different future than the one he had envisioned as he escaped Philemon. Paul wrote in 1 Corinthians 9:19, "For though I am free with respect to all, I have made myself a slave to all, so that I might win more of them." That which Paul proclaimed in respect to the Torah, Onesimus understood as the path before him. If this is so, the letter to Philemon becomes a rich exploration of how the people of the early church told the story of Jesus as if it were their own story and their own story as if it were the story of Jesus.

In this letter, Paul reminded Philemon his own debt to Paul who had evangelized him. This was not a reminder intended to "guilt" Philemon into an action that Philemon did not want to take. He wrote to place the personal request for Onesimus in the context of relationships that included Paul, Onesimus, Philemon, and the Savior. In the context of these relationships, Paul was giving Philemon an opportunity of grace.

The nature of the debt is closely tied to the acceptance of slavery. Paul knew himself to be a slave to Christ. He reminded Philemon that he too was in bondage to Christ. He then laid before him a fellow slave who had become a Christian brother. Paul pleaded for the very minimum response to the new situation of Onesimus. Rather than trying to even things up with Onesimus, Philemon was asked to let Paul be the one upon whom the debt would fall.

As in so many issues faced by the pioneer Christians, Paul did not directly counter the systemic evil of his day. There is no impassioned plea against the institution of slavery. The gospel asserted the principle expressed in Galatians 3:28. Paul believed that a person was first of all a Christian, and as a Christian that person had full freedom. To one who was surrendered to Christ, the place of slavery could be chosen as an expression of the love and submission to Christ.

We have no indication from the letter what response Philemon made to Paul's request. However, we know from the writings of Ignatius that right after the turn of the first century, the Bishop of Ephesus was a man named Onesimus. Ignatius quotes and parallels the words of the letter to Philemon in his letter to this bishop. It is hard to escape the conclusion that Paul's plea for the new relationship between Philemon and Onesimus had its desired effect. Onesimus was not only received in Colossae with regard for Paul, but he was sent back to Paul in Ephesus where his association with Paul resulted in his being chosen, after the Apostle's death, to lead the church. Who better to be the servant of the Lord and an example to the believers than one who had denied himself, taken up the cross, and followed Jesus? (Lee Gallman)

"WHO SWITCHED THE PRICE TAGS?"

LUKE 14:25-33

October 30 had special significance for Anthony Campolo when he was a boy. The night before Halloween was designated as Mischief Night. On that night, the adults of his neighborhood braced themselves for an assortment of pranks at the hands of the younger generation. They soaped windows and let air out of tires—all the typical and annoying mischief an adolescent mind could conjure up.

One year, Anthony and his best friend devised what they thought was a brilliant and creative plan for mischief. They decided to break into the basement of the local five-and-dime store. They did not plan to rob the place. Sunday school boys would never do that sort of thing. As far as the owner of the store was concerned, they planned to do something far worse. Their plan was to get into the five-and-dime store and change the price tags on some of the merchandise.

They imagined what it would be like the next morning when people came into the store and discovered that radios were selling for a quarter and bobby pins were priced at five dollars each. They wondered what it would be like in that store when nobody could figure out what the prices of things really should be.

In *The New Interpreter's Bible* commentary on the Gospel of Luke, Alan Culpepper writes, "some churches, preacher and television programs present the gospel as though they were selling a used car." No money down! Attractive terms! Low, low monthly payments! "they make it sound as easy as possible, as though no real commitment were required."

In Luke 14, large crowds of people were traveling with Jesus. Jesus turns to them and says that he wants followers, "disciples," who are willing to count the cost and pay full price in following him.

I. A Hard and Difficult Saying

Verse 26 is one of the hard sayings of the New Testament. It is difficult to understand, and it is even more difficult to practice. "Whoever comes to me and does not hate father and mother, wife and children, brothers and sisters, yes, and even life itself, cannot be my disciple."

"To hate" is a Semitic expression meaning to turn away from, to detach oneself from. What Jesus demands of disciples is that in the network of many loyalties in which all of us live, the claim of

Christ and the gospel not only take precedence, but redefines all other relationships.

Jesus adds in verse 27, "Whoever does not carry the cross and follow me cannot be my disciple." What does it mean to "carry the cross"? It means daily identification with Christ in shame, suffering, and surrender to God's will. It means death to self, to our own plans and ambitions, and a willingness to serve as God directs. A "cross" is something we willingly accept from God as part of God's will for our lives.

II. Two Illustrations

Jesus knew that the disciples would have a difficult time comprehending this hard saying. Therefore, in verses 28-32, he tells two short stories to illustrate his single point.

The first story is about a man who counts the cost of construction before building a tower. By his careful, preconstruction calculations, the man avoids littering the landscape with an unfinished tower and the harassment of his neighbors who would say, "this fellow began to build and was not able to finish."

The second story is about a king who considers going to war with ten thousand soldiers against an opponent with twenty thousand. If he is confident of a victory, he goes to war. If he realizes he cannot win the war, he seeks the alternative and "sends a delegation and asks for the terms of peace" (v. 31).

Jesus used these two examples to ask the prospective disciples, "Are you sure you wish to follow me? Is the price more than you are willing to pay?" The crowd was eager to follow, but Jesus invites them to think about what they are doing and decide if they are willing to stay with him all the way. (Bob Buchanan)

SEPTEMBER 16, 2001

❦

Fifteenth Sunday After Pentecost

Worship Theme: God never ceases looking for those who are lost and hurting, forgotten and alone. We are asked to be faithful to the task of bringing the lost home to God's welcome.

Readings: Jeremiah 4:11-12, 22-28; 1 Timothy 1:12-17; Luke 15:1-10

Call to Worship (Psalm 14:1-2, 3-7):

Leader:	Fools say in their hearts, "There is no God." They are corrupt, they do abominable deeds; there is no one who does good.
People:	**The LORD looks down from heaven on humankind to see if there are any who are wise, who seek after God.**
Leader:	Have they no knowledge, all the evildoers who eat up my people as they eat bread, and do not call upon the LORD?
People:	**There they shall be in great terror, for God is with the company of the righteous.**
Leader:	You would confound the plans of the poor, but the LORD is their refuge.
People:	**O that deliverance for Israel would come from Zion! When the LORD restores the fortunes of his people, Jacob will rejoice; Israel will be glad.**

Pastoral Prayer:

Creator God, you have entrusted the earth and air, sea and sky, to our keeping, but our carelessness and greed belie our steward-ship. The mountains quake, and the earth mourns. The whole creation awaits the glory of your deliverance from bondage and decay. Open our hearts to the freshness of your Spirit and the overflowing of your grace and love in Christ Jesus. Strengthen our resolve to work for the renewal of the earth and the restora-tion of those who do not know your care. Encourage us with what we know is sure and worthy: Christ Jesus came into the world to save. You send us to seek those who are lost and hurting, those who are forgotten and alone, those who hunger and thirst for your justice. Keep us faithful to the task that we may join the angels of God rejoicing at the feast of freedom. To the King of the ages, the only God, be honor and glory, forever and ever. Amen. (Blair G. Meeks)

SERMON BRIEFS

UNCREATING THE WORLD

JEREMIAH 4:11-12, 22-28

In the summer of 1979, decades after he had been freed from a Nazi concentration camp, Elie Wiesel returned to one. Stand-ing in the silence of Birkenau, he recalled the imagery of Jere-miah 4:23-28, and he remembered that in the smoke-filled skies above the death camps, there were no birds. They had fled the holocaust.

In this passage, the prophet foresees the destruction of Jerusalem in 587 B.C. Like the suffocating desert wind—the sirocco—which brought wilting heat to Palestine, the wind of God's judgment was going to bring about a similar suffocation of life among both people and land. A holocaust was coming. Read Lamentation 4 for details.

A number of scholars note how deliberately the language of this text echoes the creation narrative in Genesis 1. The image Jeremiah wants his readers to visualize is of the cosmos prior to

God's creative act. We recoil at such a vision. We cringe that our God could ever promise such devastation. Having ourselves witnessed the ravaged landscapes and decimated humanity of Eastern Europe in the 1940s, Southeast Asia in the 1960s, and Somalia, Bosnia, and Kosovo in the 1990s. We ask, What does it mean for God to turn away from God's own people? What could possibly justify such suffering and loss?

The contours of this entire passage suggest that the responsibility for Jerusalem's inevitable calamity falls not only to the Lord's "fierce anger" (v. 26), but the people also play a part. According to Jeremiah, their evil has taken up lodging in them (v. 14). In verse 22, according to God's indictment, God's children "are foolish" and "have no understanding. . . . They are skilled in doing evil." Commentator Mary Donovan Turner, in *The Story-teller's Companion to the Bible* concurs: "By their actions and unfaithfulness, the people of God have 'uncreated' the world" (Volume 6, Michael E. Williams, ed. [Nashville: Abingdon Press, 1996], p. 85). So we ask a second question: What does it mean for God's people to turn from God?

In 1948, not long after the Second World War had concluded, German theologian Paul Tillich agreed to the publication of a book of his sermons. The awesome truth of humanity's capability to destroy itself had been seen in the shadow of the mushroom cloud over Hiroshima. The opening sermon in Tillich's book was entitled *The Shaking of the Foundations*. One of its primary Scripture texts was Jeremiah 4:23-30. "It is hard to speak," Tillich said, "after the prophets have spoken. . . . Every word is like a hammer."

> There was a time when we could listen to such words without much feeling and without understanding. . . . There were decades and even centuries when we did not take them seriously. Those days are gone. Today we must take them seriously. For they describe with visionary power what the majority of human beings in our period have experienced, and what, perhaps in a not too distant future, all [human] kind will experience abundantly. (Paul Tillich, *The Shaking of the Foundations* [New York: Scribner's, 1948], pp. 2-3)

Tillich's words resound clearly some fifty years later. More important, consider that Tillich does not ask what it means either for God to turn away from God's people or for God's people to turn from God? Tillich deliberately avoids the inherent despair of attempting to answer either question. Instead he acknowledges that the language of the prophets which ascribed to God the power and prerogative to create and destroy is something we no longer comprehend. Yet he declares that the awful reality of our own capacity for bold creation and cruel destruction is so painfully real that our lives consist in "nothing but attempts to look away from the end!" (*The Shaking of the Foundations,* p. 11). The truth is, though, that the end will come—at God's hands or our own. So we must remember: even when we cannot find any birds on the horizon, God has promised not to "make a full end" (v. 27). God has promised to redeem and restore both creature and creation, even out of the ashes of judgment. (Mark Price)

THE FAITHFUL SAYING

1 TIMOTHY 1:12-17

Paul never gets far from a spirit of gratitude and testimony for what the Lord has done for him. This passage of scripture is a great passage of praise packaged together with the gospel. If you were writing a note to a dear friend or a group of friends, and wanted to express your gratitude, your tribute to the Lord, what would you say? Paul points out in this Scripture four things for which he offers thanksgiving to Jesus Christ.

I. He Chose Me (v. 12)

Paul never thinks he chose Jesus; it is the other way around. I never cease to be amazed at my own calling, both to salvation and to ministry as a pastor. I was a very ordinary, unpromising kid raised in a small county seat town, in a small church where I was no doubt the bane of my Sunday school teachers. But at least I never thought I chose Jesus, especially in my call to the ministry; I knew full well that he had chosen me. When we lose sight of God's calling to us in salvation, in specific forms of ministry, then we find ourselves in trouble. It is then that we tend to operate on our own strength, our own wisdom, our own pride. Let us stand amazed that he could love us and choose us, sinners condemned and unclean.

II. He Trusted Me (v. 12)

One of the great and shining truths of the gospel is that God believes in us more than we believe in God! Knowing all about them, Jesus still chose the twelve disciples. One of them betrayed him, one of them denied him with curses, and all the rest, save one, took to their heels in his hour of deepest need. But Jesus knew what he was doing. He knew what he was doing on the Damascus road when he confronted Saul and forever changed his life. Jesus forgave, redeemed, cleansed, called, and trusted Paul with the gospel. How amazing that this one who so brutally persecuted the church should be entrusted with the precious treasure of the church, the gospel. And yet Jesus has called each of us who name the name of Christian and has entrusted to us the gospel. He has entrusted to us his own reputation, for the whole world judges the gospel by the professors of it. I remember an old story about Jesus and a couple of angels looking down from the ramparts of heaven not long after the resurrection and ascension. One angel turned to Jesus and said, "Lord, it doesn't look good for the disciples. I don't know if they can successfully spread the gospel. What other plan do you have if they fail?" And Jesus is said to have replied, "I have no other plan." You and I are trusted with such a treasure!

III. He Appointed Me (v. 12)

If only we could recover a sense of being appointed in the service of the Great King! Southern Baptists have a mission training program for boys called "Royal Ambassadors." The theme song is the old hymn which affirms that "I am a stranger here, within a foreign land; my home is far away upon a golden strand; I'm here on business for my king." That's the idea; we are appointed as ambassadors for the King of all creation.

IV. He Empowered Me (v. 14)

Paul is deadly serious here as he affirms that striving would be failing, in his own strength. But in God's grace he is equipped and empowered to be an effective servant. No man or no woman is good enough, strong enough, wise enough to serve God in his or her own strength. Yet in the strength of the Lord, we go from victory to victory, in a strength and grace that is more than abundant.

V. The Gospel Condensed (v. 15)

Verse 15 is the centerpiece of the passage; the gospel condensed in weighty words. Note the *one who comes into the world*—the savior Christ Jesus. He comes *into the world*—he did not begin his existence at Bethlehem; that was merely the entrance he chose when he clothed himself in flesh and became one of us. He came into the world *to save*—to save from spiritual danger; to save us from a tragedy worse than AIDS; to save us from misery here and hereafter.

The passage speaks of the universality of sin, as Paul, the chief of sinners, confesses his sins. This summary of the gospel shows that the emphasis is on man's predicament and God's provision. It speaks of the reliability of the gospel: *It is a faithful saying*—Paul had seen the peace that the gospel brings; he had seen it in the life of the Christians he had persecuted and seen it in his own life. The gospel never fails to cleanse and bring peace to sinful men. Such a gospel is worthy of all acceptance. Acceptance by all people of all races everywhere. Such a gospel is worthy of total acceptance in the individual heart, head, and hand and throughout the wide world.

VI. A Beautiful Benediction (v. 17)

Paul soars in his benediction, and well he might, having just contemplated the glories of the gospel. But notice: *King eternal*, molding the ages of this world. *Incorruptible*, untouchable by time and sin. *Invisible*, clothed in light. *The only God!* And so he is. Amen! (Earl C. Davis)

"WHEN ONLY ONE PERSON MATTERS"

LUKE 15:1-10

In their first *Chicken Soup for the Soul* book, Jack Canfield and Mark Hansen tell the story of a man by the sea who was picking up beached starfishes one by one and throwing them back into the sea in order to save them. Even though there were more of these creatures than the man could possibly throw back into the water in time, he still believed that he was making a difference to the few that he was saving.

In Luke 15, Jesus shares three stories united by the theme of joy. Three words summarize the message of the chapter: *lost*, *found*, and *rejoice*.

The setting of the stories is mentioned in verses 1 through 2. Jesus attracted tax collectors and sinners, while the Pharisees and other religious leaders repelled them. In fact, the Pharisees and scribes criticized Jesus for welcoming sinners and sitting down at the same table to eat with them.

The first two stories, the parable of the lost sheep and lost coin, focus on God's initiative and part in salvation. The third parable, the parable of the patient father, focuses on humanity's part. It portrays God as the patient father waiting for his child to come to his or her senses and return home.

In the first parable, God is portrayed as the shepherd who seeks and gently restores the lost sheep. So strong is the love for the lost sheep that the ninety-nine are left in the wilderness while the search goes on. By leaving the ninety-nine sheep, the shepherd was not saying they were unimportant to him. The fact that the shepherd would go after one sheep is proof that each animal was dear to him.

A fourfold joy is expressed when one lost sinner comes to the Savior (vv. 5-7). There is joy in the heart of the person found. There is joy in the person who does the finding. Others join in the rejoicing of the child who once was lost. Finally, the angels in heaven rejoice. Jesus says in verse 7, "there will be more joy in heaven over one sinner who repents than over ninety-nine righteous persons who need no repentance."

Alongside the first parable that focuses on a man or shepherd,

Jesus places a story about a woman. The woman's ten silver coins represented about ten days' wages and many months of saving. Upon discovering that one of the coins is missing, the woman turns her house upside down looking until she finds the lost coin.

The parable of the lost sheep and lost coin demonstrate that every person matters to God and that God will go out of the way to reach one person. (Bob Buchanan)

SEPTEMBER 23, 2001

✤

Sixteenth Sunday After Pentecost

Worship Theme: When our culture seems to admire shrewdness more than honesty and indebtedness more than steward-
ship, we need Jesus as guide and friend, leading us to serve God's
purpose.

Readings: Jeremiah 8:18–9:1; 1 Timothy 2:1-7; Luke 16:1-13

Call to Worship (Psalm 79:1, 4-5, 8-9):

Leader:	O God, the nations have come into your inheri- tance; they have defiled your holy temple; they have laid Jerusalem in ruins.
People:	**We are become a taunt to our neighbors,** **mocked and derided by those around us.** **How long, O Lord? Will you be angry for-** **ever?** **Will your jealous wrath burn like fire?**
Leader:	Do not remember against us the iniquities of our ancestors; let your compassion come speedily to meet us, for we are brought very low.
People:	**Help us, O God of our salvation,** **for the glory of your name;** **deliver us, and forgive our sins,** **for your name's sake.**

Pastoral Prayer:
 God our Savior, your Son Jesus Christ, the one mediator
between God and humankind, gave himself that all might be

saved. Make us heralds of your truth and doers of your word that your steadfast love may be known throughout the earth. We find ourselves, O God, in a strange land, where shrewdness is admired more than honesty and indebtedness is a way of life. Be our guide, our source, and our friend. Teach us to serve your purposes and to order our lives faithfully that we may honor you. We pray for political leaders, for economists, for bank officers, that they may be friends to the poor; free us all from bondage to the master of wealth. In the midst of grief and pain, O God, we are surprised by your tears; we are confounded by your refusal to leave your hurting people. When no one can ease the distress, you are our balm. When all around us is a wasteland, you are our spring of water, our fountain of tears. Be near to us now and forever, through Christ our Lord. Amen. (Blair G. Meeks)

SERMON BRIEFS

CALLED TO EMPATHY

JEREMIAH 8:18–9:1

A man in our congregation named Charles was often quoted as saying that his favorite Bible verse was found in this passage from the prophet Jeremiah, "The harvest is past, the summer is ended, and we are not saved." I never really understood this as a favorite Bible verse. Was Charles saying this tongue in cheek, or did he truly find deep meaning and truth in these words of Jeremiah? These words are not the uplifting promises of hope and consolation that we long to hear, but perhaps these words indeed deserve a central place in the church's proclamation.

The prophet Jeremiah existed in a time of great tumult and transition. The nation of Judah was undergoing a period of political and social decline. Leaders were weak and ineffective, and all around him, the prophet saw people who were not living up to the covenant with Yahweh. The Lord calls Jeremiah to preach repentance to these sinful people, but their resistance leads toward their eventual destruction. Chapter 8 describes an upcoming military invasion from an enemy in the North. Soon, the people will undergo intense suffering and tragedy.

The amazing thing about this prophet is that he does not revel in being right. He does not stand aside and preach condemnation to the masses. At the close of chapter 8, we find him weeping inconsolably for the brokenness of his people. He knows that the judgment of Yahweh is now unavoidable, that the time for amending their ways is past, and all of this causes him deep pain.

As I hear the wailings of Jeremiah, I marvel at the power of true empathy. It is his true love and concern for the people of Judah that allows Jeremiah to anticipate, identify with, and experience the nation's suffering. As he contemplates their disobedience and its consequences, he is moved to be literally "sick at heart" over what results in the lives of his brothers and sisters. The time for hope is gone, and all that is left is mourning. The taste of salty tears, the sound of silent wonder, and the aching in the pit of Jeremiah's stomach are his only companions.

I wonder about the place of true empathy in the life of the church today. How often do we find ourselves truly mourning for the sinfulness and brokenness of our world? Do we hear the cry of our people? Do we look around and fear for the end of the summer, when all humanity will reap the harvest of our actions? I think this is the beginning point of all authentic ministry. True empathy is a vital part of our call to be the church in the world. It is only when we see the needs of the world around us that we can be moved by God to take action. We are all called to be "weeping prophets."

Perhaps we would be more faithful if we intentionally spent time in the valleys of despair. Can we risk to care as much as Jeremiah cared for his people? Are we truly sorry for a world that is marred by violence and hatred? Do we ache over the multitude of people who do not have even their basic needs met? What about our neighborhoods, inhabited with people who are lost, alone, and afraid? What about the people who need the love, grace, and peace of God in their lives? Perhaps we are too slow to mourn and too quick to sing "There Is A Balm in Gilead." Perhaps Charles was right. As the writer in Ecclesiastes says, "there is a time to weep." (Wendy Joyner)

THE PLACE OF PRAYER IN THE CHURCH

1 TIMOTHY 2:1-8

This scripture raises an interesting question: *Should the Christians of Germany have prayed for Hitler?* A study of Paul's admonition in these verses shows that it is the Christian's responsibility to pray, not for Hitler's goals and plans, but for a just government with peace and integrity. Aside from that sort of question, this entire chapter gives directions concerning public worship. It is assumed that every church will emphasize pubic worship. It has been often said that only true worship of Almighty God will save our world. Notice some aspects of public prayer touched upon in these verses.

I. All Kinds of Prayers (v. 1)

Paul tumbles all kinds of prayer out in this verse. *Supplications:* a request springing from a sense of need. People with a deep sense of need make supplications. *Prayers:* a more general term, directed toward God only. *Petitions:* We are to offer intercession for others in need as well as for our own needs. *Thanksgiving:* prayers of joy, praise, gratitude for what God has done or is doing in our life and the lives of others for whom we pray. As we think about these different aspects of prayer, one wonders if there is adequate prayer in most worship services.

II. Pray for the King (vv. 2-3)

Peter reminds us to "fear God, honor the king." Here Paul tells us to pray for the emperor. None of the emperors were Christian, and some, like Nero, persecuted the young church. We are to pray for our rulers because good government is necessary for a quiet, peaceful life. To pray for God's influence on the ruler is vastly different from praying for the will and desire of the emperor to be done, or that God will bless the schemes of the ruler. Paul's very admonition underlines the power of prayer, the transforming power of prayer. Our prayers for governing rulers is not based upon their worthiness, but on God's command for us to pray.

III. One God, One Way (vv. 4-6)

God wants all people to be saved, and somehow, beyond our knowing, our prayers are used in the economy of God to call, to transform, to change people and circumstances. And regardless of what either we or those for whom we pray may think, there is but one God. And that God created all that is, and desires that all people turn from their rebellion and be saved. The only means of salvation is through faith in Jesus Christ, the crucified one. No doubt all this sounded like the ravings of a mad man if any of the local rulers or emperors ever read it! Perhaps that is why Paul, in verse 7, is compelled to affirm he is telling the truth. After all, his gospel of salvation for all the world being possible through, and only through, a young Jew executed under Pontius Pilate and risen from the dead, must have seemed ridiculous in the Roman world. But it was true, and still is true, these two thousand years later.

IV. All People Everywhere (v. 8)

Paul's dream, his hope, his admonition is that in every church, in every circumstance, in every place God-fearing people would be lifting holy and committed hands, without anger or dissention.

There is in these words a good check of our ethics as Christians. It is hard to honestly pray about a deal in which you plan to take advantage of a customer; it is hard to lift holy hands in prayer if your marriage is being betrayed; it is hard to pray in the midst of a temper outburst. Perhaps a word about *lifting holy hands* would be in order. The Jewish idea as the hands are lifted in prayer was that of offering one's self; of asking with hands upturned to show there is no evil within; of asking with empty hands to be filled with the blessings of God. We have added to these elements that of reverence and submission. However we go about prayer, the emphasis is on *holy,* not on *hands.* God cannot put gifts in either dirty hands or heart. Perhaps a good commentary on living a quiet and peaceful life and lifting holy hands in prayer is found in Coleridge's *Ancient Mariner:*

341

He prayeth best, who loveth best
All things both great and small;
For the dear God who loveth us,
He made and loveth all.
                              (Earl C. Davis)

IF YOU HAPPEN TO BE RICH

LUKE 16:1-13

What do you make of a parable in which Jesus seems to be giving us a dishonest businessman as an example to follow? Fred Craddock (in *Interpretation: A Bible Commentary for Teaching and Preaching Luke* [Louisville: John Knox Press, 1990] pp. 188-92), tells us that this is one of two parables on money and the danger of having it to be found in Luke 16. Craddock says that the function of this first parable is to say that, if a person has money, that person can do good things with it. The second, the parable of the rich man and Lazarus, tells us that if we don't choose to do good things with what we have, we will be sorry.

I. If You Happen to Be Rich

There is a world of business and of trade, of material wealth, and of political power. There needs to be that "world" because, when it is functioning at its best, it serves us all. But that world seems to make certain promises and to impose certain expectations upon its participants. Most participants choose to let those expectations and promises govern their lives. The problem is that those expectations are often, and unnecessarily, at odds with the expectations and promises of God.

A person who is a part of that world can choose to live a life shaped by the expectations and promises of God, but it is not easy. The person who tries it is likely to find himself or herself living like an alien in a foreign land—or like an executive who has put himself at odds with his employer.

II. Choose Whom You Will Serve.

There have always been those who were parts of the world of wealth and power who used their advantages to serve the purposes of God. Wealthy benefactors have used their wealth to do good for many people. Oscar Schindler, (the historical figure upon which the movie *Schindler's List* was based), used his position to liberate some who were being oppressed and killed by the very power structure of which he was a part. How can we do that?

First, it is important to remember that it is really God and not the world of business and wealth that has given you your life and your identity. Even the wealth and advantage that you have comes from God.

Then make the necessary decision. No one can serve two masters. If you serve wealth, you will put yourself at odds with God. If you serve God, you may help to redeem the world of business and wealth and power and make it serve the purpose for which it was created.

III. Living in Two Worlds

Let me share a personal reflection. Most ministers get to do an apprenticeship in poverty during the early years of their careers. My family was just coming out of that experience and beginning to enjoy a better income when the world food crisis of the seventies happened. I saw the faces of starving children in Asia and Africa looking out at me from the covers of news magazines. I knew that something was being required of me, but what?

What should an affluent person do in a world full of hunger? Should he blame the poor for their poverty? That doesn't make sense. Should he feel guilty and not allow himself to use or enjoy what good fortune has given? That would be to waste precious things. Should he organize some grand scheme of pooling all of the world's wealth and dividing it equally? Certainly, some sharing is called for but, ultimately, pooling and dividing does not seem practical.

I finally decided that the best thing I could do was to accept what had been put at my disposal humbly and gratefully, use it to make myself a whole and effective person, and then give myself and my resources to the service of God who loves all people.

If it has been given to you to be wealthy, use your wealth for good purpose. If you do, you will find that you have made a friend of the one who can really bless you. (Jim Killen)

SEPTEMBER 30, 2001

❧

Seventeenth Sunday After Pentecost

Worship Theme: God renews our hope and assures us of our future in a land that has been redeemed.

Readings: Jeremiah 32:1-3*a*, 6-15; 1 Timothy 6:6-19; Luke 16:19-31

Call to Worship (Psalm 91:1-6, 14-16):

Leader: You who live in the shelter of the Most High,
who abide in the shadow of the Almighty,
will say to the LORD, "My refuge and my fortress;
my God, in whom I trust."

People: **God will deliver you from the snare of the fowler
and from the deadly pestilence;**

Leader: he will cover you with his pinions;
and under his wings you will find refuge;
his faithfulness is a shield and buckler.

People: **You will not fear the terror of the night,
or the arrow that flies by day,
or the pestilence that stalks in darkness,
or the destruction that wastes at noonday.**

Leader: Those who love me, I will deliver;
I will protect those who know my name.
When they call to me, I will answer them;

People: **I will be with them in trouble,
I will rescue them and honor them.
With long life I will satisfy them,
and show them my salvation.**

Pastoral Prayer:

God our only sovereign, you dwell in unapproachable light and yet you come to us with your mercy. Renew our hope, and assure us of our future in a land that you have redeemed. We praise you, Giver of life, for the joy that comes from serving you with righteousness and love, faith and gentleness. We thank you for the food we eat and the clothes we wear, for the contentment of living in your care. You call us to eternal life, and yet we confess that we are sometimes trapped by our eagerness to acquire goods we do not need. Forgive us when we let the comforts of prosperity prevent us from seeing the disparities of wealth and poverty. You bring down the powerful, O God, and lift up the lowly: Look with favor on your servants and remind us of the need for your grace. Instruct us by your prophets; open our eyes to the needy at our gates. Encourage us to grant the poor a place in our community as you have given them a place at your table. We pray in the name of our Lord Jesus Christ, to whom belongs honor and eternal dominion. Amen. (Blair G. Meeks)

SERMON BRIEFS

FOR SALE: LAND IN ANATHOTH

JEREMIAH 32:1-3*a*, 6-15

This is a curious chapter. Even a little strange. For it records how Jeremiah one day goes out and buys a field. So what?

He must have been just a little crazy. Apparently he did not even believe all the dire things he said were about to happen to Judah—that the stock market was about to crash, real estate was about to bottom out.—for the Babylonians were coming! Indeed, they were already at the city gates! There goes the neighborhood! But Jeremiah goes out and buys a field. Why?

It's a field that had been in his own family, land near his hometown of Anathoth (a few miles north of Jerusalem). Perhaps he was the oldest and had first rights to redeem it. So maybe he bought it for sentimental reasons—family and all. But the Babylonians were coming and they were not family. They would not recognize any deeds or any family sentiment. But Jeremiah buys the field anyway. Why?

Maybe as an investment, you say. Real estate is a good investment usually. But the Babylonians were coming and soon they would be the landlords.

Poor old Jeremiah. He should have stuck with preaching and being a prophet. He was no businessman. What could he have been thinking? Jeremiah was indeed interested in making an investment—an investment in the future. But it was not money he invested but something far more valuable—his faith. He was investing not in land or silver or gold, but in the Creator of all land and everything, the one who held his future and that of his people.

Jeremiah buys a field as an act of faith and an example of hope for the people who were about to lose everything, even their freedom. All that they had depended upon to give them security was about to be taken from them. Even before that happens, Jeremiah buys a field to show them his trust in God as the one who is their true source of security. Though he did not live to see it, his words came true for the day would come when "houses, fields, and vineyard would be bought and sold again" (v. 15, adapted).

How this message must have brought comfort to the people in the days and years ahead, as they said to one another, "Remember, Jeremiah bought a field in Anathoth."

Such faith in the midst of such pain and seemingly hopeless situation is astounding. It is a message I need to hear constantly. Perhaps you do too.

A friend of mine knew someone whose wife was diagnosed with cancer. It was a hard time for them—surgery, chemotherapy, anger, and depression.

Some people thought they were crazy when in the midst of all of that they went out and bought a piece of land. They called it "Anathoth."

Jeremiah buys a field when the Babylonians are at the gate. This couple buys land in spite of the sound of illness and death knocking at their door. Money and land have little to do with it, really. They are staking their claim not on land but on God. They make a deposit of faith in God's bank of goodness and love and faithfulness, no matter the circumstances.

This is a deal we cannot afford to pass up either. This is real estate we all must own a share of. It's on the market now. "Land for Sale in Anathoth." Cash or check not accepted or needed. Loans? None required. Just take out your trust and deposit it in God, and the deed is handed over to you. (Bass Mitchell)

FOR THE LOVE OF MONEY

I TIMOTHY 6:6-19

First Timothy ends with a money sermon. The difficult part in preaching this text is the barrier that money talk sets up within the congregation. "There goes the preacher moralizing about money again."

The writer of 1 Timothy will take whatever he needs from the existing culture to preach the gospel. So he borrows a proverb from Diogenes, "the love for money is the market place for all evil." He changes *market place* to *root* and gives the church a proverb for all times and places. When the proverb is quoted we often forget to mention that it is the love for money that is the root of all evil.

Quotes from the teachings of Jesus are seldom found in the pastoral letters, but this proverb parallels the saying, "you cannot serve God and mammon" (Matthew 6:24 RSV) The text also carries a bit of the cynic's bite when the author speaks of those who look to religion to yield big dividends (v. 5 NEB). There are indeed big dividends to be had from a faithful life, but the resources are not material. The writer takes aim at all of us who pray while keeping one eye on the latest gains in the stock market.

The writer causes us to ask the problem question of this century. "Why would we base our lives on anything as uncertain as money?" And we reply: "because money seems to make the world go round. Or at least that is the twentieth-century illusion regarding money."

A careful reading of the text reveals not so much a moralizing over money as a struggle with the powers of the age. First Timothy ends with what seems to be a restatement of the ending of the Sermon on the Mount. "Set your mind on God's kingdom and his justice before anything else, and the rest will come to you as well" (Matthew 6:33, adapted). Don't allow the love for the material to cause your life to be spiked on many thorny griefs (v. 10). The writer is trying to help us strike a balance. Can we strike a balance between the material and the spiritual? We must if we are to live and do well. We can have all things if we take a right relationship to God. If we fall in love with money it will have us in its clutches and bring us to ruin.

The writer directs us to the mature theology of Job's confession. "We brought nothing into the world, and for that matter we cannot take anything with us when we leave" (v. 7, adapted). Compare Job's confession with the saying, "The one who dies with the most toys wins."

By the time of the writing of First Timothy, the message of the gospel was being proclaimed to second and third generation Christians. This text is a call for a return to the original teachings of Jesus, which if followed will lead to a life of godly contentment marked by Paul's fruits of the spirit: *righteousness, godliness, faith, love, gentleness, and steadfastness* (v. 12). Here is the admonition that is needed for all times and places: do not allow the love for money to become the controlling factor in your life.

> Remember that when you leave this earth, you can take with you nothing that you have received—fading symbols of honor, trappings of power, but only what you have given; a full heart enriched by honest service, love, sacrifice and courage. (St. Francis of Assissi)

(William Cotton)

HOW TO GO TO HELL—AND HOW NOT TO

LUKE 16:19-31

What kind of a sin can cause a person to wind up in hell? It would have to be something that is evidence of some great basic wrong in a person's life. One that is mentioned often in the Bible is the failure to love your neighbors—especially your neighbors who are in need.

349

I. Symptoms Tell Us When There Is an Illness

What did the man in the parable do wrong? It was not just being wealthy that was his sin. Recently, there have been some theologies around that seemed to suggest that just being affluent is a sin in itself. But that can't be right.

If being rich was not the man's sin, what was? It was neglecting the needs of the poor man at his gate. He could not have done that if his life had not been put together wrongly. He could not have done that if there had been love in his heart.

II. There Are Poor People at Our Gates

By now, we have all heard the statistics that indicate that the gap between the fortunes of the rich and the fortunes of the poor is growing wider in our world—yes and in our country. There is evidence that the economy is working in a way that prospers the fortunate at the expense of the unfortunate. Most of us are among the fortunate. And there are some people who are terribly poor in our world.

What is the responsibility of the rich for the poor? There are many who would quickly say that the rich have no responsibility for the poor. The poor are responsible for themselves. The rich should be free to pursue their fortunes without being concerned about the poor.

According to the parable, that is not the right answer. There are lots of other passages of scripture that tell us it is not the right answer. In the parable, Abraham told Lazarus that, if his brothers would read Moses and the prophets, they would know what to do about their poor neighbors.

Evidently, that attitude can wind you up in hell. But where is that hell? It may be in the anxious, exhausting scramble after wealth that consumes some people and leaves no time or energy for living. It may be in the emptiness of having gained your goals and finding that they don't satisfy you. It may be in the addiction to upward mobility that forces us to regard "down sizing" as a threat of damnation. And it may be in the destructive civil strife and wars that can come from nations and groups exploiting one another and struggling against one another for wealth—or survival. Lots of people are suffering these kinds of hell right here in this life.

III. But What If You Don't Want to Go to Hell?

Our epistle lesson for today (1 Timothy 6:6-19) does a good job of helping us put things into perspective. It tells us that the love of money is the root of all kinds of evil and the source of lots of trouble. The wise person will organize his or her life around a relationship with God rather than around a relationship with money. If a person happens to be rich, he or she should remember to set his or her hopes on God, not upon money, and to use money to do good. Ultimately, that will lead a person into the life of love.

When you have learned to love your neighbor, you will be able to discover what to do in response to the needy who are at your gate. (Jim Killen)

REFLECTIONS

OCTOBER

Reflection Verses: "Then Moses said, 'I must turn aside and look at this great sight, and see why the bush is not burned up.' When the LORD saw that he had turned aside to see, God called to him out of the bush . . ." (Exodus 3:3-4).

Pastoring a church can be a very busy business. I don't want to encourage any whining about this, but like many other worthy vocations, the minister's job is necessarily, as they say, "time-intensive." More than this, it is unusually "interruption-intensive." On any given week, lay out your best-conceived schedule for study, worship preparation, visits, calls, counseling, programs, meetings, writing letters, and writing a sermon—but count on it falling to pieces. A "drop-in," a crisis, a conflict, a death, any number of unexpected requests for your presence and help. They all pile up and derail your agenda. Unless, of course, it's also your agenda to be the kind of human who lives and loves by being interruptible.

I often fought it when I was a pastor, fought it inwardly at least. The truth dawned slowly on me that our best chances for doing the gospel and encountering the Holy are lurking, more often than not, well off the track of our agenda.

December was my hardest month. The Christmas schedule at our place, like yours, was a killer. Extra services, sermons, programs, parties, heavy counseling, many extra visits to be made. I recall sitting at my desk on Christmas Eve morning, working on the evening sermon, and more or less panicked over the visits I still needed to make, when the phone rang—again. On the other end was a woman, a stranger to me, who said she had an elderly neighbor who was Baptist, as am I, and was unable to attend church. Her husband had dementia and had lately been cruel to her. Would I consider going to see her and taking Holy Communion?

Because it was Christmas Eve, it occurred to me that just possibly my caller had been Jesus in a clever disguise. I called the number I'd been given and spoke with the elderly woman, asking if I could come by. "That would be nice," she said; and she suggested a time when her husband would be gone. Her nurse let me in and took me back to the bedroom. There she was, ninety-one years old, beautiful, kind, and keenly intelligent. We talked for a while. She told me her life, how she had loved her years of teaching high school English, how she had loved growing up in the church, how she had gone for years to her husband's church. She had received good care there but she wasn't a member, and they had a "policy" about the Lord's Table. She had not received Communion in more than twenty years.

I asked her if I could read the Bible with her. Her face broke into radiance and she said, "Oh, yes!" I read the Christmas story from Luke, and though I'd be willing to bet she knew the story as well as I did, her face as I read was transfigured, as if hearing it for the first time. She cocked her head and sighed and nodded, and she smiled in amazement.

When at last I extended to her the tiny round tray that held the bread, she took it from my hand and raised to her lips as if to drink. Not until then did I understand that she was almost completely blind. I placed the bread to her mouth and lifted the cup to her lips, and we prayed together and we thanked God for each other and for the Christ whose hand was on us both. As I left I thought the room was trembling. I was re-created. I think perhaps that she was too.

You yourself could tell stories like that, maybe dozens of them. It's what we get to do. But have you noticed that these epiphany moments that show us what we do and prompt our deepest love for it are almost never the moments we plan? Like everyone else, we have to live by plans, goals, agendas, and scripts. But we live also by interruptions, by the unforeseen little chance that pulls on our skirts or skitters across our path. One of the great thrills of our work lies in the freedom to read the moment—not to go every direction our chain gets pulled, but to get up and improvise where we can; to make our plans but then sit loose with a sharp eye open to the opportune gospel.

It would be an interesting exercise to read through the four

Gospels with an eye to this. How many of the stories recounted there concern Jesus' response to someone who "interrupted" him? Remove those stories and there would be very little left. We have heard him say, "Follow me," and we have dutifully, gratefully thought to take our place behind him on his path. But then we notice that the way he walks is constantly leaving the path. A cry for help distracts him, and he veers off to answer; an invitation to a party is sent, and he goes off to join it; a gaggle of children shows up in the middle of a sermon, and he moves to take them in his arms. His head keeps turning, with sharp ears and keen eyes, supremely distractible. To follow him is to live in a great, improvisational freedom, and to walk in a zigzag way.

"I will turn aside to see this thing," said Moses, a good model for all those who tend a flock. The story adds a fascinating note: it was when God saw that Moses had turned aside to see that God called his name. What wouldn't you give to hear the Holy One call your name? It's possible, of course, for God to encounter us in the plans we have made and the schedules we dutifully keep. But history and experience suggest that our best chances for encountering the holy may well lie off the path of our agenda, that God loves best to call the names of those who will turn aside to see.

Maybe there's no happier or more freeing prayer we can pray than this: God, keep me interruptible. (Paul D. Duke)

OCTOBER 7, 2001

❧

Eighteenth Sunday After Pentecost

Worship Theme: We give God thanks for the faith that lives not only in our parents and grandparents, but also in our sisters and brothers throughout the world.

Readings: Lamentations 1:1-6; 2 Timothy 1:1-14; Luke 17:5-10

Call to Worship (Psalm 137:1-6):

Leader: By the rivers of Babylon—
there we sat down and there we wept
when we remembered Zion.
On the willows there we hung up our harps.

People: **For there our captors asked us for songs,
and our tormentors asked for mirth, saying,
"Sing us one of the songs of Zion!"**

Leader: How could we sing the LORD's song
in a foreign land?

People: **If I forget you, O Jerusalem,
let my right hand wither!
Let my tongue cling to the roof of my
mouth,
if I do not remember you,
if I do not set Jerusalem
above my highest joy**.

Pastoral Prayer:

God of the nations, you are the hope of all the earth. We join our voices with the peoples of far-flung lands; bless us with your streams of living water. You hear the cry of lonely cities, and you

355

promise a new city that will come from you. You travel roads with us that are filled with fear and empty of joy, and you promise a highway of praise. We live as aliens in a foreign land, yet how can we keep from singing? Give us grace to hear the "far-off hymn that hails a new creation." We pray for our faith to be increased, and yet you give us faith enough to do more than you require. We give you thanks for the faith that lives in our mothers and grand-mothers, our fathers and grandfathers, our mentors and friends. Rekindle in us the Spirit of power and love. Grant us the blessing of sound teaching and of discipline that we may guard the good treasure entrusted to us, by the power of the Holy Spirit, and through the grace given to us in Christ Jesus before the ages began. Amen. (Blair G. Meeks)

SERMON BRIEFS

LET ME LAMENT

LAMENTATIONS 1:1-6

As pastors, we are called upon to do some pretty important things—preach, teach, visit with the sick and dying, baptize, marry, administer, serve Holy Communion. But perhaps one of the most important is what I would call "letting persons lament." Each day at least one person needs to call or come by and "lament," share some burden, grieve, complain, bare his or her soul. Others need to and deep down want to but for some reason do not. They keep it inside. Others pay a lot of money so someone can listen to them lament and perhaps help them, but at least listen.

I. The Book of Lamentations

Perhaps we would prefer this book not to be in the Bible. It seems out of place, does it not? Even a little morbid? It is exactly its name—a collection of poetic "laments" mourning the fall of Jerusalem to the Babylonians in 587 B.C. The five poems that make up the book reflect the soul of a people in deep mourning. It is a book drenched in tears.

In the first poem (chapter 1) Jerusalem is personified as a woman, a destitute widow. The bitterness of Jerusalem's defeat is heightened by the remembrance of her former glory. Nothing remains of her prosperous past. The phrase "no one to comfort her" (v. 2) repeated in verses 9, 16, 17, and 21, highlights both the people's utter devastation and their need to reach out to God. They lament and rightly so.

The Bible is a very honest book. That's one reason why it speaks powerfully to each generation. And its honesty comes through in that it is not just a book of joy but also sorrow. It plainly says:

> For everything there is a season. . .
> a time to weep, and a time to laugh;
> a time to mourn, and a time to dance. . . .
> (Ecclesiastes 3:1*a*, 4)

Perhaps Lamentations was written just for the season of lamenting.

Indeed, the laments may have been written to be used in worship. They are read by Jews at the Wailing Wall each Friday and during the Hebrew month of Ab (July/August) in observance of the fall of Jerusalem. The first four laments are alphabetic acrostics, each having twenty-two stanzas beginning, in order, with a letter of the Hebrew alphabet. This helped in memorization. It is important, you see, to remember to allow time for lamenting.

II. Love Lets Others Lament

Early in my ministry, I began to resent a little when some came to me to lament. It seemed like not the best use of my time. But then I began to understand that it was one of the best uses of my time—for to allow others to lament, to express their pain and grief is to give them a gift of love. For expressing our laments, our pain is the first step toward healing.

How I cringe when someone who needs to lament is told to "get a hold on themselves" or something like that. It happens all too often when someone has died. We are uncomfortable with lamenting or at least expressing it. Perhaps this book is here to remind us that it's okay to lament and that we need to allow others time to lament too. Job's friends started out great—or they just sat and listened, letting him lament. But then they opened their mouths.

God has given us tear ducts not just to cleanse our eyes but to lament and cleanse our souls of grief and pain. And God has given us ears to listen, to allow others to lament, knowing that God also hears our laments. (Bass Mitchell)

DO NOT BE ASHAMED

2 TIMOTHY 1:1-14

Preaching from 2 Timothy raises the old discussion of who wrote the letter. I was taught that the letter was written about A.D. 150, and thus it was not the work of Paul who died about A.D. 65. However, more recently scholars have defended Paul as the author and believe that he wrote the letter to the young man Timothy during his first imprisonment in Rome. We probably will never know the author's name, but we ought not to allow these arguments to weaken the power of this personal letter that became a public instruction for those who follow Jesus.

Second Timothy provides a window through which we catch a glimpse of the evolution of tradition or the struggle to safeguard and pass the faith from generation to generation. These words grew out of the age of persecution. The young church was in trouble. The writer sits in prison trying to hang on to his disciples for the sake of the life giving story of the crucified resurrected Christ that must be told.

Witnessing to the faith in those times was no picnic, and many had fallen away. Phygelus and Hermogenes have deserted him. Demus has gone off the wrong way (4:9). Cowardliness cannot be part of the faith. So the letter is sent to Timothy, a "beloved and faithful child in the Lord" (1 Corinthians. 4:17).

Timothy is believed to have been the son of a Greek Gentile, who never converted to the faith, and a Jewish Christian mother. The author reminds Timothy of the faith of his Mother Eunice and Grandmother Lois, which tells us that he is a third generation Christian.

The situation was desperate. This might be the last generation of Christians unless some of the faithful remember and are willing to suffer for the telling of the story. Who will tell the story, who will rekindle the flame? How will the gospel be passed from one generation to the next?

This text could be a page from contemporary church experience. As we look at shrinking membership in churches, many voice the question "will the next generation have faith?" Will our children have faith? But even more to the point is Walter Brueggemann's haunting question "will the faith have children" as he makes the point of broken connections within the generations and our failure to present the gospel in new forms (*Hope within History* [Atlanta: John Knox Press], p. 92).

For a long time we took comfort in the truism that kids will grow away from the church for a time during college, but marriage and children will bring them back to church. But these days we have at least a generation that will not come back simply because they have nothing to come back to. They never were part of the church in the first place. Connections can be broken, and the faith can be lost. So faithful witnesses are needed. The story must be told. The writer describes the role that the witness must play.

A herald is needed, one who is commanded to carry and announce the message, to publish the glad tidings. An *apostle* is needed, one chosen and commissioned and sent as the personal messenger. A teacher must be found. Teachers are the ones who will help the people recall what they know and remember what is forgotten.

The writer will lay out the criteria for faithful witness. He speaks of his own suffering to offer realism to all who put their hand to the plow. He will remind Timothy that he is not to be ashamed. Timothy is unproved (1 Timothy 4:12). He is young, and he must preach to a world of intellectual snobs who will scoff. He will be subjected to the cynic's bark. After all what he is proclaiming is brand new stuff.

The very thought of telling the story of a dead Jewish criminal crucified outside the city gate who is the Lord and giver of life is absurd. Timothy's world had many gods to choose from, and they did not require suffering.

And to add insult to injury, Timothy is to follow the outline of one who is bound in chains in prison. Do not be ashamed. The foolishness of this story of the crucified one has the power to confound the wisdom of this present age.

We don't know what Timothy did, but the letter survived and so did the church. So we learn from this letter that it is left to us to stick to that outline and guard the good treasure entrusted to us with the help of the Holy Spirit. And we will trust the one who promises that we will not be put to shame (Isaiah 49:23). (William Cotton)

THE DANGERS OF SUCCESS

LUKE 17:5-10

He was young but others saw he had a gift—singing. They encouraged him to join the youth choir and to sing solos, and everyone praised him. He grew in his gift and so did the praise. He changed. He loved the praise and expected it. He had dreams of record deals and concerts with thousands of screaming fans. He would be rich. He was on his way to being successful and a celebrity (and was already acting like it) until his best friend brought him back to reality one day by saying, "You do have a gift, but it's a gift. You did nothing to earn it or deserve it. Just use it to give thanks to the one who gave it to you. Forget any recognition or rewards. All they will do is go to your head and make you forget who you really are and whose you are." That advice changed the young man. I know, for I was that young man.

In today's Gospel lesson it looks like we have two different stories—one about increasing faith and another about serving without thought of rewards. But I think they are related. Jesus is warning us about the dangers of success.

He begins by telling them to use what they have, that is, what little faith they possess. They want more faith, perhaps because Jesus had just said they were to do some difficult things, such as not offend others and offer forgiveness (vv. 1-4), and feel they need more faith to do those things. No, Jesus says. Just use the faith you have, small though it may be, for just a little faith is very powerful. That is an encouraging word to us—use the faith, the gifts you have. It matters not how much or how many. Wondrous things happen when we use what we have.

The danger comes later when the disciples actually begin to use that little faith and see such great results that they get big headed; their egos inflate and they begin to think more highly of themselves than they should. The use of their faith and gifts would have tremendous results. They would see miracles happen through them—indeed—trees would be uprooted and mountains moved. Persons would be healed. Thousands would respond when Peter preaches on Pentecost. Others would just want to touch him or stand in his shadow. Pretty heady stuff for lowly disciples.

I have seen it happen—someone begins using a gift, a mustard seed of faith, and from it great things result. One friend started a new church, and from it a TV ministry, only to let the power and prestige go to his head. Eventually, it all fell down around him. Success, even in God's kingdom, carries great dangers.

The warning from Jesus to us and the first disciples is not to let success go to our heads. Our only concern is to be obedient, to use the faith and gifts we have been given, without any thought of reward. After all, we are only doing and giving what God has given. We are only doing what's expected. No master ever thanks a servant for doing what he is expected to do. So, serve without expecting recognition or reward. And if these come, keep them in the proper perspective. Better yet, deflect them to the one who gives the faith and the gifts, the one to whom all honor and praise belong. When we can do this, then we are truly successful. (Bass Mitchell)

OCTOBER 14, 2001

❦

Nineteenth Sunday After Pentecost

Worship Theme: We offer our lives in praise and thanksgiving for God's healing power. God has made us whole through Jesus Christ who died that we might live with him.

Readings: Jeremiah 29:1, 4-7; 2 Timothy 2:8-15; Luke 17:11-19

Call to Worship (Psalm 66:1-2, 4-6, 8-9, 12c):

Leader: Make a joyful noise to God, all the earth;
sing the glory of God's name;
give to him glorious praise.

People: **All the earth worships you; they sing praises to you,**
sing praises to your name.

Leader: Come and see what God has done:
he is awesome in his deeds among mortals.
He turned the sea into dry land;
they passed through the river on foot.

People: **Bless our God, O peoples,**
let the sound of his praise be heard,

Leader: who has kept us among the living,
and has not let our feet slip.
You have brought us out to a spacious place.

People: **All the earth worships you; they sing praises to you,**
sing praises to your name.

362

Pastoral Prayer:

O God, you remain faithful even when we are faithless. Grant us the endurance of your steadfast love that we may live with Christ and join your reign of glory, through the power of the Holy Spirit. We give you thanks that your word remains unchained; grant us courage to spread its joyful truth throughout the earth. We pray for the church, that we may live in peace and harmony with one another and present ourselves to you as workers who do not need to be ashamed. We pray for the health of our community and for the welfare of the cities of our nation, whose well-being will bless us all. We pray for the sick; strengthen them in body and in faith, that they may live their lives in praise of you. We remember today, O God, our baptism, in thanksgiving for the ministry you have given us in your name; renew your Spirit in us that we may claim our gifts and use them in your service. In the name of Jesus Christ, raised from the dead, the source of our salvation, with eternal glory. Amen. (Blair G. Meeks)

SERMON BRIEFS

BLOOMING IN BABYLON

JEREMIAH 29:1, 4-7

I have a picture hanging on the wall in the church study. Those who notice it, most do not, think it kind of strange. You see, it's just a tree, a young maple tree. But it's much more than that to me and for others who know its story.

One of the things I enjoy is hiking on the mountain trails around my house. One day, years ago, I saw a large maple tree scattering its seed like tiny propellers to the four winds. Many of them fell onto a steep sandstone cliff. A shame, I thought to myself. Those seed will never survive there. But something amazing happened over the next months and years—some of those seed began to grow. Somehow they had worked their way into the cracks and crevices, started to germinate, and sent tiny roots searching for nourishment. And they grew! One of them had grown so much that a bird was building a nest in it. That is the picture I took. That is what I look at when I find myself in harsh circumstances. That is the picture I also point others to when their lives are on the rocks. It is a constant reminder that if that little tree can so bloom on a rocky cliff, then, with God's help, so can we.

I. Jeremiah's Letter

Jeremiah was writing a letter to those who had been violently uprooted from Judah and Jerusalem and transplanted in the harsh soil of Babylonian exile. How could they hope to grow there? To bloom in Babylon was beyond them. So Jeremiah shows them his own picture of a tree growing out of the rocks. They could bloom in Babylon.

II. Can't Live in the Past or the Future

But not if they tried to live in the past, the good old days of past glory, the way things used to be. Those days were gone. If they looked too much to the past, they would wither and die in the present. They could, yes, gain strength from their traditions, in remembering who they were and to whom they belonged. But they could not dwell there.

Some among them (see vv. 21-22) were telling them to look to the future. This was only a temporary set back (there may have been some political unrest in Babylon that made some of the exiled leaders think the empire would soon collapse). In other words, soon they would be going home.

So keep your bags packed, and be ready.

III. Bloom in Babylon

But Jeremiah has a very different message. It is bad news and good news. The bad is that, like a seed, they had fallen on the harshest of rocky ground—exile. And it would not be for a short time. But the good news was that if they put down roots and built, planted, married, prayed, they would and could bloom even there.

And so can you and I. I do not understand it anymore than the

maple on the rocky slopes. But I have seen it countless times—
persons fall into the harshest of soil—sickness, financial loss,
depression, grief—only to see their faith grow, their love blossom, their roots sink deeper and stronger than ever.

IV. Blooming for Babylon

Even more astounding is Jeremiah's advice to pray for Babylon, to work for its welfare, to be good citizens. In doing so they
would be a blessing to others and work for their own well-being.

So, too, as we bloom in our own Babylons, on our own rocky
cliffs, like that young maple hosting a bird nest, we can give support, help, shade and shelter to others. For we do not bloom just
for ourselves either, even in Babylon. (Bass Mitchell)

IN MEMORY—HOPE

2 TIMOTHY 2:8-15

Timothy is admonished to remember, to put his hope in Jesus
Christ raised from the dead who is also the descendant of David.
The whole gospel preached requires the preacher to make the
connection between the risen Christ and the all-too-human faith
of Israel symbolized in King David.

By the time of this writing the church was struggling with the
doctrine of the two natures of Christ. The forthcoming Marcian
heresy of disregarding the Hebrew Scriptures and thereby risking
the loss of the complete story was a great threat to the faith.
However, we must make the connection. The very man Jesus
born of the house and lineage of David is revealed in the Resurrection as the very God who is our Lord and giver of Life. We
need to find the Old Testament in the new if the right connections are to be made.

The writer of this text speaks of his suffering. He endures not
because he invites suffering, but he will take his place with the
one who suffered the death of a common criminal in order that
the elect will know the story and live.

The heart of this text is found in four couplets beginning with

THE ABINGDON PREACHING ANNUAL 2001

the word "If": If we have died with him, we will also live with him, if we endure we will also reign with him (vv. 11-12).

These words just feel good in your mouth until you come to the third "If". "If we deny him, he will also deny us." Here is a strange inconsistency. Jesus didn't deny Peter despite Peter's denial of him three times. The resurrected Christ will go in search of Peter (John 21:15). However, in the Matthew 25 account of the last judgment during the great division of the faithful from the unfaithful, the surprised goats, those who failed to find Jesus in the faces of the poor and lost, are denied entrance. Perhaps we can deny Jesus as in the case of Peter, but should we fail to find Christ in our neighbor's face the judgment is upon us.

The last couplet is equally surprising: "If we are faithless, he remains faithful—for he cannot deny himself." This verse makes the Old Testament connection with God who is long-suffering and patient with Israel. It also hearkens back to Paul's belief that we are Christ's body, and regardless of our lacking in wholeness, God will not break the relationship.

The writer uses the four "ifs" to reveal the amazing paradoxical power of Grace that comforts us in our pain, chastises us in our denials, confuses us in our efforts to do good, and finally confirms us as made in the image of God and thus we are God's children.

But we need to return to verse 8. Remember! In memory there is hope. The writer knows the power of the biblical story. Without memory, or tradition, our way of reclaiming hope will die.

Jaroslav Pelikan has defined tradition as "the living faith of the dead." In tradition the dead speak. He defines traditionalism as "the dead faith of the living" (*The Vindication of Tradition* [New Haven: Yale University Press, 1984], p. 65). When we allow the dead to speak, the word is not chained but set free. That is tradition. When we spend our time wrangling over words (v. 16), as in the case of so many meetings that we attend, the dead faith of the living is exposed. (William Cotton)

THE BEST GIFT OF ALL

LUKE 17:11-19

"Make a joyful noise to God, all the earth; sing the glory of his name; give to him glorious praise. Say to God, 'How awesome are your deeds!'" (Psalm 66:1-3a). The psalms of praise and thanksgiving express a lifestyle of great joy. Don't you wish you could go through life feeling like that? You can. God gives us many good gifts. We receive most of them gladly. But the best gift of all often goes unclaimed. It is the gift of gratitude.

I. A Story of Two Gifts

As Jesus was traveling, ten lepers came out to meet him and asked to be healed. Leprosy was a terrible and feared disease. It could cripple and kill. People who had it were often suspected of having brought God's wrath upon them because of their sins. Biblical quarantine laws required lepers to live outside of the community and to stay at a distance from everyone. It is hard to imagine anything that could destroy someone's life more completely than leprosy.

Jesus told them to go and show themselves to the priest. It was necessary for a leper to get a healing validated by a priest before he or she could return to the community. As they were on their way, they were healed. They must all have been glad. But only one chose to be grateful.

That one came back to Jesus praising God. His healing had taught him an entirely new way of relating to life. He realized that his life was a miraculous gift from God. He learned to live trusting God and celebrating life. Jesus said to that man, "Your faith has made you well." The Greek words used here are the same ones that are translated in other passages: "Your faith has saved you." Nine had received physical healing. One had received the whole new way of living in relationship with God and with life that comes with salvation.

Many who receive God's blessings only take them. Others are led by them into a life of blessedness.

II. A Reason for Gratitude

I know a person who has just come through a very painful and frightening struggle with a potentially life-threatening illness. It disabled her physically and, for a while, mentally and could easily have taken her life. But she got well and recovered her ability to live fully. Now sometimes, while doing very simple tasks, she finds herself thinking, "two years ago I could not have done this." It makes her very happy. She is grateful to God for her life and health. God is very real to her. She also feels a greater compassion for others who are going through suffering. The gratitude is the ultimate gift that pulls all of the other gifts together into a changed life.

But why aren't the rest of us just as grateful? Is our life and health any less miraculous because it has not been threatened? As long as we live, we have the good gift of life from God. And when we go to meet death in faith, we have hope as a similar gift. We too could be grateful.

III. A Gift Worth Having

But why should we want gratitude. It certainly is not in vogue.

Gratitude, as a lifestyle, is a special kind of happiness. It is happiness that does not depend upon any pride of accomplishment or pretense of deserving. It is a simple celebration of life. It is the kind of life that comes from living in faith (trust) in the grace (love) of God. It is at least part of what it means to be saved.

God has given you many gifts. Don't fail to receive the best one, the gift of gratitude that can send you down life's road singing, "Make a joyful noise to God, all the earth." (Jim Killen)

OCTOBER 21, 2001

❦

Twentieth Sunday After Pentecost

Worship Theme: God encourages us to pray with persistence and to endeavor tirelessly to tell the next generation our sacred stories of life through faith in Christ Jesus.

Readings: Jeremiah 31:27-34; 2 Timothy 3:14–4:5; Luke 18:1-8

Call to Worship (Psalm 119:97-104):

> *Leader:* Oh, how I love your law!
> It is my meditation all day long.

> *People:* **Your commandment make me wiser than my enemies,**
> **for it is always with me.**

> *Leader:* I understand more than the aged,
> for I keep your precepts.
> I hold back my feet from every evil way,
> in order to keep your word.
> I do not turn away from your ordinances,
> for you have taught me.

> *People:* **How sweet are your words to my taste,**
> **sweeter than honey to my mouth!**

> *Leader:* Through your precepts I get understanding;
> therefore I hate every false way.

> *People:* **O God, how we love your law!**
> **We meditate on your word all day long;**
> **it is always with us.**

Pastoral Prayer:

God, giver of justice, you encourage us to persist in praying and never to lose heart. Direct our prayers that we may seek your truth and live in praise of your gracious mercy. Forgive us when we act as if there were no price to pay for carelessness and greed; set our hearts toward the welfare of generations yet unborn. We thank you for your word handed down to us through the scriptures. Make us eager to tell the children our sacred stories and repeat for them your words of life through faith in Christ Jesus. God our deliverer, take us by the hand and bring us out of the land of fear and illusion. Grant us courage to live and breathe your purpose that we may come to the joy of obedience, caring for others and living in harmony with your creation. You have promised that we will all know you, from the least of us to the greatest; strengthen us in the knowledge of God through Christ your son, so that when he comes, he will find faith on earth; in his name we pray. Amen. (Blair G. Meeks)

SERMON BRIEFS

A GOD OF NEW BEGINNINGS

JEREMIAH 31:27-34

The more you read the Bible, the more you begin to see patterns in it, that is, threads woven from book to book. One such thread or theme goes from Genesis to Revelation—God is a God of new beginnings. In Genesis alone, a word that means "beginning," we see God creating new things, new creatures, and constantly giving them new beginnings—with Noah, Abraham and Sarah, then with all who followed. In the book of Revelation we see the new Jerusalem, and, indeed, a new heaven and new earth. And between these books we read story after story of the God of new beginnings. So it is hardly a surprise that Jeremiah adds to this never-ending story of new beginnings.

I. A New Beginning for Judah

The land of Judah had been devastated by the Babylonians. The people had been exiled. Even the animals had been taken. But Jeremiah sees a new beginning, a second Genesis as God will repopulate the land with people and animals. God will give them a new start (v. 27). The words about plucking up and breaking down given when Jeremiah was commissioned (1:10) are now reversed as God will plant the people and build them up. Though it took decades, many did return to the land and the nation of Israel began anew.

II. New Beginnings in Faith

But something else would be new too. The people had believed a new beginning impossible. Indeed, how could they escape their fate for they believed they were suffering for the sins of their ancestors? So what was the use in even thinking about a new beginning? Such was the depth of their despair. But Jeremiah says here that confession and repentance do matter (vv. 29-30). Accepting responsibility for their own sins and repenting in the present were meaningful actions that turned their hearts back to God and opened them to new beginnings for the future.

Indeed, a whole new beginning is what Jeremiah sees. It will be a "new covenant," or relationship unlike the one they had known based solely on obedience to laws. They had failed that one miserably. This new covenant would be more personal, written on their hearts. For they would come to "know God" intimately and deeply. They will then seek to serve and obey God out of love and out of that knowledge.

As Christians, we believe that in Christ this promise has been fulfilled, that the world has been given a whole new beginning. Paul goes so far as to say that we have in Christ been made new creations; the old has passed away, the new has come. Think of the many persons who met Jesus who must have thought that new beginnings were impossible. How many, like the blind, the lame, the outcasts, the sinners, the demon-possessed found a power in Jesus that gave them a new beginning? Remember the woman at the well? Think of the disciples themselves. Christ

371

gave them many new beginnings, especially Peter. After the death of Jesus, who would have ever thought that he or the others could hope to start again? But Easter came, the ultimate of new beginnings, and gave them and us a new beginning.

Many of us will take and drink from the cup of Christ this day and eat the bread. Whenever we do, we are reminded of the God of new beginnings, of new covenants; a God who just does not want to give up on us or let us give up on ourselves. For this God of new beginnings loves us, forgives our sins and remembers them no more. (Bass Mitchell)

ITCHY EARS OR DEAF EARS

2 TIMOTHY 3:14–4:5

My grandmother used to argue with my uncle about the Bible. She was convinced that one should never tamper with any of those inspired words. My uncle wasn't so sure the words were all inspired of God. So she would quote a part of 2 Timothy: "All scripture is inspired by God" (3:16). *All* or *every* used in this context has been a troublesome word for the church. The ongoing debate regarding the divine inspiration of scripture has often greatly misused this text. Some believe and teach that every word in the Bible is inspired, as if to say the great mystery guided the pen in the hand of the writer and sort of breathed onto the page and wrote every word down in perfect King James English. Then we are admonished to neither add to nor take from the text (Revelation. 22:18-19).

To use *all* or *every* in this way can get the preacher into real trouble. For instance, what of the ending of Psalm 137:9: "Happy shall they be who take your little ones and dash them against the rock!" Somehow that slip of the pen by an obviously angry psalmist seemed less than inspired by God. Raymond Brown reminds us that the emphasis in verse 16 should be placed not on the inspiration of each word, but on the utility of the text (*An Introduction to the New Testament* [New York: Doubleday, 1998], p. 678). All scripture is inspired by God *and is useful for teaching, for reproof, for correction, and for training in righteousness.*

Timothy, then, is to use the scripture as a means to convince, and exhort and equip. But there is also a valid reason for speaking of the divine inspiration of the scripture. At the time of the text, the age was one of pluralism. All kinds of religious experiences and options were available. There was something of a religious smorgasbord to choose from. Focus was needed. The people had itchy ears and had moved away from sound doctrine.

Timothy, then, is also to remember the faith as it was taught to him; to use Paul's outline and stay close to it.

Those times connect with our times as we watch members of our congregations go off to the bookstore and discover the New Age section. A good friend who dabbles in religious experience likes to bring me the most recent find in spirituality, which ranges from Buddha to Native American spirituality to the Gnostic Scriptures.

This kind of behavior on the part of the laity can be threatening to the preacher, and we like to accuse these folk of having itchy ears, of falling away from sound doctrine.

But I would agree with Raymond Brown that itchy ears are preferable to deaf ears. There is a spiritual awakening within our culture. If we use the Bible as a straitjacket, meaning to exclude everything but the Scriptures, folk will turn a deaf ear to us. Likewise we need to enter into conversation with those who have itchy ears. The Bible can be a strange new world when presented well, and it will cure itchy ears. Good advice is given to Timothy and to us. Keep calm and sane at all times—work to spread the gospel. And celebrate the new interest in spirituality; it can open the door to the renewal of faith. (William Cotton)

DON'T GIVE UP!

LUKE 18:1-8

The parables of Jesus have the most unlikely heroes—like a widow. It would have been difficult to find a more powerless person in those days. Yet she is held up as a model of persistence, prayer, and patience for never giving up or losing heart. We can learn much from her.

I. Don't Give Up on Yourself

She had every reason to give up. Everything was against her. Even the name "widow" in Greek is "chera," and it means "empty" or "forsaken." She was a nobody to everybody—except to herself! But she refused to play the victim. She had a sense of dignity and self-worth.

It is one thing to be seen and treated by others as a failure or a nobody. It's another to believe that. When I say to myself, "You ARE a nobody. You're a loser. Might as well give up," then I am in a world of trouble. And so many are today. They have lost so often, failed so much, been knocked down so much that they see no reason to get up and try again. They see themselves like the main character in the comic strip—"The Born Loser."

But everyone loses sometimes. All of us fail and make mistakes. We mess up. Sometimes it's not our fault and we find ourselves at the mercy of unjust persons and systems. Life is not always fair. But we do not have to accept it. Others can give up on us, but we do not have to give up on ourselves!

II. Don't Give Up on Others

This widow would not even give up on this judge, as unfeeling and corrupt as he was. She was not going to stop pestering him until he did the right thing by her.

It's easy to give up on ourselves. Maybe it's even easier to give up on others. We, too, can fall into that trap of looking down on others, of seeing them as losers and nobodies. But we cannot do that as Christians. Jesus never looked on anyone that way. Even when his own disciples misunderstood or disappointed him, he never gave up on them—just like he never gives up on us.

It's not easy. People hurt us. They let us down, even the ones closest to us. But that doesn't mean we have to give up on them. In fact, such times are when they need our patience and persistent belief in them the most.

III. Don't Give Up on God

Neither did this widow give up on God. Maybe this is why she could not give up on herself or even this judge. Maybe she could have given up on God; after all, she was a widow, and in those days to lose one's husband might be seen as punishment from God for sins (his or hers). But she did not see it this way. She had faith that God cared for her and would somehow help her.

Some people do reach the point where they think about giving up on God. Maybe some of you. Maybe you already have. Your prayers have not been answered. The tough times just keep getting tougher. But this is exactly when Jesus tells us to tough it out; to not give up. Keep on believing anyway. Keep on praying. God does care. God can be trusted to act in God's own time and way. For if a poor widow can get a corrupt judge to do what he did not really want to do, then how much more can we receive from a God who is ready, willing, and able to help us? Do not give up! (Bass Mitchell)

OCTOBER 28, 2001

❧

Twenty-first Sunday After Pentecost

Worship Theme: God gives to the whole household of faith the gift of dreaming dreams, seeing visions, and living for God's reign on earth. We approach this gift humbly, aware of all our needs.

Readings: Joel 2:23-32; 2 Timothy 4:6-8, 16-18; Luke 18:9-14

Call to Worship (Psalm 65:1*a*, 2*a*, 5, 8-9, 11-13):

> *Leader:*   Praise is due to you, O God, in Zion,
> O you who answer prayer!
> By awesome deeds, you answer us with deliverance.

> *People:*   **O God of our salvation,**
> **you are the hope of all the ends of the earth**
> **and of the farthest seas.**

> *Leader:*   Those who live at earth's farthest bounds are awed by your signs;
> you make the gateways of the morning and the evening shout for joy.

> *People:*   **You visit the earth and water it, greatly enriching it;**
> **the river of God is full of water;**
> **you provide the people with grain, for so you have prepared it.**

> *Leader:*   You crown the year with your bounty;
> your wagon tracks overflow with richness.

People: **The pastures of the wilderness overflow,**
the hills gird themselves with joy,
the meadows clothe themselves with flocks,
the valleys deck themselves with grain,
they shout and sing together for joy.

Pastoral Prayer:

Generous God, your goodness is like abundant rain that comes early and late, bringing a plentiful harvest. You have dealt wondrously with us, and we praise your name; you are our God and there is no other. Pour out your Spirit on us that we may fully proclaim your words of life. Give to the whole household of faith—young and old, daughters and sons—the gift of dreaming dreams, seeing visions, and living for your reign on earth. We pray for all who endure hardships in their ministries. Lord in your mercy, hear our prayers for congregations in countries where churches are suppressed; for relief workers struggling against storm, famine, and disease; for teachers and students in schools where fear rules; for those who protect our country; for all who face misfortune, conflict, and loss. Rescue them from the lion's mouth and save them for your kingdom. Forgive us when we do not see our own failings and are too proud to ask for your mercy; teach us the humility of your Son Jesus Christ, who was humble that he might be exalted. To him be the glory forever and ever. Amen. (Blair G. Meeks)

SERMON BRIEFS

THE DIFFERENCE IN PROPHECY
AND PREACHING

JOEL 2:23-32

The danger of Bible study is in the new and unanswerable mysteries that can be generated when searching for answers to life's questions. It is a wonderful sort of danger, for the Holy Scriptures are intended to both inspire and to challenge, to motivate and to consternate. Like the time a person asked the question, "What *is* the difference in prophecy and preaching?"

I. Good Preaching Comforts the Afflicted

There is an old adage, attributed to Dr. Tex Sample (but he says that it predates him), that goes, "Good preaching comforts the afflicted and afflicts the comfortable." The primary task in biblical preaching is to comfort the afflicted. Preaching must offer hope to offer comfort. It must help the listener to lift up their eyes in order to see their salvation. For Christian biblical proclamation—the preaching of God's Word—to be genuine and true, it must be rooted in the hope that is born at Christmas, resurrected at Easter, and empowered at Pentecost.

I stood before a packed sanctuary of mourners, grieving the untimely death of a mother of teenagers. The woman had collapsed in the stands during her daughter's drill team competition. She had been the victim of an aneurysm. Questions of theodicy arise at a time such as this, so I addressed them head-on. We do not know the answers to many of life's mysteries, but we can place our hope and our trust in the God who is with us. There is hope for grieving families, hurting bodies, disturbed minds, and troubled souls, because Jesus Christ is a real person and the resurrection is true. Good preaching comforts the afflicted.

II. Good Preaching Afflicts the Comfortable

I like the story told by Dr. Michael Reeves about the pastor who, one particular Sunday, decided to change the way the offering was dedicated. He had the ushers bring the plates to him after they were passed, but instead of singing the Doxology, he took the plates and turned to face the cross. The pastor held up the meager offering given by an affluent congregation and said, "Lord, no matter what we say or do, this is what we think of you!" I wonder how many people wanted the plates passed again?

When I say that good preaching should afflict the comfortable I mean *convict* those who are complacent, apathetic, arrogant, self-righteous, or self-centered. I am not referring to punishment, nor am I suggesting that the preacher invoke unhealthy guilt. There are some occasions when we have a twinge of guilt as a motivator to change. This is different from manipulative, negative, unhealthy guilt. Good preaching may evoke this, but mostly, it inspires and points the way to truth that is not masked by affluence, poverty of spirit, or self-indulgence.

III. Preaching That Is Prophetic Offers a Vision That Is of God

Most every preacher whom I know wants to be prophetic instead of pathetic. They want to say something that is significant—an idea that challenges the head and invokes the heart. For this to happen, the Holy Spirit *must* be involved! The prophet Joel paints a scene of plenty and blessing as a gift from God. It is God's response to the people's repentance. On the heels of this time of plenty, God will "pour out my spirit on all flesh" (v. 28). For Joel, "all flesh" probably referred to the Jews; but later, Peter would expand that understanding to include all people of every nation. It is the spirit of God that gives us power, vision, and the gifts to do God's work.

In 1995, the former pastor at the downtown church where I serve helped to paint a vision for expansion to a growing southern part of the city. We would be one church with two locations; not a relocation, but a stronger outreach to where the people were. It seemed a far-fetched dream, but land was donated, people gave gifts large and small, and in 1999 a large, multipurpose facility opened. What had been a vision became reality. It was prophetic and will allow this church to reach persons who would never come downtown to worship. Preaching that is prophetic offers a vision that is of God. It is a vision that challenges, convicts, uplifts hope, and reflects the loving promises of an amazing God. (Gary G. Kindley)

HOLD NOTHING BACK

2 TIMOTHY 4:6-8, 16-18

The author of 2 Timothy closes the letter with a toast—his life is poured out like a libation. Cheers! Here's looking at you!

But libation taken seriously also means a life poured out in the form of costly sacrifice like wine spilled on the altar. This text rhymes with Romans 12 where Paul admonishes the faithful to present their very "bodies as a living sacrifice" to God (12:1). Hold nothing back.

The writer tells of his struggles: "I have fought the good fight, I have finished the race, I have kept the faith." The crown awaits the writer. Is this some kind of holy boasting, self-righteous crowing? I think not. Here is a desperate man who will use every occasion, even the risk of arrogance, as a means to preach the salvation story and to encourage the fainthearted.

Many of his disciples have left him. He uses the language and metaphor of the Olympic games to give Timothy a pep talk. Timothy knows about the long distance runner who if he is to win must find the strength that he doesn't have. The runner must save up for that last kick needed to push beyond his or her endurance, and at the breathless point of needing oxygen, will finally feel the finish line string snap. In that moment of ecstasy he knows that the race is run, the fight is finished, and the faith is secure.

Poet Donald Hall in telling of his struggle to write a good poem tells would-be poets to hold nothing back. Put everything out that can possibly belong in that poem or story. Don't save anything for the next one. That's the only way to work. That is the only way to live (Bill D. Moyers, *Language of Life: A Festival of Poets* [New York: Doubleday 1955], p. 157).

Martin Buber said it even better, "Remember, the good is the enemy of the best." In a world that will put up with "that's pretty good," 2 Timothy challenges us to do our best, to pay up personally even to the point of pouring out our lives as living sacrifice.

A friend tells of a young man who canceled his cable television subscription because he wished to make a sacrificial gift to his church each month. The cable person called to discover why the cancellation. The young man explained that he did it so he could make a sacrificial gift. "Sir, said the representative, can you give me another reason, we don't have a category for sacrifice on our cancel list." So it goes.

The writer ends the letter with one true boast—to God be the glory. He means the God who made the sacrifice that is demanded and proved in the death and resurrection of Jesus,

that the faithful will be delivered from every evil attack and kept
safe. Glory to God forever. Amen. (William Cotton)

SOMETIMES THE ONLY WAY UP IS DOWN

LUKE 18:9-14

I was recently in a hospital that was undergoing major renova-
tions, and I needed to get to one of the upper floors but the ele-
vators were not working. I came to a hallway and knew I had to
go up one flight of stairs. But the stairs were blocked off and a
sign said, "to go up you must go down the stairs. At the bottom of
the stairs look for further instructions." I followed the directions
and eventually made it to my destination.

I could not help thinking of this when I read today's parable
concerning the Pharisee and the tax collector. For it seems to
have a similar message, "sometimes the only way up is down." Or,
as Jesus says it, "For everyone who makes himself great will be
humbled, and everyone who humbles himself will be made great"
(v. 14 NIV, paraphrased).

In God's sight, the only way up is down—to humble ourselves,
to not think more highly of ourselves than we should, to see ourselves as we are—sinners in need of God's grace. No one stands
so tall in God's eyes as one who kneels in humility. This kind of
genuine humility is like throwing a rubber ball to the ground,
which makes it rebound upward.

I. Humility Training

Comparisons. A constant source of humility is to consider
whom we compare ourselves to (although a sure sign that one is
humble probably is that you do not compare yourself to others).
The Pharisee came off fairly well in his own eyes by contrasting
himself with a tax collector. How many of us make such favorable
comparisons for ourselves? But if it's humility we wish and need,
we should compare ourselves with the right person—Christ. Difficult to come away from that comparison feeling superior, isn't
it?

Trainers. Once Muhammad Ali got onto a flight that was about to take off, and he was told to put on his seatbelt. He replied, "superman don't need no seatbelt." The flight attendant replied, "superman don't need no airplane either." He put on the seatbelt.

God has a way of providing persons to teach us humility.

See the Truth. Humility comes from seeing the truth about ourselves. A painter once painted a perfect picture of a king. But the king hated it. The king had scars on his face from battles and a wart on one cheek. The painter left them off. He made the painter put them back. He wanted to be seen for who he truly was. A good, honest look in a spiritual mirror from time to time does wonders in fostering a spirit of humility (which is not seeing yourself as unworthy or more lowly than you should, but simply seeing your scars and warts as well).

II. Humility Produces Fruit

Humility puts us in a position to bear fruit for the Kingdom. It's difficult for even God to do through us if we do not know how much we truly need and depend upon God. I wonder if that's not the real problem of the Pharisee—he does not really need God. He was a self-made man. Notice how many times he says "I". He came not to confess his need but to profess his sufficiency, confident in his own goodness by telling God and everyone else, "God, you're sure fortunate to have me on your side."

I was in an apple orchard not too long ago. Have you ever noticed that the branches with the most fruit hang lowest to the ground? God, the great Orchard Owner, lifts up those lowly branches because God knows that's where the fruit will be. (Bass Mitchell)

REFLECTIONS

❧

NOVEMBER

Reflection Verses: "Comfort, O comfort my people, says your God. . . . Get you up to a high mountain, O Zion, herald of good tidings; lift up your voice with strength . . . lift it up, do not fear; say to the cities of Judah, 'Here is your God!' " (Isaiah 40:1, 9).

It's hard to read Isaiah 40 and not hear George Frideric Handel humming in your ear. This is where the *Messiah* begins. Remember how he set the opening lines? When the Overture is finished, the strings begin a quiet, stately pulse. Suddenly they stop—as a pure tenor voice sings three simple notes, descending like a hand on the shoulder: "Comfort ye." Soon the music takes a dramatic turn. The tenor sounds like a man running into the room with startling news: "the voice of him that crieth in the wilderness, 'Prepare ye the way of the Lord. Make straight in the desert a highway for our God.' " The music quickens, and the tenor belts out the great vision: "Every valley shall be exalted, every mountain and hill made low, the crooked straight and the rough places plain." When he sings of the valleys, the music lifts the valleys up. When he sings of the mountains, the music brings them down. And when he sings of the crooked, the music is crooked at first, then straight and clear and plain.

There is one performance of *Messiah* that I'll never forget. What made it so memorable was the illness of the tenor. It was in the church of my youth. I was in the choir. Two of the soloists were professional imports; the other two were talented nonprofessional members of the church. The tenor was one of these. He had been sick all week, and we all wondered if he'd be up to it; but when the time came, he was in his place. When the orchestra finished the Overture, he stood. But when he opened his mouth to sing, "Comfort," what came out was not comfort at all. His voice was raspy, cracked, excruciating. We wondered if he'd stop

383

and sit down. The conductor looked at him with raised eyebrows full of permission, but he kept singing, cracking, breaking all the notes like vases. We all developed a sudden interest in our shoes. We squirmed as he kept assaulting those impossible notes, for six torturous minutes. He sang about valleys coming up but they stayed low; and the mountains wouldn't budge for him; and by the end, all the rough places seemed rougher than they'd ever been before.

He was a good man. In his right voice he could sing the piece beautifully. But on this night before all these expectant faces, he couldn't get it right, and he just kept singing. I'm glad now that he did. His public agony with these words has become a kind of inspiration to me.

Preachers are given a commission that is beyond us. We are pointed to fathomless mysteries, then required to say them in words. We inhabit a world of unspeakable evils and unutterable grief, a world also glowing with holy fire and infinite love, trembling with the ineffable. We are commanded to stand on our little clay feet in front of people who, like us, are searching, struggling, and dying—and speak for them all that is terrible and wonderful in their lives, all the while pointing to the impossible promises of God. We get to attempt this every week.

"Cry out!" said the Voice to the prophet. "What shall I cry?" the prophet shot back, the weekly refrain of many a preacher. But this prophet isn't looking for just another text or theme; he's looking for a reason. "All people are grass!" he cries—we're all withering like grass and wilting like flowers. We're pretty for a day, then we die. God, look at all this death! Look at all these ruined hopes. Comfort *these* people? How? Who will believe it? "What shall I cry?"

But the Voice doesn't take no for an answer. *"Get up. Get up to a high mountain and cry out good tidings."*

God, we can't, our voices will crack. *"Lift up your voice!"*

God, our hope is weak. *"Lift it up with strength!"*

But we are afraid! *"Lift it up, be not afraid. Say to the people: 'Here is your God!'"*

The Voice of our calling turns out to be dismissive on the subject of our personal fears and inadequacies. God shows no concern over our cracked voices, doesn't seem to care that we will miss many notes in this grand music. It all starts to sound like that old commercial for a certain brand of athletic shoes: "Just do it!" Get over yourself. Ready or not, dive into your part.

People like us are prone to introspection. We should be. But like most good things, self-study can grow perverse. Stare into the mirror long enough, noting imperfections, tracing scars, caressing wounds, lamenting all the marks of somebody's sins— and before long, you've stared yourself out of the job, or completely forgotten what you're here for. Even what passes for "devotional time" can easily contort, reducing our concern to the very small size of ourselves.

Well here's a news bulletin. We're not that big a deal. It's not about you, and it's not about me. There is a world full of suffering and wrong, and there is God. God has a Word for the world, and is not waiting for perfect voices to intone it. The only voices available are our kind of voices—badly flawed, and so what? Our voices aren't the thing, the Music is.

Fred Craddock has told how as a young pastor, like most of us, he took himself too seriously. An older man gave him some advice. He told him that before leaving the house in the morning he should pray, asking God to help in everything he said or did to do his very best. Then as he put on his hat to leave, he was to say, "Here goes nothing!" Of course.

Lift up your voice. Lift it up with strength. Be not afraid, lift it up. (Paul D. Duke)

NOVEMBER 4, 2001

❧

Twenty-second Sunday After Pentecost

Worship Theme: We thank God for the fellowship of the saints, for those who are called in God's name to lives of praise, showing by their acts of mercy that Jesus is now among us.

Readings: Habakkuk 1:1-4, 2:1-4; 2 Thessalonians 1:1-4, 11-12; Luke 19:1-10

Call to Worship (Psalm 119:137-144):

> *Leader:* You are righteous, O LORD,
> and your judgments are right.
> You have appointed your decrees in righteousness
> and in all faithfulness.

> *People:* **My zeal consumes me**
> **because my foes forget your words**
> **Your promise is well tried,**
> **and your servant loves it.**

> *Leader:* I am small and despised,
> yet I do not forget your precepts.
> Your righteousness is an everlasting righteousness,
> and your law is the truth.

> *People:* **Trouble and anguish may come upon me,**
> **but your commandments are my delight.**
> **Your decrees are righteous forever;**
> **give me understanding that I may live.**

Pastoral Prayer:

God of all the saints, we give you thanks for the faithful witnesses now and in ages past who surround and encourage us by

386

their abundant faith and their steadfast love. We remember with thanksgiving our loved ones who have died; let your light shine on them and, by the power of your resurrection, bring us together at last to your joyful home. Give us the wisdom, O God, to see Jesus now among us and, truly seeing him, to renew our promises to serve others in your name, caring for the poor, the prisoners, the outcasts, the sick, and the grieving. We thank you for your church, for the fellowship of those who are called in your name to lives of praise. Make us worthy of your call and grant us the power of your Spirit to live by our faith. Grant us grace to glorify your name, according to the grace of our God and the Lord Jesus Christ. Amen. (Blair G. Meeks)

SERMON BRIEFS

THE RIGHTEOUS SHALL LIVE BY FAITH

HABAKKUK 1:1-4; 2:1-4

His people were living under threat. They seemed powerless to do anything to avoid or avert the siege that was about to be laid upon them. And Habakkuk did not understand. Why do the wicked have all the trump cards and the righteous suffer persecution? And why did his pleas for mercy seem to fall on divine ears that had gone deaf? "O LORD, how long shall I cry for help, and you will not listen? Or cry to you 'Violence!' and you will not save? . . . The wicked surround the righteous—therefore judgment comes forth" (1:2-4).

From Job to Habakkuk to Christ's cry from the cross to Rabbi Harold Kushner, those who think deeply cannot forever fail to wonder why bad things happen to good people. As a member of my church says: "Everytime I read about a child who is killed in a wreck, I wonder why so many Mafia bosses live to be ninety. Where is the justice in that?" I appreciate her sentiment and, in honesty, more than once I have asked the same question.

For Habakkuk, however, this was not merely a theological point to ponder. It was not parlor chitchat for when the preacher visits. To Habakkuk, this question was serious business. His people and their future were hanging in the balance. The threat of violence was real. Psychologists tell us that family members watching a loved one struggle with a terminal illness go through "anticipatory grief." Habakkuk was there. His was anticipatory grief for the overthrow of his people. And he took it seriously. So he went up on the city wall to be alone and talk with God.

"I will stand at my watchpost; and station myself on the rampart; I will keep watch to see what he will say to me" (2:1) And the Lord replied to Habakkuk, among other things saying: ". . . the righteous live by their faith" (2:4). It is not a specific answer to the theodicy question, but perhaps all the answer Habakkuk and we can handle.

In truth, suppose God did explain to us the reasons for evil. Suppose we were told why children are killed and Mafia bosses live to be aged, why wars are waged, why cancer, why arthritis, why people are inhumane to other people who had done nothing to provoke such treatment. Suppose you and I were given an answer to the question "Why?" Would our suffering then be any less painful or traumatic? Of course not. The question is not one of data but one of faith. The question is not "Why?" but rather "How?" or "What next?" "How do I survive the pains of this existence?" "What do I take from this experience that can enrich or enhance my future living?" To know why we hurt makes hurting no less painful. But to learn and grow from the experience makes us more fully human and more essentially alive. And that requires moving from "Why?" to "What?"

> "I will stand at my watchpost;
> and station myself on the rampart;
> I will keep watch to see what he will say to me."

And the Lord answered: "the righteous live by their faith."

(Michael B. Brown)

SOME SEEDS GROW

2 THESSALONIANS 1:1-4, 11-12

I'm sure that Paul's feelings are sometimes described in the words of the old spiritual: "sometimes I feel discouraged and think my work's in vain. . . ." Surely that is the way Paul felt as he was forced to hastily leave Thessalonica after having planted a church in possibly only three or four weeks (Acts 17:1-8). Like all evangelists and pastors who lead revivals and renewal meetings, we know that the zeal will cool, and sometimes we leave the church wondering if the meeting will bear fruit. We are sometimes haunted by Mark Twain's statement about the local revival meeting: "Everybody got saved last week; they'll be sinners again before this week's out."

But apparently the Thessalonian church was well planted, and the fellowship not only survived the persecution and harassment of the local synagogue and the civil authorities, but it began to have a reputation for love and growth and godliness. Paul's point in the verses we focus upon today includes at least three points and a prayer!

I. Unexpected Growth in Unexpected Places

First, he says that the faith of this church has grown, and that in itself was remarkable. Second, along with the growing faith there is a growing sense of love and fellowship. We tend to marvel at this and wonder, *How could a church grow in faith and love under such circumstances?* It is precisely adverse circumstances that most often draw a church together and lead them to higher levels of love for each other. It has been said that the worse thing that could happen to the Christian church was the conversion of the Emperor Constantine. For from this point onward, the church was the "in" group. The Thessalonians, hastily planted and left to the grace of God, endured and grew stronger in adversity. And that led Paul, in the third place, to say how proudly he and his companions spoke of the Thessalonian church, as they taught and preached in Corinth and Athens. One of the things most pastors do not do well is to speak of their spiritual pride in their people. I have not been good at that throughout my ministry. But I have tried, in recent years, to let my people know how proud I am of them.

II. A Pride That's Right

Probably every pastor has an experience akin to my experience when, after a long time as pastor of a large and respected church,

I went out with a small group to start a new church. I marvel, six years later, at the courage, commitment, and spiritual depth of that group who left multimillion-dollar facilities to go meet in a schoolhouse. I try to tell my church how proud I am of them. Every pastor would honor God by so doing, and with Paul teaching the people that their spiritual growth and love is all part of a wonderful plan of God.

When I read this first chapter of 2 Thessalonians in the light of the circumstances of the founding of the church, I am reminded of how, every spring, I plant several hundred zinnias, daisies, and other flowers—by digging a hole, sprinkling a bit of plant food and a dollop of water, and then jamming the plant into the hole. Amazingly, most of them live and thrive, through the dry times and the floods; standing against the rabbits and the bugs and the grandchildren. And all through the summer, I rejoice and reflect on the tenacity of these flowers. That's akin to what Paul is doing.

III. He's Got the Church in His Hands

But flowers are one thing, and the church is another. Paul's mind and heart is on the plan of God that he sees unfolding in the Thessalonian church. Oh, that is not to say that Paul is blind to the problems of the church—most of which appear to be the result of spiritually youthful zeal. But he says in verses 11 and 12 that his prayers for this church have a definite focus. He prays that God may count them worthy of the high calling to come to Christ, to be in Christ, to bear fruit for Christ, to be Christ's at his appearing. Paul's message is this: *we pray . . . that God may count you worthy of your calling, and fulfill every desire for goodness and the work of faith with power.* Their worthiness of their calling will be seen in God's granting of their desire for goodness, and their desire to do great things for God. And this worthiness, this standing firm, this fulfilling of their witness of love and gospel, will lead to the glorifying of the name of Jesus.

Sometimes we work for years and see little visible results; sometimes as in the case of the Thessalonians, a little seed is planted and left to the grace of God, and it grows into a mighty tree. It keeps me in touch with my frailties and weakness; that is also Paul's testimony. (Earl C. Davis)

UP A TREE

LUKE 19:1-10

Jesus was coming to Jericho. The streets were crowded. Every-one wanted to see this man who just the day before had given sight to a blind beggar. Even Zacchaeus, the notorious tax collec-tor, wanted to see Jesus. I can't imagine that he had any friends. Few people were hated more than tax collectors. He knew peo-ple hated him, made snide remarks, laughed at him behind his back. Yet they also feared him. He had power. But he was also short of stature. And perhaps that was an embarrassment to him. It gave his enemies one more thing to use to make fun of him. Maybe that was one reason he became a tax collector—it made this little man feel like a big man. But it did not win him any friends. He was short and could often be overlooked. But not as a tax collector. That got him noticed, even if it came with a heavy price.

Curious, though, he decides to climb a tree that day, not caring perhaps that it would give people more reason to ridicule him. And could it be that he climbed that tree not just to see Jesus but in hopes that Jesus would see him? Deep inside Zacchaeus wanted, needed, hoped to be seen! For no one ever really saw him, not the real him. They could not see past their hatred to his heart, to his pain and loneliness.

And wonder of wonders, Jesus does see him! Perhaps Jesus asked someone near by who he was and then was warned to stay away from him because he was a sinner. But such a man up a tree was a most curious thing. Even Jesus didn't see that every day. And the heart of Jesus was touched. When he looked up, he did not see just a short tax collector, but a man who was searching, longing to be seen, to belong. So Jesus tells him to come down, for he's going to eat with him. Wonder what the crowd said when they heard that?

Do not miss the significance of this act. Eating with someone in those days was an act of profound friendship. A meal was a sacred time, reserved only for the closet of friends. To take a meal with someone was to say that you were friends forever. It established life-long bonds. Jesus invited himself to Zack's house.

And Zack knew exactly what that meant. He was, for the first time in his life, offered friendship, love, acceptance—the things he had most longed for and could never buy with all his money. But now, through this man from Nazareth, it all was offered to him without cost.

Such love, such acceptance profoundly changed Zacchaeus. He would go out and try to undo the harm he had caused. He would become a friend to others, not preying upon them. "Salvation has come to your house today," Jesus tells him, "for you, too, are a child of Abraham, Zacchaeus. You are part of God's family. You belong. You just strayed from the fold for a time. But now you've come home" (vv. 9-10, paraphrased).

In Jericho, Jesus looks up a tree at a man who climbed up there to see and be seen. Wonder of wonders, this Jesus was even then on the path to Jerusalem where he, too, would climb up a tree where he could see everyone, even you and me, and there offer us what we all need more than anything else—a love that accepts us, a friendship that welcomes us, a grace that forever changes us. (Bass Mitchell)

NOVEMBER 11, 2001

❧

Twenty-third Sunday After Pentecost

Worship Theme: We are children of the resurrection, members of God's new household, and Jesus shows us a new way to love in thanksgiving for God's great gift of life.

Readings: Haggai 1:15*b*–2:9; 2 Thessalonians 2:1-5, 13-17; Luke 20:27-38

Call to Worship (Psalm 145:1-5, 17-21):

Leader:	I will extol you, my God and King, and bless your name forever and ever.
People:	**Every day I will bless you, and praise your name forever and ever.**
Leader:	Great is the LORD, and greatly to be praised; his greatness is unsearchable. One generation shall laud your works to another, and shall declare your mighty acts.
People:	**On the glorious splendor of your majesty, and on your wondrous works, I will meditate. The LORD is just in all his ways,**
Leader:	The LORD is near to all who call on him, to all who call on him in truth. He fulfills the desire of all who fear him; he also hears their cry, and saves them.
People:	**TheLORD watches over all who love him, but all the wicked he will destroy. My mouth will speak the praise of the LORD, and all flesh will bless his holy name forever and ever.**

Pastoral Prayer:

Living God, we come to you as children of the resurrection, alive in your Spirit, mindful of your constancy, and thankful that you have chosen us. When we are alarmed and shaken in mind, we turn to you for assurance of your love and salvation. Give us confidence; give us courage to hold fast to the traditions. Give us teachers who show us your truth. Forgive us when we are preoccupied with useless questions and fail to be amazed at the great gift of life you offer us. Open our eyes to the new thing you are doing; astonish us with the joy and peace of your new creation. Save us from our complacency; keep us alert and ready, knowing that once again, in a little while, you will shake the heavens and the earth and the sea and the dry land, and you will fill your house with splendor. Grant us grace to obtain the glory of our Lord Jesus Christ, in whose name we pray. Amen. (Blair G. Meeks)

SERMON BRIEFS

FRESH STARTS AND SECOND CHANCES

HAGGAI 1:15*b*–2:9

Amid the battered ruins of their existence, the people of God assumed their future was completely behind them. It was their lot to suffer, to be left out and left behind, and to be abused. It seemed they would forever be mere puppets in the hands of a more powerful political empire. But God spoke to them through the prophet Haggai, telling them of fresh starts and second chances. Basically he reminded them of the Exodus (2:5-6). And Haggai encouraged them that what God did once, God could do again.

There is an old adage that says: "Life is ten percent circumstance and ninety percent attitude." Or again: "God plus one make a majority." When we know that God is with us and for us, then regardless of circumstance our attitude can become victorious.

A man awoke from a coma to find his wife sitting by his bed.

He motioned her to him. "Dear," he said, "you have been with me through so much. When I decided to start a business, you stood beside me, even though the endeavor was a foolish idea. When the business failed, you stood beside me. When I took another job in an industry I knew nothing about, you stood beside me. When I got fired, you still stood beside me. When I went to work third shift in a convenience store, you stood beside me. When I got shot in a robbery attempt, you stood beside me. You know what?"

"What dear?" she whispered.

He said, "I think you're bad luck!"

It was a matter of attitude. Some would have seen the light of her faithfulness and support. He focused on the darkness of his circumstances. He saw the glass half full.

It would have been easy for Haggai's people to see the glass as half empty, to focus only on the darkness of their circumstances. But the prophet reminded them of God's faithfulness, how God had stood beside and delivered them in days past. And Haggai believed that which God had done before, God would do again. "Yet now take courage . . . for I am with you, says the LORD. . . . I will shake the heavens and the earth and the sea and the dry land; and I will shake all the nations, so that the treasure of all nations shall come, and I will fill this house with splendor, says the LORD of hosts. . . . The latter splendor of this house shall be greater than the former . . . and in this place I will give prosperity" (2:4-9). God can move into situations of need and fear and work the miracle of new beginnings.

I have always appreciated the fact that graduations are called "commencement" exercises. To commence is to begin. That which one might interpret as "the end" (graduation) is in fact a new beginning. So it is with people of faith. God can move into our fear, our loss, our grief, our guilt, our despair, our sin, and our struggles with the promise of fresh starts and second chances, new beginnings and greater victories than we had ever dared to dream about. Each time we think we see a dead end ahead, by God's grace it may be a new commencement. God's power and our attitude can make it happen. (Michael B. Brown)

THE SKY IS FALLING

2 THESSALONIANS 2:1-5, 13-17

Remember the nursery story about chicken little? *The sky is falling; the sky is falling!* Well, both the Thessalonian church and you and I know that feeling. Remember the hype and hysteria in some religious circles about Jesus returning at the dawn of Y2K? Frankly, there isn't much difference between the question posed in these verses by the Thessalonians and the ever-present question in our times about the return of Jesus; it is merely a matter of *whether* and *when*.

I. The Setting of the Thessalonian Question

It seems that some members of the young church were getting hot and bothered by rumors, perhaps proclaimed by "spiritual" folk who prophesied, or by folk purporting to have seen a letter from Paul, or a report from Paul, *that the Lord had already returned.* And apparently there were those who were very concerned and upset. It was like wondering if the rapture had come and you were left behind. So the question to Paul was whether Jesus had actually returned. Paul's advice to this young, easily impressed church is still good advice for our times.

II. A Doctrine of the End Time

When we study this second chapter, we see that Paul reminds them that *Satan's last stand, his last big push, has to happen before Jesus returns.* (1) There has to be a falling away of Christians, Paul says. (2) "the Man of Lawlessness," the one who pretends to be God and persuades many others to accept him, must appear. (3) This evil one, this evil power, is presently being restrained, says Paul. This means that it is already at work even as Paul writes and continues to create confusion and evil in our world. (4) Sometime in the future, says Paul, this evil one, this *Antichrist*, will be revealed and unmasked for who he is, the tool of Satan, and he will be destroyed by Jesus' coming.

A couple of questions always arise when we deal with this passage: *Who is this "Man of Lawlessness,"* this counterfeit Christ? Usually identified with the Antichrist of the book of Revelation and the number 666, the efforts to name this tool of the devil are legion. Everyone from the Pope to Muhammad, from Napoleon to Martin Luther, from Hitler to Gorbachev (whose birthmark was seen to be the mark of the beast); from Henry Kissinger to Reagan (whose three names all had six letters and who recovered from a serious wound) have been suggested. We simply don't know who Paul was talking about, but *he clearly felt that the Thessalonian church members knew to whom he was referring.* A second question is *what holds that evil tool of Satan back?* The most popular suggestions are that this one is restrained by the Roman Empire, or by the Holy Spirit, or by the proclamation of the gospel. Again, we simply don't know what Paul was referring to.

III. Stick to Sound Doctrine

But more broad, and more important than whether we can identify this person or power, are the lessons Paul teaches that church in that situation. First, Paul says, remember that I taught you about all this when I was with you. *Stick to sound doctrine.* Notice that although Paul has apparently discussed his views on this unfolding scenario with the church, he doesn't try to identify the evil one, nor does he try to set a date for all this to happen. The most you and I can say is that our world is certainly *growing more evil, more morally confused, more anti-God and more pro-Satan,* and that this judgment is not the usual "this next generation is going to the dogs" kind of talk.

There is a tremendous growth of evil in ways unknown to former generations, and *we can draw the conclusion that it won't be as long until Jesus returns as we may have thought.* And with Paul, we need to be saying to each other: *Keep the focus on Jesus.* Do not focus on the devil and his work but on Jesus and his coming and his kingdom. We need to remember the little chorus that was popular when I was in college that told us to look full in Jesus' "wonderful face."

And the things of earth will grow strangely dim
In the light of his glory and grace.

IV. The Deceptive Power of Evil

A second lesson Paul points out is this: *Be aware of the deceptive power of evil.* Whether you and I have a complicated scheme of the end times or not, we need to hear Paul's word about a vast power of evil that counterfeits Christ. Surely that has been true in all ages, and is no less true in our times. The devil is smart enough to disguise himself as good—indeed, the Word says he can appear as an angel of light—and smart enough to use puppets that look for all the world like Jesus! I think of how in our *movies* prostitutes and lawbreakers are so often portrayed as the only ones who have a warm and generous heart, and therefore all else is excused. I think of how our courts' interpretation of *freedom of religion,* which looks good on the surface, has become the vehicle to deny and undermine Christianity even in our land. I think of *politicians* who speak with a religious tongue and live like the devil underneath it. I marvel at the *idolizing of evil, corrupt and indifferent people* on a trivial basis, as we do in the sports world. In all these ways and many more, I think we can see how evil disguises itself as good, and destroys our society.

V. Are You Ready?

The most important lesson Paul stresses to these Thessalonian folk caught up in their end-time excitement is this: *We need to prepare, rather than being caught up in wild excitement and speculation.* We are those chosen by the living God for salvation and sanctification and victory and glory through Jesus (2:13-16). Are you prepared if Jesus should come back today? If there is to be an increase of evil in the closing time—are you ready for persecution? Have you identified yourself with righteousness, with Jesus and his church? (Earl C. Davis)

THE POWER OF LIVING DOUBT

LUKE 20:27-38

This text "happens" on Tuesday before Jesus was arrested on Thursday and killed on Friday. Jesus' opponents are trying to trap him. They first question his authority (Luke 20:1-80). Then, they ask the question of paying taxes (Luke 20:20-26). Our text raises questions concerning the resurrection. Advent is near and the theme of judgment at Christ's coming is upon us. The theme of resurrection seems fitting, for there we find power in the midst of doubt.

I. What About the Sadducees?

The Sadducees raise the question of the resurrection, but they do not seem to grasp the significance of what is taking place. They are easy to dislike because, as Luke bluntly says, they do not believe in the resurrection (v. 27), and they are trying to trap Jesus. Yet, they need to be understood. The Sadducees were the conservatives of their day who had been in existence some two hundred years. Their mission was to preserve and conserve the Jewish way of life in the land that God had given them. They even accepted foreign rule as long as it meant that the tradition could be kept alive. The Sadducees were not perfect. They entered into unholy alliances for the sake of order and to preserve their self-interests. Yet, they sensed danger in this "resurrection" idea. For them it was not scriptural. They only accepted the first five books of the Old Testament and they did not find resurrection there. Resurrection was too speculative for them. It was morally risky. If there is another world beyond this one, why should people live responsibly now? In addition, they had political concerns. If the "good stuff" comes later, why not risk losing one's life in revolution? Ideas like resurrection could endanger all they loved. Their doubt had the noblest of aims and it came from a desire to conserve and not lose what God had given them. Though their motives were not pure, their concern was legitimate.

II. Two Kinds of Doubt

One kind of doubt is a dead/killing doubt. This kind of doubt says there is no God. There is no meaning or purpose in life. Society witnesses to this kind of doubt in its despairing behavior such as substance abuse, senseless killing, promiscuous behavior, the attitude that anything goes behavior because all is permissible. Life has no value and hopelessness abounds.

A second kind of doubt is faithful doubt. This is the kind of doubt the Sadducees had, who trusted God and did not need resurrection just to fill personal needs. They stress responsible life now, and so are trying to get Jesus to show how unsound this resurrection business was. In response, Jesus shows them resurrection from their own Scripture (v. 37). Yet he also points out that the Sadducees' question reveals the same error that led them to their doubt to begin with. They imagine resurrection life as being essentially like this one. Heaven does not equal earth taken to perfection. Life in God is not an extension of this life. Resurrection is complete transformation. The only thing that holds this life together with the next is God, the God of Abraham, Isaac, and Jacob. That is enough for real, true belief and hope. (Marcia T. Thompson)

NOVEMBER 18, 2001

❦

Twenty-fourth Sunday After Pentecost

Worship Theme: Jesus calms our fears in the face of uncertainty and disaster, promising to give us words and wisdom and to teach us to live in faith, caring for the good of all.

Readings: Isaiah 65:17-25; 2 Thessalonians 3:6-13; Luke 21:5-19

Call to Worship (Isaiah 12):

Leader:	You will say in that day: I will give thanks to you, O LORD, for though you were angry with me, your anger turned away, and you comforted me.
People:	**Surely God is my salvation;** **I will trust, and will not be afraid,** **for the LORD GOD is my strength and my might** **and has become my salvation.**
Leader:	With joy you will draw water from the wells of salvation. And you will say in that day: Give thanks to the LORD, call on his name; make known his deeds among the nations. . . .
People:	**Sing praises to the LORD who has done gloriously;** **let this be known in all the earth.** **Shout aloud and sing for joy, O royal Zion,** **for great in your midst is the Holy One of Israel.**

Pastoral Prayer:

God our creator and redeemer, we come in thanksgiving for your abundant gifts and in expectation that you will make all things new. Forgive us for the former ways of pride and selfishness; make us eager for them to be forgotten. Create us anew as you delight that we may love and serve you our whole life long. Renew your earth, O God, and all who live in it. Too many children die every day; too many mothers are denied the care they need for themselves and their children; too many old people are alone and in need. Grant that our infants may thrive and our elderly enjoy the blessings of a long and healthy life. Give us the wisdom and courage to share the wealth of this land; grant that those who build houses may live in them and those who plant our farmlands may have enough to eat. Bless your church that we may not be irresponsible or burdensome to each other; teach us to live in faith, caring for the good of all. Give us peace at all times and in all ways, through Jesus Christ, the Lord of peace. Amen. (Blair G. Meeks)

SERMON BRIEFS

THE AGE TO COME

ISAIAH 65:17-25

These words speak of the age to come in which all existing conditions will undergo complete transformation. In that day, there will be joy and peace. The sound of weeping will no longer be heard in the streets. People will live to be one hundred years old. Each person's enjoyment of the fruit of individual labor is promised and expected. Generations will live together simultaneously. Human desires will be fulfilled even before they have even been expressed. What is your vision for the age to come? Even more important, is God calling you to do something to hasten the coming of the new age?

What about *freedom from grief?* We see grief in a thousand ways every day. Children continue to be gunned down in the streets. Wars continue over who will possess a certain parcel of land. Senior citizens go to bed hungry and hurting, not only because there is no food, but because they crave a loving embrace. What are you going to do to hasten the coming of the new age when there will be no grief? Remember, "faith without works is dead."

What about *premature death?* Do you remember the names of Bufford O. Furrow, Jr., Alan Eugene Miller, Mark Barton, Benjamin Nathaniel Smith, T. J. Solomom, Eric Harris, Dylan Klebold, Sergei Barbarin, Russell Eugene Weston, Kipland Kinkel, Mitchell Johnson, Andrew Golden, Michael Carneal, and Luke Woodham? One thing they had in common was their execution-style killings of many innocent people throughout the United States during the last three years. These included schoolmates, business associates, family members, people known and unknown to them. These men have become a strange symbol of those in the *old* age who are responsible for so much premature death.

But before we let our anger get the best of us, or we become arrogant about our own supposedly good intentions and behavior, let's remember that Scripture has this awful indictment, "All who hate . . . are murderers."

In the new age people will live out the full span of their lives. What are you doing to make that happen? While the arguments over gun control continue, is there something we can do to stop the plague of premature death that is upon us as a race? What about being more attentive to what people are really saying to us, instead of writing it off as that person just having a bad day? When we sense that someone is on the edge, why do we not take steps to intervene? It takes courage to live in the new age. We will not move into the new age without both personal and corporate pain? A question to ponder: Is it worth it?

And finally, in the new age *oppression and exploitation* will no longer be realities. These evils remain so prevalent, that to mention them calls to mind the many ways we participate in their continuance in the world. If you could do one thing to alleviate this kind of suffering in our world, what would it be? To have no answer proves how widespread this problem is. The age to come, if we can believe the prophet, will focus on God-inspired solutions. (Jim Clardy)

GUIDING WORDS

2 THESSALONIANS 3:6-13

It was bound to happen. There was something in the Thessa-lonian church akin to the situation in the elementary school class-room when the teacher leaves the room. It seems the immaturity of everybody comes out! In the case of this church, the bigger issue in Paul's mind was the question of the return of Jesus. But we see in this third chapter that *orthodoxy* goes hand-in-hand with *orthopraxy*. Right thinking has to be accompanied with right actions.

I. Godly Folk Can Wobble

In this third chapter Paul asserts his apostolic authority (v. 6). He does not ask the church; he does not suggest to the church— he commands the church to separate itself from unruly members. Clearly Paul is thinking here of unethical behavior. Perhaps he has in mind some of those who have upset the church and done seri-ous damage to the fellowship and spiritual growth of the group by their talk about Jesus already having come. But it is more likely that Paul, as in his first letter to the Thessalonian church, has broader ethical concerns. So let us hear well this word that the church is the "unleavened lump," the sanctified and called-out body. We will also remember that in the correspondence to the Corinthians, Paul first urges disciplinary action on a brother; then he urges the church in a later letter to receive the repentant brother back into the circle of fellowship, lest Satan take advan-tage of his broken spirit and feeling of being outcast. Just so, as we hear Paul urging a life of separation from the world and condemn-ing those who "wobble" in the faith, themes that we all know and need to be emphasized in our times, let us also take seriously the teaching, not only of our Lord but also of Paul, on forgiveness.

II. Follow the Leader!

What an amazing passage of scripture: Follow me; I have noth-ing to hide, I will not lead you astray (vv. 7-9). I have always appreciated Paul's willingness to put himself up as a model for the saints to follow. I fear that the lives of many of us as leaders of God's people could not stand that kind of scrutiny. It is a sad fact that in the church, among the leadership both in the pulpit and in the pew, too often there is no desire to urge the brethren to follow our example in spiritual discipline, in financial commitment, in modeling Christian roles in the home and community. Can we imagine the impact a pastor and his congregational leaders would have if they boldly told the congregation, "You have us for an example, a model. Follow us in spiritual zeal, in modeling a Christian lifestyle, in finding freedom from the materialism of this world!—Our churches would be transformed. May that be your prayer and mine.

III. Individual Responsibility

And yet, in light of Paul's exhortation to use him for a model, Paul also rings the changes on the responsibility of the individual to lead a godly life (vv. 11-12). I remember from years ago a situation in which a man in a church I pastored had been away for some years and came back to find that everything had changed. He began to quietly undermine by comments about the present pastor and staff not being "spiritual," and the church not being spiritual. Frankly, it worked on me; I knew my shortcomings better than anyone, and I had to wonder if the man was right! And then he did something that set me free. In a fit of fresh zeal, he rose in a meeting to say that the Lord had convicted him to begin tithing his income to the church! I realized that while I was trying to live to the light I had, this man was simply a busybody who was not being spiritually honest. He was not even living as he knew he should! I think that sort of thing is what Paul is speaking about here. Somebody in the Thessalonian church was surely embarrassed when Paul's letter reached him or her! Lazy folk, hiding behind a guise of spirituality, were apparently stirring up the church and certainly sticking their noses into things that were none of their business. Paul urges these people to work for their living and keep their mouths shut.

Paul closes our scripture passage with the admonition: Do not be weary in doing good (verse 13). It's a word all God's people need to hear. We need to keep in touch with ourselves spiritually, lest we burn out and grow weary of well doing. Some of the saddest memories for any pastor are of those folk who grew tired, who burned and burned like the candle at both ends, and finally burned out. Sometimes they can be retrieved; sometimes they are lost to that particular church. Let our zeal be grounded in spiritual depth. (Earl C. Davis)

THE POWER OF LIVING FAITHFULLY

LUKE 21:5-19

In order to understand the passage it may be helpful to note that the events described in the text happen on Tuesday of Holy Week. The foreshadowing of things to come is very real. Jesus is using every opportunity to teach his disciples. Trying to prepare them for his death, resurrection, and return, he wants them to be ready for the uncertainty that will come for them very soon.

In verses 5 through 6, people are speaking of the temple's beauty. Jesus speaks to his disciples and tells of its destruction. To the disciples, the destruction of the temple was unthinkable, yet it happened within the lifetime of some of the disciples. It was truly the "end of the world," the end of the visible testimony to God's presence. The destruction of the temple was like having the props for their faith kicked out from under them. Jesus is thinking and speaking deeper than mere props. Jesus talks about faithful Christian life in those times when nothing built by human effort is available. Christian faith, which might at one time have comforted in times of trial, now is the cause of trials. Jesus knows his disciples will have such times of uncertainty.

Jesus warns his disciples (and us) in verse 8 to "Beware that you are not led astray." He tells them that while many people will come and predict the end of time, he himself does not know when it will take place. The tone, however, leaves a sense of urgency. Jesus says in verse 9, "Do not be terrified" of all the disasters that will happen. War, sickness, earthquakes, and famines are going to happen and have happened in some part of the world through all the generations.

In verse 13, Jesus tells the disciples (and Christians everywhere) persecution will give opportunity to "testify." God will give the words required for each occasion. There are many places in the world where being a Christian can be a reason for imprisonment and even death. In China and other Asian countries, Christians gather in illegal house churches. They "testify" to us of the urgency of faithfulness, because faithfulness leads to eternal life (v. 19).

A living faith has a sense of urgency, a passion for life, and the ability to see every opportunity in our lives as an opportunity to "testify." We have become lazy in America. Because of our freedom, we have seen the church decline as the central focus, and other interests have come to the fore. We are being "led astray" by other things that draw our attention to the possibility of happiness and hope. Unfortunately most are looking for those things in the wrong places. What are those things that are leading us astray from Jesus? What would happen if all of a sudden the faith that has brought comfort in times of trial becomes the cause of trials and hardships? Would you still faithfully follow?

The girl at Columbine High School two years ago, who in face of death said she was a believer, "testified" faithfully. A humble woman named Mother Teresa "testified" faithfully by giving her life to those who were helpless and dying. Both witness to us that we need to always be ready and should "testify" with our very lives. A song that was performed on the television program, *Touched By An Angel,* might be a fitting prayer for us all:

For as long as I shall live I will testify to love
I'll be a witness in the silences when words are not enough.
(Paul Field, et al. "Testify To Love," *Touched By An Angel: The Album* [Sony Music Soundtrax, 1998])

(Marcia T. Thompson)

NOVEMBER 25, 2001

❦

Christard the King/Reign of Christ Sunday

Worship Theme: God sent the beloved Son Jesus, who left his throne in glory, to live among us and be called a king like no other; a king who reigns with justice and humility, exalting the lowly.

Readings: Jeremiah 23:1-6; Colossians 1:11-20; Luke 23:33-43

Call to Worship (Song of Zechariah, Luke 1:68-79):

> *Leader:*   Blessed be the Lord God of Israel,
> for he has looked favorably on the people and redeemed them.
> He has raised up a mighty savior for us
> in the house of his servant David,

> *People:*   **as he spoke through the mouth of his holy prophets from of old,**
> **that we would be saved from our enemies**
> **and from the hand of all who hate us.**
> **Thus he has shown the mercy promised to our ancestors,**
> **and has remembered his holy covenant,**
> **the oath that he swore to our ancestor Abraham,**
> **to grant that we be rescued from the hands of our enemies,**
> **might serve him without fear,**
> **in holiness and righteousness**
> **before him all our days.**

> *Leader:*   And you, child, will be called the prophet of the Most High;
> for you will go before the Lord to prepare his ways,

to give knowledge of salvation to the people
by the forgiveness of their sins.

People: **By the tender mercy of our God,**
              the dawn from on high will break upon us,
              to give light to those who sit in darkness and
              in the shadow of death,
              to guide our feet into the way of peace.

Pastoral Prayer:

God our shepherd king, you have promised a reign where we
will no longer feel afraid or be dismayed. Gather us now and lead
us home at last. We give thanks that you rescued us and trans-
ferred us into the kingdom of your beloved Son, through whom
and for whom all earthly power was created. We praise you for
sending Jesus, who left his throne in glory to be called king by
those who honored him with branches and by those who gave
him a crown of thorns. Make us strong with all the strength that
comes from his glorious power. We pray for all who this day call
on Jesus to hear their cries, for he is a king like no other, a king
who listens all day long. He breaks the power of oppression and
calls his saints from everywhere; no one works like him. Teach us
to embrace all people in his name and to nourish his justice in
the world. Give us grace to serve his endless reign that all things
may be reconciled to God through Christ our head, who makes
peace by the blood of the cross. Amen. (Blair G. Meeks)

SERMON BRIEFS

THE PROMISE AND RESPONSIBILITY
OF LEADERSHIP

JEREMIAH 23:1-6

Within the Old Testament, the word shepherd is often used as
a metaphor for the king or governing class of officials within the
land. As a prophet during one of Judah's most tumultuous times

politically and socially, Jeremiah had much to say about the quality of leadership that the king and his fellow leaders had exercised. These verses contain words of strong condemnation for the past and present leadership of the nation of Israel. However, once the past and present concerns have been voiced by Jeremiah, words of hope for the future are spoken.

In verses 1 through 3, Jeremiah begins with words of judgment spoken against those who had ruled unjustly. The king and his advisors, as shepherds, were to look out for the well-being of the people. Their chief concern was to be the welfare of those people within their care. However, the Lord pronounces judgment upon the rulers, for as he looks over the kingdom he sees nothing but destruction and a scattered, fearful bunch who have been driven from their homes. It was a dark time in the nation of Judah, and there was little hope that things would be quickly remedied.

Yet, verses 4 through 6 paint a different picture for the future. The Lord himself promises to gather the remnant of the flock and bring them back to the fold. He will raise up new shepherds who will truly shepherd the people, including "a righteous Branch, and he shall reign as king and deal wisely, and shall execute justice and righteousness in the land. In his days, Judah will be saved and Israel will live in safety. And this is the name by which he will be called: 'The LORD is our righteousness'" (vv. 5-6). What encouraging words to speak to a nation that is cynical and hopeless! The leaders of the past who were unjust and unwise will not have the last word. The last word belongs to God, who is working to do a new thing in Israel. This word is a word of hope for people who need security and welfare in their life as a society.

The "raising up of a righteous Branch" has Messianic overtones for those of us living after the time of Christ, yet most scholars believe that Jeremiah was not looking that far into the future. Deliverance for the people of Israel was needed in very concrete ways, and one of the best ways that God could provide for them was to give them leaders of integrity and honor. The hope of Jeremiah was indeed that "Judah will be saved and Israel will live in safety" (v. 6). A king who would execute justice and righteousness in the land was the only way that this society would indeed live in safety. The hope is for a leader who would call upon the Lord to be their righteousness and their strength.

Jeremiah's word speaks to us about the great responsibility and the great promise that lie at the heart of leadership. Any person who is entrusted with the care and welfare of people—a parent, teacher, pastor, or president—must attend to their job with the utmost concern. God's harshest judgment is perhaps reserved for those who have not attended to their responsibilities, and have in fact done harm to those who are most dependent upon them. God seeks even now to raise up men and women who will execute fairly and administrate rightly. In the midst of the busyness of work, school, and home, God calls out leaders who realize their ultimate dependence upon "The Lord who is our Righteousness." These words of Jeremiah serve as a powerful reminder of where the people of God and their leaders can find true safety and rest. (Wendy Joyner)

ENDURING STRENGTH FROM THE SUPREME SAVIOR

COLOSSIANS 1:11-20

The painfully true confession of ministers is not desirable to hear, at least not for those who are suffering. The truth is most ministers face people in the midst of adversity and difficulty with a desire to give them a quick fix. "take two spiritual aspirins and see me next Sunday." Paul is less hopeful for a fast cure to Christian adversity. This text stands as a challenge to those who desire to offer encouragement to those suffering. The truth is, there is no easy way out.

I. A Significant Prayer (vv. 11-12)

Paul prays that the Colossian believers will be made strong and be prepared to endure all things. Not just endure all things, but to do them with patience, joy, and gratitude. Quite a tall order for believers in the first century who may have lost their lives for this item called Christian faith!

Paul does not pray for what we all secretly crave. You know the prayer, "Lord, take this thorn from me! Get me out of here!" No, instead he prays for strength and preparation for the difficulties. Strength is certainly always welcomed, but "preparation" for hardship sounds like "boot camp." Preparation calls forth images of practice and in this case means that we may learn from smaller difficulties how to face larger difficulties. He does not pray us out of the difficulties (cf. Romans 5:3-5).

Perhaps the practice of endurance is needed not for the survival through difficulties but the posture during them. Paul prays that the Colossians would exemplify endurance marked by patience, joy, and gratitude to God. *Patience* is demonstrated toward others, *joy* is an inner personal posture, and *gratitude* relates to our relationship with God.

II. The Source of Strength (vv. 13-20)

God is to receive thanks in our endurance of difficulties because despite the immediate circumstances, God enables believers to partake in the benefit of God's saints. God's is a work that is wholly one-sided. It is the Lord who rescues us and transfers us into the kingdom of Jesus Christ (v. 13). Through Christ, believers have redemption and the forgiveness of sin. For that act of God in Christ, we are to be thankful even when enduring difficult circumstances. Somewhere in the midst of the gratitude, the joy, and the patience, a believer finds strength outside the human realm.

The source of the strength is in the one who has accomplished redemption and forgiveness of sin for the believer. He is a "redeemer" because he is the agent of creation. One would have to ignore Paul's clear intention in verses 15 through 20 to fail to recognize that if he is not the creator, then he is not the redeemer. Thus Jesus must be kept in the proper perspective given the heresy to which the Colossian believers were exposed.

Jesus Christ is the image of the invisible God. That is, he is the direct and perfect reflection of the Father. If one has seen Jesus, one has seen the Father (John 14:8-11). Moreover, he is the first-born of all creation, but that is not to say that he was created. In him all things, spiritual and physical, were created. He created them for his own purposes. Paul stretches the modern scientific mind here to hold to a redeemer who is such by his position as

REFLECTIONS

❦

DECEMBER

Reflection Verses: "Zechariah said to the angel, 'How will I know that this is so? For I am an old man and my wife is getting on in years.' The angel replied, 'I am Gabriel. I stand in the presence of God, and I have been sent to speak to you and to bring you this good news. But now, because you did not believe my words, which will be fulfilled in their time, you will become mute, unable to speak, until the day these things occur'" (Luke 1:18-20).

The first person we meet in Luke's Gospel is a clergyperson, and the first part of the Advent/Christmas story becomes a great joke on him. Would you like a part in the Christmas pageant this year? Who would you like to be—a shepherd, an angel, Mary? If you're clergy, Luke says, "No, here's your part. Come on stage dressed as you are, like a preacher. You're the one who in the line of duty gets the very first report of good news. Then you stand there in the Holy Place telling Gabriel himself that you need a sign. Then you're struck dumb, dummy, sent to the back of the class, with nine months of your own pregnant silence to pay attention and maybe learn something."

I guess we shouldn't be all that hard on Zechariah. Luke says that both he and Elizabeth were righteous and blameless. And the story really needs to put a sock in his professional, male mouth, to clear the stage for the soaring exchange between those two impossibly pregnant, prophetic women. Besides, we understand his position. When it's your job to say the holy words, make the holy gestures, and generally run the business of the holy place, it can come as a terrible shock that the Holy actually happens. More specifically, you get so used to managing sacred speech and action, it's easy to be unprepared for the sacred to break through in spite of you with huge surprises.

Strictly speaking, Zechariah's sin is not that he questioned Gabriel or God. After all, Mary had a question for Gabriel too: "How can this be, since I am a virgin?" Her question expresses bafflement, amazement, a realistic, brassy biological doubt. But notice the difference in the question of the old priest. "How will I *know* that this is so?" This is the question of a manager. It's not the expression of doubt; it's an insistence on verification, an itch for that much control. Mary may have been troubled, but this man is anxious; and his anxiety goes grasping.

By his own admission, Zechariah is an old man. Maybe he has simply seen too much disappointment in his life not to go grasping for a manageable certainty. Maybe Elizabeth's heart had been broken too many times for him to go telling her this news without being double sure that it's true. Maybe, too, he has heard more than his share of religious humbug in his day—smiling true believers promising how soon God will make it all better. Our profession puts us in a prime position to witness both humbug and heartbreak. Spend enough time in priesthood and not only will you see your own heart broken, you may come to suspect that you've been a bit of a humbug yourself. No wonder our ranks are filled with the cynical and depressed. The church is full of Zechariahs, men and women at the altar feeling old, hard pressed to believe in the arrival of anything splendidly new.

Like him, our anxiety has a way of rendering us mute. A worried congregation waited for Zechariah, their faces lifted in expectation, needing the blessing from their priest. But when he emerged, all they got was a man gaping like a fish and waving his arms in the air. An anxious priest forfeits the power to bless. How easily pastoral speech itself becomes a kind of mute arm-waving. Rivers of proper words spouted by preachers devoid of their own passion or hope or astonished faith will be like video with the sound turned off. Nothing that matters will get heard; the people will leave without benediction.

So what's an old priest to do? Maybe we could start by pondering a literal answer to Zechariah's question. "How will I know that this is so?" What Gabriel could just as well have told him is that he most certainly *would* know. He would know when his wife started puking in the mornings, and when her belly started swelling, and when she placed a howling son in his arms. He would know not by insisting on confirmation but by waiting for it to come in its own time. We managerial types don't excel at waiting, but there's no bypassing Advent. We begin to uncurl our anxious fingers from today's frustration by opening receptive hands for tomorrow's revelation. Trusting God can mean trusting time. We wait.

And maybe we follow Zechariah by undertaking a new kind of silence. The story frames his muteness as a punishment, but we could just as easily understand it as a gift, perhaps a cure. To an anxious, controlling religious professional comes the mandate: Hush! Close your mouth and open your eyes. You're not in charge after all, and you have nothing to say until you have paid attention to the mysteries unfolding before you.

If it's your job in this season to stand and proclaim the promises and to call a people into watchful waiting, can you imagine a more crucial preparation than to observe your own watchful silence, with open hands toward tomorrow's fulfillments?

When Elizabeth's baby was born and Zechariah's time-out was over, the first word to rush with the Spirit from his mouth was, "Blessed!" And it came in the form of a song. When we priests grow silent enough to wait for the promises, and watch for them, and wish for them, we will regain the power to bless. It will be music in everyone's ears, especially our own. (Paul D. Duke)

DECEMBER 2, 2001

❦

First Sunday of Advent

Worship Theme: The God of peace calls us to join the streams of people from all nations who will exchange their swords for plowshares in anticipation of Christ's coming reign of glory.

Readings: Isaiah 2:1-5; Romans 13:11-14; Matthew 24:36-44

Call to Worship (Psalm 122):

Leader: I was glad when they said to me,
"Let us go to the house of the LORD!"
Our feet are standing within your gates, O Jerusalem.
Jerusalem—built as a city that is bound firmly together.

People: **To it the tribes go up
the tribes of the LORD,
as was decreed for Israel,
to give thanks to the name of the LORD.
For there the thrones for judgment were set up,
the thrones of the house of David.**

Leader: Pray for the peace of Jerusalem:
"May they prosper who love you.
Peace be within your walls,
and security within your towers."

People: **For the sake of my relatives and friends
I will say, "Peace be within you."
For the sake of the house of the LORD our God,
I will seek your good.**

Pastoral Prayer:

God of peace, you call us to your holy mountain to join the streams of people from all nations who will exchange their swords for plowshares and their spears for pruning hooks. Grant that we may walk in your paths, leaving the shadows of confusion and discord to live in the light of your presence. We pray for all who work toward the day when we will study war no more: for those who negotiate treaties, those who teach conflict resolution, those who show the ways of peace to the children, those who bring your justice and mercy. We thank you for the promise of Jesus' coming again in glory as he once came in lowliness and need. Because we do not know the day of our Lord's coming, wake us up from our sleep that we may live honorably and put on the clothes of light. Because salvation is nearer to us now than when we first believed, keep us awake that we may lay aside all our sorrow and put on the Lord Jesus Christ, in whose name we pray. Amen. (Blair G. Meeks)

SERMON BRIEFS

GOD'S HOUSE IS A PEACEFUL HOUSE

ISAIAH 2:1-5

What would you do if you were God? John Mortimer's barrister *extraordinaire*, Horace Rumpole, once mused on such a question. "Would I," he ruminated,

> have cobbled up a globe totally without the minus quantities we have grown used to, a place with no fatal diseases or traffic jams. . . ? Above all, would I have created a world entirely without evil? And, when I come to think rather further along these lines, it seems to me that a world without evil might possibly be a damned dull world—or an undamned dull world, perhaps I should say . . ." (*Rumpole on Trial* [New York: Viking Penguin, 1992], p. 1.)

Thankfully, the world isn't so dull, damned or undamned. A report filed in last year's newspapers concerning Sharon Stone was most touching. The Hollywood actress gave up her collection of firearms to the Los Angeles County Sheriff's Department, following the shooting and killing of students at Columbine High School in Littleton, Colorado.

In Atlanta, Georgia, that same month, a local church sponsored a gun "buy-back" day on the heels of a shooting incident at Heritage High School in nearby Conyers, Georgia. People came from near and far with pistols, sawed-off shotguns, even miniature submachine guns. For every firearm delivered, each man or woman received fifty dollars. The weapon was carefully checked, then placed in an eighteen-gauge brushed steel casket, which was later buried.

Congress began explorations into the subject of violence in the media. The number of violent acts witnessed on a given day of television programming is staggering; it's even worse with 150 to 500-channel satellite television. One wonders about the environment of teenagers like T. J. Solomon. He broke into his stepfather's gun cabinet, withdrew the .22-caliber shotgun, which he fired at will into the Heritage High student body before morning classes, as well as a .357 magnum snub-nosed pistol, which he was relieved of before further injuries could be inflicted.

Our children are not exempt from this. Far too many stories are documented in which children under twelve years of age discover a loaded handgun in a desk or dresser drawer, in the top of a closet, or under a bed, then go outside to "play" with it. Several years ago, the *Free Press* reported that a youngster in Detroit, Michigan, who killed his cousin, was completely unaware a single bullet was in the revolver at the moment he pulled the trigger the fourth or fifth time.

We live in a vicious world—or, at least, it seems that we do. It isn't the world that is vicious; it's that we are, at least potentially. It is said that Adolf Hitler could not hold a conversation. He carried off the veil of omniscience by memorizing huge lists of facts and used these to embarrass his underlings and keep the reins of power tight. This is not particularly engaging; instead, it is smothering. Psychologist James Hillman put it well when he remarked that if we do not learn from that demonic character, we might vote into power someone who wins a TV trivia contest.

> If [a] clue to psychopathy is a trivial mind expressing itself in high-sounding phrases, then an education emphasizing facts rather than thinking, and patriotic, politically or religiously correct

"values" rather than critical judgment may produce a nation of achieving high school graduates who are also psychopaths. (*The Soul's Code: In Search of Character and Calling* [New York: Random House, 1996], p. 225)

But God has established a house not made with hands where peace is the prime directive. Final arbitration between the nations and Israel will take place therein. The people of their own accord—or so they think—shall come to learn of the ways of God. People will come from near and far to be educated and judged.

And as a result of their willingness to learn, they will be transformed. They will change from a people of the spear and sword to a people of agrarian peace, perhaps taking on the image of Grant Wood's 1930 Midwestern farming couple of "American Gothic" fame. And they will no longer learn war. (Eric Killinger)

IT'S TIME!

ROMANS 13:11-14

"You know what time it is," commented Paul to his readers in Rome (v. 11). Whether they did or not, do we? What Paul meant by these words is not so obvious to us. The dual focus of Advent on the first and final comings of Christ provides a good opportunity to reflect upon time and our relation to it.

This age, to which we are not to be conformed (Romans 12:2), measures life by marking the chronological passage of time: one has lived so many years; the days pass in increments of seven, thirty, three hundred sixty-five, punctuated from time to time by "holidays"; only x more shopping days until Christmas! There may be a sense of a goal in time so marked—getting a driver's license, turning twenty-one, graduating, getting a promotion, retiring. Yet, time seems to devolve into a cycle largely devoid of meaning. Time passes and so do we, and we are gone and our places know us no more. In the desire for our lives to count for something, we work toward making our place bear the mark of our having been here.

When we transpose this perspective on time to the realm of the eschatological, we risk distortion. In the reckoning of the world, this Advent, one in a succession of Advents, should see something that we have done to "bring in the Kingdom." As we see continued evidence of *fallenness* and *unredeemedness*, we can become despondent, as though our lives really make little difference.

This is a flawed perspective. Each Advent is new and even though we encounter themes of judgment, it is not mere negativity with regard to the way our lives have been. Why is this? Advent partakes of time in the world reflected in the Bible and liturgy. Time in this world is a matter of ripening, of coming to fullness. In his letter to the Galatians, Paul spoke very plainly of this (cf. Galatians 4:4-5; also Philip H. Pfatteicher, *Liturgical Spirituality* [Valley Forge: Trinity Press International, 1997], p. 107). Time calls us, therefore, not to frantic attempts to make meaning, but to expectancy for the revelation of God's meaning. Attempts to make meaning are exercises in idolatry wherein we attempt to create our own salvation. We are called rather to await that which meets us from God's future, seen most fully in Christ.

This sense of time is a freeing judgment, a "no" that brings with it a "yes." It relativizes all of our achievements. On the one hand, it relativizes the good we have accomplished. All our accomplishments, no matter how grand, lack ultimacy and can become idols in our hands. Advent speaks a stern and somber "no" to them. Yet on the other hand, all the wrong that we have committed is also relativized. It is not excused or passed over, but subjected to judgment that holds forth the possibility of new life. A historically oriented sermon on this passage may be preached by focusing upon St. Augustine, who wrestled long and hard with matters of achievements for both good and evil and his relation to God. His conversion was sealed when he read these words from Romans in Alypius's garden. Augustine recounted this narrative of spiritual journey in the first eight chapters of his *Confessions*, with the climax coming in chapter 8. Reflecting on the event, Augustine wrote, "I was mad and dying; but there was sanity in my madness, life in my death. . . ." (*The Confessions of St. Augustine*, trans. Rex Warner [New York: Mentor Books, 1963], p. 175). He was met by a possibility not his own, and so by a future he could not make, but could only receive as a gift from God. Such is the word of Advent.

Let us therefore be contrite but without anxiety, For Powers and Times are not gods but mortal gifts from God; Let us acknowledge our defeats but without despair, For all societies and epochs are transient details, Transmitting an everlasting opportunity that the Kingdom of Heaven may come, not in our present And not in our future, but in the Fullness of Time. (W. H. Auden, *Collected Longer Poems* [New York: Random House, 1969], p. 163.)

(Philip E. Thompson)

THE CRIME OF DELAY

MATTHEW 24:36-44

Some experiences in life are those "Never to be forgotten" ones that cause a person to say, "I'll never forget when. . . ." The horrible event is over, but the shadow remains.

Jesus' story in this text reminds me of one of those, "I'll never forget when . . ." chapters in my life. A few short days after moving into the first home we owned in our ministry, we experienced a break-in while we were away overnight. My wife returned home and entered the house by the side door. She sensed something was wrong, then discovered someone had kicked in our back door. After calling the police we found that little had been stolen, but the intruder had trashed the bedroom while rummaging through our belongings. We lost what most victims lose—our security of privacy. For months it was difficult to enter the house without wondering who might be lurking behind the couch or standing in the shadow of the closets. Immediately after the break-in we beefed up security by installing sensor lighting, fixing the broken door, and changing locks. Like the owner of the house in Jesus' story, had we known the time the thief was coming, we would have stayed home, left the lights on, played loud music, and borrowed a pit bull from one of the neighbors to greet the thief.

Jesus informs his hearers that he would return at the least expected hour and our crime would be to delay our action of preparedness.

423

I. Preparation Includes Prioritization

First things first should be our motto. Jesus placed the idea in perspective when he said, "seek first the kingdom of God and his righteousness. . . ." Kingdom priorities include:

- Salvation—becoming Kingdom bound (John 3:16).
- Sanctification—becoming holy (Hebrews 12:14).
- Faith—living by hope not sight (2 Corinthians 5:7).
- Grace—living worthy of our calling (Ephesians 4:1).
- Commitment—to the person of Jesus (Matthew 9:9).
- Worship—a right attitude toward a Holy God (Revelation 4:11).
- Scripture—the craving of absolute truth (1 Peter 2:2-3).
- Prayer—the two-way communication with Almighty God (Ephesians 6:18).
- Servanthood—the search to become great through becoming less (John 3:30).

Are you living with Kingdom priorities in your heart or the anti-God ho-hum priorities of the world?

II. Preparation Includes Proaction

Shakespeare's *Hamlet* is about a gifted young prince who possessed sensitivity, wit, and exceptional intelligence. People looked to him as their leader. But Hamlet had one noticeable flaw: he could not bring himself to take action.

At the genesis of the play Hamlet encounters his murdered father's ghost. The spirit relates that Hamlet's uncle—his father's brother was the villain who killed him. Hamlet screams outrage and revenge upon his uncle. Throughout the play Hamlet does nothing to seek the revenge promised to his father.

Hesitation plagues Hamlet. He talks about revenge, thinks about it, imagines it, plans it, but never does anything about it.

Frustrated by his son's procrastination the father's ghost reappears to Hamlet and basically says, "For Pete's sake, quit talking and get on with it."

Christians all too often hesitate, doubt and retreat when God calls for action!

- How many people would become Christians if Christians evangelized?
- How many people could be fed and clothed if Christians took the social gospel seriously?
- How many people could be healed if Christians interceded for wellness?
- How many children would be protected if Christians would not turn their heads?
- How many teenage pregnancies would be avoided if Christians pushed for abstinence?
- How many deaths by drunk drivers would be stopped if Christians proclaimed temperance?

For God's sake, it's time to quit talking and get on with it!

III. Preparation Includes Positiveness

Negativity destroys accomplishment of any goals. When we examine the scripture text, Jesus definitely relates the fact that sometime he is returning. What a positive eternal event it will be—for those who are ready for his return any hour of the day or night? I want to be like the one man working in the field or the woman grinding with the hand mill who are taken by God. How exciting that day will be for those prepared for their trip to an eternally positive destination. Are you positive you are ready? (Derl Keefer)

DECEMBER 9, 2001

❧

Second Sunday of Advent

Worship Theme: The God of promise intends for all creatures to live together in harmony. God sent John to prepare the way for Christ's coming reign of equity and mercy.

Readings: Isaiah 11:1-10; Romans 15:4-13; Matthew 3:1-12

Call to Worship (Psalm 72:1-7, 18-19):

Leader: Give the king your justice, O God,
and your righteousness to a king's son.

People: **May he judge your people with righteousness,**
and your poor with justice.
May the mountains yield prosperity for the people,
and the hills, in righteousness.

Leader: May he defend the cause of the poor of the people,
give deliverance to the needy,
and crush the oppressor.

People: **May he live while the sun endures,**
and as long as the moon, throughout all generations.
May he be like rain that falls on the mown grass,
like showers that water the earth.

Leader: In his days may righteousness flourish
and peace abound, until the moon is no more.

426

People: **Blessed be the LORD, the God of Israel,
who alone does wondrous things.
Blessed be his glorious name forever;
may his glory fill the whole earth. Amen and
Amen.**

Pastoral Prayer:

God of promise, your plan for creation is to bring all creatures together in harmony: the wolf and the lamb, the leopard and the kid, the calf and the lion. Give us the trust and joy of a little child, and lead us to live in peace with one another in accordance with Christ Jesus. Grant that we may join with all earth's inhabitants and in one voice glorify God. You sent your messenger John to preach repentance and prepare the way for Christ's coming: Flood our lives with the light of your presence that we may find a new way to live and await with gladness the coming in glory of Jesus our Redeemer. Extend your hand to us, O Lord; bring equity to the poor, mercy to the outcast, endurance to the discouraged, and steadfastness to the weak. Bring to earth the fullness of your knowledge as the waters cover the sea. We give you thanks for your gracious assurance that the root of Jesse shall come. Bring us at last to your glorious dwelling; in the name of Jesus Christ, in whom we hope. Amen. (Blair G. Meeks)

SERMON BRIEFS

A PORTRAIT OF THE CHRIST

ISAIAH 11:1-10

There are many portraits of Christ. None is better than this word picture painted for us by Isaiah. Written seven centuries before he came, it perfectly describes him.

I. He Will Have a Great Mind (vv. 2-3*a*)

Everyone acknowledges the wisdom of Jesus. Agnostics acknowledge the wisdom of Jesus. Atheists acknowledge the

427

wisdom of Jesus. He showed a comprehensive knowledge of God. He showed a thorough understanding of man. His sermons were deep; his parables practical and pointed.

II. He Will Show a Great Sense of Justice (vv. 3*b*-4)

Injustice was common in Isaiah's time and in Jesus' time. Injustice is still common today. It was the poor especially who were ill-used in those days. There was a need for a just judge, an impartial judge. There will always be such a need. There will always be a need for punishment for the wicked. No thinking person can just dismiss the awful deeds of the merciless as if they were insignificant. Can you imagine a Heaven to which everyone is admitted? Can you imagine a Heaven that included Atilla the Hun, Adolf Hitler, Joseph Stalin, and Saddam Hussein? If "man's inhumanity to man" is never ever punished then justice does not exist in the world; it is only a figment of someone's idealistic imagination. So here, equity for those who have been ill-used is balanced by retribution for those who have mistreated them.

III. He Will Usher in a Great Peace (vv. 6-9)

What a lovely picture here! Natural enemies (wolf and lamb, leopard and kid, calf and lion) live together in peace. It must have been this way in the Garden of Eden! While we will not take this picture literally, we will certainly take it seriously. History notes a period of relative calm in the western world and calls it *Pax Romana*: the peace of Rome. But it was an enforced peace, and not a lasting peace. The *Pax Jesus* (the peace of Jesus) will be real and eternal. We do not see this peace in world situations today, but we will see it someday. Meanwhile we have a foretaste of it in our hearts. In the Bible it is called "the peace that passes understanding."

IV. He Will Bring a Great Vision (v. 10)

The first readers of this verse were startled by it. They never thought of the Gentiles as a matter of concern to God. Gentiles were of little concern to them! But here, in the midst of one of their greatest books, is this promise that the Gentiles will come to acknowledge the God of Israel. It was another way of saying that "all nations" should hear about God (Luke 24:47). The Lord Jesus made crystal clear what should have been understood from this text. "Everybody ought to know who Jesus is!" Everyone should have the opportunity to believe in the Christ and to love and serve him. We wonder how the Jews missed that! But then we wonder how we too sometimes miss it. Our circle of concern should be as large as God's! That's more difficult now than it ever was, because we know so much of the news of the world. Difficult or not, our concerns should mirror his! (Robert C. Shannon)

THE WITNESS OF WELCOME

ROMANS 15:4-13

You could, with justification, decide not to preach on this lesson. Wedged between lessons that offer much more familiar Advent themes (the shoot from Jesse, the "Peaceful Kingdom," John the Baptizer's call to repent), the Romans lesson lacks the sense of urgency we tend to associate with Advent. What's more, some crucial omissions have been made in the assignment of verses. Verses 1 through 3 are required to add the lesson's necessary context.

I would suggest that, being careful to add the first three verses, this lesson may be fruitfully employed to illumine the Christian life. In so doing, it sheds light on and receives light from the Isaiah and Matthew lessons. As evocative and captivating as the image of the "peaceful kingdom" is, what does it have to do with real life? What keeps it from being simply a dream, the stuff of wishful thinking? Also, as often as we hear of its necessity, what does it mean concretely to "repent" or turn toward the future that is coming from God? This lesson indicates that the life of the community that is indeed turned toward God's future revealed in Christ will reflect the peace that is brought by that future.

Christ did not seek to act for his own benefit (v. 3), but stood in radical solidarity with others, particularly the poor, the outcast, and sinners. His life was turned from self-interest to the future, peaceful reign of God. For us to "welcome one another" (v. 7) is for us to live likewise. We turn from narrow self-interest, no longer looking for our own gain and benefit, but orienting our lives toward the good of others, and so toward God (1 John 3:11-19). We will be turned toward that promised future. This is to repent. Living in reconciliation and forgiveness, our lives will reflect the reconciliation of Jew and Gentile that God effected in Christ, fulfilling the promises to the chosen people. When the Christian community lives by overcoming divisions, it becomes the tangible sign on earth of God's peaceful kingdom that will be made full in the final restoration of creation. (Philip E. Thompson)

IGNITING THE FLAME

MATTHEW 3:1-12

One has to like John the Baptist's straightforward approach to life. His preaching and message to the people were simple, austere, and right to the point: "change your life." The message cannot be any simpler.

John's bluntness offended the religious leaders when he dared to call them a brood of vipers or snakes.

He tells the people he is simply a messenger from God, but that Jehovah has on the scene a main character coming who is the Messiah. This appointed one will then "ignite the kingdom life within you, a fire within you, the Holy Spirit within you, changing you from the inside out" (*The Message*, p. 17). The Spirit is the personification of Jesus, the Messiah.

Scientists explain that fire has three distinct rays:

- One that is a chemical change produces the tempering of steel and turns wood into ashes.
- One that is caloric produces heat.
- One that is luminous produces light.

These three aspects also give a clue of the function of the Holy Spirit as it enters a person's life.

• The Flame of the Holy Spirit burns up sin producing purity.
• The Flame of the Holy Spirit within produces power.
• The Flame of the Holy Spirit illuminates perpetually.

I. The Flame of the Holy Spirit Burns the Sin of Impurity Producing Purity

The nature of sin presents itself like a two-headed serpent. The outer conduct is the result of the carnality that lies beneath the surface. It is the matter of transgression as well as disposition.

There are the sins of the flesh and the sins of the spirit that must be dealt with before the spiritual house is clean. When God's Holy Spirit comes he will arrange the house as he sees fit and then take out the trash and burn it!

David's anguished cry of Psalm 51 is a prayer of holy desire for purity, "blot out my transgressions" (v. 1 NIV) and then, "create in me a pure heart, O God" (v. 10 NIV). The Psalmist realized that his fleshly transgression of adultery stemmed from an inner carnal condition of sin. We should echo his longing for heart purity.

II. The Flame of the Holy Spirit Burns Within Producing Power

The New Testament draws a line in the sand at Pentecost. On one side of that line is found spiritual inadequacies, moral fumbling, denial, and defeat. The best illustration of this is the picture of the disciples huddled in the upper room of Jerusalem with the masses passing by daily and no word from the allies of Jesus. As the disciples looked back all they could see was the horror of the crucifixion. They also remembered the resurrected Jesus who gave them an incredible homework assignment—to preach the gospel to every nation. Jesus stayed with them for forty days giving them the message but not the power or courage to proclaim it. On the day of Pentecost John the Baptist's prophecy was fulfilled. As God poured out the Holy Spirit upon the spiritual cowards gathered in prayer, God doused them with spiritual adequacy, moral certainty, the power of redemptive evangelistic offense, and victory. God did not take away their humanness, but cleansed them to correct their disposition to sin. In that moment God's holiness was shared with them.

431

The Holy Spirit helped these disciples to live a lifestyle that was holy, pleasing, and acceptable unto God—which was their reasonable service. Today in this new millennium God will do the same for anyone who desires to be holy. Holiness unto the Lord ought to be our watchword and song.

III. The Flame of the Holy Spirit Illuminates Perpetually

One of the chief qualities of fire is its ability to light other fires. A tiny spark can ignite a great blaze. Several years ago on the out-skirts of Los Angeles someone threw a smoldering cigarette along the road. It set fire to a few dry leaves, and they in turn set the trees on fire. Soon there was a tremendous conflagration that swept through the woods, consuming hundreds of acres of fine timber, and threatening many homes. It took scores of firemen and forest rangers and the equipment of several townships to quench the blaze. The financial loss was estimated in the millions of dollars, all the result of a tiny spark from a lighted cigarette!

The fire of the Holy Spirit has the ability to spread. It lights a flame on the altar of an individual and through him it spreads to the members of his family. It lights a flame on the altar of a pas-tor's heart and through him, sets fire to the whole congregation. It sparks the life of some layman, and through him starts a spiri-tual blaze in the whole community.

Our prayer must be for God to ignite the flame in us today! (Derl Keefer)

DECEMBER 16, 2001

❦

Third Sunday of Advent

Worship Theme: The God of hope promised a Savior, and the young girl Mary humbly heard God's voice. God fills the world with joy at Christ's coming to bring down the proud and raise up the lowly.

Readings: Isaiah 35:1-10; James 5:7-10; Matthew 11:2-11

Call to Worship (Song of Mary, Luke 1:46-55):

Leader: My soul magnifies the Lord,
and my spirit rejoices in God my Savior,
for he has looked with favor on the lowliness of
his servant.

People: **Surely, from now on all generations will call
me blessed;
for the Mighty One has done great things
for me,
and holy is his name.
His mercy is for those who fear him
from generation to generation.**

Leader: He has shown strength with his arm;
he has scattered the proud in the thoughts
of their hearts.
He has brought down the powerful from their
thrones,
and lifted up the lowly;
he has filled the hungry with good things,
and sent the rich away empty.

People: **He has helped his servant Israel,
in remembrance of his mercy
according to the promise he made to our
ancestors,
to Abraham and to his descendants forever.**

433

Pastoral Prayer:

God of hope, you promised a Savior, and the young girl Mary humbly heard your voice. Is this the one to come or are we to wait for another? He healed the blind, cleansed the lepers, raised the dead, and brought good news to the poor. Is this the one to come or are we to wait for another? The hungry are filled with good things, and the rich sent away empty; the powerful are brought low and the lowly lifted up. Is this the one to come or are we to wait for another? Grant us grace to know the one who comes in your name, bringing your love to a weary world. Give us courage to prepare for your reign of justice and mercy by opening our hearts to all people. May we, with Mary, answer your call, "Here I am, the servant of the Lord." Keep us on your Holy Way; redeem us and guide us to your home where deserts bloom and waters break forth in the wilderness. Fill us with all joy and peace in believing so that we may abound in hope by the power of the Holy Spirit, in the name of Jesus Christ. Amen. (Blair G. Meeks)

SERMON BRIEFS

GOOD TO THE POINT OF ABSURDITY

ISAIAH 35:1-10

Isaiah 35 is a vision overstated. Could circumstances really turn out so well for the Judean exiles to whom the message was delivered? Surely the prophet exaggerates his case. Yet we come back to these words, as generations before us have, because we sense that God's work is not finished. We hope for still more.

I. Isaiah Exaggerates

Our text today comes near the end of the first part of the book called Isaiah. It is part of the transition from the prophecies of doom addressed to Judah in the eighth century to the prophecies of hope addressed to the exiles in the sixth century. The first part of Isaiah ends with a story of deliverance and warning. The Assyrian king laid siege to Jerusalem during the reign of Hezekiah. His effort was unsuccessful, however, and the people of Jerusalem saw the hand of God in their deliverance. Isaiah 36 recounts this, but chapter 39 foreshadows the Babylonian threat that would later succeed where the Assyrians failed. Jerusalem would be destroyed and its inhabitants taken into exile.

The vision of Isaiah 35 is placed to set these events into a larger perspective. It is as if the writer is saying, "You think God did something great when the Assyrians came? Just you wait! You'll see greater things than that!" Readers are prepared for the message of hope to come, even before they hear the warning.

The vision really is a grand one: The desert blooms. The blind see. Burning sand becomes pools of water. And the exiles return safely to everlasting joy and prosperity. In a sense the vision came true. The exiles did return eventually. They rebuilt Jerusalem and the Temple. Those who returned experienced a second Exodus, again passing through the desert and becoming Israel. But clearly the vision is hyperbole. Things were not as wonderful, as easy, or as permanent as Isaiah 35 suggests.

II. Exaggeration Is Necessary

If Isaiah 35 described the return from exile in accurate detail, we would consider it an interesting artifact, but not the word of God to us. For what it does, it has to be overstated. It points us forward to the further work of God. It says to us, "You think God did something great when the exiles returned? Just you wait! Greater things are ahead."

This vision left the people thirsty for more, a still better life. Such hopes generated the electric atmosphere in which Jesus ministered. Jesus found people eagerly looking for God to do more. Christians naturally saw Jesus' death and resurrection as the greatest of God's saving acts. And yet they recognized that God is not finished with what Jesus started. We say, "Christ has died. Christ is risen. Christ will come again." We too look for more.

We recognize in Jesus' birth a mighty act of God, not entirely unlike the way Judeans looked at deliverance from the Assyrians. Just as the book of Isaiah points to a further work of God, the

435

Christian looks to God for a completion of the work begun by Jesus. Any vision of this work is necessarily overstated because we have no better way to describe it. We lack the capacity and imagination to truly know how God will consummate history. We cannot define eternity in an accurate, technical way. So we take what we know and imagine it good to the point of absurdity. This does not give us knowledge of the counsels and intentions of God; but it gives us hope, hope warranted by what God has already done.

Isaiah 35 is grossly overstated. And thank God it is, for it points us in the right direction. (David Mauldin)

THE LORD'S COMING AGAIN

JAMES 5:7-10

As we have come into a new millennium, there has been a great deal of emphasis upon the end of time, the time toward which all creation is moving and when our Lord will return claiming the faithful, subduing the enemies of God, and heralding the beginning of a whole new relationship with God. Many claim they know the signs and can predict the time. In their claim is the hope it will come soon, for there is a certainty that the one speaking will be among those God claims.

What we have experienced and are experiencing in this emphasis is a kind of impatience with God. We want God to intervene, to break down the things which are so counter to what God intended us to be and do, and to claim us for a life which is greater than anything we could imagine or think. We are not alone in this; for the early Christians, this anticipated coming had greater immediacy.

The writer of James advises the early Christians to have patience. He uses that wonderful image of the farmer waiting with patience for the crop. Planting in faith that the seed, soil and weather would all cooperate so that there would be an abundant harvest. There has to be trust in the provisions of God to make the harvest possible.

So it is with the Lord's coming again. There is much to do as we move toward that day. There is much to be done in the world, in us, in the communities of faith. As the Lord patiently and persistently moves toward that day, so should we, in patience, persistently do those things which bring the world and people of the world into relationship with God through Jesus Christ that emanates the purposes of God found in creation and in the redeeming work of Christ. This patience being urged implies that we are to be especially attentive to our own relationships with God. "Strengthen your hearts" is the advice of the writer of James. It raises the image of exercise that strengthens our physical heart and body so that it is healthier and ready for the strenuous and trying moments of life. Such exercise enables us to endure longer and with greater sustaining power. So it is that we are to give time to strengthening the inner life so we focus in the right place, drawing on the resources of God which we see more readily, and sensing that entrustment of our lives to God, for whatever comes, whenever it comes.

Patience also implies giving attention to the relationships within the community of faith of which we are a part. I appreciate the candid, straightforward way the writer of James puts it: "do not grumble against one another so that you may not be judged." Finding fault with one another is an indication that we have lost sight of the One we anticipate coming. It is focusing on us rather than upon the Lord who is coming. As one friend said, "We need to ask, 'What do my comments about others, my attitudes toward others, and my treatment of others say about my relationship with God through Christ?'" The apostle Paul, in his letters, urged us to seek unity through the Holy Spirit.

The joy is that if we can be patient, allowing God to work toward our Lord's coming in God's own time, we will find ways to strengthen our relationships with God and also work toward a community of faith which reflects the presence of Christ's Spirit among us. It enables us to anticipate a time, whenever God determines it will be, when God will reign and the powers of evil will be subjected to God's reign, forever and ever. (William Miller)

THE SERVANT JOHN

MATTHEW 11:2-11

The average person may have looked at John the Baptist as a star shining in the wilderness. He had a large audience to speak to daily from Jerusalem, Judea and the entire area of the Jordan. He experienced remarkable results from his preaching as people confessed their sins and were baptized by him in the Jordan River. John had a unique personality and demeanor, wearing clothing made of camel's hair and wearing a leather belt around his waist. As a Nazarite he let his hair and beard grow giving a wild appearance. His preaching was straightforward and unrelenting, with no apology. He even had King Herod's secret admiration. The commoner enjoyed the criticism John openly gave the hypocrites of the religious circle—Pharisees and Sadducees.

John never looked upon himself as a star, but as a servant of God. John's excellence of life was not his dynamic, persuasive and direct preaching, but his willingness to serve God.

I. Servanthood Can Include Suffering

John lived in the open wilderness. The fresh air, the freedom to go when and where he wanted to live like he desired were all a part of the aura that surrounded him.

As the preaching became too close to Herod and Herodias's situation, suffering became a part of his servanthood, and John found himself in prison.

Oswald Chambers wrote, "to choose to suffer means that there is something wrong; to choose God's will even if it means suffering is a very different thing. No healthy saint ever chooses suffering; he chooses God's will, as did Jesus, whether it means suffering or not" (R. Kent Hughes, *1001 Great Stories/Quotes* [Wheaton: Tyndale House Publishers, 1998], p. 405).

Today, you, like John, may find yourself in a "prison" of isolation, neglect, abuse, hatred or a multitude of other "prisons." God sends his messenger to tell you that things may seem dark, but persevere. Miracles are happening and your miracle is that God is with you through it all.

438

II. Servanthood Includes Ministry

John had a ministry from God. His particular calling was to be a prophet meaning a person who speaks for God. The customary Hebrew word for prophet is derived from a verb meaning, "to bubble" or "pour forth." That described John! He bubbled with God's Presence and declared the message God wanted spoken. John's concept of religion differed from the religious leaders of the day. He understood the message to mean that religion came from the heart and not just the law. He preached about righteousness, holy living, experience and repentance!

His ministry included the role of forerunner of Messiah Jesus. The Baptist grasped the ministry of the Messiah to release the people from the true captives of the land and heart—Satan.

To what ministry has God called you today—teaching, janitoring, ushering, choir or orchestra member, nursery attendant, evangelism or bus driver? What about life's ministry? We must minister to people in our secular jobs as well. Have you prayed about where God wants you to minister today?

III. Servanthood Includes Faith

Amid all John's doubts and questions Jesus saw his faith. Jesus looked far beyond John's superficial doubts and saw the integrity, honesty and faith of the man. The Baptist had long preached and sacrificed for God's people and wanted assurance of the legitimacy of Jesus' ministry.

Jesus was not offended, but rather sent the messengers back with a list of items that would verify to John the faith he had placed in Jesus.

Our faith is never misplaced when it is in Jesus. "Servanthood not stardom is our goal" (Christopher Morley). (Derl Keefer)

DECEMBER 23, 2001

❦

Fourth Sunday of Advent

Worship Theme: The God of light sends a Savior, who enlightens our hearts and dispels the shadows of ignorance and sin. We want to be ready for Christ's coming in glory.

Readings: Isaiah 7:10-16; Romans 1:1-7; Matthew 1:18-25

Call to Worship (Psalm 80:1-5, 7, 17-18):

Leader:	Give ear, O Shepherd of Israel, you who lead Joseph like a flock.... Stir up your might, and come to save us!
People:	**Restore us, O God;** **let your face shine, that we may be saved.**
Leader:	O LORD God of hosts, how long will you be angry with your people's prayers? You have fed them with the bread of tears, and given them tears to drink in full measure.
People:	**Restore us, O God of hosts;** **let your face shine, that we may be saved.**
Leader:	But let your hand be upon one at your right hand, the one whom you made strong for yourself. Then we will never turn back from you; give us life, and we will call on your name.
People:	**Restore us, O LORD God of hosts;** **let your face shine, that we may be saved.**

440

Pastoral Prayer:

God of light, your church joyfully awaits the coming of its Savior, who enlightens our hearts and dispels the shadows of ignorance and sin. We want to be ready when the long night ends with the dawn's first rays. We want to be ready when the storm clouds break and the rainbow's light shines. We want to be ready when valleys are high, hills are low, and highways are straight. We want to be ready when justice rolls down like the waters of a stream. We want to be ready when the sick are healed and the hungry filled. We want to be ready when all tears are wiped away and our joy is like the morning. We want to be ready when God's glory is revealed, when Jesus our Savior comes. We want to be ready to live so that your reign of justice will touch all earth's people. We want to be ready to celebrate the birth of Jesus, your Son and our Redeemer. We want to be ready to welcome Jesus' coming again in glory. With your Spirit's help, may we walk always in your light, through Jesus' name. Amen. (Blair G. Meeks)

SERMON BRIEFS

THE PATIENCE OF GOD

ISAIAH 7:10-16

I. We Can See God's Patience with Israel

While the coming destruction of the nation of Israel may seem to suggest impatience on the part of God, the opposite is the case. God gives Ahaz a sign even though he will not ask for a sign. God will not abandon his people. Even in distress they are to remember that they are the people of God, and God will not abandon them. Certainly they had tried God's patience. He had delayed the judgment the nation deserved, but now it must come. Like Israel we try God's patience. As a nation we try God's patience. As a church we try God's patience. As individuals we try God's patience. No aspect of God's character is more amazing. Stubbornly he keeps working with us and for us—even when we accept his gifts casually and accept his grace casually.

II. We Can See God's Patience Through the Years

The prophecy in these verses had both an immediate and a distant fulfillment. If you hold two objects in front of you one cannot tell how far apart they are. So they could not tell that seven hundred years lay between the first fulfillment and the second. Those who believed the promise must have grown restless, expecting the Messiah to come in their day. But generations had to pass before Jesus came. Galatians 4:4 says that "when the fullness of time had come, God sent forth his Son." Matthew 1:23 says that the Lord Jesus Christ was the ultimate fulfillment of these encouraging words. For seven hundred years they were "standing on the promises."

Christians, too, are standing on the promises. Our Lord will return. Believers have cherished the promise for twenty centuries. We don't know how many more years will pass but we know that eventually God will do what God promised, and Christ will return. "The Lord is not slow about his promises" (2 Peter 3:9). God waits that others may have time and opportunity to repent and come to God.

III. We Can Learn Patience from God

We who would be godly must learn how to be patient. We must be patient with God. God may not answer our prayers immediately, but *will* respond. God lets the world go on its way, with all its want and suffering and need. We wonder why God does not say, "Enough!" We wonder why God doesn't bring it all to an end. But we must be patient with God. And we must be patient with one another. All of us are growing spiritually. Some are growing faster than others. Some, like children, grow a while, stop growing, and then start growing again. If Almighty God can be patient with us, surely we can be patient with one another. Hebrews 10:26 says that we need patience. Hebrews 12:1 says we run with patience. James 1:4 says we should let patience have her perfect work. (Patience is a recurring theme in the book of James. See 5:7, 5:8, 5:11.) Second Peter 1:6 says we should add to our faith and virtue patience. Jesus praised the patience of the church at Ephesus. It is a neglected virtue. God is our example. Jesus is our example. Let us all learn patience! (Robert C. Shannon)

SET APART

ROMANS 1:1-7

It might be easy to read the beginning of the letter of Paul to the church at Rome and say with some frustration, "How can I preach on this text? It is the salutation to a long theological letter!" It might be easy to skip, but if we look a little closer we may find ourselves amazed at how much Paul packed into the introduction of this letter. It was a custom that ancient Greek letters began with the name of the person who sent the letter and the name of the recipient with a short greeting. In the letter to Romans, Paul expanded his introduction considerably. He wanted to catch the attention of his readers. Within the introduction, Paul expressed his Christian faith in a short synopsis of what he would later expound upon in the letter.

I. God's Promises

Paul began the letter in the regular manner of letter writing in that day. He gave his name as the sender of the letter. Instead of following immediately with the recipient, though, Paul made a short statement of self-identification. He used the words "apostle," "servant," and a saint "set apart" (v. 1) with the purpose to proclaim God's good news in Jesus Christ. This "gospel of God" (v. 1), this good news was promised in the scriptures, the sacred writings of the Jews (v. 2). Much can be said on the basis of this theme. Throughout the Old Testament, God promised many things to God's chosen people. Promise and covenant are connected. The content of the covenant is promise. God was and is steadfast in God's promises. There are many examples of covenant/promise. In this letter, Paul will write about covenant and promise in reference to Abraham (Genesis 12:1-9). This story and others throughout the Old Testament point to the promise made through covenant and how God was faithful to the promises found in Scripture.

II. God's Promise Fulfilled in Jesus

In verses 3 through 4, Paul gave in a nutshell the truth that the rest of his letter would address: the good news, the truth concerning Jesus Christ. The prophets of the Old Testament had foretold Jesus' coming. The Gospels themselves would later sound the theme that Jesus is the fulfillment of God's promise to God's people. For example, the book of Matthew makes many connections to the fulfillment of God's promise in Jesus as told by the prophets. Matthew 1:22-23 says, "All this took place to fulfill what had been spoken by the Lord through the prophet. . . ." (Other references to the promise of Jesus written by the prophets and referenced by Matthew are 2:5-6, 2:17-18, 3:3, 4:14-16, 12:17-21, 13:14-15, 13:34-35, 15:7-9, 21:4-5, 26:31.) In these few verses, Paul expressed much of his belief. Jesus came to earth. He was human, a descendant of David. God's promise for salvation is fulfilled through the death and resurrection of Jesus Christ our Lord.

III. All Are Redeemed in Jesus and Called to Be Saints

Paul, however, does not stop there. Through God's grace, the Gentiles are included in the promise. It was part of the promise long ago. In Abraham, "all families of the earth shall be blessed" (Genesis 12:3). Jesus has come and is the final redemption for all creation. Paul lets the "cat out of the bag" before he ever begins his theological discourse. All are invited to "belong to Jesus Christ" (v. 6), to be set apart as "saints" (v. 7) who belong to God and serve God. Paul invited his Roman readers and us to consider the promise fulfilled in Jesus. How do we belong to Jesus Christ? Are we "set apart" for God's service? (Marcia T. Thompson)

CHRIST THE BABY—CHRIST THE KING

MATTHEW 1:18-25

The Reverend Billy Strayhorn told the story of a four-year-old boy watching his mother change the baby. When she overlooked sprinkling the baby's backside with baby powder and hurriedly put him into his diaper, the four-year-old hollered, "Hey, Mom, you forgot to salt him!"

Strayhorn asked, "Have you ever noticed how babies can turn ordinarily intelligent men and women into complete morons as they make all those googly noises and funny faces? I've often wondered what the babies think of it all."

This is Christmas, the season of the baby, the Christ Child. Babies equal hope, they equal the future, and they spice up our lives. Christ the baby has become Christ the King.

I. Christ the King Is the Messiah

This is a cosmic event—sending Jesus into our world. It is God invading mankind—and it is not science fiction!

The early Christian message concentrated on this proclamation: the eternal God who no man has seen or can see; who lives in a light that no man can approach; has unveiled God's self; and, in a manifestation of Grace, has become audible, visible, tangible. In Colossians 1:15 Christ is called "the image of the invisible God." In Jesus Christ it was not simply a ray of the light of the glory of God that penetrated time. God turned fully toward man in this life that was full of grace. Jesus has come not only to be God-Messiah to the Israelites and to the Gentiles, but also to be Savior!

II. Christ the King Is the Savior

It is not just a cosmic event that transpired that cold winter's night in Bethlehem of Judea that angels sang about to some shepherds. It is a personal event that can transpire in our hearts.

A Calcutta paper relates that recently a young Brahman came to the house of a missionary for an interview. In the course of the conversation he said: "Many things that Christianity contains that I find in Hinduism; but there is one thing that Christianity has and Hinduism has not." "What is that?" the missionary asked. His reply was striking, "A Savior."

To the message of God's incarnation in the logos become flesh, the New Testament adds the *reconciliation*. Jesus was the Savior of the lost, those gone astray, the fallen, the refuse of life, the dregs, the moralistic, the humanitarian—but lost. God did not separate from them; God associated with them and broke

445

bread with them. In order to make possible this forgiveness, and for the sake of this alone, Jesus had to go the way of the cross— to his last breath. Jesus loved people with a divine love that sought sinners. On the cross he still prayed for his enemies; he received the lost thief into his fellowship and wrestled him from hell. We must recognize and proclaim him as our Redeemer-Savior-Friend.

A Portuguese captain of an African slave ship was trying to escape an English vessel that was attempting to save the slaves. As the English vessel pulled alongside the Portuguese ship, the slave runner captain gave guns to the black slaves and told them to fight for their lives because the Englishmen had come to kill them. Terrified and confused the slaves did as they were told" thinking that they were fighting for their lives. They killed and wounded their friends who had come to set them free!

We shake our heads and groan at the picture. Yet, my friends, many of us are doing the same to Jesus. We have become so deluded by Satan's lies. God wants the best for our lives, but Satan has lied to us and confused our thinking. We want to believe in the raw sinful habits that Satan has told us are fine. So we resist God's voice of condemnation. Satan tells us not to worry about our sin now—we have plenty of time to "make it right with God" someday. So we wallow in our sin—and the right time never comes. Jesus as Savior, has come to set you free—yet we kill him by our rejection. Why are you rejecting the very one who has come to redeem you?

To fall into the hands of God—to stand before the judgment seat of God—is a fearful thing. It is only through the word and work of Christ that we receive the assurance that we go— redeemed.

Is Jesus *your* Savior—your personal Savior today? He wants to be.

III. Christ the King Is the Companion

The word *Immanuel* is taken from Isaiah 7:14 and means "God with us." He has delivered us from our enemies and will be with us as our companion protector.

Fichte, the philosopher stated: "Only the metaphysical saves us—not the historical." According to this view, a historical event can illuminate a truth, but it cannot be its basis.

In the biblical witness of prophets and apostles a totally different view of time and history confronts us. Time is like a stream that constantly pushes forward until through the power of God it has reached its goal in the consummation of all things.

Events may occur that impel the current of history forward. Whenever such an event has occurred, everything thereafter is different.

The old world order is shaken in its foundations—God's new eon has dawned and will be our companion. (Derl Keefer)

DECEMBER 30, 2001

❧

First Sunday After Christmas Day

Worship Theme: The God of joy sent Jesus, who calls us sisters and brothers and shares with us all things, even our death. God promises that we will also be raised with Christ and will be God's children of glory.

Readings: Isaiah 63:7-9; Hebrews 2:10-18; Matthew 2:13-23

Call to Worship (Psalm 148:7-13):

Leader: Praise the LORD from the heavens;
           praise him in the heights!
           Praise him, all his angels;
           praise him, all his host!
           Praise him, sun and moon;
           praise him, all you shining stars!
           Praise him, you highest heavens,
           and you waters above the heavens!
           Let them praise the name of the LORD,
           for he commanded and they
           were created.

People: **Praise the Lord from the earth,**
           you sea monsters and all deeps,
           fire and hail, snow and frost,
           stormy wind fulfilling his command!
           Mountains and all hills, fruit trees and all
           cedars!
           Wild animals and all cattle, creeping things
           and flying birds!

Leader: Kings of the earth and all peoples,
           princes and all rulers of the earth!

Young men and women alike,
old and young together!

People: **Let them praise the name of the LORD,**
for his name alone is exalted;
his glory is above earth and heaven.

Pastoral Prayer:
God our joy, we give you thanks for your gracious deeds and
your praiseworthy acts. You have lifted us up and carried us
through all our days. In this season of glad shouts and songs, we
are truly grateful for your gentle touch and the calm of your
voice. In the midst of happy echoes, we hear the cries of those
who are even now in death's shadow, remembering that at your
Son's birth was also heard the lamentation of Rachel weeping for
her children. Be with all who grieve in this holy season and with
those who are dying while others are alive with anticipation at the
beginning of another year. Free us from slavery to the fear of
death. Let us hear again the angel's greeting: "do not be afraid,"
and live in the assurance that Jesus, who came not to a prince's
cradle but to the cross, calls us sisters and brothers and shares
with us all things, even our death. Grant us grace to know your
promise that we will also be raised with Christ and that you will
finally destroy the one who has the power of death. Lead us to
your streams of living waters and bring your children to glory at
last; through Jesus Christ our Lord. Amen. (Blair G. Meeks)

SERMON BRIEFS

AN OLD HYMN WITH A NEW MEANING

ISAIAH 63:7-9

This is a hymn of gratitude for the kindness and mercy Yahweh
has shown Israel. If we were to compare it to the structure of one
of our modern hymns, several verses could be pointed out.

The first one is an affirmation that *God has been Israel's Savior*
(v. 8). Whether we think of Israel's deliverance from the captivity

to the Babylonians, here in the immediate context, or the rescue from Egypt, or any number of other acts of mercy, the theme of "Yahweh as Savior" is a chord played throughout Israel's history.

These questions come to mind. Can we think now of God as the savior of the nations? Does God's acts of saving mercy extend to nations we do not normally consider Christian?

The second verse of our hymn is the clear message that *God participates in the suffering of God's people* (v. 9). I remember once hearing a comment on this verse that went something like this: "In Israel's adversity God was no adversary."

One might want to read again, at least, portions of the book of Job, to catch something of the dynamic of the adversarial role of God in people's lives. Of course, the drama ends with the startling truth: "In adversity God is no adversary."

The third verse has the wonderful image of a *parent lifting a child from danger or unpleasant circumstances with strong arms and carrying that child to safety* (v. 9). A church I once attended was celebrating its one hundredth anniversary. Much of the history was presented on video. The story included comments about many persons in the past who had served faithfully but also included words about persons presently in attendance at the church. We were told that four children come to the church every Sunday but without their parents.

The visiting speaker for the day said to me after the service, "On my way home I'm going to stop by and visit the parents of those children." His intent was not to make a scene or preach at the parents for not attending church with their children, but simply to be an encourager. This unselfish act was made more moving because he didn't even know those children's parents. The speaker illustrated that he was committed to the children of our world, and serves for us as a reminder of our call to care for the children.

Visualize, if you will, an image of children being carried from unpleasant circumstances with strong arms to safety. Perhaps there is no greater challenge the church could receive today than to become known as the strong arms that carry children to safety. (Jim Clardy)

A COMMUNITY OF CHRISTIANS

HEBREWS 2:10-18

Suffering has had a varied role in the history of the church. The church has tried to grasp how suffering is to fit into our lives through studying the initial example of Jesus. It is clear that Jesus chose to suffer and die as an expression of his obedience to God. It is also clear that when Christians were confronted with the choice of turning aside from the gospel or enduring suffering, they were to choose in favor of the gospel and in so doing, embrace suffering. What is not clear is the way Christians who are not caught in threatening situations are to relate to suffering.

Some, especially in the earliest days of the faith, became so fixated on a martyr theology that they sought out suffering and death as a guarantee of their salvation and of their special place with God. Marks of identification with Christ's suffering, the stigmata were highly prized.

Some in our less threatened times have turned away from suffering as a mark of spiritual blessing and have proclaimed a "gospel" of blessing. The triumph of Jesus over the forces of sin, death and suffering is viewed as complete and God wishes nothing for Christians but health, happiness and material prosperity.

Hebrews 2:10-18 calls the church back to the meaning of suffering without romanticizing the experience.

The primary "actor" in this passage is God. God is the Creator, the One "for whom and through whom all things exist." God is also the One whose loving purpose is to draw many into "glory," into relationship with God. God also is the power behind the completion of Jesus through suffering. It is not appropriate for us to imagine a heavenly council in which a plan is put forward to run Jesus through some maze of suffering as if God were a mad scientist, experimenting on a rat. The writer of Hebrews did not hesitate to place the words that the Hebrew scripture attributes to God in the mouth of Jesus. The unique role and identity of Jesus, fully human and fully divine is maintained throughout Hebrews.

Suffering created the Christian community. We are who we are through the sacrifice of Jesus. Jesus did not create a company of

451

disciples who would propagate his ideas; he created a community of people who have been transformed through his death. Jesus' completion (being made perfect) through suffering is a call for others who must be sanctified to share in suffering as well. The humble, oppressed and despised community of Christians are called Jesus' brothers and sisters because they share with him these experiences.

Jesus' victory over sin and death is not something added to the experience of the cross by God. God did not look on as Jesus was faithful unto death, and then as a consequence of his faithfulness, grant the conquest over evil. It was in the very act of Jesus' obedience that sin and death were defeated. Neither Hebrews nor any other Christian scripture solves the mystery of salvation. God is intimately involved in human salvation, not as a spectator but as a participant.

Hebrews helps the Christian seeking to understand salvation to gaze at the mystery from a different perspective. All the theories of the "how" of salvation should be taken together without seeking to fold one into another. The one offered here, that of the "sacrifice of atonement," is sometimes taken in isolation from others. When this happens, the great truth of the mystery of salvation is distorted. Ultimately, the question of salvation's "how" is overwhelmed by salvation's "who." Too much time and energy has gone into worrying through theories which in the final analysis are best left in the heart of God.

What Hebrews does is to connect the suffering of Jesus with the experiences of the Christians to whom the message is intended. Their (and our) sufferings are gathered into the greater purpose of God in such a manner as to identify them with Jesus' successful endurance and triumph. The completeness of Jesus' humanity enabled him to be both the example and enabler of the Christian's victory. (Lee Gallman)

365 DAYS OF NEW BEGINNINGS

MATTHEW 2:13-23

In a Charlie Brown cartoon several years ago Lucy approaches Charlie and happily yells out, "Merry Christmas!" Then in the spirit of the season she says, "I think we ought to bury past differences and try to be kind." Charlie Brown philosophically asks, "Why does it only have to be this time of year? Why can't it be this way all year long?"

Lucy looks disgustedly at him and replies, "What are you, some kind of fanatic?"

It would be fantastic if Christmas *could* last all year long! The truth is most of us have already begun our journey down from the mountaintops of our "Joy to the World" and "Peace on Earth" to the valley of the shadow of fast-paced lives.

The obscure event of a hurried flight of Joseph, Mary, and Jesus into Egypt opens a highway before us to 365 new Christmas beginnings!

I. A New Beginning of Trust

Joseph's sensitivity to God demonstrates his total trust in God's prompting and direction.

- Joseph's trust led him to take his family out of harm's way (v. 14)
- Joseph's trust led him to be a part of prophecy (v. 15)
- Joseph's trust led him back to Israel at the proper time (v. 19)

Following God's leadership takes unadulterated trust—not on occasion—but daily! We cannot expect to hear God speak in a crisis if we don't recognize his voice in the calm.

Jeanette Strong illustrates the concept of trust. She explains that when her son was a toddler she had problems washing his hair. He sat in the tub while Jeanette put shampoo in his hair. As the water was poured on, he would lean his head down getting water and shampoo in his eyes causing him to cry. She would try to explain to him that he needed to just look straight ahead and avoid getting the shampoo in his eyes. He would nod his head as if he understood and put his trust in Mommy. As soon as the rinse water started, his fear would overcome his trust, and down would go his head and the shampoo brought more tears.

She said that during one of those bouts in the tub God began to speak to her heart. It was as if God was saying, "I love you.

Trust me." She writes, "sometimes, in a difficult situation, I panic and turn my eyes away from him. This never solves the problem; I just become more afraid, as the 'shampoo' blinds me." I'm sure my lack of trust hurts God very much, but how much more does it hurt me?"

She then makes a great point as she writes, "Now when I find myself in a situation where it would be easy to panic, I picture my son sitting in the bathtub, looking at me, learning to trust me. Then I ask God what I should do. Sometimes the answer may seem scary, but, one thing I'm sure of 'he'll never pour shampoo in my face!'" (James Hewett, ed. *Illustrations Unlimited* [Wheaton: Tyndale House, 1988], pp. 479-80).

II. A New Beginning for Family

The exciting genesis of family life started that first Christmas day, but the moment came when reality settled in their minds and hearts. Nurturing this young child would be their responsibility for a lifetime. They were ordained to responsibility for the child. Now it meant fleeing from home and interrupting normal family life as they make a home in far away Egypt.

If we are to experience new beginnings with our families, it involves teaching children early about Jesus, praying with spouses, and attending a house of worship—even if the children wiggle during service.

Charles Swindoll is credited with writing the six characteristics of a "strong family":

- Strong families are committed to each other.
- Strong families spend time together.
- Strong families work at communication.
- Strong families express appreciation.
- Strong families are committed to spiritual values.
- Strong families work toward solutions when crisis comes.

If any of these is not prevalent in your family situation—jump-start a new beginning—Now!

III. A New Beginning for Spiritual Life

I believe the journey to Egypt strengthened Joseph and Mary's spiritual resolve. These two people were already spiritually sensitive! Few of us have bonafide angels appearing to give detailed instructions from God? Nobody else in all the world was invested with the care of God's son but Joseph and Mary. God wouldn't just lend his one and only Son to some strangers—would he?

But Joseph and Mary *were* human. Spiritual growth and understanding must *never* stop! The short period Joseph is on the earthly scene with Mary grasping spiritual truths becomes evidence that they continued to grow. Spiritual power develops through the pressure of hard places—Mary and Joseph understood that fully! Do we? (Derl Keefer)

BENEDICTIONS

Advent Season

Here in this place we have seen an intimation of the presence of Christ. As we leave this place of worship, we once again meet ourselves. Help us to see Christ in each of our brothers and sisters. And as we encounter a needy world, may we do our part to make the rough places smooth, so those around us will see God's saving work.

Go from this place of worship,
Knowing that you also
Are blessed of the Lord.
Christ whose presence is among us,
Go with each of you,
Into your home and community,
Into your work and play,
Until you can say, wherever you move,
"Surely the Lord is in this place."

Christmas Season

There's a void to the stillness at the end of this season. As our fellowship is concluded and we leave this sanctuary, we go from here to the strange dullness of the after-Christmas lull combined with the hesitant anxiousness of beginning a new year.

Yet even in the midst of this sentimental turmoil, the peace of Christ can settle, calm, and enliven our depressing anxiousness.

May our lives be enriched by all that is good. May our fellowship be sweetened by sincerity and kindness. And may the reality of the blessedness of the Christian life bring an ever present glow to our hearts.

Through Jesus Christ our Lord. Amen.

Now may God who has begun a good work in you, continue to work in you his perfect will, even as he promised, so that you may fulfill God's purpose with joy and have a sense of his presence with you always.

Season After the Epiphany

"May the Lord direct your hearts to the love of God and to the steadfastness of Christ" (2 Thess. 3:5).

Go forth from here
As those who hear the call of Christ,
As those who respond to that call,
As those who live in the high calling of God
In Christ Jesus.
And may the knowledge and forgiveness of Christ
Be shed abroad
Wherever you move.

And now may the rich blessings of God
And the grace of our Lord Jesus Christ
And the abiding presence of the Holy Spirit
Go with you
And be yours in increasing measure.

Lenten Season

We have professed our faith here in the presence of brothers and sisters.
We have offered both ourselves and our possessions as gifts to our God.
And we have received from the Lord's hand bountiful mercy and grace.
Let us go forth to continue this cycle of giving and receiving,
as we celebrate and live each day the faith we have professed this morning.
May our hearts and voices be continually before our Lord.
May we dwell in the shelter of the Almighty, and walk in God's presence with joy.

Go with us, O God, in the shelter house of your protection.
Let us dwell in your presence this coming week,
So that we can be instruments for gathering your people
Through the respect and love we show to all we meet.
Amen.

This is the day that the Lord has made.
Let us continue in it,
With our gladness and rejoicing,
Honoring our risen Savior.
Alleluiah!

Easter Season

"Now may the God of peace, who brought back from the dead
our Lord Jesus, the great shepherd of the sheep, by the blood of
the eternal covenant, make you complete in everything good so
that you may do [God's] will, working among us that which is
pleasing in [God's] sight, through Jesus Christ, to whom be the
glory forever and ever. Amen" (Heb. 13:20-21).

Season After Pentecost

Trust God for the past—for the forgiveness of past sins, the healing of past hurts. Trust God for the present—for meeting daily
needs, for guidance in daily living. Trust God for the future—for
help with tomorrow's troubles, for the hope of eternal life. In a
world of uncertainty, God's love is sure. Past, present, and
future—God's love remains forever. Amen.

May you "lead lives worthy of the Lord, fully pleasing to [God],
as you bear fruit in every good work and as you grow in the
knowledge of God. May you be made strong with all the strength
that comes from [God's] glorious power, and may you be prepared to endure everything with patience, while joyfully giving
thanks to the Creator, who has enabled you to share in the inheritance of the saints in the light" (Col. 1:10-12).

Go from here
To the work and witness of life
Knowing that the living Christ

Goes with you.
And may Christ himself
Present you holy and unblamable
And unreproachable in God's sight.

Special Occasions

Now go forth from here
And may the Spirit of Christ go with you every moment.
May peace on earth and goodwill toward all persons
Be your experience and the experience of all Christ's disciples.

"May the God of hope fill you with all joy and peace in your faith,
that by the power of the Holy Spirit, your whole life and outlook
may be radiant with hope" (Rom. 15:13 JBP).

Eternal Savior, we have seen in your victory
Our hope realized, our faith confirmed, our strength renewed.
As we go from here
May the victory of the risen Christ be our victory.

Go forth from here in the power of the ascended Christ who said,
"Go therefore and make disciples of all nations." Go with the
presence of the ascended Christ who said, "I am with you
always." Go with the purpose of the ascended Christ who assures
you that he will confirm the message in the lives of all those who
hear.

You have been given the gift of the Holy Spirit.
Go forth empowered and equipped by the Spirit
To be Christ's body, doing Christ's work in the world.

TEXT GUIDE*
THE REVISED COMMON LECTIONARY (2001)

Sunday	First Lesson	Second Lesson	Gospel Lesson	Psalm
1/7/01	Isa. 43:1-7	Acts 8:14-17	Luke 3:15-17, 21-22	Ps. 29
1/14/01	Isa. 62:1-5	1 Cor. 12:1-11	John 2:1-11	Ps. 36:5-10
1/21/01	Neh. 8:1-3, 5-6, 8-10	1 Cor. 12:12-31a	Luke 4:14-21	Ps. 19
1/28/01	Jer. 1:4-10	1 Cor. 13:1-13	Luke 4:21-30	Ps. 71:1-6
2/4/01	Isa. 6:1-8 (9-13)	1 Cor. 15:1-11	Luke 5:1-11	Ps. 138
2/11/01	Jer. 17:5-10	1 Cor. 15:12-20	Luke 6:17-26	Ps. 1
2/18/01	Gen. 45:3-11, 15	1Cor. 15:35-38, 42-50	Luke 6:27-38	Ps. 37:1-11, 39-40
2/25/01	Exod. 34:29-35	2 Cor. 3:12-4:2	Luke 9:28-36 (37-43)	Ps. 99
3/4/01	Deut. 26:1-11	Rom. 10:8b-13	Luke 4:1-13	Ps. 91:1-2, 9-16
3/11/01	Gen. 15:1-12, 17-18	Phil. 3:17-4:1	Luke 13:31-35	Ps. 27
3/18/01	Isa. 55:1-9	1 Cor. 10:1-13	Luke 13:1-9	Ps. 63:1-8
3/25/01	Josh. 5:9-12	2 Cor. 5:16-21	Luke 15:1-3, 11b-32	Ps. 32
4/1/01	Isa. 43:16-21	Phil. 3:4b-14	John 12:1-8	Ps. 126
4/8/01	Isa. 50:4-9a	Phil. 2:5-11	Luke 22:14-23:56	Ps. 31:9-16
4/13/01	Isa. 52:13–53:12	Heb. 10:16-25	John 18:1-19:42	Ps. 22
4/15/01	Acts 10:34-43	1 Cor. 15:19-26	Luke 24:1-12	Ps. 118:1-2, 14-24

*This guide represents one possible selection of lessons and psalms from the lectionary. For a complete listing see *The Revised Common Lectionary.*

Sunday	First Lesson	Second Lesson	Gospel Lesson	Psalm
4/22/01	Acts 5:27-32	Rev. 1:4-8	John 20:19-31	Ps. 150
4/29/01	Acts 9:1-6 (7-20)	Rev. 5:11-14	John 21:1-19	Ps. 30
5/6/01	Acts 9:36-43	Rev. 7:9-17	John 10:22-30	Ps. 23
5/13/01	Acts 11:1-18	Rev. 21:1-6	John 13:31-35	Ps. 148
5/20/01	Acts 16:9-15	Rev. 21:10, 22-22:5	John 14:23-29	Ps. 67
5/27/01	Acts 16:16-34	Rev. 22:12-14, 16-17, 20-21	John 17:20-26	Ps. 97
6/3/01	Acts 2:1-21	Rom. 8:14-17	John 14:8-17 (25-27)	Ps. 104:24-34, 35b
6/10/01	Prov. 8:1-4, 22-31	Rom. 5:1-5	John 16:12-15	Ps. 8
6/17/01	1 Kings 21:1-21a	Gal. 2:15-21	Luke 7:36-8:3	Ps. 5:1-8
6/24/01	1 Kings 19:1-15a	Gal. 3:23-29	Luke 8:26-39	Ps. 42 and 43
7/1/01	2 Kings 2:1-2, 6-14	Gal. 5:1, 13-25	Luke 9:51-62	Ps. 77:1-2, 11-20
7/8/01	2 Kings 5:1-14	Gal. 6:(1-6) 7-16	Luke 10:1-11, 16-20	Ps. 30
7/15/01	Amos 7:7-17	Col. 1:1-14	Luke 10:25-37	Ps. 82
7/22/01	Amos 8:1-12	Col. 1:15-28	Luke 10:38-42	Ps. 52
07/29/01	Hos. 1:2-10	Col. 2:6-15 (16-19)	Luke 11:1-13	Ps. 85
8/5/01	Hos. 11:1-11	Col. 3:1-11	Luke 12:13-21	Ps. 107:1-9, 43
8/12/01	Isa. 1:1, 10-20	Heb. 11:1-3, 8-16	Luke 12:32-40	Ps. 50:1-8, 22-23
8/19/01	Isa. 5:1-7	Heb. 11:29–12:2	Luke 12:49-56	Ps. 80:1-2, 8-19
8/26/01	Jer. 1:4-10	Heb. 12:18-29	Luke 13:10-17	Ps. 71:1-6

*This guide represents one possible selection of lessons and psalms from the lectionary. For a complete listing see *The Revised Common Lectionary.*

461

Sunday	First Lesson	Second Lesson	Gospel Lesson	Psalm
9/2/01	Jer. 2:4-13	Heb. 13:1-8, 15-16	Luke 14:1, 7-14	Ps. 81:1, 10-16
9/9/01	Jer. 18:1-11	Philem. 1-21	Luke 14:25-33	Ps. 139:1-6, 13-18
9/16/01	Jer. 4:11-12, 22-28	1 Tim. 1:12-17	Luke 15:1-10	Ps. 14
9/23/01	Jer. 8:18–9:1	1 Tim. 2:1-7	Luke 16:1-13	Ps. 79:1-9
9/30/01	Jer. 32:1-3a 6-15	1 Tim. 6:6-19	Luke 16:19-31	Ps. 91:1-6, 14-16
10/7/01	Lam. 1:1-6	2 Tim. 1:1-14	Luke 17:5-10	Ps. 137
10/14/01	Jer. 29:1, 4-7	2 Tim. 2:8-15	Luke 17:11-19	Ps. 66:1-12
10/21/01	Jer. 31:27-34	2 Tim. 3:14-4:5	Luke 18:1-8	Ps. 119:97-104
10/28/01	Joel 2:23-32	2 Tim. 4:6-8, 16-18	Luke 18:9-14	Ps. 65
11/4/01	Hab. 1:1-4; 2:1-4	2 Thess. 1:1-4, 11-12	Luke 19:1-10	Ps. 119:137-144
11/11/01	Hag. 1:15 b –2:9	2 Thess. 2:1-5, 13-17	Luke 20:27-38	Ps. 145: 1-5, 17-21
11/18/01	Isa. 65:17-25	2 Thess. 3:6-13	Luke 21:5-19	Isa. 12
11/25/01	Jer. 23:1-6	Col. 1:11-20	Luke 23:33-43	Luke 1:68-79
12/2/01	Isa. 2:1-5	Rom 13:11-14	Matt. 24:36-44	Ps. 122
12/9/01	Isa. 11:1-10	Rom. 15:4-13	Matt. 3:1-12	Ps. 72:1-7, 18-19
12/16/01	Isa. 35:1-10	James 5:7-10	Matt. 11:2-11	Luke 1:47-55
12/23/01	Isa. 7:10-16	Rom. 1:1-7	Matt. 1:18-25	Ps. 80:1-7, 17-19
12/30/01	Isa. 63:7-9	Heb. 2:10-18	Matt. 2:13-23	Ps. 148

*This guide represents one possible selection of lessons and psalms from the lectionary. For a complete listing see *The Revised Common Lectionary*.

CONTRIBUTORS

Don M. Aycock
First Baptist Church
501 Oak St.
Palaka, FL 32177

Gerald L. Borchert
Northern Baptist Theological
  Seminary
660 E. Butlerfield Rd.
Lombard, IL 60148-5698

Michael B. Brown
Centenary UMC
P. O. Box 658
Winston-Salem, NC 27102

Bob Buchanan
Parkway Baptist Church
5975 State Bridge Road
Duluth, GA 30155

Linda McKinnish Bridges
9071 Auburn Grove Court
Mechanicsville, VA 23116

Joseph Byrd
Stewart Road Church of God
1199 Stewart Road
Monroe, MI 48162

Jim Clardy
Murfreesboro District
316 W. Lytle St., Suite 202,
Murfreesboro, TN 37130

William Cotton
Grace United Methodist Church
3700 Cottage Grove
Des Moines, IA 50311-3699

Joseph Daniels
Emory UMC
6100 Georgia Avenue, NW
Washington, DC 20011

Earl C. Davis
Trinity Baptist Church
8899 Trinity Road
Cordova, TN 38018

Paul D. Duke
Mercer University
3001 Mercer University Drive
Atlanta, GA 30341-4115

Paul L. Escamilla
Walnut Hill United Methodist
  Church
10066 Marshall Lane
Dallas, TX 75229

Lee Gallman
Columbia Drive Baptist Church
862 Columbia Dr.
Decatur, GA 30030

Kay Gray
Hamilton UMC
3105 Hamilton Church Road
Antioch, TN 37013

Wendy Joyner
Fellowship Baptist Church
466A Hwy 280
East Americus, GA 31709

Derl Keefer
Three Rivers Church of the
Nazarene
15770 Coon Hollow Road
Three Rivers, MI 49093

Jim Killen
Trinity United Methodist Church
P.O. Box 5247
Beaumont, TX 77726-5247

Eric Killinger
408 E. Boyd Road
Hogansville, GA 30230

Gary G. Kindley
First United Methodist Church
508 N. Gray Street
Killeen, TX 76541

Mickey Kirkindoll
First Baptist Church
P.O. Box 395
Jefferson, GA 30549

David Mauldin
Brentwood Cumberland
Presbyterian Church
516 Franklin Road
Brentwood, TN 37027

Tommy McDearis
Blacksburg Baptist Church
550 N. Main
Blacksburg, VA 24060

Blair G. Meeks
501 Clear Spring Court
Brentwood, TN 37027

William Miller
Christ United Methodist Church
508 Franklin Rd.
Franklin, TN 37069

Bass Mitchell
Rt. 2, Box 68
Hot Springs, VA 24445

Carol M. Norén
North Park Theological Seminary
3225 W. Foster Ave.
Chicago, IL 60625

Kathleen Peterson
Palos UMC
P.O. Box 398
Palos Heights, IL 60463

Mark Price
Westwood Baptist Church
8200 Old Keene Mill Road
Springfield, VA 22152

Vance P. Ross
First UMC Hyattsville
6804 Calverton Drive
Hyattsville, MD 20782

Mary Scifres
3810 67th Avenue Court N.W.,
Gig Harbor, WA 98335

J. Michael Shannon
First Christian Church
200 Mountcastle Drive
Johnson City, TN 37615

Robert C. Shannon
P. O. Box 716
Valle Crucis, NC 28691

Thomas Steagald
P.O. Box 427
Marshville, NC 28103

CONTRIBUTORS

Marcia T. Thompson
Robert's Chapel Baptist Church
P.O. Box 128
Pendleton, NC 27862

Philip E. Thompson
Robert's Chapel Baptist Church
P.O. Box 128
Pendleton, NC 27862

Eradio Valverde
6800 Wurzbach Road
San Antonio, TX 78240

INDEX

❦

OLD TESTAMENT

NEW TESTAMENT